T0325472

The Universal Tactics of Successful Trend Trading

The Universal Tactics of Successful Trend Trading

Finding Opportunity in Uncertainty

By

BRENT PENFOLD

WILEY

This edition first published 2021
© 2021 John Wiley & Sons, Ltd

Registered office
John Wiley & Sons Ltd, The Atrium, Southern Gate, Chichester, West Sussex PO19 8SQ, United Kingdom

For details of our global editorial offices, for customer services and for information about how to apply for permission to reuse the copyright material in this book please see our website at www.wiley.com.

Wiley publishes in a variety of print and electronic formats and by print-on-demand. Some material included with standard print versions of this book may not be included in e-books or in print-on-demand. If this book refers to media such as a CD or DVD that is not included in the version you purchased, you may download this material at http://booksupport.wiley.com. For more information about Wiley products, visit www .wiley.com.

Designations used by companies to distinguish their products are often claimed as trademarks. All brand names and product names used in this book are trade names, service marks, trademarks or registered trademarks of their respective owners. The publisher is not associated with any product or vendor mentioned in this book.

Limit of Liability/Disclaimer of Warranty: While the publisher and author have used their best efforts in preparing this book, they make no representations or warranties with respect to the accuracy or completeness of the contents of this book and specifically disclaim any implied warranties of merchantability or fitness for a particular purpose. It is sold on the understanding that the publisher is not engaged in rendering professional services and neither the publisher nor the author shall be liable for damages arising here from. If professional advice or other expert assistance is required, the services of a competent professional should be sought.

Library of Congress Cataloging-in-Publication Data is available:

Names: Penfold, Brent, 1962- author. | John Wiley & Sons, Ltd., publisher.
Title: The universal tactics of successful trend trading : finding opportunity
  in uncertainty / Brent Norman Lindsay Penfold.
Description: [Hoboken] : [Wiley], [2020] | Includes index.
  Identifiers: LCCN 2020020364 (print) | LCCN 2020020365 (ebook)|
  ISBN 9781119734512 (hardback) | ISBN 9781119734550 (adobe pdf) |
  ISBN 9781119734499 (epub)
Subjects: LCSH: Portfolio management. | Stock price forecasting. | Investments.
Classification: LCC HG4529.5 .P444 2020 (print) | LCC HG4529.5 (ebook) |
  DDC 332.64—dc23
LC record available at https://lccn.loc.gov/2020020364
LC ebook record available at https://lccn.loc.gov/2020020365

Cover Design: Wiley
Cover Image: © champc/Getty Images

Set in 10/12pt, SabonLTStd by SPi Global, Chennai, India.

Printed and bound by CPI Group (UK) Ltd, Croydon, CR0 4YY

10 9 8 7 6 5 4 3 2 1

To my beautiful family,
Katia, Beau and Boston,
the three best trades I've ever made.

CONTENTS

ACKNOWLEDGEMENTS

The only acknowledgement I'd like to make is to everyone who bought my earlier book *The Universal Principles of Successful Trading* (*UPST*) (Wiley, 2010).

If that is you, then a big, big thank you.

If it's not you, then a big thank you anyway for picking up this book!

This book has come about only because of the success of *UPST*.

Since its publication in 2010 *UPST* has become an international best seller having been translated into Polish, German, Korean, Japanese and simplified and orthodox Chinese.

If it wasn't for its success this companion book would never have been written.

So, a big thank you to all the traders out there who helped *UPST* become the success it is today.

PREFACE

BUCKLE UP

This book is about practical trend trading.

But wait. Before you decide to attempt trend trading, or continue trend trading, you will first need to do a little 'speed' review and 'speed' self-analysis to determine whether you're suitable for it. It would really be pointless continuing with this book if deep down you weren't suited to trading with the trend. Hence this little 'heads up' before you start.

Now, if after your speed review you decide trend trading is not for you then no worries. Well done on being truthful to yourself, your risk capital and your family.

If you do decide you're up for it, and if you persist, then well done—you will be rewarded. However, the key word is 'persist'. Although simple, trading is not easy, particularly trend trading. You will need to learn to endure its unpleasantries. It won't be a smooth ride without its bumps. But if you persist and are sensible, you will be rewarded. So why not buckle up and let me give you a little speed introduction to the world of professional trend trading.

THE FIRST AND MOST IMPORTANT FACT ABOUT TREND TRADING

Let me start with the unpleasantries. Trend trading is undeniably miserable. Yep, I said it. Miserable. Miserable with a capital 'M'.

It's a miserable existence where you can expect to suffer 67% losses on all your trades. You'll be spending more time losing then winning. A lot more time losing. If you're still with me then you'll need to be aware of the following:

- You won't be trading to make immediate profit. No.
- You won't be trading to prove your market analysis correct. No.
- You won't be trading for the action, or thrill of being in the market. Don't be stupid.
- You'll only be trading in what you believe is the general direction of the market's trend, which quite often will be wrong. Get used to it.
- You'll only be trading for the opportunity to earn expectancy, not profit. That's right.
- Expectancy comes from both your winning and losing trades. Yes, it does.
- Expectancy can only accrue over a long period of time covering many losses and a few wins. Did I say it was miserable?

Know and accept this and you'll be prepared.

I'm not saying this to be a kill joy. I'm saying it to be realistic and to tell you how it is. I don't want you to develop a satisfactory trend-trading methodology only to see you throw it away following a dreadful losing streak of 10, 20 or 30 losing trades. It will happen. Don't think it won't. The market's Mr Maximum Adversity will ensure it does.

Remember, life as a trend trader is miserable. You'll always be losing. It's repetitive and boring. You'll be placing the same orders and entering the same trades over the same portfolio of markets time and again. It's a constant wash cycle of rinse and repeat. It's repetitive, it's boring and it's painful. You'll constantly suffer drawdowns. Some quite deeply. It's more mind numbing then mind stimulating.

However, despite its challenges, it is also profitable, and at times, very profitable.

But only if you stick with it during the turbulent times. Survive the turbulent times and you'll be around to enjoy the good times.

You will need to employ appropriate money management. You'll need to trade small relative to your risk capital. You will need to ensure your risk-of-ruin (ROR) is at 0%. You will need to ensure you're a good loser, both in never moving your stops and never letting the losses get you angry. You will need to suffer the bad times. You will need to learn to endure the darkness that will inhibit your world from time to time. Do all that and you will come out the other end with a surprising result.

I hope that if you embark on this trend-trading journey that you will remember these few words.

I hope you will remember them when you're in a deep dark place that all trend traders inhabit. When it appears to be the darkest, I hope you will remember that successful trend trading is all about survival, avoiding risk of ruin, being a good loser and following a good trade plan. I hope you'll remember you're only trading for the opportunity to earn expectancy, not immediate profit. That expectancy can only accrue over a long period of time executing many, many trades. It may take a whole year. It may take a couple of years. This is because you don't know which market or markets will decide to trend or when they'll decide to trend. But if you can learn to ride and stay on the bumpy equity curve you will be rewarded when a new equity high is reached.

Are you still up for trend trading?

No? No worries and well done on being decisive, and honest.

Yes? Well done and welcome to my painful world of trend trading. I hope you enjoy the ideas I'm going to share with you.

HOW TO MAKE MONEY TRADING

Now that I've got you quickly briefed and soberly onboard (and remember to keep that buckle tight), let's cut to the chase. You're reading this book for one reason only, and it's the same reason why I'm writing this book. You want to know how to make money trend trading.

Well I'm going to show you how.

But you'll need to stick with me as I progress through the book. When you finish, you'll need to independently verify and validate everything I say. It's no good me telling you what works and what doesn't. It's up to you to tell yourself by doing the work. Defy human nature and put the effort in. Do that, execute correctly and you'll be rewarded.

Good luck.

Brent Penfold
Sydney, Australia

INTRODUCTION

This book has a dual objective.

A REALIST BOOK

Firstly, I hope it will become a popular book based on its own merits. I hope in time it will become seen as a realistic and honest voice on trend trading. And just like trend trading, one that will stand the test of time.

A COMPANION BOOK

Secondly, I also hope this book will be seen as a necessary and deserving companion to my previous book, *UPST*. A natural extension and compliment to the universal principles of successful trading that I extensively wrote about in *UPST*.

THE MISSING CHAPTER

With *UPST* I took a holistic approach to discussing the process of trading that follows a number of immutable core principles. Principles that are applicable to all traders regardless of the market, instrument and timeframe, technique or analysis they follow. Following a good process of trading is primary to the secondary issues of markets, instruments, timeframes, techniques and analysis.

Being a holistic-type book I spent little time on the most interesting part of trading—the analysis and development of trading strategies. I spent little to no time on dissecting market structure, identifying appropriate setups and applying sensible trading plans.

As a side-bar it still amazes me that *UPST*, a trading book that basically doesn't discuss in detail market structure, analysis, setup criterion, entry, stop and exit techniques was so popular. In a nut shell, it doesn't dwell on the interesting side of trading—the analysis, investigation, development, reviewing and finalization of trading strategies. No. The book concentrates on the dry aspects of trading, the universal principles of successful trading. Material that I personally cherish above all else, but material nevertheless I know not to be particularly exciting. From a material perspective, this book will be far more interesting, not more important, but far more interesting compared to *UPST*.

Now back to point.

UPST is a more holistic, theoretical type book. This book will be a more practical, how-to guidebook on trend trading. It will be a natural extension and complement to *UPST*, where I will attempt to take the principles I shared regarding methodology and apply them in a practical manner to investigate, review and develop a robust trend-trading methodology.

Although I wrote extensively about 'methodology' in *UPST*, I did not provide a practical turn-key strategy example to demonstrate my ideas. This book will provide the practical turn-key strategy example to do just that, to demonstrate what I was saying. To give you an example of what I discussed in *UPST*.

I suppose you could view this book as the missing 'practical' chapter of *UPST* that will provide an example of an objective and independent trading methodology.

MY OBJECTIVE

As I've mentioned, my objective is to make this book:

1. An important, honest, informative, practical and helpful book for the serious trend trader, which can stand on its own merit and be robust enough to last the test of time.
2. An important and complimentary companion book to *UPST*, its missing chapter so to speak.

Accordingly, it will have a singular, narrow focus on the 'method-ology' side of trading. It will not touch upon the other universal principles of successful trading—those are comprehensively covered in *UPST*.

Wish me luck.

NOT ENOUGH TO BE SUCCESSFUL

Please understand that this book is not a silver bullet. By itself it will not be enough to make you a successful long-term sustainable trader. Although I believe this is a good book, it will not be enough on its own to help you learn how to become a successful and sustainable trader. A trader who can survive despite the inevitable losses, inevitable drawdowns, inevitable doubt and inevitable pain that all traders are intimate with. No, this book will not be enough. However, in combination with my previous book *UPST*, I believe it has the potential to transform a losing trader into a long-term sustainable winning one. If you haven't already done so please read *UPST*.

This book only covers one component of the universal principles of successful trading, 'methodology', you'll need all the others to hope to achieve sustainable trading success.

THERE WILL BE DUPLICATION

Let me apologize now as there will be some duplication with *UPST*.

Although this book has a narrow focus, there will be times where I'll need to touch upon other areas that are detailed in *UPST*. So, there will be some duplication. My apologies now for the duplication you will come across here and there. However, please understand that the duplication is necessary to help explain, emphasise and resonate a point I'm trying to make. It will not be duplication for the sake of 'padding'. In actual fact I want this traders' 'hand book' to be relatively small, as it's designed to complement *UPST*.

READERS OF DIFFERENT EXPERIENCE

I hope this book will have something for everyone.

For those readers relatively new to trading there is some good news and some bad news. The bad news is that I will be covering a lot

The Universal Principles of Successful Trading

1. Preparation	2. Enlightenment	3. Developing a Trading Style	4. Selecting Markets	5. The Three Pillars	6. Trading
Maximum Adversity Emotional Orientation Losing Game Random Markets Personal Boundary Best Loser Wins Risk Management Trading Partner	Avoid Risk of Ruin - Best Loser wins - Money Management Holy Grail = E x O Simplicity - Support/Resistance - Trend where majority fear - Validation - T.E.S.T	Style - Trend Trading - Swing Trading Timeframe - Intra day - Short-term - Medium-term - Long-term	Characteristics Single markets Multiple markets	Trading's Three Pillars 1. Money Management 2. Methodology 3. Psychology 1. Money Management - Fixed Risk - Fixed Capital - Fixed Ratio - Fixed Units - Williams Fixed Risk - Fixed Percentage - Fixed Volatility 2. Methodology Approach - Discretionary - Mechanical Method = Set-up + Trade Plan + Validation Set-up Analysis - which market theory? Trading's Pandora's Box - Astrology - Cycles - Dow Theory - Elliott Wave - Fibonacci - Fractal - Geometry - Indicators - Market Profile - Patterns - Seasonals - Statistical - W.D Gann Trade Plan Entry + Stop + Exit Validation - E(R) T.E.S.T (Thirty Emailed Simulated Trades) 3. Psychology Managing Hope, Greed, Fear and Pain	Putting It All Together Monitor Performance Positive Re-Enforcement Equity Momentum

This book only covers one component of the universal principles of successful trading.

Yep, just like School it's a lot of hard work!

FIGURE I.1 This book alone is not enough to make you successful; you will also need to know the universal principles of successful trading, which I extensively wrote about in *UPST*.

of information. And I say a lot. So, you'll need to concentrate. That's the bad news. The good news is that it's all good information!

For the more experienced reader, I hope the ideas I share here will resonate with you and either reinforce what you already know to be true or encourage you to revisit and reinvestigate and then reconsider the ideas I share here.

EVIDENCE, NOT OPINION OR MYTH

It's my preference here to deal only with evidence. Not opinions. Not myths. Much of what is written, spoken or animated about trading is based on the author's, presenter's or editor's opinion with a few well-chosen chart examples thrown in. Unfortunately, these opinions wilt under scrutiny.

In this book it's my preference to discuss only those ideas that can be distilled down into clear and unambiguous objective rules. Rules that can be hard coded in appropriate software to determine their historical significance. It's my preference to demonstrate the historical profitability (or loss) of all ideas I share that I believe are worth discussing.

Too often the most enthusiastic talking heads, engaging writers or charismatic presenters capture traders' attentions. Many confuse the 'confidence' displayed as valuable and actionable knowledge. However, it's usually impossible to make money from these sweeping opinionated views. Unfortunately, it's the lack of granularity that allows these repeaters and amplifiers to continue to express their views. Lack of detail avoids accountability, which is good for them. Sadly, the lack of detail is usually ignored by less experienced traders, who generally pay for their ignorance in trading losses. They usually decide to buy the 'hot' share the next day without any consideration for where to place a 'stop' or what expectancy they're trading for?

In this book I will attempt to code my ideas, whether good or bad, to illustrate their historical profitability (or loss). And while I'm here, I should also add an important warning that historical performance of any idea is no guarantee that the same performance will continue into the future.

NOTHING NEW AND SHINY

If you've picked up my book looking for a new trading idea then I'm sorry to disappoint you, because I don't have one. What I'm going to share with you is not new. What I'm going to share with you can be referenced in other books. I have nothing new to show you. I'm simply standing on the shoulders of others who have gone before me. However, what I will say is that I'll be standing on the strong shoulders, not the weak ones.

So unfortunately, if you are looking for a new trading idea, then this book might not be for you.

However, if you're looking for good ideas, then I may be able to help you. I will be sharing a number of them. But remember they won't be new. Some, one in particular, is old and simple. Actually, it's very old and very simple. An idea that is so old and obvious that most traders discount its usefulness. To most 'old' and 'simple' means 'unfashionable' and 'not profitable' and therefore 'not' useful.

But let me tell you, 'old' and 'simple' is the new 'good' and 'robust'. By the end of this book (if you're still with me) I hope to convince you that 'old' and 'simple' will become the new 'fashionable' and the new 'useful' and the new 'essential' in trading.

I wish I could entice you with a new idea. A shiny and mysterious new idea that would lift your hopes for a better and more profitable future that would activate your feel-good neurotransmitters. But I can't. There would be nothing better for this book's success then a new idea wrapped in mystery. But unfortunately, I don't have one.

I like old and I like simple trading ideas.

SIMPLE IS BEST

I like 'simple' ideas for the obvious reason that they are 'simple'. Now, there are many reasons why traders lose. But one reason they lose is that the majority of traders mistrust the obvious, they mistrust simple trading solutions. They can't believe trading can be simple, so they seek clues and advantages in the new and the complex.

Believe me when I say simplicity works. Simple means you have avoided the trap of excessive curve fitting. You have avoided the miss-step many make of either intentionally or unintentionally curve fitting their strategy to historical data. Simple means fewer moving parts, which means less can go wrong moving forward. To me, simple does not mean less but 'more' in trading. And by 'more' I mean more 'robustness'—the single most important attribute of any trading strategy. Robustness to last the test of time. Robustness to not only make money today, but tomorrow and into the future. So, what I will be sharing is simple. Therefore, please do not mistrust what you're about to learn but embrace it for one of its greatest strength—simplicity.

So, if you're not necessarily looking for a new idea, but seeking help to be introduced to or reminded about what works, then this book may quietly surprise you.

NOT PERFECT

In addition, the ideas I will be sharing with you are not perfect. They do lose. They do experience drawdowns. They will hurt you. They will leave you uncertain, disappointed, frustrated and, at times, furious. But they have an edge, a positive expectancy. Good traders can make money from an edge.

KEEPING IT REAL

I'm writing this book for the serious trader. Not for the rainbow chasers. This book is about how to chip away to get ahead. It's not about revealing trading secrets. It's not about selling false hopes and it's not about publishing nonsense. It's not about showing you how to 'hit' a mythical 'home run' in trading. No. It's about keeping it real for the serious trader. Yes, what I will share with you is not shiny and new. Yes, what I share with you will at times leave you battered and bruised. But that is part and parcel of trading. It's not all sunshine and high fives. Trading successfully for long periods of time will have its dark and uncertain times. I can promise you that what I will be sharing with you between these pages will leave you shaken and doubtful at times, but at least what I will be sharing is real and has an edge.

SUCCESS WILL COME

If you understand, respect and embrace the importance of money management and its significance in being one of the chief weapons against ROR, then what I will share with you in this book will help you navigate the volatile world of global markets. But first you will need to understand, respect, embrace and execute the universal principles of successful trading that I have extensively written about in *UPST*. If you can, and if you can combine them with what I'll be sharing with you in the following chapters, then you may pleasantly surprise yourself with where you arrive. At a destination that I hope will be safe, and one that will be called sustainable trading.

MY BACKGROUND

I've been involved with the markets for over 35 years, since I joined Bank America as a trainee dealer in 1983. Since my first trade I've probably tried just about every technique there is to trading. If there was a book, a seminar, a workshop or a software program that could help my trading, I either bought it, attended it or installed it. During the 1990s in my quest to find an edge, I felt like I was walking through a revolving seminar door. I attended many well-regarded seminars. I attended the Turtles seminar with Russell Sands, learnt PPS with Curtis Arnold, studied geometry with Bryce Gilmore and attended Larry William's Million Dollar Challenge (MDC) seminar. I picked up useful bits here and there and it was Larry William's MDC seminar that reinforced my work with short-term mechanical price patterns.

As a trader I trade a portfolio of uncorrelated systematic (or algorithmic) trend and counter-trend strategies across multiple time frames (short term, medium term and long term) over a portfolio of global index, currency and commodity futures. My portfolio contains over 30 markets. For index futures I trade the SPI, Nikkei, Taiwan, Hang Seng, Dax, Stoxx50, FTSE, E-Mini Nasdaq and E-Mini S&P 500 index futures contracts. For currency futures I trade the main currency pairs against the US dollar, which include the Euro Currency, British Pound, Japanese Yen and Swiss Franc. For commodity futures I trade the three most liquid futures contracts in the US within the interest rates, energies, grains, meats, metals and softs market segments.

I trade my portfolio on an almost 24/7 basis, where a day doesn't go by without one of my many futures orders being triggered somewhere around the world.

I'm principally a pattern trader. Apart from using the average true range and a 200-day moving average, I focus purely on price. And please do not read too much into my use of a 200-day moving average. There is nothing magical about me using 200-days. It's just a length I have always used. I don't even know whether it is the optimal length to determine the dominant trend, and nor do I care. The last thing I would want to do in my trading is start using 'optimized' variables, as its one of the quickest routes to the poor house. And please understand that those strategies of mine that use the 200-day moving average don't use it to find trade setups. They don't use it to find entry, stop or exit levels. They just use it to determine the dominant trend.

THIS BOOK IS NOT ABOUT FUTURES TRADING

Despite myself being a futures trader, please do not think this book is about futures trading. Yes, many of the examples and portfolios used to share and illustrate ideas will involve futures, but only because they are a device of convenience for myself. What I will be sharing in this book, similarly to what I did with *UPST*, is a focus primarily on the process of good trading. Not on secondary issues such as individual markets and instruments. This book is not about trying to convert you to futures. Futures is just my preferred instrument to trade. You will have your own preferred markets and instruments to trade. So, please don't think this book is designed to attempt to convert you to the markets and instruments I trade. No. I'm writing this book to encourage you to focus first on the process of good trading rather on any individual market, instrument, technique or timeframe. It's just that the majority of examples involve futures, and I use futures because it's convenient for me.

So, please understand that this book will be focused on the correct process of good trading, regardless of market, instrument or timeframe. The markets and instruments shown within these pages are for illustrative purposes only, and in their turn become secondary in importance to following good trading principals.

PATHWAY TO SUSTAINABLE TRADING

I hope this book can become a sensible stepping stone on your pathway to sustainable trading. I certainly believe it's possible to reach your destination if this book is used in combination with my previous book, *UPST*.

I have a lot to share with you over the following pages. Let me give you a brief outline of what I'll be discussing.

In Chapter 1 I begin by outlining how difficult it is for you and I to succeed as traders.

In Chapter 2 I offer a number of key messages covering knowledge, risks, application and execution.

In Chapter 3 I share with you the appeal of trend trading and why you should seriously consider it as a trading technique.

In Chapter 4 I give a brief outline of why trends exist.

In Chapter 5 I share my thoughts on why so many fail at trend trading.

In Chapter 6 I review a number of different trend trading strategies to demonstrate the various techniques that exist.

In Chapter 7 I discuss the importance of measuring strategy performance on a risk-adjusted basis.

In Chapter 8 I share a toolkit that traders can use to help them review, develop and select strategies to trade.

In Chapter 9 I finish the book with an example of using the toolkit to develop, what I believe is, a sensible and sustain trading strategy.

JUST MY OPINION

As you read through my book please always remember and understand that what I write is only one person's opinion. Mine. I only represent one trader's view and please don't accept, just because I write something, that it's necessarily true. I'm certainly no guru and nor do I believe anyone can claim that mantle in trading. I'm just writing what I believe to be true. So, please don't take offence to anything I write, it's just what I think and it's ok for you to disagree. I won't be offended, I promise. The only caution I'll make is that you will need to produce the necessary substantiation to counter my position as my ideas/position will be supported by historical evidence and actual trading experience. So, if you do find yourself disagreeing with my ideas, then you will need to produce the necessary verification to support your view. It won't be enough for you to rely purely on gut feel or personal opinion. Remember, our gut feelings and our personal opinions are generally held captive by our cognitive biases, which can and do play havoc with our trading decisions. So be warned!

Just as what I write represents only my opinion, please accept that it's not my intention to convert you to my way of thinking or trading. I'm only writing to share with you my thinking and approach to trading. What you do with it is your choice.

Once again, please remember that just because I write something it doesn't necessarily make it true. Although I believe in my heart of hearts that what I write is true, and I will have the evidence to support it, it doesn't necessarily mean you should accept it as true on face value. Certainly, welcome my ideas and opinions, but remember to validate all ideas before implementing them in the market.

ALL ROADS LEAD TO ROME

As we know, there are many roads that lead to Rome. Similarly, in trading, you need to remember and understand that there are many different ways to trade. I'm just showing you one way, one approach I use. I'm not saying my approach is the only way and I'm not saying my approach is the best way. All I'm doing is showing one road I travel. It doesn't mean you have to go the same way. However, if you do find yourself lost on your trading journey at least you'll know my approach is one option available to you.

REPETITION

My writing style is to reinforce ideas through repetition, so please let me apologize now for the repetition you're about to see throughout my book. And believe me, I am repetitive. I've been criticized for the way I write and teach, but I can only do want makes sense to me. It's just the way I roll. I'm not a professional educator or writer. I just trade and I'm happy to put pen to paper to share my thoughts, even if they're a little disjointed, circular and repetitive. I wish I could say something once and be content (which would make Katia happier for sure)—however, it's not how I'm wired. So, if repetition is going to annoy you then please accept my sincere apologies now.

QUESTION AND VERIFY EVERYTHING

Please do not accept what I or another author writes on face value. Certainly, welcome all opinions and thoughts you hear, see or read about trading, but please, please reserve your opinion until you have first questioned and independently validated the idea.

Only your questioning, review and independent validation will demonstrate whether an idea of mine or another's has truth and, more importantly, value in your hands. It will only be through your own efforts that you will be able to determine what is truth or fiction. Do the work and you will be rewarded.

LET'S GET STARTED

I hope you will welcome the ideas I share with you in this book and if you have any questions please do not hesitate to contact me via my web site www.indextrader.com.au.

To begin your journey, I want to discuss our living paradox where it's both the best of times and the worst of times to be a trader. Confused? Well, let me give you a big welcome to my contradictory world of trading.

CHAPTER 1

The Paradox

NIRVANA AND DESPAIR

Today we live within a trading paradox where it's both the best and the worst of times to be a trader.

Today we've never had it so good. With the advent of the internet, development of high-speed wireless networks and proliferation of smart phones with even smarter online trading applications, traders can buy and sell just about any instrument, in any market, across any exchange, at any time.

When I compare it back to the early 1980s, when I thought wearing a data pager was an unfair advantage, today feels totally futuristic with all the technological wizardry available at our finger tips.

Today we have multiple online discount brokers with both web-based and smart phone applications. We have inexpensive historical and real time data with automated trading programs. There are multiple charting programs with hundreds of indicators. We have multiple markets to trade ranging from forex to financials to commodities. We even have cryptocurrencies to trade. There are multiple instruments we can trade from options to warrants to futures to shares and CFDs.

But it does not stop at the electronic wizardry available.

Traders have never had it so good with the enormous vault of available trading knowledge. Today there are multiple trading theories to consider, multiple trading newsletters to subscribe to, multiple trading authors to read, multiple financial shows to tune into, multiple trading educators to listen to and multiple trading workshops to attend.

Really, there is no reason or excuse for a modern trader to fail. It's the best of times.

But unfortunately, it's also the worst of times.

Just ask the majority of traders. Why? Because despite the advancements made in technology and trading knowledge, the majority of traders today still lose. It's an unfortunate situation where over 90% of active traders fail. Just like they did back in the 1980s when I thought wearing a data pager was both hip and advantageous. So, for the majority it's the worst of times.

It's the paradox us traders live in.

IT'S ALSO A CONFUSING TIME

Not only is it the worst of times but it's also a confusing time. It seems the world excels in confusion and uncertainty. It throws up so many questions with few good answers.

Whenever I try to puzzle out the world's riddles I usually end up with a sore head. Who knows the answer to the big macro issues? I don't think anyone really does. I mean who knows for sure whether the European Union will hold together? Who knows whether the United States will get hold of its debt and deficit? Who knows whether China will return to trend growth? Who knows whether Japan will find a resolution to its demographic struggles? Who knows whether the world will return to normalcy following the Coronavirus pandemic? And who knows if central banks will normalize monetary policies or keep supplying their opioid cocktail of cheap and abundant money? Will they continue to enable the market's liquidity-drug-addicted dependency or will they restore risk to its previously respected and proper pedestal? I certainly don't know.

But the questions don't stop at the macro level. They also mount up at the micro level, where trading throws up its own avalanche of questions.

Out of the hundreds of markets available which ones should we trade? Should we trade local or international markets? Should we trade consumer discretionary, consumer staple, energy, financial, health care, industrial, information technology, materials, metals, mining, telecommunication, utility or commodity markets? Within each market segment which individual businesses or markets should we select?

But the questions don't stop there.

Which instruments should we trade? Shares, options, warrants, contracts for difference or futures?

Should we use fundamental or technical analysis or a combination of both? If it's technical analysis, should we use cycles, patterns, indicators, astrology, geometry, Dow Theory, seasonals, Market Profile, Elliott Wave or WD Gann? Just to mention a few.

As I said, so many questions, and they don't stop.

Are the markets bullish or bearish? Should we trade with or against the trend? Should we be a short-term, medium-term or longer-term trader? How much should we risk? Where should we enter, place our stops and exit?

As I said, there are so many questions to answer. Is it any wonder that so many traders today are so confused?

HOW I CAN HELP YOU

Well I'm here to help you.

But an important qualifier before I do. I need to let you know that I don't know everything there is to know about the markets. I wish I did, but I don't. When I was younger, I thought I knew everything there was to know. As I've got older, I've got wiser! So, to be up front I have to tell you that it's an unfortunate truth that after 35+ years in the markets, and ten years since I wrote *The Universal Principles of Successful Trading* (hereafter, *UPST*), I still don't know everything there is to know about trading and the markets.

However, I know you're looking for answers.

What I can do is share part of what I do. And I do make money trading. So, what I can tell you is this. If I can make money trading, so can you. If I can make 20–30% annual returns with *manageable* risk, so can you. And that is the important word, *manageable*. I'm not some amazing trader with unique and exclusive knowledge. No. I'm just like you. I may have more experience and more market scars then you, but I'm still normal. I'm no special trader with Marvel super hero powers or insights. I'm just an ordinary person who has gained some knowledge with a lot of experience along the way.

So please believe, despite what your experience has been so far, that it is possible to trade successfully.

HOW TO TRADE SUCCESSFULLY

I'm writing this book for one reason and one reason only. To show you how to make money trading with the trend. Put simply, profitable trend trading is dependent upon the understanding and acceptance of the universal truth and universal principles of successful trading. You will need to read, comprehend, embrace and execute the universal truth and principles of successful trading. If you get the universal truth and principles right the profits will follow. They have to. Ignore them and you'll continue to struggle. Period. No discussion. No ifs. No buts. No excuses. This applies to all traders in all markets, across all timeframes and all instruments.

For the universal principles of successful trading you will need to read my previous book, *UPST*.

For the universal truth you will need to read Chapter 2.

SUMMARY

Despite it being both the best and worst of times to be a trader, I believe there is a safe pathway forward to help you navigate your way towards a sensible destination. A pathway that will go a long way to answering many of the confusing questions we traders have to answer each day. A pathway that will allow you to find opportunity in uncertainty. A pathway that I hope, even with my limited knowledge, will lead you to a rewarding position of sensible sustainable trading. That pathway will commence in Chapter 2, where I want to share with you a number of key messages.

CHAPTER 2

Key Messages

Those that fail to learn from history, are doomed to repeat it.
Winston Churchill (1874–1965)

I want you to learn from my experiences. If I can help you avoid the mistakes others (and I) have made in the past then I will certainly have helped you along your pathway towards sustainable trading. I just need to get my thoughts down in a coherent order. Wish me luck.

It's well accepted knowledge that over 90% of active traders lose. To avoid the same fate, it's important for you to know and to remember the past. Know it and you may just avoid repeating the same mistakes others have made. And traders are experts at repeating the same old mistakes, over and over again. To help you avoid the same fate it's important to pause and take a look back at all the carnage that technical analysis, trading and the markets have left behind.

The best way I know to share my experiences and knowledge of the past is to present them as key messages.

These key messages represent core knowledge and values I believe in. Strongly believe in. I'll apologize now if some of them offend you; however, I can only share what holds true for me. For my trading compass they show the true north. I hope they can also help you navigate your journey towards sustainable trading.

The key messages I'd like to share with you can be grouped under four areas:

- knowledge,
- risk,
- application and
- execution.

Let's take a closer look.

KNOWLEDGE

This is an obvious place to start, in your head. It's the moment before you insert your key into the ignition. My key knowledge messages include:

- acknowledge and accept everyone loses,
- expect and accept 67% losses,
- accept technical analysis has little value,
- seek evidence,
- accept no one can predict the future,
- time to get serious,
- stop trading what you think,
- read *The Universal Principles of Successful Trading*,
- become a cynic,
- 0% risk-of-ruin (ROR) is king,
- compound annual growth rate (CAGR) is queen,
- the only secret,
- accept the truth about trading,
- acknowledge being a discretionary trader is difficult,
- follow the smart money,
- placebo traders,
- be sensible with indicators and
- the biggest crime.

Let's look at each in turn.

Acknowledge and Accept Everyone Loses

Yes everyone. Even the winners lose plenty of times. If you trade, you will lose. If you already trade then you already know the truth of my words.

There are few absolutes in trading. However, there are some hard and generally immovable and unavoidable truths about trading. Losing is one of them. To repeat:

- you will lose trading and
- you will lose often.

So, don't spend an inordinate amount of time and effort trying to devise ways to avoid *all* losses. Losses are unavoidable. If you spend too much time and energy trying to eliminate losses then you will only create issues of excessive curve fitting down the track. An issue that I will discuss further in detail and one that you should attempt to avoid at all costs.

Losing is the cost of doing the business of trading so you'll need to accept it, get used to it and eventually (try to) become comfortable with it.

Expect and Accept 67% Losses

This book is about trend trading. I've mentioned before an immovable and unavoidable truth about trading with the trend. You can expect to lose on average around six to seven times out of every ten trend trades. That's almost a bankable guarantee.

If you can't accept losing 67% of the time when trading with the trend, then you shouldn't be trading. And don't think counter-trend or swing trading is going to save you if you can't trade with the trend. Sure counter-trend trading makes money, but it's not the safest way to trade. The safest way is to trade with the trend. Trends move markets and are the basis of all profits. Being on the right side of a moving market is where the majority of profit will come from. Counter-trend trading against the trend is hard with limited profit potential.

You will need to ignore the majority of trading books that perpetuate the rainbow myth. Trading is not all about banking profits and getting rich. You need to accept the reality that trading is first about survival, about avoiding ROR. It's about surviving long enough to enjoy the wins when they come along. Trading is about experiencing, dealing with and surviving the continual loses and drawdowns it inflicts. Trading is about dealing with the doubts that drawdowns inflict upon your methodology. Trading isn't about enjoying the brief sunshine new equity highs produce. Trading is about inhibiting and surviving the dark, gloomy and often despondent isolated places regular drawdowns throw you into. Surviving long enough to be present to enjoy the good opportunities when they come along and deliver the well-deserved new equity highs. New equity highs that quickly disappear before throwing you back into drawdown. Trading, like a washing machine, is set on a constant cycle of rinse and repeat as you're regularly thrown between drawdowns and new equity highs.

I'm harping on about losses because that is the reality of trend trading. Although the idea of trading is relatively simple, it's not easy when your regular companion of day-to-day engagement with the market is constantly recording losses. As I've said before, it's my preference to make you aware of the challenge of trend trading so you don't lose heart and throw away your strategy following 10, 20 or 30 consecutive losses.

Accept Technical Analysis Has Little Value

Remember the past. Please never forget it. If you do, you'll be in a heap of trouble. The chief protagonist of the past is the chameleon called technical analysis.

Technical analysis refers to the practice of looking at past prices to predict future prices. And who wouldn't want to know the future? It's the ultimate proxy for a crystal ball. But you need to be careful as technical analysis represents a living paradox where, on the one hand, it promises good insights into market behaviour while, on the other, it's pulling money out of your pockets.

Wherever you look within the large field of technical analysis you'll find a history of failure. A killing field of false techniques, failed strategies, dead dreams, ruined ambitions and empty trading accounts. The technical analysis landscape is littered with more failed methodologies and trading strategies then you can hope to count. Approaches that only ever looked good on a few well-chosen charts. Excessively curve-fitted and data-mined strategies with too numerous and too overly optimized variables. Methodologies without any anchored reasoning. Techniques absent of any shred of evidence that they had ever worked in the past, let alone hope to work in the future. Failure wherever you look.

It's an unfortunate reality that the field of technical analysis is better known for its failures than its successes. With over 90% of active traders losing, it paints an unflattering picture.

Despite the marketing hype, it's rare to find ideas within technical analysis that have real substance. Yes, there are pockets of gems among the rubble, but they're hard to find. The best I can do is to describe the general field of technical analysis as enthusiastic opinion. There is no doubt the various authors believe what they write and share. There is no doubt the examples they show look authoritative. The only problem is their ideas only appear authoritative in an anecdotal manner on a few well-chosen charts. Rarely do they show equity curves demonstrating their idea's historical and hypothetical performance.

If they do, they usually contain too many overly optimized variables. Unfortunately, we the traders are too accepting and too trusting so we believe the advocate's persuasive voice to the detriment of both our trading accounts and trading souls. So, you need to be aware of this bleak landscape before you lean too heavily on technical analysis. You've been warned.

Seek Evidence

The best stance you can take to safeguard yourself against much of the questionable areas of technical analysis is to adopt an evidence-based approach. Certainly, listen to or read whatever takes your interest. But before you commit money you should first independently verify the idea. You need to gather independent evidence that an idea or tool, once incorporated into a strategy, has value in your hands.

Once the idea is coded up, you'll need to calculate its expectancy and your ROR. If it's at 0% you'll then need to complete an equity curve stability review (more about that in Chapters 5 and 8) to see how sensitive your ROR is to changes in variable values. If successful, you will then need to complete a T.E.S.T (Thirty Emailed Simulated Trades) with your trading partner.

Do all that and you'll (hopefully) avoid 90% of the past mistakes all traders make. Traders who are too trusting of technical analysis and too clueless about their ROR or the fragility of their strategy's equity curve.

You need to stop expecting technical analysis to navigate you to safety. Certainly, there are elements that are good, but they represent a small niche within a large field of alternative and competing and sometimes diametrically opposed approaches (take, for example, Livermore's Reaction Model in Chapter 6 vs Elliott Wave Theory). The only way you'll be able to sort the wheat from the chaff is to gather evidence.

Evidence requires:

- A complete turn-key trading strategy with clear and unambiguous rules for:
  - when to trade,
  - where to enter,
  - where to place stops and
  - where to exit.

- A money management strategy with clearly defined units of money.
- Creation of a historical equity curve allowing you to calculate:
  - expectancy and
  - ROR.
- Completion of an equity curve stability review to gauge the sensitiveness of your strategy's alternative equity curves to changes in variable values.

Once acceptable evidence is gathered, you'll then be in a better and safer place to cast judgement on the particular area of technical analysis you're reviewing.

Accept No One Can Predict the Future

If you didn't already know then please let me tell you. There is no such thing an all-seeing crystal ball. No one can predict the future. It's best to ignore all predictive type approaches like WD Gann, Elliott Wave and astrology.

(Now I think I've definitely offended some people with that comment. If that includes you, then please accept my apology and please understand my comment only reflects one person's opinion, and I'm no authority on the markets. As I said earlier, I don't know everything there is to know about the markets so I could well be wrong in my comment. However, from my experience, my comment holds true for me.)

Now back to Gann, Elliott and astrology. Their attraction is their perceived ability to determine the direction of future prices. I know first-hand the appeal of having a crystal ball. For many years, before I switched to focusing on mechanical price patterns, I was a disciple of Elliott Wave. I get the comfort these strategies offer by taking away the uncertainty of tomorrow. The only problem is it's a false comfort. They have little to nil 'reliable' predictive power. Certainly, they can be correct from time to time, making them at times irresistibly appealing, but so can a broken watch when it works twice a day.

It's best to accept that no one can predict the future with *reliability*. Being right occasionally is not enough.

However, their lack of consistency isn't the real villain in this play. The real culprit is how they take the trader's focus away from the present to focus on the future. Focusing on a future date builds up the expectation and emotional investment in the outcome.

Bewitching and indoctrinating both their unconscious and conscious minds into believing the prediction will come true, only to see it doesn't, where traders will continually adjust stops to give the prediction more time until it's too late when the stop becomes a catastrophic loss.

And this is the big irony.

Predictive strategies generally are counter-trend strategies. They're usually looking for a reversal against the trend. They are anti-trend. While trend traders make most of their money doing nothing as a trend continues and continues and continues, the predictive traders are busy attempting to catch the reversal, only to be stopped out again and again and again.

From my experience, it's best to leave the predictive methodologies to those who gaze at the clouds and focus on the present. Don't make the mistake that so many traders make and continue to make.

Time to Get Serious

You will need to review your motives for trading. Hopefully you'll not be trading for the excitement or adrenaline rush trading can offer. Hopefully you'll not be trading for the cerebral challenge of solving the market's Rubik's cube. Hopefully you'll not be trading to prove to those around you that you're the smartest and hopefully you will not be trading simply to prove that you are right.

I hope you'll be trading for the sole purpose of making money. Nothing less and nothing more.

Stop Trading What You Think

You think you're smart. And you are smart. However, intelligence in many other parts of your life doesn't necessarily transfer well over into trading. Just look at your trading account. Trading what you think is costing you money. Your partner knows it. Your accountant knows it. And I suspect, deep down, even you know it. So, it's best that you stop trading what you think this very second. Have you stopped? Good.

This may sound strange; however, I'm going to say it (and hey, why not, it's my book!).

In trading, generally speaking, thinking costs money. I said what?

Successful sustainable traders generally execute repetitive behaviour that requires relatively little thinking and much 'doing'.

Doing like collecting data, looking for setups, executing trades and managing positions. Much is normalized repetitive behaviour identifying preferred and recognizable setups and applying consistent and sensible trade plans. Very little is off-piste, left-of-field, creative, deep thinking.

They did their deep thinking when developing their trading methodology.

When trading they're usually focusing 100% of their effort and energy on perfect execution of their trade plan. I do and it's a grind. Day in day out, recording fills, collecting data, running models, managing open positions, adjusting stops, reviewing new setups and entering orders. It's a job. At the time of writing I have 86 open orders in my Interactive Brokers' Trader Workstation platform. Executing my multiple trade plans is time consuming, repetitive, boring and a grind. It's a job. However, apart from my energy and effort, all it requires from me is concentration. It doesn't require 'thinking'.

So, please stop trading what you think and start thinking about developing a sensible robust and positive expectancy trend-trading methodology. Once developed, just concentrate on executing your trade plan. Don't think too much about the markets outside your trade plan. Certainly, think deeply when developing additional strategies or looking at ways to improve your primary approach. But when trading, it's best to think less and concentrate more.

As a reminder you should also remember that you don't trade to satisfy your personal view of the market. You don't trade to pick market direction. You don't trade to prove your view right. You only trade for the opportunity to earn expectancy. Expectancy can only come from your trade plan, not your personal view. I'll say it again, your personal view is worthless, just ask your partner and accountant. Your personal views cost money.

You will have to learn to trade what is in front of you according to your positive expectancy trade plan, and not what you think.

Read *UPST*

I'll say it again (and again—see, I said I was repetitive). This book, despite my best of intentions and its good content, isn't enough for you to succeed in the markets. It only provides one stepping stone along your pathway towards sustainable trading. This book is about tactics, strategies. It's about developing a positive-expectancy trend-trading methodology. Although very important, it's not the be all and end all for trading. You will also need to know, comprehend, embrace, dream about and execute, execute and execute the universal principles of successful trading to survive and prosper in the markets. If you haven't already, please read my previous book *UPST*. This book, despite its good contents, in isolation will not make you either profitable or sustainable. If you haven't already, please, please, please read *UPST*. Combine it with this book and then you'll be well on your path towards sustainable trading.

Become a Cynic

I'd like to encourage you to become a cynic when it comes to trading ideas. This is because not all ideas are created equal. As I've mentioned, the field of technical analysis leaves much to be desired. Definitely welcome all ideas, and I hope you welcome mine. However, be cynical towards all ideas, including mine, until you have independently verified and validated them. Learn to validate what you trade and trade what you validate. Do not accept any trading idea on face value, despite how convincing it reads, sounds or looks. Please become a cynic and learn first to investigate, back test, validate and validate all ideas before you consider placing real money behind them.

So, once more, let me please repeat that what I write is only my opinion. And just because I or another author writes something doesn't necessarily make it true. Only you can verify and validate my ideas. Only you can determine the value of my suggestions. Only you can determine if what I say is true. Defy human nature, do the work and you'll be rewarded.

0% ROR is King

In my opinion, ROR is the most important concept in trading. The most important. Nothing comes close. Not methodology. Not setups. Not entry techniques. Not stop techniques. Not money management. Not psychology. No. ROR is numero uno.

ROR is a statistical concept that will tell a trader the probability that they, according to how they trade, will ruin their trading account. Or in layman's terms, go bust. ROR combines two important components of trading: expectancy and money management. It combines the amount of expectancy a trader can hope to earn per dollar lost from their methodology with the amount of capital they're prepared to risk per trade according to their money management strategy. Combining expectancy and money management will produce a statistical ROR. If a trader wishes to enjoy longevity in the markets, they must commence trading with a 0% ROR. No ifs. No buts. There is nothing to discuss. It's non-negotiable. So, any ROR above 0% is too high. Certainly, a trader with a 50% ROR will reach their point of ruin quicker than a trader with a 2% ROR. However, even with a low 2% or 1% ROR a trader is still guaranteed to go bust—it'll just be a matter of time.

Every trader, if they have aspirations to succeed, must know what their individual percentage ROR is for either their individual or portfolio of strategies when combined with their money management strategy. If their ROR is above 0% then they have no business trading. And if they do, then they'll deserve the negative results they get.

As I said, 0% ROR is king.

To receive a more detailed explanation of ROR please refer to my previous book *UPST*.

CAGR is Queen

If 0% ROR is king, then CAGR is queen.

CAGR refers to compound annual growth rate, or the annualized return your strategy earns over the period in question. It's the indisputable measure of a strategy's efficiency in generating profit.

After you survive in trading your next objective is to make money and the CAGR is the final arbiter on a strategy's net dollar performance. Although it doesn't address the level of risk incurred to achieve the performance, the CAGR is the definitive straight line between starting and end capital.

It's also important not to confuse the CAGR or annualized returns with 'average' returns. While average returns are used for calculating some performance metrics, it's not a return that should be used to gauge and compare a strategy's performance.

Let me explain. The average return is exactly what it says. If you start trading your strategy with $25,000 and it grows 100%, you'll end the year with $50,000 in your account. If during the following year your strategy suffers a 50% drawdown, you will return to your original capital of $25,000.

So, over the two years, your CAGR or annualized return, is 0%. You haven't made or lost any money.

However, an unscrupulous strategy developer or vendor, only interested in maximizing sales, may publish the strategy's average annual returns as being 25%. A 100% gain in year one followed by a 50% loss in year two results in a net return of 50%, when divided by two years, produces an average return of 25%. The number is called the average annual return, and it's misleading if it's being used to present a strategy's performance. Because wouldn't your trading account be more than $25,000 if after two years you had averaged 25% per year?

What you're interested in is what your strategy has realized on an annual compounded basis, the CAGR or annualized return, which in this example is 0%.

Please remember CAGR is queen for total strategy performance and consciously ignore average annual returns when measuring strategy results.

The Only Secret

Secrets, secrets, secrets. Oh, who wouldn't want to know trading secrets? Hey, I'd love to know them! Well after being involved in the markets for over 35 years I feel there is only one real secret. It's simply this:

The best loser is the long-term winner.

This quote is applicable to an ex-Chicago Board of Trade pit trader called Phantom of the Pits.

I think he has hit the proverbial nail on the head with his quote. Most traders are bad losers. They hate taking losses, moving stops and looking for any excuse to keep a trade alive, finding all sorts of reasons to rationalize their actions. They'll ignore a losing position until it becomes so big that they can no longer ignore it and are forced to stop themselves out at a catastrophic loss. Most people are only bad traders because they are bad losers. Behavioural finance calls this the disposition effect, where traders are disposed to avoiding loses at all costs. You will need to reprogram your mind to neutralize it.

Learn to welcome your losses and learn to become a good loser. I do and I am. I'm a gold medallist at losing. I'm a very active trader and I lose on generally half my trades. So, I lose a lot. If I wasn't a world champion at losing, I wouldn't be here, right now, at home writing this. So please, please learn to welcome your losses and become a good loser. Losing is part and parcel of the business of trading. It's the heavy cost of inventory you have to finance. Become a good loser and you'll take a giant step towards success. It's really the only true secret to successful trading.

If you can't see yourself being a good loser, then you can't possibly learn to trade with the trend. Remember trend traders can generally expect to lose on six to seven trades out of every ten. Trend trading demands you become a good loser. If you can't see yourself being one then please put this book down, turn around and be thankful you're walking away from an experience you'd rather forget!

Accept the Truth about Trading

Let me tie together a number of these key messages. Individually they're powerful, but together they're monumental as they strike to the truth about trading.

Contrary to popular trading literature, profitable trading is not about picking winners, picking tops or picking bottoms. Nor is it about knowing and mastering your inner self. No. You now know that trading, particularly with the trend, is miserable and painful. It's full of uncertainty and drawdowns. In time you'll learn it lacks dopamine and serotonin. If that wasn't challenging enough it also has a mathematical ROR attached. I've certainly painted you a bleak landscape, which I hope has concentrated your attention. I now want to narrow my grim observation into a pinpoint focus. To help funnel your energy, resources and concentration to where it counts.

In case you have any doubts, please let me emphasize that profitable trading is not about any of the misconstrued and popular misconception perpetuated by trading literature. That is, profitable trading, as I've said, is not about picking anything. Not about picking winners, picking tops or picking bottoms. No. It's not about mastering your inner self. It's not about finding a magic indicator or having the perfect entry technique. No. Profitable trading is not about being the smartest trader. It's not about being right and it's definitely not about knowing trading secrets. No.

In my opinion, the universal truth is that profitable trading is based on two key factors:

1. The math.
2. Being the best loser.

Simple. This is how I survive and make money trading. This is where you will need to be before you commence trading. This universal truth is based upon the universal principles of successful trading (please refer to *UPST*). Let's take a closer look at each.

The Math

Profitable trading is simply about the math, where you need to commence trading with a 0% ROR. You will need to learn how to correctly calculate it. If it's not at 0%, or if you're unable to calculate it, then you have no business trading. If you do trade then you'll deserve the disappointment you'll experience.

The math of profitable trading is to trade with a 0% ROR.

Calculating it begins with knowing the percentage return you can expect to earn for every dollar you lose based on your trading methodology. You will need positive 'expectancy' from your methodology (setup, entry, stop and exit). It's also about knowing what amount of your risk capital you are prepared to risk on each trade. It's about knowing the number of units of money you have to trade with. You will need good money management.

The mathematical combination of your expectancy and money management will generate a percentage probability of ruin. This is the math of profitable trading, combining a positive expectancy strategy with a sensible money management strategy. To be profitable you will need to commence trading with a 0% ROR. This is the math of profitable trading.

Being the Best Loser

Profitable trading also needs you to resist the disposition effect of hanging on to losing trades. Remember the only real secret to profitable trading is that the best loser is the long-term winner. You will need to learn to welcome your losses because you cannot avoid them in the business of trading. You will need to learn how to endure the pain of losing as it will become your constant companion. You will need to learn to never move a stop but stick to your trade plan. You will need to learn to ignore hope, fear and greed. You will need to learn to stop overthinking and focus on executing your trade plan. You will need to develop a proper mindset. You will need to have a good trading psychology.

The Universal Truth about Trading

Profitable trading is not about picking winners, tops or bottoms but simply;

#1 The MATH

$$\text{\$\$ Trading = positive expectancy + units of money}$$
$$\text{\$\$ Trading = 0\% risk-of-ruin}$$

#2 Being the BEST LOSER

- Welcome your losses.
- Endure the pain of losing, it's part of trading.
- Ignore hope, fear and greed. Stick to your plan.
- Develop a proper mindset.
- Develop a good trading psychology.

The universal truth is based upon the universal principles of successful trading.

UPST = Money Management + Methodology + Psychology

FIGURE 2.1 The universal truth is that profitable trading is not about picking winners, tops or bottoms. It's about the math and being the best loser.

I suggest you photocopy Figure 2.1 and stick it above your trading screen.

Acknowledge Being a Discretionary Trader is Difficult

There are two types of traders. They usually fall under the labels of either 'mechanical' or 'discretionary' traders.

First up please be aware that 'mechanical', 'systematic', 'quantitative' and 'algorithmic' are all interchangeable labels. They all refer to the same type of trader. Although 'algorithmic' does imply the addition of automatic electronic online order execution when a setup appears and is triggered. All these labels refer to the same type of trader. A trader who has a 100% objective strategy with clearly defined and unambiguous rules on when to trade, where to enter, where to place stops and where to exit. There is no discretion in their trade plan.

Now all traders, regardless of the mechanical or discretionary label, should have a complete trade plan that encompasses setups, entries, stops and exits.

A mechanical, systematic, quantitative or algorithmic trader has no discretion on whether or not they will trade a setup when it appears. They will follow their trade plan faultlessly without fear or favour. When a setup appears, they will trade it, regardless of market conditions or news headlines. An algorithmic trader in addition will have their online trading platform programmed to monitor their setups and automatically execute their orders online.

On the other hand, a discretionary trader will retain the final authority on whether or not they'll follow or execute their trade plan. They'll make the final decision. They'll use their discretion on whether or not to pull the trigger.

In my opinion, it's very difficult to succeed as a discretionary trader. I'd encourage everyone to consider trading on a systematic or mechanical basis. Not a discretionary basis.

Let's have a look at why.

Both traders are generally the same except for two areas:

	Trade Plan	Evidence
• Mechanical trader	Complete	Yes
• Discretionary trader	Incomplete	No

Mechanical traders have complete trade plans. They usually have less rules, where the trade plans can be measured for historical performance. They follow an evidence-based approach.

Discretionary traders generally have incomplete trade plans, as proponents usually have a 'but wait' excuse for delaying execution. Their incomplete trade plans usually have more rules (falling into the trap of excessive curve fitting) and are not measurable (due to incompleteness) for historical performance. They don't follow an evidence-based approach.

Both traders have trade plans. One complete, and one a work in progress. While the systematic trader will know theirs, the discretionary trader doesn't. I believe the 'discretionary' label is polite speak for a trader who is unprepared. Having an incomplete trade plan means they're unaware of their expectancy or ROR. Hey, they may not even know what 'expectancy' and 'ROR' mean?

This is why I believe it's usually more difficult to succeed as a discretionary trader. They're generally ignorant of their expectancy and ROR, trading blind with only faith and hope behind them. While, on the other hand, a mechanical trader knows their expectancy and ROR, trading with purpose and historical evidence, which gives them confidence.

Discretionary traders, being ignorant of their expectancy and ROR, have no historical evidence to tell them whether or not their trade plan has an edge. They're trading blind. Being blind makes it difficult to succeed in trading.

Take the following discretionary strategy as an example.

A discretionary trader may decide to trade breakouts from traditional congestion patterns such as flags, pennants and triangles in the direction of the trend. For the dominant trend they may choose to use a 200-day simple moving average. Once in a trade they may decide to use a daily close in the opposite direction beyond a short-term or medium-term moving average as their stop.

Now I don't have a problem with this particular approach and I can actually see many merits to the strategy (please refer to Curtis Arnold's Pattern Probability System (PPS) strategy in Chapter 6). However, for most discretionary traders who follow such a methodology I'd imagine they wouldn't know the expectancy of such a strategy. I think I could say with confidence they probably wouldn't even know how many 'flags', 'pennants' or 'triangles' existed in their preferred portfolio's historical data set? They'd be ignorant of the number of historical opportunities upon which they're basing their decision to trade. Not only that, they'd also be relying on those historical patterns to be overall profitable. Having faith in a couple of well-chosen chart examples isn't enough.

In addition, a discretionary trader is relying on their ability to visually identify their preferred patterns. A difficult enough task at the best of times when subjective opinion is required. And an almost impossible task when all your cognitive biases come to bear on your conscious mind. Expectation is a powerful force. It acts on your perceptions as much as gravity acts on us. It's a force. And when you expect to find a flag, pennant or triangle, guess what, you will find one, regardless of whether or not one exists, as we tend to see what we expect to see. It's a big problem for the discretionary trader. Well unfortunately it isn't sufficient to rely on your visualization skills to find patterns to support a strategy.

To know a strategy's expectancy you need to have scoured your portfolio's entire historical data set for all the congestion patterns. And you need to objectively define the patterns. Near enough isn't good enough. The patterns need to be accurately coded up so there are no 'ifs' or 'buts' or cognitive 'expectations'.

Next the trader will have to work out how to measure the impact of their subjective 'but wait' discretionary moments. I have no idea how to measure the impact of such a discretionary overlay. But let's assume the discretionary trader does.

Once the entirety of a discretionary trade plan is complete an historical profit and loss analysis, along with an equity curve, should be created and the resultant expectancy and ROR calculated.

Then the questions start. Does the methodology have a positive expectancy? Yes or no? If yes, what is the strategy's ROR once it's combined with a preferred money management strategy? Is it at 0%? If yes, are there enough trading opportunities to make the strategy worthwhile to trade? If yes, you're moving forward. You will then need to determine its level of robustness, which will come down to a question about its historical equity curve. Is it stable or fragile? Please note I'll be spending more time later discussing 'robustness'. But the point here is that a strategy's usefulness starts first with whether or not it has a positive expectancy and 0% ROR. Most discretionary traders cannot answer that question. Period. And that is not good enough.

Without that information it's hard to succeed as a discretionary trader.

So, it's an unfortunate occurrence that the majority of discretionary traders generally trade on hope. They hope their trade plan has a positive expectancy. They hope they won't go bust. Without knowing their expectancy or ROR discretionary traders are essentially gamblers, relying on unproven theories that in turn rely upon a few well-chosen picture-perfect chart examples.

I think deep down discretionary traders don't want the 'evidence' spot light shining on them. They would prefer to operate in the shadows where they can't be called out. They'll regularly use the old cliché excuse:

... you can't judge me on my imperfect application of a perfect theory...

Yes, I've actually seen that excuse used. Most, but not all, discretionary traders, I believe, are a little delusional. They become unwilling captives of their cognitive biases, believing in their ability to perfectly recognize and perfectly trade all future setup patterns (i.e. flags, pennants and triangles etc.). They have an overwhelming (false) belief in their confidence to identify tradable patterns.

So, in my opinion, it's very difficult to be a successful discretionary trader, not impossible, but difficult. A trader without knowledge of their expectancy and ROR is really trading in the dark. They're trading on faith that their preferred methodology has a tangible edge.

For the new or struggling trader, I would suggest they learn how to develop a mechanical or turn-key strategy where nothing is left to interpretation. Once completed and satisfied that their strategy delivers the appropriate expectancy, opportunities, ROR and robustness, then they could decide on how to trade it. Take every signal like a mechanical or algorithmic trader does, as I do myself, or do as Larry Williams does and trade the mechanical signals on a discretionary basis. Like Larry they could become discretionary mechanical traders. But first they would need a systematic, mechanical strategy to allow them to calculate their individual ROR and various performance metrics.

Follow the Smart Money

If I haven't convinced you of the merits of trading on a systematic/mechanical/algorithmic basis then you should look towards the professionals and see what they do (Figure 2.2).

According to BarclayHedge (www.barclayhedge.com) systematic trend followers had seen their assets under management grow from $22 billion in 1999 to over $298 billion by 2019. Over the same period, they estimate discretionary traders had only grown their assets under management from $8 billion to $12 billion.

Clearly, if the weight of professional money is behind systematic trend trading then shouldn't you sit up and take notice? I implore you to. If you are serious about achieving success in trading then please focus your attention and energy on becoming a mechanical/systematic/algorithmic trader.

It's only through following precise evidence-based and measurable rules that you will be able to calculate your expectancy and ROR, and know whether or not you're trading with purpose or merely gambling.

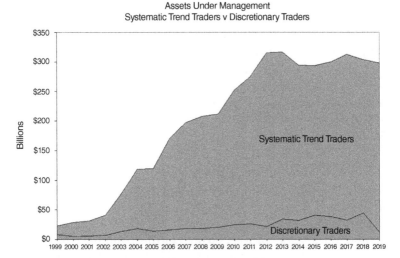

FIGURE 2.2 If you're undecided about whether or not you'd prefer to be a systematic or discretionary trader, you could do far worst then follow what the professional money does, trade on a systematic basis!

Placebo Traders

I want to make one qualification to my concerns about the diffi- culty in succeeding as a discretionary trader. In my previous book, *UPST*, I discussed those successful traders who enter the market based on unproven theories yet continued to make money. Traders blindly trading with success without knowing either their expectancy or ROR.

I referred to those traders as 'placebo' traders.

Trader's whose confidence to trade was misplaced on unsub- stantiated ideas. I came to the acceptance that it didn't really matter why a trader entered the market, as long as their accumulative wins were larger than their accumulative losses. Even if a trader's faith in a particular market theory was misplaced, did it really matter how they entered if they still won due to their good trading instincts? Instincts that ensured their wins paid for all their losses? Of course it doesn't matter.

However, these placebo traders are the exception to the rule, where the majority of traders lose. I see them as being exceptionally good natural traders, knowing to cut losses short and letting profits run. Unfortunately, for the rest of us mere mortals it's not that easy.

So, I still stand by my assertion that it is difficult to succeed as a discretionary trader and that most traders should first become competent at being a mechanical or systematic trader. However, I do acknowledge that there is a small niche of naturally gifted traders. Traders who are chemically wired to be exceptional traders, who don't need a structured systematic methodology producing a positive expectancy and 0% ROR to succeed.

Be Sensible with Indicators

Please be sparing with indicators. Generally, I'm not a fan of subjective variable dependent indicators. Yes, I do use some indicators in my strategies such as the average true range and moving average indicators; however, as a general rule, I'd prefer to deal with 100% price. The big problem with variable dependent indicators is that they usually lead to equity curve instability, a situation best avoided. To my mind they represent the proverbial poison chalice where they'll excite you on the one hand with what appears to be a useful insight only to see their usefulness vanish, usually at your cost.

The Biggest Crime

The biggest crime you can commit in trading is to lose your entire risk capital. Over 90% of active traders have committed it. And over 90% of active traders will continue to commit it. Please do not commit this crime yourself. Your best defence is to ensure your ROR remains at 0%. Make it your personal goal to become not only an expert in ROR but also an expert practitioner. Better yet, consider having '0% ROR' tattooed on the inside of both your eyelids to ensure you even dream about it. A painful thought? Absolutely. But one less painful then actually committing the crime.

Well, this brings me to the end of my key 'knowledge' messages. My next key messages refer to 'risk'.

RISK

This is the time when you'll need to check if you're driving with airbags. Apart from losing money, there are other risks you'll need to be aware of and be on guard for. If this was an audio book I'd insert:

... danger, danger Will Robinson ...

to alert you to the risks ahead. And the risks I'm talking about aren't related to strategy performance or volatile markets. There are other and just as important risks that you need to be aware of. They include:

- the storytellers,
- the Holy Grail,
- you and
- the four horsemen of strategy apocalypse.

The Storytellers

Beware of the experts.

You know who they are. The self-proclaimed experts. The noise makers. The talking heads. The clever editors and the persuasive communicators. I'm talking about those well-groomed studio hosts of financial news services who generously offer their insightful opinions. I'm talking about those bold headlines insinuating bold predictions. I'm talking about those harried looking brokers being interviewed at the close of markets. I'm talking about those persistent email publishers espousing strong market views and forecasts. And I'm particularly talking about those economists, both real and self-proclaimed, advocating their 'economic' thoughts. Those attractive faces with entertaining and authoritative voices and words who actually believe what they say. You know them. The infotainers, the repeaters, the amplifiers, the fiction peddlers and the revisionists. The distracters. The storytellers.

The storytellers who occupy the airwaves, internet and print. They populate the communication channels from TV to radio, through books to newsletters, from podcasts to YouTube. You have seen them, heard them and read them. They'll offer up enthusiastic commentary and clever and entertaining prose disguised as useful information. Their recency bias usually encourages them to falsely perpetuate and extrapolate the recent past. They become victims of their own confirmation and anchoring biases when advocating their pet and entrenched views. They become the champions of the herd and its consensus thinking, the biggest red flag to an angry market. A market whose nature is to punish the consensus. They think the market's Mr Maximum Adversity is a fairy tale character.

You will have to learn to ignore the storytellers. You now have to take full responsibility for your own fate and lock yourself into a virtual hermetically sealed cocoon where you can only hear yourself and not all the distracters out there. They're all noise and none of their commentary represents actionable information.

Those talking heads of financial news services are possibly your biggest risk with their breathless and excited announcements of tick-by-tick moves. Those earnest economists, echoing their own faith-based doctrine, confuse dogma with useful evidence-based facts. These peripheral market participants, despite their impeccable grooming and authoritative sounding financial advocacy, offer no more than puff punditry. Trivial popcorn to placate the average viewer.

To stay your own course, you will have to learn to ignore them despite their convincing narrative. A narrative that only acts as a siren call, which will lure you to your financial demise. Their opinions are not anchored with any positive expectancy and nor does their opinion represent any actionable knowledge.

It's all noise and it's not actionable information.

The storytellers' noise is just enthusiastic opinion. It's simply hubris. Please remember enthusiastic and well-articulated commentary is not useful and actionable information, it's only someone's 'opinion' divorced from any semblance of expectancy.

One particular group of storytellers you need to be very wary of are the really serious, really well-groomed, really well-educated and accredited and really well-spoken economists. I believe they are the most dangerous. Not because their opinions are less accurate than any of the other distracters but because their occupation affords them unworthy gratis, which leads people to take them seriously. You need to understand that despite their university education, their area of expertise—economic knowledge—is just like religion, it's faith based. There is no hard science or evidence to support their preferred school of economic thought. They, like a poorly developed trading strategy, have too many variables and too many assumptions baked into their preferred theory on how economics and the world works. However, their 'respectability' of being university educated along with their sobering 'economic' language and distinguished-sounding employer suggests there is substance to their opinions and their forecasts. This 'respectability' unfortunately attracts traders with the same cataclysmic outcome as moths that are attracted to light.

If you doubt my poor opinion of their poor opinion then please refer to David Reifschneider and Peter Tulip's 2017 paper titled 'Gauging the Uncertainty of the Economic Outlook Using Historical Forecasting Errors: The Federal Reserve's Approach'. At the time of publishing this paper David Reifschneider worked for the US Federal Reserve while Peter Tulip worked for the Reserve Bank of Australia. Both heavy hitters and trained economists. Their paper concluded that economists can't forecast. Their study compared forecasts of important economic indicators (like unemployment, inflation, interest rates and gross domestic product etc) and then compared those forecasts to the actual outcomes. The result? You guessed it. There were widespread errors! Yep, economists, despite their good education, sombre appearance, economic speak and good manners, can't forecast! Their economic models are kaput. Their opinion isn't worth the paper it's written on. You're better off with a coin toss.

You need to remember market commentators, observers or pundits, infotainers, repeaters, amplifiers, fiction peddlers and revisionists usually have, but not always, an ulterior motive. Their motive is to build your trust, a potential customer. They're looking to appear knowledgeable and confident so that you will feel knowledgeable and confident. They're trying to cultivate trust—to become so trustworthy that you'll purchase something from their business. Whether it's a bank loan or a cable or streaming or advisory subscription service. They have an ulterior motive. They're no more than dopamine peddlers. The people we should listen to or read are the actual traders, and preferably successful traders, not the animated and well-spoken mannequins filling up our smart screens.

It's best to ignore the storytellers.

The Holy Grail

Another huge risk you face is to believe that a mythical Holy Grail trading strategy exists. That painless strategy with 100% accuracy and 0% drawdown. You know the one.

So, let's address that particular elephant in the room. The unhealthy, unrealistic and unholy obsession with pursuing the Holy

Grail. Many traders believe there is a universal secret out there that will reveal and unlock the market's mysteries to the delight of both their trading accounts and egos. If only they could locate it. And it's not from their lack of trying!

This belief that there is a perfect strategy out there for you to either buy or develop will be a constant risk to you. It's a timewaster, a distraction and enabler of procrastination. It's a huge rabbit hole you don't want to fall into.

You need to stay anchored in the present and stop procrastinating as you idle your time away dreaming about finding or developing the perfect strategy. The one you can clearly see becoming your own virtual ATM. You need to drag yourself back and focus on the now, the present.

The present manifests itself in the bills you have to pay. That's the reality of life where we all reside. No doubt you've caught yourself day dreaming, idly dreaming the time away believing there is an easier way to trade, if only you could find it. Rabbit holes may make a pleasant distraction—however, they don't help to pay the bills.

Opinions, beliefs, declarations or intentions of what you're going to do doesn't contribute to the bank account. It's trading a robust positive expectancy strategy today that has a 0% ROR. That is what will build your account over time, not idly thinking about what you want to do.

With this book you'll have no excuse not to find a robust positive expectancy strategy, independently validate it, select a manageable portfolio, complete a T.E.S.T and place yourself in a position to trade it with a 0% ROR. None. It will only be your will, or lack of will, that will hold you back. But only if you accept the present.

However, I'm a realist and I know most of you will still keep a small candle burning in the deepest recesses of your minds for that mythical strategy. Hence, rather than attempt to shut it out completely, let's try to give it some clarity, so you could possibly find a sensible place to keep that candle burning. A place safe enough that it doesn't burn your house down!

First of all, the Holy Grail will mean something different to different traders. It may be the ultimate 100% accuracy strategy that doesn't lose and represents the mythical and proverbial money tree. To others it may be a reasonably accurate strategy with minimal drawdown. Regardless of the degree of 'Holy', the idea is that it represents a robust methodology that is painless to trade. That it's a joy to enter the market with.

So, each of us will have our own degree and definition of paradise trading.

It's my honest belief that such an 'easy' and almost 'perfect' trading strategy does not exist, and its pursuit is pointless, harmful and energy and resource sapping.

Pointless because you and I don't need a Holy Grail strategy to make money. An ordinary robust strategy will work just fine.

Harmful because it will distract you from getting on with the business of trading today. Harmful because the task of finding perfection is an impossible task. Its objective is as impossible as finding the end of a brilliant rainbow. Being in an endless circle of frustration would knock any rational person off their centre. Harmful, as I said.

Energy and resource sapping because it would be an infinite herculean task to achieve. And that's the point, it would in all likelihood be an impossible task to complete.

However, I also understand human nature and how we're all inquisitive.

So, for the moment, let's assume and accept that a Holy Grail strategy does, in whatever degree or definition, exist. For example, let's assume James Simons' Renaissance Technologies very secretive Medallion Fund does possess such a fabled Holy Grail strategy, or portfolio of Holy Grail strategies. According to a Bloomberg article published in 2016, the fund's annualized return (CAGR), before fees, between 1988 and 2016 was 80%! I think such a result would warrant the 'Holy Grail' label being applied.

So, rather than hypothesizing about the existence of a Holy Grail strategy, there appears to be evidence—and I grant its only based on a single Bloomberg article (although Renaissance Technologies is the envy of its Hedge Fund peers)—that such a money-making strategy, or portfolio of strategies, does exist.

So, let's accept that a Holy Grail strategy exists, and that the carrot is firmly planted in Medallion Fund. Now we can all calibrate our research and fantasy compasses towards Setaukets, Suffolk County, Long Island in New York where Renaissance Technologies is located.

So, there we have it. The Holy Grail does exist and we know where it is.

Now to be a realist.

To ever hope to achieve what the Medallion Fund has achieved, I think it's only logical to accept you would have to duplicate their setup. And that's the kicker. According to Bloomberg, among the roughly 300 staff they employ 90 hold PhDs in mathematics and physics. That's the level of effort and expense you'd have to incur to hope to duplicate what they have, which for most of us would be an impossible task.

So, my point is this. Even if we accept the existence of a Holy Grail, it's a pointless task to even attempt to pursue it unless you're a billionaire yourself. So, give it up. Let go of the dream and focus on the present where there are now, today plenty of robust trend-trading strategies with plenty of positive out-of-sample performance ready to work for you. I will review a number of them for you in Chapter 6. You just need to stop staring over the fence and focus on your own backyard.

So, to ensure we get it out of our system, please let me rinse and repeat. If we accept a Holy Grail strategy does exist, let's also acknowledge that:

It'll be too costly in time/effort/resources to unearth it.

And let's also acknowledge:

1. It's unnecessary to know for success.
2. It'll be more worthwhile to focus on what works now.
3. It'll be more worthwhile to focus on what has worked in the past.
4. If it has worked in the past it'll be more likely to work in the future.

So, we traders need to 'compartmentalize' reality and our hopes.

For reality we need to focus on the now, the present. Focus on what works. Focus on practical, established and robust trading ideas. Focus on making money now to pay the bills now.

For hope we need to put aside time for research. Put aside time to (attempt) to discover the elusive Holy Grail. But only put time aside for research if you're successfully making money in the present, now.

In a nut shell, if you're a treasure hunter at heart, you need to accept there is no Holy Grail strategy today. It may exist tomorrow, but definitely not today. So please accept the present and focus on making money now and don't lose yourself down tomorrow's fanciful rabbit hole. Chasing or waiting for perfection is a pipedream. There is no perfect strategy today. There are good strategies, but not perfect ones. You do have to suffer pain to be profitable. Don't risk losing yourself down the endless rabbit hole believing there is a profitable and painless Holy Grail money-making strategy out there for you today. It's a time waster. Anchor your focus on reality, stay in the present—and only allow 'hope' to appear once you have successfully become a sustainable trader.

You—Wanting to be Relevant

Believe it or not, but you present another big risk to yourself.

As individuals we wish to be recognized and valued. It's no different with trading. To be valued we believe we'll need to create our own strategies.

The issue you will have to address and control is relevancy. Your own personal ego may be your biggest obstacle to success. You. Your need to be relevant. Your need to have your work valued and recognized. Traders feel their work and effort to succeed in the markets should be recognized and rewarded. They want to receive a dividend for all their efforts. And the best way to be recognized, to receive a reward for effort expended, is to trade their own strategy. Since most strategies suffer from data mining and excessive curve fitting it's not a positive reward, but negative. So, traders continue to tweak and adjust, continue to brain storm and construct, and unfortunately, continue to suffer. They stay trapped in this endless loop because they believe they deserve a positive reward for all the effort and financial pain they have invested to become successful traders. And in their mind, the only reward suitable is to actually trade their own strategy, even when there are fine, not perfect, but perfectly fine and well-established strategies with positive out-of-sample performance to choose from.

It's a paradox where the only reward a trader should be concerned with is a growing account balance. Yet they place more importance on doing it via their own development efforts. All because they want to be relevant. Does it really matter who designed the strategy as long as it helps you make money? It's best not to pander to your ego.

Later I'll share with you what I believe may be one of the best publicly available trading strategies there is. There's no secret about it. It's very well known. It's a strategy that should become every trader's benchmark against which they should compare their own development efforts. If they're unable to develop a better methodology then, in my opinion, they should trade it. It's simple. It's robust. It shouldn't matter who developed it. It should be preferred over any personal development that is inferior.

The moral of my efforts here is that to ignore well-established robust strategies, to satisfy your self-worth and to pander to your ego is foolish.

If you suffer from the need to be relevant, remind yourself that you are, because your choice of strategy to trade, your choice of money management strategy and your execution is 100% you. Without 'yourself' you'd be trading with a ROR above 0%. So, you *do* count.

So, please accept that many good trend-trading strategies have already been developed, some time ago and not by you or me. You will need to learn to leave your ego at the door. You will have to fight the need to make yourself and your efforts relevant. Don't try to extract a dividend from all the effort and knowledge you have gained from all the trading books, strategies, seminars, workshops, software and webinars you have purchased, attended, installed and viewed. If you come across a robust and simple idea that your own efforts cannot surpass then please push aside your pride and ego, believe what you see, and use it.

The Four Horsemen of Strategy Apocalypse

Finally, you should keep an eye out for a huge risk ahead of you that I call the key predictors of strategy failure, the four horsemen of strategy apocalypse (Figure 2.3). They are:

1. Data mining.
2. Excessive curve fitting.
3. Latest or newest trading idea.
4. Missing equity curves.

Data Mining

Data mining occurs when performance results appear on only a few select and well-chosen markets. It's no more than old fashion cherry picking, where the developer shows their strategy's performance on the best performing markets. This can occur when a strategy's historical results are shown on only a few (perfect) markets or only on an individual market sector (like only currencies, or only interest rates). Now, I know that individual markets can and do have their own odd idiosyncrasies, as well as market sectors. Where, for example, index markets are quite distinct from others as they're always back filling (mean reverting), making it hard for traditional trend-trading strategies to be successful. I personally trade different strategies on

---

Key Predictors of Strategy Failure

The Four Horsemen of Strategy Apocalypse

1. Data mining.
   Signs are;
     i. Few markets.
     ii. Select markets.
     iii. Sector dependent markets.

2. Excessive curve fitting.
   Signs are;
     i. Too many rules.
     ii. Too many variable-dependent indicators.
     iii. Different variable values for buy and sell setups.
     iv. Different variable values per market.

3. New.
   Signs are;
     i. Marketing hype heralding the virtue of a latest discovery.
     ii. Lack of out-of-sample data.

4. Missing equity curve.
   Signs are;
     i. No equity curve = No strategy.
        No strategy means absence of clearly defined
        trading rules.

FIGURE 2.3 When you see the Four Horsemen of Strategy Apocalypses galloping towards you, run!

indices as opposed to other markets. However, as a good general rule, it's better to see a strategy's performance over an entire universal portfolio of diversified markets, and not a specifically chosen handful. Versatility across a portfolio of markets is one of the key attributes of winning strategies. Versatility eliminates the risk of data mining. Winning strategies are based on sound ideas that should work across any freely traded market. Only seeing a few well-chosen markets should make you suspicious of either your own development efforts or others.

Excessive Curve Fitting

In statistics data consists of signals and noise. Market data that reflects the dominant trend represents good signals. All the back filling, twists and turns represent noise for the trend trader. Overly curve-fitted strategies attempt to capture every dip and rally in the market. Traders should design their strategies to capture only the meaningful signals in historical data, not the noise as it has no predictive power for the trend trader.

Now, curve fitting will always exist in all strategies as a level of curve fitting is required to capture meaningful market signals. So, curve fitting will always be present in any strategy. You will always require an idea of what signal you want to capture and a way to capture it if you wish to develop a strategy. Without the idea and way to capture it there is no strategy. So, curve fitting will always be present. All traders do it. Most traders overdo it. The good traders always look to minimize it. You can fall into the trap of excessive curving fitting, where you attempt to capture every dip and rally in the market (i.e. the noise) when you either end up with or see strategies that have:

- a preference for complexity over simplicity,
- too many rules with too many filters,
- too many indicators with too many adjustable variables,
- different variable values between buy and sell setups and
- different variable values across different markets.

Or, in short hand, strategies that are too complex as opposed to being simple. The complexity introduced is designed to avoid, cut out or skip performance-damaging loses while capturing home run, celebratory and skyrocketing performance enhancing profits. Loses that will inevitably reappear in the future because the complexity will not be able to avoid them. Profits that will inevitably fail to materialize because the complexity will not be able to recapture them. Both negative outcomes that will damage a trader's account and confidence.

The Latest and Newest Trading Idea

This is a biggy. This is a hard one to defend as you'll be up against all the clever endorphin-charged marketing magic the unscrupulous developers employ. You'll recognize it when you see marketing hype heralding the virtue of a latest discovery. Their clever marketing is designed to trigger the opioid receptors in our brains that release those euphoria-embracing endorphins. To give us a natural high, which they hope will lead to an impulse buy, just one click away. And it's a difficult impulse to deny. The attraction to something 'new' is a powerful motivator as the idea of new gives the hope that it will replace the pain and disappointment of 'old' experiences. Experiences such as continual losing. Who wouldn't want something new to erase past negative experiences?

Another trick to be aware of is the 'denial' approach marketers use: the suggestion that you need the 'latest' otherwise you'll be left behind. To 'deny' yourself would be unfair. Take this clever but manipulative pitch:

> *You need ongoing, current, cutting-edge trading strategies. Without them you'll fall behind and slip into the abyss of mediocre traders who never quite make it to the top.*

"Wow!" hey? Who doesn't want the opportunity to stay ahead? No one wants to fall behind let alone slip into the abyss! It's such a reassuring and intuitive sounding statement that it would capture the majority of newbie traders. You need to be aware of these types of pitches as they are dangerous at worst and misleading at best. They appeal and comfort your need to have certainty by attaining the latest, newest strategies. It implies yesterday's strategies with their accompanying losses will be destined for the bin, never to be seen again because you'll no longer be using yesterday's trading information. It's 100% rubbish. What you need is what works, what can be supported by out-of-sample evidence. And the older the idea, the more out-of-sample evidence you'll have to build your confidence.

So please try to stay alert to any dazzlingly 'new' trading discoveries, which are absent of any out-of-sample performance, and keep your endorphins in check.

Missing Equity Curve

Finally, another clear sign of future strategy failure is the absence of an historical equity curve. The absence is a telling sign. It occurs either because the strategy is too subjective without clear and obvious rules to code up or the developer knows on close inspection it's a losing proposition. So, regardless of how compelling the narrative is or how good the chosen chart example looks to support a trading idea, unless an historical equity curve along with a calculated expectancy and ROR is present, it'll be no more than a pipedream and one best left alone.

This brings me to the end of my key risk messages. Next, I want to share my application insights.

APPLICATION

This is where the rubber hits the road. My key application messages include:

- develop your verification skills, get software now,
- less is more,
- robustness is gold,
- embrace the old, it's the new fashionable,
- resist the new,
- develop turn-key strategies and
- trade a portfolio of turn-key strategies.

Let's look at each.

Develop Your Verification Skills, Get Software Now

If you're serious, really serious, you will want the right tools. You will need the right software tools to verify trading ideas. Without evidence your methodology has a positive expectancy and a 0% ROR—then you are straight out gambling. No ifs. No buts. Period. You deserve the results you get.

It's time to change that.

It's time to develop a useful and necessary skill. You must learn how to code up methodologies. You must learn how to create historical equity curves, perform profit and loss analysis and calculate performance metrics. To do this you'll need to buy and learn how to use appropriate backtesting software. Without appropriate software you won't be able to efficiently verify a trading idea. So, learn how to start coding up trading ideas that resonate. Start creating equity curves. If you don't believe me then please read my interview with Brian Schad in Chapter 12 of *UPST*.

Now the bad news is that it will take time, effort and frustration. Learning how to code doesn't occur over night. You'll need to lean in because without software skills you will struggle to independently verify ideas. The good news is that with suitable software skills you'll be in a far more knowledgeable and confident place where you'll be able to make far better decisions.

I use VBA (Visual Basic Application) for Excel to code up and test my trading ideas. Learning how to code using Excel macros was the best thing I ever did. It made me independent and gave me the skill set to examine any trading idea that came into my head. I'm not suggesting you go off and use Excel's VBA as I know there are plenty of good third-party programs out there that allow you to code trading ideas. However, I am suggesting that if you don't already have the coding skills you should be looking to acquire them!

To find what's available its best to do a simple Google search. However, to help you along I recently held an all weekend online workshop with traders from around the world (they came in from Canada, the United States, Poland, Australia, Brazil, Hong Kong and Japan). During the workshop I asked my traders what software they used and I'm happy to share their responses with you. There was a varied list of software—however, as a starting point you may like to review the following off the shelf trading packages:

- AmiBroker,
- Channalyze,
- MultiCharts,
- Trade Navigator,
- Tradeguider,
- TradeStation and
- Trading Blox.

Out of this list the more popular packages being used among my traders were TradeStation, MultiCharts, Amibroker and Trading Blox.

Apart from these third-party packages some of my traders have elected to code my strategies straight from the following programming languages:

- Visual Basic,
- Python,
- Java and
- Ruby.

Now, what is interesting, and a valuable insight I am very happy to share with you, is that although a few of my traders are programmers by profession, others, like myself, are not. Yet they, like me, made the effort to learn how to code straight from a programming language. What is also interesting is that it wasn't only the enthusiastic home-trained coders who decided to write their own trading programs but also the professional programmers. This is an email I received from one of my traders, who by profession is a programmer;

> *Hi Brent,*
>
> *I use TradeStation/MultiCharts for anything that requires heavy visualization or automation, but it's not good for portfolio-level simulation or execution.*
>
> *I use Trading Blox for portfolio-level simulation, but it's not good for visualization, and they require you to pay yearly for the IB integration.*
>
> *I also use Excel to verify the individual signals/debugging.*
>
> *I've been working to develop my own backtest platform using Java ... it's called Pathfinder =)).*
>
> *In backtesting your systems, I actually got fed up with the TradeStation/Trading Blox limitations and I've decided to do all my testing and automation using Pathfinder after I'm done with this round of backtesting. I should have done this a long time ago. I was actually inspired with what you said during the seminar and saw what you've built, given that you're not even a programmer!*
>
> *Thanks*
> *M.L USA.*

It's certainly nice to leave an impression on someone. And it actually reminded me of myself when I got my inspiration to start building my own VBA Excel model. Please refer to my interview with Larry Williams in Chapter 12 of *UPST*.

Like myself, the following trader has knuckled down to become a self-taught programmer:

> *Hi Brent,*
>
> *I wouldn't say that I am a developed programmer yet. I have been learning Python for the last couple of months, and have just coded 5 of your strategies in the last few weeks (to the point that it can check the data and generates orders if satisfied by one click). I am finishing the other 4 strategies in the next 2-3 weeks so the whole IDX portfolio will run from Python by just few a clicks.*
>
> *Cheers*
> *J.W Australia.*

However, this trader, also self-taught, has taken it to another level:

Hi Brent,
Some notes on software development:

- *Your structured, simple and straight forward approach to trading really resonated with me.*
- *I purchase Microsoft Visual Studio and two books on VB.NET programming.*
- *I read chapter one and did all the exercises in the book . . . and kept working through the books on my kitchen table, each night after the kids were in bed.*
- *I mapped out what I needed the software to do—I focused on 'the HOW':*
  1. *Open a text file and load into an array (I use US date time on my computer).*
  2. *Perform calculations—setups, entry levels, stop, entry date, exit level, exit date, net position for each long and short side of each system.*
  3. *Create the text for the orders.*
  4. *Record the trade history and calculate the performance metrics.*
  5. *Open an excel file, paste arrays into the excel file, close and save it.*
- *I broke this down into small steps and tested a small program for each step (e.g. open a file and read each line)—Google is a great resource for finding out how to do things.*
- *I audited the output to make 100% sure the program worked correctly— encountered and corrected a lot of bugs.*
- *I needed my wife to place the orders each day . . . so I needed to simplify the process (to make her life easy) . . . I wrote an MT4 script to read a CSV order file and place orders automatically.*

Nothing that anyone else couldn't do—just like eating an elephant . . . small bites and one bite at a time . . . and just keep chipping away at it over about 3 years.

Cheers
T.W Australia.

Well there you go readers. Defy human nature. Do the work. Take small bites. Persist and you'll be rewarded. It is possible to learn how to code trading ideas to create equity curves, perform profit and loss analysis and calculate the resultant expectancy and ROR. And if the resultant robustness analysis suggests stability in your equity curve then you can also learn to code your strategies to automatically produce orders. And if you don't believe me that it's possible, then just re-read the comments above. They are from real people, real traders, with real ambition. They are the people to listen to. Not the repeaters, amplifiers, infotainers, distracters and revisionists.

Remember you're smart? Good, because you are. You are smart enough to now know not to trade what you think. Now take your smarts and start teaching yourself how to code ideas either with an off-the-shelf third-party package or straight from a programming language. Remember you are smart. I've shown how other traders have done it, so you can too. The only reason you won't is because you're:

- too time constrained and rely on a third party for help,
- not as committed to trading successfully as you thought,
- plain lazy,
- not as smart as I give you credit for, or
- unfortunately, you're subconsciously into trading for the thrill of gambling.

It is never too late to start. Just take small bites at a time.

(Now I just have to see whether I can enrol Katia into placing my orders, wish me luck there!)

Less is More

Strategy failure is illustrated by equity curve instability. Instability that is usually caused by excessive curve fitting. Excessive curve fitting creates too much complexity. 'Complexity' is adult speak for too many components (rules and filters) and too many indicators with adjustable variables. This is why I'm generally not a fan of indicators where traders can spend too much time tweaking each and every variable to create their dream equity curve. A dream that usually turns into a nightmare as regularly as night follows day.

I will be spending more time on the issue of excessive curving fitting and the resultant complexity, equity curve stability/instability and strategy failure later on.

However, at this point, a key application message is to keep your methodology simple. Remember less is more. Please look to keep your strategy simple, objective and consistent because complex, subjective and inconsistency kills. Only deep pain and deep disappointment will be found in complexity.

I personally think the following quotes are some of the best I've ever read about trading. The first is from Tom DeMark, the world-renowned market analyst who has worked for many of the big names like Paul Tudor Jones and Steve Cohen. He remarked in Art Collins' book *Market Beaters* (Traders Press, Inc. 2004):

> *The bottom line was, after 17 programmers and 4 or 5 years of testing, the basic 4 or 5 systems worked best.*

Tom DeMark was referring to the time he worked for Paul Tudor Jones. While at Tudor Investments he created four or five basic systems. After creating the strategies, the firm brought in 17 programmers to examine optimization models, artificial intelligence and anything possible that had to do with higher-level math. And that's when he made his observation that, after 17 programmers and four or five years of testing, the *basic four or five systems worked best.* As I said, I think his observation is very insightful and the moral of the message is to not look for answers in complexity.

Please avoid complexity and embrace less is more when developing ideas to trade. And if you don't believe me, then please listen to Tom DeMark.

Robustness is Gold

Robustness is defined by a stable, upward sloping equity curve on out-of-sample data. A tradable robustness should be the Holy Grail objective of every methodology. Robustness is gold in trading, it's to die for. Naturally, all methodologies believe they work but in application they don't. So, a methodology that simply works, has worked since it was released or has worked since the idea was published is rare, very rare and therefore worth its weight in gold. Robustness is what keeps you going during those inevitable and painful drawdowns. It's what keeps your confidence up when you begin doubting your strategy.

Robustness and stability are interchangeable.

Robustness—the Number One Attribute

Robustness should be the first attribute you look for in a strategy. It's singularly the most important attribute any strategy can have. Unless a strategy can continue to perform well into the future it's worthless.

Its ability to perform will be a direct function of its robustness. You will need to learn how to identify it. Whenever I review an idea, despite how compelling it is, unless I see robustness, I'll ignore it. I hope you do as well.

Robustness—Ranks Ahead of Performance Metrics

Robustness trumps performance metrics. Don't be convinced otherwise. If you aren't already aware, you will be in time, there is a dazzling array of performance metrics out there. As traders you can get carried away with the choice of measurements available. From an extensive array of ratios (Sharpe, Sortino, Calmar, Mar, Treynor and Martin) to Van Tharp's Quality System Number to Jensen's Alpha and Modigliani to expectancy, ROR, reward/risk ratio, profit factor, the Ulcer Performance Index, maximum drawdown and CAGR you'll soon realize the world of system performance can get pretty cluttered.

However, the unfortunate truth is that the majority of performance metrics are superfluous if a strategy is not robust enough to see a positive upward sloping out-of-sample equity curve. It doesn't matter how shiny and impressive performance metrics look if a strategy has no legs. So, please understand that no amount of marvellous metrics will help lift a falling equity curve.

In my opinion, robustness trumps the majority of performance metrics.

However, if you find there are a number of robust strategies competing for your attention then certainly an array of performance metrics is useful in ranking the methodologies. I'll be sharing the performance metrics I use later in Chapter 8.

But unfortunately, for most strategies below the line, they are simply not robust enough and have little or next to no indication of being robust. Excessive curve fitting and data mining sees enthusiastic ideas crumble under the market's onslaught. No amount of above-the-line positive performance metrics will help a south bound equity curve. If you feel compelled, certainly review and give consideration to those performance metrics that grab your attention; however, understand they're all superfluous if your strategy is not robust to begin with.

Robustness—Time is Priceless

What is priceless when reviewing a strategy is time since release date.

The more time, the more out-of-sample results there is. The more time, the more evidence there is a strategy is robust. The more time, the more confidence a trader has that their strategy will trade out of future drawdowns (Figure 2.4)—because confidence is everything when you're in a long, deep, dark drawdown. Belief that your strategy will recover and return to a new equity high. The confidence to stick to your strategy's trade plan comes from its out-of-sample performance. The more time in the market, the more evidence. The older the strategy the better. The more confidence you have in your strategy, the higher the likelihood that you'll continue to trade your strategy out of its drawdown.

Robustness—R-Squared Tradability

I've mentioned that the Holy Grail objective of all strategies should be a tradable robustness. So, when robustness does exist it's preferable

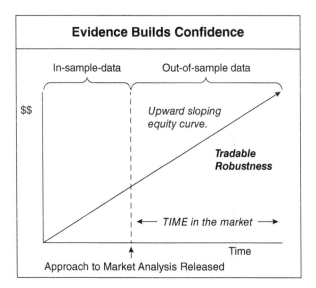

FIGURE 2.4 The longer a strategy idea has been known, the more out-of-sample performance data there is and the more confidence it gives the trader.

that the robustness is tradable. For the average retail trader, a strategy, despite its compelling robustness, is all academic if it has institutional size drawdowns. For you and I, we need to keep it real.

One metric I use to gauge tradability is the R-squared calculation. It measures how close an equity curve fits a regression line. A 100% reading suggests the equity curve is very smooth, representing a straight line. A low reading suggests the equity curve is very bumpy and difficult to trade. I generally prefer strategies with 90+% R-squared readings.

Robustness—How to Measure

There are only two approaches you can use to measure a strategy's robustness:

1. evidenced based and
2. indicative (faith) based.

Robustness—Evidence Based

The only undeniable proof, or evidence of robustness, is positive out-of-sample performance. A positive upward sloping equity curve post release date. The ultimate authority. Out-of-sample results. It's simple, pure 100% evidence. It's fact. There is no denying the strategy is robust. Nothing beats out-of-sample performance. No clever algebraic performance metric. No compelling and overwhelming trading logic. No consensus building, overly enthusiastic and authoritative advocacy. No slick and clever cognitive manipulative marketing. It's all superfluous to out-of-sample performance.

The best strategies with plenty of out-of-sample performance are the older, established methodologies. Old ideas that have lasted the test of time. Utilizing an old or established trading principle offers the trader plenty of out-of-sample data to *demonstrate* the stability of their strategy's equity curve. The more out-of-sample data, the more time a strategy has to demonstrate its stability and robustness.

If good out-of-sample performance exists, everything else is redundant. Opinions about the strategy. Marvellous metrics. Cautionary comments. Dubious doubts. Partial praise. Hesitant hedging. All redundant. All pointless. If a strategy can deliver positive out-of-sample performance then it's robust. No ifs. No buts. Just robust with a capital 'R'. In Chapter 6 I'll review a number of well-established trend-trading strategies. As you'll see, the majority have positive out-of-sample performance. They are robust. There is no denying their performance. Now, whether their performance is at an acceptable level is another question all together, which I will address later in the book. However, for evidence of robustness, the majority of strategies I'll review have it in spades.

Robustness—Indicative (Faith) Based

If a strategy has no history then by definition it's new. New strategies cannot provide evidence of out-of-sample performance, or robustness, because none exists. However, this shouldn't prevent traders from attempting to develop or review new strategies. And there is no reason why new strategies can't be robust if they're versatile and follow good design principles.

Trading a new strategy is really based on faith. A developer, by ensuring versatility and following good design principles, will hope their new strategy will be robust. Robust enough to avoid the twin evils of strategy development—data mining and excessive curve fitting. They will *hope* stability will occur in their new strategy's equity curve. It is possible.

The trick is to avoid the twin evils of strategy development. One can be eliminated while the other will always be present. Experienced traders will look to minimize curve fitting while less experienced traders will overdo it.

There are two key indications of robustness:

1. versatility and
2. good design.

Versatility—Avoids Data Mining   Versatility refers to a strategy's profitability over a diverse portfolio of universal markets. Versatility is a good indication of robustness as it suggests a strategy has avoided data mining where it will only appear to work on a number of well-chosen, cherry-picked markets.

Good Design—Avoids Excessive Curve Fitting   Signs that a strategy has followed good design principles is a good indication of robustness, as it suggests the strategy has avoided excessive curve fitting.

Good design principles include:

- Measurability
  - Provides complete trade plans with clearly defined, unambiguous and objective rules for:
    - when to trade,
    - where to enter,
    - where to place stops and
    - where to exit.
  - Allows calculation of a strategy's expectancy and a trader's ROR.
- Simplicity
  - Favours less is more.
  - Favours simplicity over complexity.
  - Favours objectiveness over subjectiveness.
  - Favours rigidity over flexibility.
  - Favours sound, boring and logical ideas over thrilling, exciting and esoteric ideas.
  - Has few rules.
  - Has few indicators.
  - Has few variables.
  - Has the same values for both buy and sell setup.
  - Has the same values across all markets
  - Avoids excessive curve fitting.

If these indications are present then a strategy can be considered potentially robust. That's it. Versatile, measurable and simple. Particularly simple. Less is more.

If you don't believe me then please listen (again) to Tom DeMark's earlier remark:

> *The bottom line was, after 17 programmers and 4 or 5 years of testing, the basic 4 or 5 systems worked best.*

For me personally, as a mechanical/systematic or algorithmic trader (whichever label resonates with you), I believe Tom DeMark's comment, is the best insight I've ever read about trading. Answers are not found in complexity.

When you decide to put pen to paper so to speak, you will come to this fork in the road. You will need to decide which path to take. The well-trodden evidence-based path with old, boring and proven ideas that can demonstrate stability over out-of-sample data. Or the fresh indicative/faith-based path with promising possibilities—and hope your skills will be enough to create a strategy with a stable enough equity curve that avoids data mining and excessive curve fitting. This fork in the road will present you with a simple binary choice. Will you choose evidence over faith or hope over pragmatism? My preference is to choose demonstrable evidence over faith's internal hope.

Embrace the Old, it's the New Fashionable

Yes. As you know, I like 'old' ideas. I like them for the plain reason that they are 'old'. Old means time in the markets. Time legitimizes established theories. Time demonstrates an idea's robustness over out-of-sample data. Time means longevity. Longevity means profitability. Profitability means robustness, the singular objective of all trading methodologies. The more time there is, the more robustness—and the more robustness there is, the more confidence I have. Evidence of out-of-sample robustness can only come from old, established ideas.

The moral here is don't forget the past. So, you'll need to dust off your older technical books and revisit their ideas with the intention of gathering evidence on whether they work or not. You should refer to books published before 2000 as they will give you at least 20+ years of out-of-sample data. If the books have an idea worth coding, 20+ years of data is plenty enough to gauge robustness.

In Chapter 6 I'll be reviewing a number of different trend-trading strategies, the majority of which have out-of-sample performance. I know it won't be an exhaustive list; however, it'll certainly be a good place for you to start. But regardless of where you start, make sure you do start by embracing the old. New ideas can't demonstrate robustness with out-of-sample data, as it doesn't exist for 'new'. Learn how to locate, review and verify old ideas, because that is where the rich and very valuable out-of-sample data exists.

Resist the New

As you will soon learn there are plenty of well-established and robust trend-trading strategies for you to consider. There really is no need for you to develop your own and risk falling into the relevancy trap. In my opinion, you should ignore the latest, younger and newest exciting trading idea and focus on the tried and tested.

There are two very important reasons to resist 'new' trading ideas:

1. no evidence of robustness and
2. your powerful neurotransmitters.

No Evidence of Robustness

Always remember that new ideas, as I've just mentioned, despite their compelling attraction, by definition can never give you rock solid out-of-sample performance. They can never provide hard evidence of robustness—that desirable attribute we all want in our strategies. New strategies can only offer *hope* that their equity curve will remain stable, robust, into the future. There certainly are 'indications' you can look out for that could suggest robustness, such as versatility and good design, as I've already discussed. However, from a general understanding, if you pursue new ideas, you're doing so based on faith that their equity curves will remain stable.

As I've mention ad infinitum, there are enough well established and robust trend-trading strategies out there to review and consider without you having to reinvent the wheel and go alone with no hard evidence of robustness.

Now, I know all old ideas at one point in time were new. I get that. I shouldn't be too critical of new. I do understand this. However, I also understand that I'd prefer not to be a guinea pig in a new experiment when there are plenty of old and proven strategies to review and trade. I'm quite happy to let others play first adopters as they tip toe along the bleeding edge of new possibilities.

However, having said that, if a new idea grabs your attention then certainly give it consideration—but make sure there are indications of robustness and a successful equity curve stability review before you place real money behind it. But never forget that, if you do, you're giving up on a solid well-established old evidence-based approach for what might turn out to be a pie in the sky. In my opinion, it's an easy choice. Always go for the proven out-of-sample strategy over a promise. It's best to shun the new.

Your Powerful Neurotransmitters

Secondly, 'new' can hijack your neurotransmitters making you susceptible to clever marketing campaigns. Before you know it, after an enthralling website has grabbed your attention and kept you captivated, you're purchasing the latest and newest trading solution. You are buying not because you know it's robust (which should be the only reason for buying a trading solution) but because your neurotransmitters are making you 'feel' good about buying. It's hard to resist feeling good.

Let's take another look at the clever and manipulative pitch I showed earlier. It has a very persuasive message:

> *You need ongoing, current, cutting-edge trading strategies. Without them you'll fall behind and slip into the abyss of mediocre traders who never quite make it to the top.*

Who wants to fall behind? I don't. Who wants to make it to the top? I do. Who needs 'cutting-edge' trading solutions? I'll take two please; where do I sign up?

Clever marketers aim to hack into our positive neurochemicals that trigger our dopamine and serotonin neurotransmitters. Powerful neurotransmitters that make us feel good. Hey, who doesn't want to feel good? And it's hard to resist the neurotransmitters that make us feel good.

Suffering losses during a prolonged drawdown can be damaging to the spirit. Losses can lead to procrastination, self-doubt and lack of enthusiasm—a state of mind that is linked to low levels of dopamine. You can start to feel like a failure, isolated and depressed. Isolation and depression are linked to an absence of serotonin.

Vendors and marketers know this. So, they design their offer to sell you something new. To give you hope. To lift you out of your depression. Marketers know offering a 'new' cutting-edge strategy with the promise of riches will give prospective customers a natural dopamine hit. A hit that will lift their spirits, confidence and enthusiasm. They know that you seeing an offer of cutting-edge solutions will allow you to visualize the benefits to you—success. Success in trading means money in your account. And not just money but big money. Well, apparently, your brain can't determine the difference between what is real and what is imagined, so your brain will produce serotonin making you feel good about the imaginary money you're about to make. Or, in others words, really good. So good in fact that you'll seriously consider purchasing the latest cutting-edge solution. Marketers know all this. They know you will feel good, they just hope you will feel good long enough to purchase their new cutting-edge offer. 'New' trading offers are simply short-term, dopamine-driven, marketing efforts. Buyer beware!

New in trading is generally good for vendors and bad for traders.

So shy away from the new and resist the urge of hope and good feelings that new inspires. New is only good for promoters who prey on people's lack of dopamine and serotonin.

Please don't be seduced and fooled by the lift in your neurochemicals that 'new discoveries' in trading creates. I know they're powerful neurotransmitters, I get that and I've succumbed to them in the past. Haven't we all. But you have to be strong enough to ignore their powerful effects. Remember new, by its very existence, can never offer hard out-of-sample evidence to demonstrate robustness. The best it can offer are indications of robustness. It's best to avoid new trading solutions.

Develop Turn-Key Strategies

A turn-key, or complete, strategy is ready for immediate use. A strategy with complete and objective rules for setups, entry, stop and exit levels. A strategy that does not require any interpretation.

There are two very important reasons for using turn-key strategies, either on a discretionary mechanical or 100% mechanical basis:

- Risk-of-ruin (ROR) and
- cognitive biases.

ROR

Every trader's number one objective is to commence trading with a 0% ROR. The risk of you ruining your trading account is a mathematical function of the combination of how you trade (methodology) and how much capital you risk per trade (money management). Any ROR above 0% is a guarantee that a trader will go bust. A trader with a 30% ROR will certainly reach their point of ruin much earlier than a trader with a 1% ROR. However, a trader even with a low 1% ROR is still guaranteed to eventually go bust. It will just be a matter of time. If you wish to enjoy a long-term sustainable trading career then you'll need to know what the likelihood is of you going bust, given the way you wish to trade and how much capital you wish to risk per trade. The only way to properly calculate your ROR is to have a complete turn-key strategy where all the rules are precisely and accurately spelled out.

Remember, it's difficult to succeed as a discretionary trader. Most discretionary traders have incomplete trade plans that are not measurable. Without measurability discretionary traders are unable to calculate either their expectancy or ROR. Which, in my opinion, is a catastrophic situation.

If you wish to trade then you will need to know your combined methodology and money management's ROR. The only way you'll be able to correctly calculate it is to develop a complete turn-key trading strategy. No ifs. No buts. It's non-negotiable. Regardless of whether you call yourself a discretionary, mechanical or discretionary mechanical trader, you need to ensure you commence trading with a 0% ROR. That is mandatory to survive in trading. It's an iron-clad rule not open for discussion. Remember ROR is king. And ROR can only be calculated from a complete strategy where all the rules are clearly and objectively defined for setups and trade plans (entry, stop and exit). Only complete or turn-key strategies can be coded up and backtested for profitability, expectancy and ROR. General ideas about setups and general approaches for entry, stops and exits are too loose and too vague to code up and therefore too amateurish and too carefree to consider for trading. They may be good enough to sell books and webinars, but they are not good enough to trade in real markets with real money.

If you're serious about trading you will need to develop complete turn-key strategies to know your individual ROR. Now you may decide to trade them on a discretionary basis, picking and choosing your signals, but at least you'll know the basis of your trading will have a kernel of ruin protection in it. If it's not 'turn-key' you'll be trading in the dark gambling on your luck.

Cognitive Biases

Our minds are powerful things and that's generally a good thing. However, for trading it can open a whole can of worms. When it comes to trading, the absence of clearly and unambiguous rules for setups and trade plans opens the door for our minds to be influenced by our various cognitive biases. Thoughts that are skewed. As I've discussed earlier, this is a huge problem for discretionary traders because people tend to see what they want to see. Our minds are full of cognitive obstacles that are difficult, if not impossible, to navigate.

Let's take a look at the tricky selection, confirmation and recency biases we all carry around.

Discretionary traders can suffer selection bias when they'll only remember the picture-perfect chart examples when justifying a trade.

They'll conveniently ignore all the other chart examples where the patterns failed. Discretionary traders can also suffer from confirmation or information bias where they'll only review or pursue information that supports what they believe. They'll ignore all else. If they're long they'll only review bullish news. Discretionary traders can also suffer from recency bias where they'll expect a recent profitable chart example to repeat, ignoring all previous chart examples in the data set, which may have been losses.

Now, discretionary traders may advocate for their ability to be conscious and in control of their cognitive biases, but reality and good intentions are rarely the same. As I've mentioned before, discretionary traders can suffer from expectation bias where they will find what they're looking for. Take the following paragraph as an example:

> *I cnduo't bvleiee taht I culod aulaclty uesdtannrd waht I was rdnaieg. Unisg the icndeblire pweor of the hmuan mnid, aocdcrnig to rseecrah at Cmabrigde Uinerrvtisy, it dseno't mttaer in waht oderr the lterets in a wrod are, the only irpoamtnt tihng is taht the frsit and lsat ltteer be in the rhgit pclae. The rset can be a taotl mses and you can sitll raed it whoutit a pboerlm. Tihs is bucseae the huamn mnid deos not raed ervey ltteer byistlef, but the wrod as a wlohe. Ins't that aaznmig?*

This paragraph comes from Paul Ciana's book *New Frontiers in Technical Analysis* (Wiley, 2011). Ciana used the above paragraph to demonstrate how powerful our minds are at bringing order out of chaos. And I have to agree with him on that point. It is amazing that we read the above and make sense of it! But it's also terrifying as it goes to show how powerful our minds are at attempting to create order that we understand. Our expectation bias will have us seeing what we want to see, just like cloud reading.

And this is a strong criticism of technical analysis and why it's difficult to succeed at discretionary trading. Many believe identifying patterns on charts is similar to identifying patterns in the clouds. It all depends on an individual's subjective and cognitive challenged interpretation. Being reliant on interpretation therefore makes technical analysis (and cloud reading) too subjective and too unreliable to be taken seriously.

Turn-key strategies remove any room for your cognitive biases to work. There are no gaps or grey areas they can wriggle into. The trader will know with absolute certainty whether a setup exists or not and where trades should be entered, stopped or exited.

Turn-key strategies can protect a trader from their bias filled imagination.

Now you may ultimately decide to be discretionary in the application of your mechanical turn-key strategy, but at least your strategy will be a complete strategy with (hopefully) a positive expectancy and 0% ROR. Discretionary traders can advocate managing their own cognitive biases; however, at the end of the day, ROR is king, and the only way you can accurately measure it is from a turn-key strategy. Turn-key strategies present a win–win outcome. They not only allow individual strategy ROR to be calculated but they also enable you to ring-fence yourself against your own very powerful and very imaginative, but ultimately damaging, cognitive biases. To me that's a handsome win–win.

Trade a Portfolio of Turn-Key Strategies

Diversification works. Diversification of methodology, timeframe and markets. I encourage you to strive for diversification in technique, timeframe and markets. With this book I'm looking to start you at the beginning. To put you on a pathway towards sustainable trading. The best place to start is trading with the trend. It's the safest way to trade. Once—and only once—you have achieved sustainable trading with the trend should you then look to develop a sensible counter-trend strategy.

Eventually all successful traders move towards trading a portfolio of uncorrelated strategies that are diversified by both technique and time. They will include trend and counter-trend strategies over the short, medium and long term. Trend and counter-trend strategies are uncorrelated and complement each other. When markets are choppy and costing the trend trader money, their counter-trend strategies should be doing well, back filling the losses caused by trend trading.

Diversification works. I do it. In time, you should too. Trading multiple uncorrelated strategies over multiple timeframes and over multiple markets will give you more trading opportunities, diversification against individual strategy and individual market failure and a smoother equity curve. Diversification provides better risk management. But first, focus on achieving sustainable trading by following the trend.

This brings me to the end of my key application messages. Next, I want to share with you my thoughts on execution.

EXECUTION

This is where you hope to stay on the road! The key execution messages include:

- endure the pain,
- deal with drawdowns,
- accept uncertainty, it's the norm,
- accept constant change, its life,
- ignore the future,
- focus on yourself,
- be content and
- embrace humility.

I'll look at each in turn.

Endure the Pain

Pain? You probably thought trading would see the end to your pain. The pain of not having enough money. The pain of not having enough flexibility in the day to pursue your own interests. The pain of being beholden to an employer.

Well I'm sorry to be the bearer of bad news (again).However, pain is your new silent partner in the business of trading. Like any partner in a business you will need to become familiar with its idiosyncrasies and learn how to cohabit.

So, if you wish to trade, you will need to say hello to 'pain', wash your hands thoroughly, give it a firm handshake, pull it in for a Coronavirus free firm hug and welcome it openly into your life. Pain will become your constant companion. Learn to embrace it like a good friend.

Don't believe me? Try this. When you lose money, it will obviously hurt. When you lose money for a number of months, it will definitively hurt. When you make money, you'll think about how much more money you could have made if you had just stayed in the trade a little bit longer. It will hurt—really, really hurt. When you spend considerable time and energy studying a plausible theory on trading and it doesn't pass your minimum strategy requirements, it will hurt. When you spend a lot of money on what you think are reputable seminars and you lose money implementing the ideas learned, it will hurt. When you spend considerable time and energy researching, developing, programming and testing an idea and it comes up with a negative expectancy, it will hurt. When you spend a huge amount of time and energy over many years working to improve your edge and fail, despite all the time and energy you have spent, it will disappoint you and it will hurt. When you're trading with the trend and losing on 67% of your trades, it will hurt. When you're trading and in drawdown, which you are for most of the time, even with a higher accuracy methodology, it will hurt. When you withdraw funds to pay yourself or tax it will impact your position sizing, and the aggravation you feel about missing out on potential extra profit by trading smaller will hurt. And when it occurs during a drawdown, it will really, really aggravate and really, really hurt. When you're out of the market looking and waiting for that next trade, the anxiety you feel about not being in the market and potentially missing out on the next big trade will hurt. And when your partner is planning another overseas holiday at a time that you're convinced the markets will experience a significant shift, the thought of travelling in the near future and being out of the market, even before the holiday is confirmed, tickets bought and hotels booked, will hurt. Really hurt.

Please, please, please. Do not see trading as your ticket to a deserted, palm tree–lined tropical beach lagoon where you won't have a care in the world. No. It's an activity that takes effort and perseverance, that requires a high level of pain tolerance. You have been warned.

Deal with Drawdowns

I can't talk in general terms about the pain of trading without specifically mentioning drawdowns. Every trader hates them, particularly when over 90% of traders never recover.

One guarantee I can give you is that your next drawdown will be a lot closer than you think. So, rather than hope it will be a distant experience its best to plan for its inevitable arrival. The question becomes: What can a trader do about it? Luckily there are some steps you can take to manage them.

Firstly, do you throw out your strategy and start again? No. Drawdowns are part and parcel of trading. They may be irritating and painful at times, but (hopefully) they're only temporary.

Do you review your strategy? Certainly. I'm always scrutinizing what I'm doing, squinting my eyes and twisting my head as I ponder whether my models can be improved without falling into the trap of excessive curve fitting. Most times I come away shaking my head thinking no. Generally, my strategies are simple and price dependent without undue influence of traditional variable dependent lagging indicators. There's usually nothing for me to tweak, which is what I like.

Do you consider that the markets have fundamentally changed and so do you change your strategy? No, no, no. Or should I say yes, yes, yes. The markets do and have changed. There are new markets and new instruments and new innovations in the markets all the time. From electronic trading to high frequency trading to almost 24-hour trading in some markets. Yes, markets do change. But they're always changing, that's what is constant about them. Nothing stays the same. But the more markets change, the more they stay the same. It's just the names and events that change. The savings and loans crisis of the 1980s. The 1987 share market crash. The 1991 Japanese real estate collapse. The 1994 and 1997 Asian currency crises. The Long-Term Capital Management debacle in 1998. The 2000 dot com bust. The 2008 US housing bubble and resultant global financial crisis. The 2020 share market crash and Coronavirus pandemic. While the names and events change, the result is always the same. Normalcy. Surprise. Shock. Volatility. Normalcy. Surprise. Shock. Volatility. Normalcy. Rise and repeat.

Markets regularly rotate through cycles of stability, instability and back to stability, instability and so on, just like civilizations through ancient and modern history. It's rinse and repeat. It's just the players and events that change. So, in my opinion, the markets haven't changed.

Your strategy needs to be good enough to cope with all market conditions and all market sentiments. Just take Richard Donchian's Four-Week Rule strategy, which he shared in 1960. The strategy is always in the market and will enter, or stop and reverse, at a four-week breakout. Take a look at its performance in Figure 2.5.

The results are all out-of-sample as the strategy was published in 1960. As you can see the equity curve is rising despite talk of difficult and changing markets. Despite all the surprising financial shocks since the 1970s. According to the rising equity curve, markets have not changed over the past 40 odd years. Nothing has changed despite experiencing the greatest concentration of financial shocks the world has ever seen.

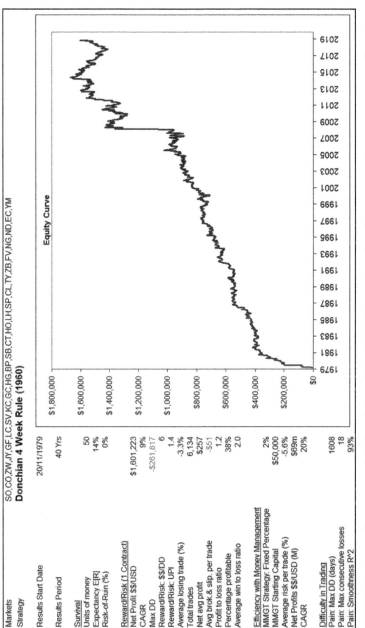

| Markets | SO,CO,ZW,JY,GF,LC,SV,KC,GC,HG,BP,SB,CT,HO,LH,SP,CL,TY,ZB,FV,NG,ND,EC,YM |
| Strategy | **Donchian 4 Week Rule (1960)** |

Results Start Date	20/11/1979
Results Period	40 Yrs
Survival	
Units of money	50
Expectancy E[R]	14%
Risk-of-Ruin (%)	0%
Reward/Risk (1 Contract)	
Net Profit $$/USD	$1,601,223
CAGR	9%
Max DD	-$261,817
Reward/Risk: $$/DD	6
Reward/Risk: UPI	1.4
Average losing trade (%)	-3.3%
Total trades	6,134
Net avg profit	$257
Avg brok.& slip. per trade	-$51
Profit to loss ratio	1.2
Percentage profitable	38%
Average win to loss ratio	2.0
Efficiency with Money Management	
MMGT Strategy Fixed Percentage	2%
MMGT Starting Capital	$50,000
Average risk per trade (%)	-5.6%
Net Profits $$/USD (M)	$69m
CAGR	20%
Difficulty in Trading	
Pain: Max DD (days)	1608
Pain: Max consecutive losses	18
Pain: Smoothness R^2	93%

FIGURE 2.5 Performance of Richard Donchian's 1960 Four-Week Rule strategy demonstrates markets have not changed over the last 40 years, despite the array of financial crises that have occurred. It supports the old adage that 'the more markets change, the more they stay the same'.

If there ever comes a time that I accept a particular strategy of mine is broken (with a permanently falling equity curve), I'll never blame the market. If it fails, it will simply be because my strategy wasn't good enough. Full stop. No convenient excuses such as the markets have changed.

Do you build new strategies to diversify or reduce the risk of individual strategy failure? Certainly, and that is what I do. I trade a portfolio of uncorrelated but complementary (trend/counter-trend) strategies over multiple time periods (short, medium, long term) over a diverse portfolio containing 30+ markets. However, there is no reason why I can't add to or improve on what I have. And really this is what I spend the majority of my time on, researching, programming and testing new trading ideas. I'm always looking to improve my mouse-traps, even when the majority of the ideas and effort come to nothing.

Do you add more markets to diversify your market risk? Absolutely, and that is what I do. I trade a portfolio of diversified markets to reduce the risk of individual market failure.

Do you reduce your position size? Certainly, and that is what I do. My money management rules dictate that I reduce my position size when I'm losing.

Do you just stop trading? Yes and No. Yes if your equity momentum has shifted negative for a particular strategy and no if it hasn't. It's what I do.

So, while drawdowns are as inevitable as the change in seasons, there are plenty of actions you can take to dampen them. The trick is to build a well-diversified and low-correlated portfolio of strategies and markets, which will help lessen their impact.

Embrace Uncertainty, it's the Norm

Look. As I said earlier, I'm not trying to be a kill joy here. I know, I know, I know. If talking about losing, misery, ROR and pain wasn't negative enough, I'm about to trumpet on about 'uncertainty'. Yeah, I hear you and I understand your irritation—however, I have to bring the false 'shine' on trading back to a realistic 'matt' finish.

So please let me continue.

Another stumbling block for traders is the uncertainty they feel about the future. We all worry about tomorrow. The worry about whether current conditions will lead to a market crash or a financial catastrophe or an unspeakable mishap somewhere around the world like the 2020 Coronavirus pandemic. The world is full of uncertainty and the anxiety it causes. I mentioned earlier how it's a confusing world with too many big questions to answer. As I said, I haven't solved those riddles. However, I do know with certainty that there will always be uncertainty around the world. So, you will need to accept that it's the norm. If you don't, procrastination will slay your missed opportunities. Worry has the potential to distract you from executing your trade plan.

First up, you have to accept you have no control over the future—tomorrow—despite all the worry you have.

Secondly, you have to acknowledge there will always be uncertainty about the future and accept that change from the current status quo will always happen. In one respect it is one thing you can be assured of. You have to accept that nothing is linear. Nothing exists in perpetuity. The world swings between stability and instability. There is no certainty about tomorrow. Accept it. If you can learn to both welcome and embrace uncertainty then you will not be paralysed by the fear uncertainty creates. You will not be disadvantaged by the indecision and procrastination fear causes. You will not miss out on opportunities caused by procrastination.

Uncertainty is the enabler of procrastination. Procrastination is one of the traders' deadly sins. It's a cycle you want to avoid. A cycle where uncertainty leads to procrastination, which in turns leads to missed opportunities. Missed opportunities lead to pessimism.

The best thing to do is to accept the fact that uncertainty is the reality of trading. No one knows the future so stop looking for certainty before you place a trade. Certainty is an illusion.

Please accept that your individual worry will have no impact on the likely outcome of any change event. The only impact it will have is to create hesitation and procrastination and prevent you from executing your trade plan.

So, please learn to embrace uncertainty. It has always been, is currently and will always be the 'normal' in trading. The cold hard truth is that you will need to learn to accept uncertainty as your constant companion. You will need to accept that you'll never be comfortable trading. As soon as you learn to accept it the better off you'll be. Expect doubt and expect worry. It's a fact of the markets. Don't let uncertainty, procrastination and pessimism stand in your way. The moral is not to look for certainty and comfort in the world of trading. It doesn't exist. Also understand that where uncertainty exists, opportunities can be found.

Embrace Constant Change, it's Life

Tomorrow is very unlikely to resemble today as 'change' has been the constant theme throughout life on earth. I know most of us are uncomfortable with and fear change. However, it's been the only constant or certainty throughout history. I suppose constant 'change' and 'uncertainty' go hand in hand. Constant change is another enabler of procrastination. Procrastination, as you know, is one of those traders' deadly sins.

Like uncertainty, constant change, or the fear of change has the power to render the trader mute and transform them into the proverbial deer caught in the headlights. Whenever you catch yourself worried about a potential problem and thinking discretion is the better part of valour, come back and read this section.

History is littered with change, yet we're still all here. Yes, some financial events have been volatile, some have led to crashes like the 2020 pandemic, but if you follow a sensible trade plan, you'll find in most instances that you'll be on the right side. Change, and the volatility that results, is good for profits. And if by chance you are on the wrong side, your stop will protect you.

Please don't let your fear of change stop you from being successful in trading.

Always remember, constant change has been with us since man and woman walked the earth. Change has been the regular theme and companion of humanity throughout time. Change has seen various ice ages come and go. Change has seen the rise and fall of civilizations. Change has seen the rise and fall of fortunes. Change has seen fiat money come and go throughout the ages. Change has seen a constant parade of financial crises. Change has seen nations default regularly throughout their histories. Change is a well-documented observation about market behaviour. The 'status quo' is regularly interrupted. From seasons, to civilizations, to financial markets and fortunes, nothing travels along a linear road. It ebbs and flows, meandering along and around trend paths that eventually terminate, sometimes violently. Change reflects a regular cycle of stability leading to instability leading to stability and so forth. It's set on a constant wash cycle of rinse and repeat. The only constant is that change from the present state is certain.

You will need to learn that constant change and constant uncertainty will be your constant companion. So, stop worrying about what you have no control over and get used to the constant uncertainty that rules our world. Don't let your worry about change and uncertainty lead to peak pessimism, which in turn will lead to peak procrastination and peak disappointment.

Ignore the Future

Despite many attention-grabbing headlines, no one can tell the future. No one. Remember there is no such thing as a crystal ball. Deep down you already know this. However, despite your pragmatism, you can't help but keep a small candle burning in the back of your mind in that small place where optimism outweighs pessimism. Well it's best to snuff out that little candle of hope. It's time to remind yourself you're an adult. There are no more fairies down at the bottom of your garden. It's time to wake up and smell that particular essence of life. It's not roses. It's more nine parts reality and one part distraction.

As traders we must acknowledge:

- we don't know the future,
- we don't know from where or when our winning trades will come from,
- we don't know for how long or how short a trade will last and
- we don't have any control over what the markets will do.

So, please stop worrying about something you have no control over. It's best to ignore the future.

Focus on Yourself

Now something positive. You're the only one you have control over. Not the markets. Not your strategy's future performance. No. Only yourself. You. Executing your trade plan. You. Finding your setups. You. Entering and managing trades. You. Managing your position sizing according to your risk capital and money management strategy. As traders you need to ignore the future and just focus on yourself. As traders you need to focus on controlling your risk and money management, which will keep you in the game long enough to enjoy the good wins.

Be Content

Next, you will need to learn to be content. It's highly likely that you'll never be a rock star trader—however, there is no reason why you can't become a competent and sustainable trader.

As a trader you will need to accept that you'll never catch every big move. You will need to learn to be content with the trades you make. As a trader you will come to realize that you don't need to be in every big move to successfully manage your risk capital with a modest expectation. As a trader you will come to realize that you don't have to be in the market every day. As a trader you will come to realize and accept that you will miss many good moves and that it's ok. As a trader you will have to learn to be content with what you have.

Embrace Humility

When you start winning please remember the times when you were losing. You will need to keep a level head in this business of trading. You will need to fight your impulse to share your good trades with anyone who will listen. When the successes arrive, I hope that you will embrace humility. If you don't, the market's Mr Maximum Adversity will send a tsunami of pain your way. And he'll do it at a time when you'll least expect it.

I particularly like the following insight from Andrea Unger, an exceptionally talented trader who has on four occasions won the World Cup Championship of Futures Trading®:

> *If you want to succeed as a trader you must always stay humble. Being humble will ensure you always remain respectful of the market and its potential to hurt your account. Being humble ensures you will always be aware of who is in control of your environment. And guess what, its not you. You are not the boss. The market is. Being humble will allow you to acknowledge you're only a drop in the ocean of traders.*

Being humble will allow you to remain open, flexible and adaptable so you can learn from both your winners and losses. Being humble will ensure you're continuously open to learning, and that's a powerfully important ingredient to long-term trading success.

On that quote it brings me to the end of my execution messages.

SUMMARY

Apologies for such a long, and I know at times repetitive, monologue. But I had to get my thoughts down on paper. I know there is a lot to absorb here and I know it's unlikely you'll agree with everything I've said. No worries. However, feel free to review this chapter as often as you like and, I believe, in time more and more of my messages will resonate with you.

With most of my key messages (hopefully) onboard, I now want to share with you some insights into why trend trading is so appealing.

CHAPTER 3

The Appeal of Trend Trading

So, what's all the fuss about trend trading? Why must it be the first strategy to master in trading? Well I'm glad you asked! Let's take a look. But first, let me address the irony that surrounds trend trading.

IT'S A PUNCH AND JUDY SHOW

The irony and paradox of trend trading is that traders continually receive mixed messages.

On the one hand they are regularly warned that past performance is not indicative of future performance. It's impossible to time the market. Chasing manager performance is pointless. Literature and academia's Random Walk Theory say just that, prices are random. They don't have any predictive powers. It's a waste of time developing trading strategies based on past prices. A dart throwing chimp could do an equally good job. The Efficient Market Hypothesis shouts efficiency, efficiency, efficiency, saying there is no valuable information to exploit in past prices. You can't earn an excess return above the market's return. It's senseless reviewing past prices to predict future prices.

They're told the market is random, there are no trends, do not follow the trend.

While on the other hand, they're told there is a mountain of evidence, some of it going back centuries (hey, take a look for yourself in Appendix A), demonstrating that trend trading produces excess returns above the market. And not just across one or two markets but across all markets, across all countries and across all market cycles. They see a whole industry of commodity trading advisors (CTAs)

64

extracting both high fees and excess market returns. They see high profile trend trading managers like David Harding, Bill Dunn, John Henry and Ed Seykota consistently outperform the markets. They can see the trend in their performance.

They're told to follow the trend, the trend is their friend.

Argh, what to do?

Traders can be forgiven for thinking they're an extra in a Punch and Judy show. Being slapped and punched from pillar to post with each equally forceful (don't follow yesterday's performance, its random) and convincing (follow yesterday's performance, the trend is your friend) view. They (or should I say we) literally feel punch drunk with conflicting messages.

Well, let me see if I can help sort the wheat from the chaff. But before I begin let's have a quick overview of what trend trading is and why trends are important.

WHAT IS TREND TRADING?

In a nut shell trend trading is an approach that uses past prices to make buy and sell decisions. Trend followers will buy markets that are going up and sell markets that are going down. The 'trend' will determine a trade's direction.

The trick here is to correctly define the trend.

There are two styles of trend trading:

1. momentum trend trading and
2. relative strength trend trading.

Each has its own variety of techniques as you can see in Figure 3.1. Trend trading relies on three golden tenets:

• follow the trend,
• cut losses short and
• let profits run.

These are the three core value drivers of all successful trend trading strategies. These tenets do not try to predict market moves but only react to them, with the aim of capturing returns from large, outsized moves.

TREND TRADING STRATEGIES

- Momentum Trend Trading

  <u>Relative Momentum</u>
  - Rate of Change Systems

    - Relative Price Move
      - Hearne 1% Rule (1850)
      - Gartley 3- and 6-Week Crossover (1935)
      - Donchian 5- and 20-Day Crossover (1960)
      - Golden 50- and 200-Day Crossover

    - Relative Time Move
      - Calendar Rule (1933)

  <u>Absolute Momentum</u>
  - Breakout Systems

    - Price Breakouts
      - Ricardo Rules (1800)

    - Swing Breakouts
      - Dow Theory (1900)

    - Congestion Breakouts
      - Livermore Reaction (1900)
      - Darvas Box (1950)
      - Arnold PPS (1987)

    - Channel Breakouts
      - Donchian 4-Week Rule (1960)
      - Dreyfus 52-Week Rule (1960)
      - Turtle Trading (1983)

    - Volatility Breakouts
      - Bollinger Bands (1993)
      - ATR Bands

  - Retracement Systems
    - Elder's Triple Screen Trading System (1985)
    - Mean Reversion

- Relative Strength Trend Trading

FIGURE 3.1   There is a vast array of techniques within the universe of trend trading.

WHY ARE TRENDS SO IMPORTANT?

Trends are important because they move markets and are the basis of all profit. Trends refer to the dominant direction a market moves in over a particular timeframe. The objective of trading, once survival is achieved, is to make money. The easiest way to make money is to trade in the direction markets move, that is, their trend.

Trends identify the *lines of least resistance* where the profits are easiest.

It's difficult to accumulate profits by always selling in an uptrend. Not impossible, but it is difficult. Better to trade in the direction where there is least resistance (the trend) and collect the easier profits. The trick here is to identify the trend! In Chapter 6 I'll be showing how alternative strategies attempt to identify the trend.

Now that we know a little more about what trend trading is and why trends are important, let's begin to discuss in detail why trend trading is so appealing.

THE APPEAL OF TREND TRADING

In my mind there are five good reasons why trend trading is appealing:

1. It's durable.
2. It works.
3. It's best practice.
4. It simplifies the trading process.
5. It's difficult.

I'll start with its durability. This will require a look back at history.

It's Durable

A great appeal of trend trading is that it isn't a new idea. No. It's a very old idea that you will soon see has its roots in centuries past. An old idea that, despite its long history, is still profitable at the time of writing, and I suspect will continue to be profitable.

I like ideas that are old and durable. Although there are no guarantees that trend trading will continue to be profitable into the future, the odds suggest it will. For evidence-based traders like myself, the more evidence I have for an approach that works, the better. I have no interest in being an early adopter. I have no interest in being a bleeding edge guinea pig. I have no desire to end up like those early explorers who may have won the hearts and minds of an appreciative populace only to end up face down and expired!

Nope. I prefer to tread along well-trodden and well-sign-posted pathways. Pathways that are well recognized, such as trend trading.

Trend trading may not be shiny and brand new. It may not be the talk of the town. It may not be fashionable. But at least it's got a past that can be scrutinized and relied upon when trading gets difficult.

Nothing gets thrown away quicker than a new trading idea that starts losing money.

Trading an old idea infuses confidence in a trader. Certainly, old ideas can and do lose money, but at least you can have confidence the old idea in all probability will come good in time. New ideas don't have the same established heritage to rely on.

Let's see how old trend trading is.

History of Trend Trading

The earliest record of any technical analysis has been attributed to a Japanese rice merchant called Munehisa Homma. He is thought to have developed candlestick charts around the mid-1750s. The earliest record of any reference to trend trading involved a gentleman called David Ricardo. It occurred a long time ago in 1838. I told you trend trading was old.

David Ricardo (1772–1823)   David Ricardo was an Englishman. He began life as a broker, became a trader and share manipulator and then did a nice pivot to become a respectable economist and politician. It's believed he amassed his wealth following his own three golden tenets of successful trend trading (and certainly his sharemarket manipulation didn't hurt).

James Grant wrote about David Ricardo in his 1838 book *The Great Metropolis, Volume 2*:

> *I may observe that he amassed his immense fortune by a scrupulous attention to what he called his own three golden rules, the observance of which he used to press on his private friends. These were,*
>
> - *Never refuse an option when you get it*
> - *Cut your losses short*
> - *Let your profits run on.*

Well how about that. Straight off the bat. There you have it. Two of trend trading's three golden tenets right there. Cut your losses short and let your profits run. Although no date has been attributed to David Ricardo's golden rules, I'm happy to hazard an estimate of say around 1800. Yep, I'll to go with that.

So, how about that. The two guiding lights to trend trading, although not widely published at the time, have been in existence for over two centuries.

Two momentous ideas that are still as effective today as they were back then.

As an aside, don't think David Ricardo was some Robin Hood–type figure, benevolently sharing a rich man's ideas with the poor. No. He was an early sharemarket manipulator who made a large part of his fortune from spreading false rumours of a French victory at the Battle of Waterloo. This naturally caused a market panic, after which he bought shares at a deep discount before news of a British victory reached England. But no doubt, after buying them cheap, he held onto them, letting his profits run!

Let's now examine some other notable 'trend' traders.

Pat Hearne (1859)

Pat Hearne (1859)   Pat Hearne was a famous American gambler and crime figure. He was also a share trader who is reported to have probably devised the first systematic trend trading strategy as reported in William Fowler's 1870 book *Ten Years on Wall Street*. Fowler reports on Hearne's strategy:

> *Pat Hearne, the late noted sporting man, was wont to operate thus. He would buy 100 shares of some stock, and when it rose one percent he would buy another 100 shares, and so on. As soon as it fell one per cent he sold the whole.*

Although technically pyramiding, it was still a strategy designed to follow the trend, letting profits run and cutting losses short.

William Fowler (1833–1881)

William Fowler (1833–1881)   In the same book Fowler records two of the three golden tenets of trend trading by writing:

> *A most weighted maxim, verified by Wall Street experience, is this:*
> *'Cut your losses short and let your profits run'.*

So, it appears these golden tenets have been known for a very long time, again appearing in print in 1870. Remember the first recording was in James Grant's 1838 book.

Charles Dow (1851–1902)   Dow Theory is a corner stone of technical analysis. Its name comes from Charles Dow, cofounder and first editor of *The Wall Street Journal*. Dow is considered by many to be the father of technical analysis. Although he never referred to his work as Dow Theory, its focus was centred on the identification of trends. He published his market ideas in a number of articles he wrote for *The Wall Street Journal* between 1900 and 1902. Following his death, both William Hamilton and Robert Rhea expanded and refined his ideas. It was after his death that the term 'Dow Theory' was used to defined his work.

A significant part of his work was his peak and trough trend analysis, where a bull market was defined by higher highs and a bear market by lower lows. Each respective market remained in existence until a change in trend occurred.

This aligns with trend trading's maxim of letting your profits run.

Dow Theory's peak and trough trend analysis is possibly the first objective attempt at mechanically defining a 'trend'. In addition, it may also possibly be the second systematic trend trading model to be devised after Hearne.

So, there we have it. We have three definitive publications recording the three golden tenets of trend trading in 1838, 1870 and 1900. In print, clearly articulated and without any ambiguity.

But references to trend trading doesn't stop there.

Arthur Cutten (1870–1936)   During the 1920s Arthur Cutten became widely known as one of the largest commodity speculators in the United States. Although hugely successful, he came undone during the 1929 sharemarket crash where he is reported to have lost most of his fortune. In an article he wrote for the *Saturday Evening Post* on 3 December 1932, titled 'The Story of a Speculator' he stated:

> *Most of my success has been due to my hanging on while my profits mounted. There is the big secret. Do with it what you will.*

Cutten obviously didn't adhere to Ricardo's golden rule of cutting losses short during the 1929 crash, but he certainly knew how to let his profits run. Cutten was definitely a trend follower.

Richard Wyckoff (1873–1934)   Richard Wyckoff was a trader, broker and newsletter writer on Wall Street. His central belief was that shares had a tendency to trend together in established bull or bear markets. Consequently, he only went long when the broad market was trending up. He only went short when the broad market was trending down. In addition, he would only buy the strongest share, or short the weakest share, within its industry demonstrating his belief in the idea of relative strength.

As you can see, his central approach to investing was to follow established relative trends. He was so successful that he ended up owning nine and a half acres in the Hamptons.

Jesse Livermore (1877—1940)

Jesse Livermore is possibly the most famous share trader of his time. It's believed he is the central character of Edwin Lefèvre's 1923 book *Reminiscences of a Stock Operator*. Livermore became famous for making and losing not one but two multi-million-dollar fortunes. Some believe he made over $100 million from the 1929 crash. It's believed Livermore had lost most of his fortune before his death in 1940. Lefèvre's book is possibly one of the most highly read trading books in existence. If you haven't already read it make sure you do. Many believe it's a thinly disguised biography of Livermore. In it there are a number of key quotes that today are attributed to trend trading. They include:

> *Always sell what shows you a loss and keep what shows you a profit. That was so obviously the wise thing to do and was so well known to me that even now I marvel at myself for doing the reverse.*
>
> *After spending many years in Wall Street and after making and losing millions of dollars I want to tell you this: it never was my thinking that made the big money for me. It was always my sitting. Got that? My sitting tight!*

He certainly knew the power of cutting losses short and letting profits run, two golden tenets of trend trading.

Livermore wrote a book about trading called *How to Trade in Stocks* (Duell, Sloan and Pearce, 1940). In his book he makes direct reference to following the trend:

> *It may surprise many to know that in my method of trading, when I see by my records that an upward trend is in progress, I become a buyer as soon as a stock makes a new high on its movement, after having had a normal reaction. The same applies whenever I take the short side. Why? Because I am following the trend at the time. My records signal me to go ahead!*

In a nutshell, Livermore subscribed to the three golden tenets of trend trading: follow the trend, cut your losses short and let your profits run. He also admitted his failures in trading were attributed to him not following his own rules of cutting losses short and letting profits run.

Although Livermore was a celebrated share trader, he unfortunately took his own life in 1940. Many believe the wild swings in his wealth took their toll. However, to his credit he didn't lose everything, leaving a $5-million estate to his wife Harriet Noble.

George Seaman (1933)   Unfortunately, I couldn't find references to the birth and death of George Seaman; however, he did write a sharemarket book in 1933 titled *The Seven Pillars of Stock Market Success*. In the book he recommended traders buy stronger shares during a bull market and sell weaker shares during a bear market. Seaman believed in the benefits of relative strength trend trading, which aligns itself with the golden tenet of letting profits run.

George Chestnutt (1885–1956)   George Chestnutt was a successful fund manager who ran the American Investors Fund for many years starting in the 1930s. He is reported to have written:

> It is better to buy the leaders and leave the laggards alone. In the market, as in many other phases of life, the strong get stronger, and the weak get weaker.

Chestnutt was another investor like Wyckoff and Seaman who focused on relative strength trend trading where the core objective is to let profits run.

Robert Edwards and John Magee (1948)   Robert Edwards and John Magee wrote the seminal book *Technical Analysis of Stock Trends*, first published in 1948. It's still in print today and I believe it's now up to its eleventh edition. Their book helped to popularize what have now become known as traditional trend continuation and trend reversal chart patterns such as triangles, pennants, flags and head-and-shoulders. The pair also defined the concept of trend lines based on swing points and helped promote Dow Theory. Edwards and Magee were champions of trend trading and of educating others in the importance of trading with the trend.

Harold Gartley (1899–1972)

Harold Gartley was a Wall Street broker and technical analyst. He is best known for his 1935 book *Profits in the Stock Market*. He covered Dow Theory, triangles, moving averages and gaps. Gartley may be attributed with being the first to reference 'mechanical' trading when he states, when referring to his three-week and six-week dual moving average crossover strategy:

> *As a mechanical system for stock trading, requiring only one simple study which should not take more than 15 minutes a week, it has turned in an excellent profit during the last six hectic years.*

Not only has Gartley identified the importance of trading in the direction of the trend but he had also looked at systemizing a trend trading strategy. In Chapter 6 I'll review Gartley's strategy to see how it has performed 85 years after its publication.

Nicholas Darvas (1920–1977)

Nicholas Darvas was a professional dancer. He was so good he was regularly invited to tour the world. He was also an avid share trader. During the 1950s Darvas was able to make over $2 million trading shares. In 1960 he wrote *How I Made $2,000,000 in the Stock Market*, in which he shared the strategy he used.

His method became known as the Darvas Box strategy. It was a simple breakout strategy designed to trade in the direction of the trend. Following a congestion of prices, Darvas would visualize a box containing prices and buy a breakout of the box. The method was designed to capture trends, letting profits run while cutting losses short.

Darvas was a trader who was able to successfully enshrine the golden tenets of trend trading into a systemized trend-trading strategy.

Richard Donchian (1905–1993)

Richard Donchian was a commodities and futures trader who in 1949 opened the first publicly managed futures fund called Futures Inc. In addition, he developed trend trading strategies. His trading philosophy was based upon a belief that commodity prices moved in long, sweeping bull and bear markets. Writing in the 1957 *Commodity Yearbook* he stated:

> *Every good trend-following method should automatically limit the loss on any position, long or short, without limiting the gain.*

During the 1960s he became well known for a couple of trend-trading strategies that he developed and shared with subscribers of his weekly 'Commodity Trend Timing' newsletter. One was a dual 5-day and 20-day moving average crossover strategy, while the other was a breakout strategy that has become known variously as either the Donchian Breakout Channel or Four-Week Rule. Both were mechanical strategies where a trader's discretion wasn't required.

In my opinion, his Four-Week Rule (please refer to Figure 2.5 in Chapter 2) is one of the most successful trend-trading strategies to have been developed.

Donchian epitomized trend trading by enshrining trend capture, cutting losses short and letting profits run in his trading strategies.

Jack Dreyfus (1913–2009)   Jack Dreyfus was another successful investor who operated on Wall Street during the 1950s and 1960s. He was known as the 'Lion of Wall Street'. His Dreyfus Fund, between 1953 and 1964, returned 604% compared to Dow Jones Index's 346%. Many believe he was a trend follower who invested in shares that were making new 52-week highs.

Being a breakout investor firmly places him in the trend trading camp where his success speaks for itself.

200 Years Young and Still Going Strong

If we can accept David Ricardo was cutting his losses short while letting his profits run in 1800, then we can say with confidence that the idea of 'trend trading' has been known for over 200 years. Each following century has contained successful trend followers where today, I will argue, it's still a legitimate and successful strategy.

Being over 200 years old the idea of trend trading is possibly the most durable idea in finance, where very little is long-lasting. As you'll learn, I like durable ideas and trending trading is certainly durable. Being durable makes trend trading appealing.

Now that we understand that one of the great appeals of trend trading is its durability, we need to move on to the next immediate reason for its appeal, which is because it simply works. To understand how, we first need to discuss the science behind it. This is of utmost importance, as there is a whole chorus of dissent out there dissuading people from becoming active traders. We need evidence to understand why trend trading works. Yes, we of course want to see the money—however, having 'science' in our corner is also handy. So, let's look at the science first, and then the actual making of money next.

APPEAL OF TREND TRADING—IT WORKS, JUST LOOK AT THE SCIENCE BEHIND IT

Another appeal of trend trading is that it works. To understand why, we need to look at the science. This is terribly important because there is an all-powerful academic hierarchy who dismiss active trading. They say it's a senseless pursuit and time waster. Let's first try to understand the academic resistance against trend trading.

Theory Says You Can't Beat the Market

Let me try to summarize the academic position. In a nut shell academia says you can't beat the market. They say it's random. They say it's efficient. The theory says price changes follow a normal distribution, which is clever academic speak for 'random'. Since prices are random then any attempts to predict future price movements, say via trend trading, is a senseless waste of time. Ergo trend trading can't work. You can't use past prices to predict future prices.

Let's spend a little time unpacking the academic theory.

The Random Walk Theory

The Random Walk Theory (RWT) states that market prices are serially independent (that's some more clever speak for random), where today's price change will be unrelated to yesterday's price change. Being serially independent implies that they follow a normal (random) distribution where price changes will be constant through time, falling symmetrically either side of an average. It's pointless to look at past prices to predict future prices.

The Efficient Market Hypothesis

The Efficient Market Hypothesis (EMH) states that all markets are properly priced as they reflect all available information. It believes an investor or trader cannot make abnormal returns studying information that is already absorbed and correctly reflected in the market.

In addition, since prices can only be impacted by the arrival of new information, which is unknown until it appears, it believes prices are also random (similar to the RWT) because the arrival of new information is random. Markets are both efficient and random. It's pointless to look at past prices to predict future prices.

Key Assumption is Randomness

The key assumption for both theories is that price changes are random and markets are efficient. They're efficient at absorbing new information. They're efficient at adjusting prices rapidly and correctly.

The big take away is the strong belief that price changes are random. If prices are random, then there is no way anyone can use past prices to predict future prices, which is the bedrock of trend trading. If prices move up, higher prices are expected. If prices move down, lower prices are expected. But if prices are random, then no one can expect higher prices to follow a rally, or expect lower prices to follow a fall.

The big implication is that *random* prices *must* follow a normal distribution. A normal distribution implies randomness where price changes must occur in a constant and even fashion through time and must fall symmetrically either side of an average. The distribution must follow the shape of a bell curve.

This is a key-stone belief of many well-respected and accepted financials models. They're built on the assumption that price changes are normally distributed (i.e. random). That is their ironclad argument as to why trend trading is a waste of time and why it can't work. Traders cannot use past prices to predict future prices if prices are random. It's senseless to rely on a coin toss to make trading decisions.

Many Models Rely on Markets Following a Normal Distribution

This key assumption that price changes follow a normal (random) distribution is imbedded in many important models, as shown in Figure 3.2.

I suppose we can't be surprised that these models rely on the normal distribution function as distributions are representations of life. Markets are simply a single representative of a huge collective voice of many investors and traders. Everything in life that surrounds us

Financial Models Built on the Assumption Price Changes are Normally Distributed	
RWT	Random Walk Theory
EMH	Efficient Market Hypothesis
MPT	Modern Portfolio Theory
CAPM	Capital Asset Pricing Model
Options	Black & Scholes option pricing
VAR	Value at Risk

FIGURE 3.2 A key-stone assumption of many financial models is that changes in market prices, or returns, follow a normal (random) distribution.

falls into a distribution of some sort, so why not the markets, which represent the millions of transactions that occur every day between buyers and sellers.

And the most common distribution in life that surrounds us is the normal distribution where events occur randomly in a symmetrical manner either side of an average. From our height, weight and IQs any variable with a large enough sample size will follow a normal distribution.

What are the Benefits of a Normal Distribution?

Knowing that a time series follows a certain distribution allows people to use that distribution's function to estimate the likely outcome of a certain variable. It can be used to estimate student results, car accidents, insurance claims, mortgage defaults and deaths. It can also be used to predict the likelihood of a sharemarket crash.

The good news is that the normal distribution function works well when the events themselves behave well.

For example, if we accept the theory's belief that market price changes are random and follow a normal distribution, we could use the normal distribution function to estimate the likelihood of how often the market may rise or fall by 1%, 2% or 5%.

The bad news is that if the event in question, like price changes, isn't normally distributed as thought, the estimates will be wrong, and I mean really wrong. And this is a serious issue for those financials models that rely on the key 'normal distribution' assumption. But more about that later.

First, let's try to understand more about what is meant by a normal distribution?

A Normal Distribution

A normal (random) distribution is one where, given a large enough sample size, a variable's outcome (height, weight, IQ or daily/weekly/ monthly price changes etc.) will be constant through time and will fall symmetrically either side of an average. Each outcome will be serially independent (random). Half the outcomes would experience negative changes. The other half would experience positive changes. The average value should be very close to its median. The distribution will follow the shape of a bell curve where 99.7% of all outcomes should fall within three standard deviations of the average.

A variable is assumed to be normally distributed where:

- 68% of all values should fall within one standard deviation of the average,
- 95% of all values should fall within two standard deviations of the average,
- 99.7% of all values should fall within three standard deviations of the average and
- 99.9% of all values should fall within four standard deviations of the average.

If a variable, like price changes, is believed to be normally distributed, then it would expect very few outliner events beyond three standard deviations from the average and almost none beyond four standard deviations.

The Bell Curve

A bell curve chart is exactly what it says, a 'bell'-shaped curve. The chart in Figure 3.3 illustrates what a normal bell-shaped distribution should look like.

The normal distribution is called a bell-shaped distribution because the random outcomes will be constant through time and fall symmetrically either side of an average. Half the outcomes will be negative changes, while the other half will be positive changes.

Sorry to labour the point but it's important to know what a normal (random) distribution is and what it looks like in order to understand

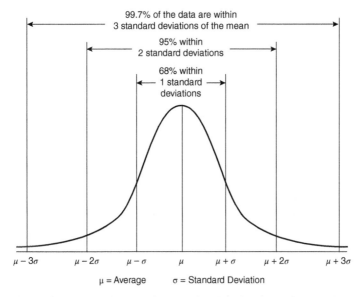

FIGURE 3.3 According to theory, the distribution of price changes follows a normal 'bell curve' (random) distribution.

academia's opposition to trend trading. A normal distribution is a key assumption that underpins many financial theories or models and is therefore the key argument for why it's pointless to use random past prices to predict future prices (i.e. trend trading).

Let's take a closer look into these theories beginning with the one first formulated, the RWT.

RWT

In 1863 Jules Regnault, a French broker, is credited as being the first person to suggest market prices were random. He was followed by another Frenchman, Louis Bachelier, a mathematician who published his PhD thesis *The Theory of Speculation* in 1900. He concluded that market prices were random, implying it was a waste of time studying past prices to predict future prices. Burton Malkiel, in his 1973 *A Random Walk Down Wall Street*, again advocated the random nature of markets, while trumpeting the share-picking qualifications of a dart-throwing chimp.

The chief takeaway is that price changes are serially independent (random), so it's pointless studying past prices to predict future prices.

Random outcomes follow a normal distribution.

EMH

The EMH was developed by Eugene Fama in 1965. It states that markets are efficient because they reflect all available information, rapidly, efficiently and correctly adjusting prices to any new information that appears. As a result, EMH believes it's impossible to make abnormal returns in excess of market returns as all prices instantaneously reflect all information.

There are three forms of EMH. Weak, semi-strong and strong. Each form builds on the previous form.

The weak form says prices reflect all *past* available public information. It says you can't use past prices to predict futures prices. This is in direct conflict with trend trading. The semi-strong form adds to weak form, saying prices also reflect all *current* available public information and will instantaneously adjust when new public information becomes available. The semi-strong form discounts the value of fundamental analysis. The strong form continues to build on the others, believing prices reflect all current available *private* information (i.e. insider knowledge).

EMH says prices efficiently reflect all available information and that only new information can impact or shift prices. Accordingly, since new information is unknown and occurs at random, then future price changes must also be unknown and must also occur randomly.

The chief takeaway is that you can't study any information to beat the market as its all instantaneously reflected in market prices. Since new information occurs randomly, so must the resultant price changes. Price changes are therefore serially independent (random), so it's pointless studying past prices to predict future prices.

Random outcomes follow a normal distribution.

Randomness is King

Both the RWT and EMH wrap themselves in the 'random' blanket. They unequivocally believe it's pointless to study past prices to predict future prices when the market has a mind of itself. How could anyone possibly think to outwit it, surely pure folly?

Their key-stone argument is that markets are random, where price changes follow a normal distribution. Therefore, any effort to attempt to beat an unbeatable market is a waste of time, resources and sanity! The key-stone assumption underpinning their argument is that price changes follow a normal (random) distribution. Please keep that thought in mind—prices changes follow a normal distribution—front and centre as we continue.

Let's now take a graphical look at what constitutes a perfect, efficient and random market (as defined by the RWT and EMH).

A Perfect (Random) Market

By definition a perfect market is a random market. In a perfect, or random market, price changes will follow a perfect normal (random) bell curve distribution.

Since the theory states that markets are both efficient and random, I want to create a fake market to simulate their key-stone assumption that price changes follow a normal distribution (due to their randomness).

If the RWT and EMH want to embrace randomness, so can I. I can do randomness. With the help of Excel's random number generator, I will simulate the tossing of two dice.

One dice will be treated as generating negative down moves (−1%, −2%, −3%, −4%, −5% and −6%) while the other will be treated as generating positive up moves (1%, 2%, 3%, 4%, 5% or 6%). Each random toss will sum the two dice. The final sum will be between −5% and 5%.

Consequently, the result of each random toss of my two dice could be:

−5%, −4%, −3%, −2%, −1%, 0%, 1%, 2%, 3%, 4% or 5%.

My model will generate 9,600 random tosses to approximate the amount of daily market data covering 40 years.

The sum of each random toss will be accumulated into a time series.

Figure 3.4 shows my first fake market.

Wow, not bad. Plenty of trending opportunities there to trade. But don't be impressed. Remember it's simulated. It's random. It's fake! Since it's simulated by a random number generator, I can easily create another fake market. Try the market in Figure 3.5.

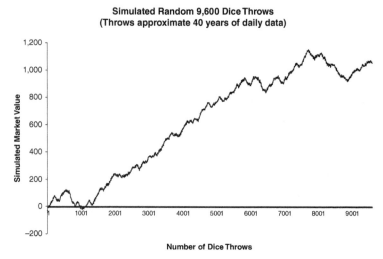

FIGURE 3.4   This simulated market, despite its strong looking trends, is fake, where the changes in prices (dice throws) follow a normal (random) distribution.

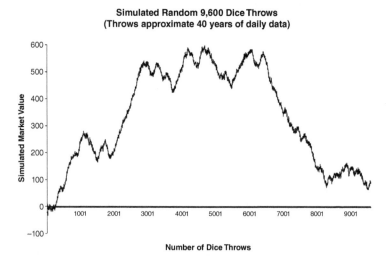

FIGURE 3.5   This is another simulated market, where the changes in prices (dice throws) follow a normal (random) distribution.

Well, not as good as my first attempt, but over a simulated period of 40 years there does appear to be plenty of good trending opportunities to trade.

So, how about that?

Both fake markets have been created the same way, according to the RWT and EMH, to simulate how markets are thought to behave where price changes, both in magnitude and direction, occur in an efficient (instantaneously) way when new information randomly (dice throws) appear. And like many real markets, they both look completely different.

My fake markets, I believe, are well simulated.

Now, despite their different shapes, both fake markets appear to show plenty of trending opportunities, just like real markets.

Or do they?

According to the RWT and EMH, it wouldn't matter if these fake markets did or did not exist as they are no different to real markets. Simulated or not, according to the RWT and EMH, price changes will follow a normal distribution. Price changes will be serially independent (random) and constant through time. They'll fall symmetrically either side of an average, where half will be negative and half will be positive. There will be no bias either way, meaning it's impossible to develop strategies that rely on prediction to earn excess returns.

To repeat. The main lesson from the RWT and EMH is to accept the observation that price changes are normally distributed (i.e. random). That being the case there is no point in trying to earn excess returns beyond the market, or in other words, don't try to time the market. Don't try to develop trading strategies like trend trading, which attempt to predict future prices (trends) based on past prices. It's pointless.

So, despite my simulated dice throwing looking like terrific markets, they, like real ones, are (supposedly) normally distributed (random) making them impossible to predict and actively trade for an edge.

The best way to view the serial independence or randomness of price changes is to view a histogram of distributions. Take a look at the histogram in Figure 3.6 showing the distribution of my simulated dice throws.

I've overlaid a bell-shaped curve on the histogram in Figure 3.6 to illustrate how nicely my dice-throwing price changes follow a normal and random 'bell curve' distribution.

But what does it all mean?

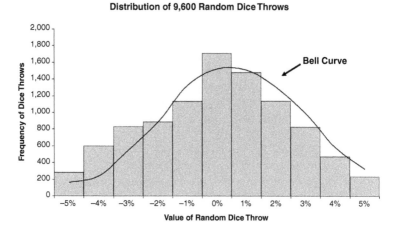

FIGURE 3.6   The histogram of dice throws shows the changes in values follow a normal 'bell curve' distribution.

The histogram shows for my fake market that the majority of price changes from my dice throwing, just like real price changes, are constant through time, are serially independent (random) and fall symmetrically either side of an average where half experience negative changes, while the other half experience positive changes. There is no bias to either positive or negative changes. There are very few outliners on the edges. The dice-throwing price changes look constant, random and normally distributed. There is no serial dependence between prices changes.

A Tale of Three Pictures

I have three different looking charts illustrating the same simulated time series. I have two inspiring (but fake) line charts illustrating many significant trends and I have a histogram summarizing the distributions of my random dice throws.

Although the pictures are of the same time series, they tell two different stories.

While the line charts suggest there are good profits to be made, the histogram tells a completely different story.

The histogram of distributions is not telling any story about 'easy' profits. It demonstrates that the distribution of price changes is serially independent.

Looking at the histogram you will notice the most frequent dice thrown resulted in 0% return. For most of the time my fake market went nowhere. And looking at either side of the 0% move, you can see the other dice throws are distributed symmetrically around the 0% move, implying the total number of all negative percentage dice throws are approximately the same as all the positive percentage dice throws. The distribution follows a perfect normal (random) distribution. Randomness rules.

Let's look at the actual frequency numbers of each percentage dice throw in Table 3.1.

Well how about that.

The histogram numbers show a telling story. The down moves appear to cancel out most of the up moves. In other words, most of the percentage movement has been up and down without actually going anywhere! The random dice generator, and hence my fake market, has worked very hard to gain very little.

So, let's go back to the key assumption embedded within the RWT and EMH.

Are price changes, as simulated by my dice-throwing exercise, serially independent (remember that is clever academic speak for 'random')? Are markets essentially random? Do markets follow a

TABLE 3.1   The frequency of dice throws shows the down moves generally cancel out the up moves, signifying that changes follow a constant and symmetrical normal (random) distribution.

Sum of Dice Throw	Number of Dice Throws			
−5%	281			
−4%	601			
−3%	831	Down	3735	39%
−2%	886	Moves		
−1%	1136			
0%	1709	0%	1709	18%
1%	1481	Moves		
2%	1141			
3%	828	Up	4156	43%
4%	474	Moves		
5%	232			
Total	9600			

normal (random) distribution? Are we wasting our time developing strategies that rely on studying past prices to predict futures prices to beat the market?

Based on the above observation of seeing how the histogram of percentage up and down moves cancel each other out, with price changes close to the average you could support such an opinion. That despite the simulated time series line charts showing directional price movements, the individual price changes, just like a real market, are random—as demonstrated by their equal spread either side of the average.

This is what the RWT and EMH believe. This is their foundation stone.

If markets and prices are both efficient and random, the distribution of their daily, weekly, monthly, and quarterly price changes should follow a normal bell curve random distribution where all the up and down moves would essentially cancel themselves out. Price changes would be constant through time and fall equally either side of the average. We would expect to see 68% of all price changes fall within one standard deviation of the average percentage return. We would expect to see 95% fall within two standard deviations and 99.7% within three standard deviations. We would expect it to be almost impossible (99.99%) to see a move beyond four standard deviations.

A normal distribution says we cannot make abnormal returns in excess of the market's return.

A normal distribution says markets and prices are random and as such it is pointless to study past prices in the hope of predicting future prices. With serially independent price changes there are no price trends. Don't follow the trend. Trend trading is pointless and writing a book about it is even more pointless! I'm a Goose!

Or is it, and am I?

Are Markets Really Normally Distributed?

Well, we've just had a short introduction to market theory where its key-stone argument is that market returns, or price changes, follow a normal (random) distribution. Market returns are random. With that being the case, it's pointless to develop trading strategies such as trend trading, which rely on predicting future prices based on past prices, because prices are random. You can't predict the future. You can't beat the market. Don't try to time the market. You're a knuckle head if you try. You're wasting your time.

Daily Gold Prices (1998 – 2020)

FIGURE 3.7 Over the last 22 years gold appears to have shown a number of significant trends.

To help us gain a better insight, let's leave the theoretical simulated fake markets behind and take a look at an actual real market. Let's see whether real life matches academic life. For my real market I'll use gold; please refer to Figure 3.7.

It appears that if an investor or trader had bought gold around 1998 and held their position up to 2020, they would have been well ahead despite the large pullback in 2015. One could be forgiven for thinking it looks pretty easy to do well in gold.

However, we now know there is another and more informative way to look at a market, and that is a histogram of the market's daily price changes or returns. Viewing the same data from a different angle may reveal that making money in gold isn't so easy.

The histogram in Figure 3.8 shows the distribution of gold's daily returns between 1998 and 2020. It shows the number of days when a particular percentage move was made. Starting in the middle, you can see the daily 0% change was the highest recorded change (or no change). It moves to the right, showing the positive up moves in quarter percentage increments (0.25%). The negative moves shift to the left. The height of each column represents the number of days the move was made, its frequency of occurring.

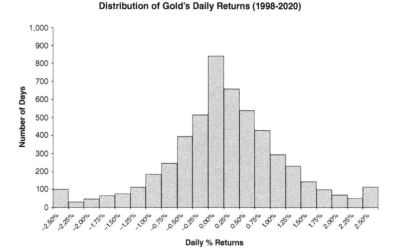

FIGURE 3.8   A histogram of gold's daily price changes, or returns, over the last 22 years.

The histogram tells a completely different story to the line chart. It doesn't tell a story of 'easy' profits.

The highest and central column represents the average daily 0% change that went nowhere. Being the highest column means it's the percentage change that occurred most often.

The histogram appears to be distributed quite symmetrically either side of the average 0% change. It shows the positive daily up moves on the right being approximately the same as all the daily percentage down moves on the left. It appears to be a normal (random) distribution that follows a bell curve.

Let's look at the actual frequency numbers of each daily percentage move in gold in Table 3.2.

Well how about that. Table 3.2 shows a telling story. The number of up moves essentially equals the combined 0% to down moves across the last 22 years of data. In other words, most of the market movement over the last 22 years has gone nowhere! The markets have been working very hard for no gain. We can see out of the 5,231 daily closes in gold that for over 840 days, or for nearly 16% of the time, gold's daily prices have worked hard just to move sideways.

TABLE 3.2   The frequency numbers of gold's daily price changes, or returns, reveals the up moves have generally been cancelled out by the down moves.

Gold's Daily Returns	Number of Days			
−2.50%	100			
−2.25%	30			
−2.00%	47			
−1.75%	66			
−1.50%	75			
−1.25%	112			
−1.00%	184	Total		
−0.75%	246	Zero to		
−0.50%	395	Down		
−0.25%	513	Moves	2608	50%
0.00%	840			
0.25%	658			
0.50%	539	Total		
0.75%	427	Up		
1.00%	293	Moves	2623	50%
1.25%	231			
1.50%	143			
1.75%	98			
2.00%	70			
2.25%	50			
2.50%	114			
Total	5231			

So, let's go back to the original key assumption embedded within the RWT and EMH.

Are markets normally distributed? Are they essentially random? Does gold's daily returns (as our proxy for real markets) follow a normal bell-shaped distribution? Are gold's daily returns distributed equally in a constant, symmetrical and serially independent (random) way either side of an average, where most of the values (99.7%) will fall within three standard deviations (−3.2% and +3.2%) of its average (0.03%)?

Based on a quick glance of the histogram in Figure 3.8 you could easily answer yes. However, on closer inspection it may appear gold is not as normally distributed as first thought?

Let's look again at the histogram.

The question we need to answer is whether gold (as our proxy for all markets) is normally distributed? We want to know because if it is then we'll know it's pointless wasting our time developing trading strategies that attempt to predict future (trending) prices based on past prices to make excess returns above the market.

Is Gold Normally Distributed—Does it Fit Under a Bell Curve?

An easy way to answer this question is to simply overlay a normal bell-shaped curve over the top of gold's daily returns histogram. If gold is normally distributed the bell-shaped curve should fit snuggly over the histogram.

Using gold's average daily return (0.03%) and its standard deviation (1.08%) it's relatively straight forward to generate a bell-shaped curve. Using Excel's random number generation function I've constructed a bell-shaped normal distribution curve where 68% of all returns fall within one standard deviation of the average, 95% within two standard deviations and 99.7% within three standard deviations. I've then overlaid my bell curve distribution over the histogram.

Let's have a look at Figure 3.9.

What da? Ermm, interesting? Although at a first glance gold's histogram appeared to follow a normal (random) distribution, overlaying a bell curve suggests otherwise. As you can see, the histogram *doesn't* fit snuggly under the bell curve. The middle low percentage daily changes appear to occur far more frequently than a normal distribution would expect, far exceeding the top of the bell curve. In addition, gold's daily returns are showing far more daily occurrences than a normal distribution would expect beyond three standard deviations (−3.2% and +3.2%). There appear to be fat tails at the edge.

Looking at how the histogram does not fit snuggly under the overlaid bell curve distribution, we can see gold's daily returns, or price changes, are *not* normally distributed.

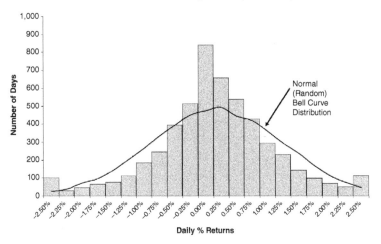

FIGURE 3.9 Despite the theory, gold's daily returns do not fit under a normal (random) 'bell curve' distribution.

Fat Tails—the Only Time You'll Like the Word 'Fat'

Please refer to Figure 3.10 and you'll notice the edges are marked 'fat tails'.

Fat tails represent far more occurrence of large price changes than one would expect if prices were normally distributed and followed a bell shape curve. Fat tails, or tail risk, are the risks of extreme outcomes. Fat tails are often referred to as black swan events, like the 2020 Coronavirus-triggered sharemarket crash, that are meant to occur rarely. The term 'black swan' was popularized by Nassim Taleb's book *Fooled by Randomness: The Hidden Role of Chance in Life and in the Markets* (Random House, 2001). Fat tails refer to an important part of market behaviour. The regular occurrence of unexpected over-sized moves. Oversized moves not expected by a normally distributed market.

If gold is representative of all markets, then the existence of fat tails in its daily price changes disproves the belief that market prices are normally distributed and validates trend trading strategies that seek to exploit large directional moves.

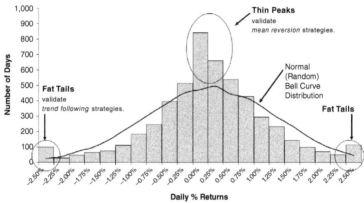

FIGURE 3.10   The existence of thin peaks and fat tails demonstrate gold's daily returns do not follow a normal (random) 'bell curve' distribution.

Thin Peaks

In Figure 3.10 you'll also notice I've marked the middle area where the histogram exceeds the bell curve. Thin peaks represent many smaller than average moves. There are far more of them than we would expect to occur if markets were normally distributed. If gold is representative of all markets, then the existence of thin peaks in its daily price changes also disproves the belief that market prices are normally distributed and validates mean reversion strategies that seek to exploit reversions to the mean. Thin peaks encourage traders to collect easy premium income from option selling. However, they forget all about fat tails where larger than expected price moves occur more frequently than expected, wiping out the option seller.

Trading Strategies

As I've suggested these two anomalies—fat tails and thin peaks—both relate to an important part of market behaviour that can be exploited by well-designed trading strategies. The existence of fat tails and thin peaks undermines academia's key-stone argument that market prices follow a normal (random) distribution. Fat tails and thin peaks are a double slap down to the ivory tower brigade. Consequently, the existence of fat tails legitimatizes the development of trend trading strategies that are designed to capture outsize moves. The existence of thin peaks legitimatizes the development of counter-trend (swing) strategies that are designed to capture moves that revert to the mean.

So, Are Markets Normally Distributed? Are They Perfect?

Based on our understanding of the theory and the distribution of gold's daily price changes, it appears gold fails the normal distribution assumption. This opens the door for traders to develop both trend-trading and mean-reversion strategies to take advantage of the respective fat tails and thin peaks. It appears that excess returns are available for enterprising traders.

However, the only stumbling block is my current sample size of one market, gold.

A sample size of one is not enough to throw out the normal distribution assumption (is that a sigh of relief I can hear from the ivory tower?).

Let's now take a look at my universal portfolio of 24 markets and see whether as a group their prices changes or returns follow a normal distribution and behave as the theory suggests. I know my sample size of 24 markets falls short of the required 30 to make any findings statistically significant. However, I feel it's large enough for my purposes as I believe my portfolio is both diversified and universal enough to be representative of 'markets'. We'll take a look at the 24 markets and see whether their price changes or returns are normally distributed or have similar characteristics as gold. The markets I'll use are summarized in Table 3.3.

Are the Universal Portfolio's Returns Normally Distributed?

For data I've used 22 years of physical spot prices between 1998 and 2020. The 24 markets covering 22 years gives me plenty of daily closing prices. I'll reference my portfolio of 24 markets as 'P24'.

Let's first look at a histogram of my portfolio's daily percentage returns or price changes, measuring the percentage gain or loss from one day to the next (Figure 3.11).

TABLE 3.3   My universal portfolio contains 24 of the most liquid and diverse markets traded on the Chicago Mercantile (futures) Exchange.

Universal Portfolio - P24	
Sector	**Market**
Indices	Nasdaq-100
	SP500
	Dow Jones
Interest Rates	5-Year Treasury Notes
	10-Year Treasury Notes
	30-Year Government Bonds
Currencies	Euro Currency
	Japanese Yen
	British Pound
Metals	Copper
	Gold
	Silver
Energy	Crude Oil
	Natural Gas
	ULSD - Heating Oil
Grains	Corn
	Soybeans
	Wheat
Livestock	Feeder Cattle
	Lean Hogs
	Live Cattle
Softs	Sugar
	Coffee
	Cotton

At first glance the histogram appears to show that my portfolio's daily returns are normally distributed, with price changes being constant through time and falling symmetrically either side of the average. Let's look at the actual frequency numbers for each daily percentage return in Table 3.4.

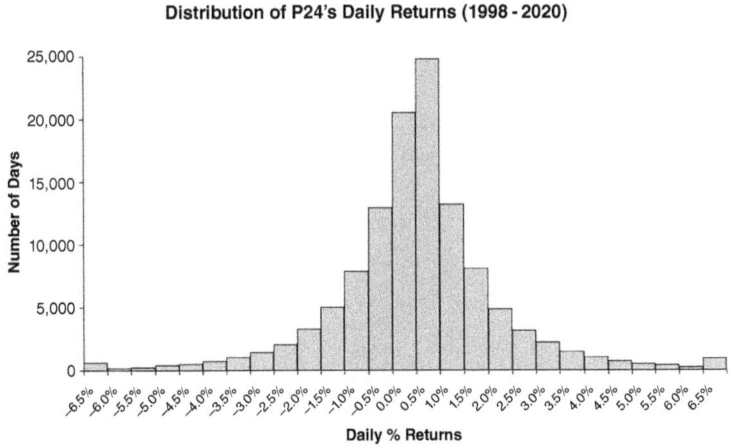

Distribution of P24's Daily Returns (1998 - 2020)

FIGURE 3.11 The daily price changes, or daily returns, of my universal portfolio of 24 markets appear, at first glance, to follow a normal random bell curve distribution.

There seems to be little bias between the negative and positive moves with the total number of negative to zero daily percentage moves being offset by the total number of positive daily percentage moves. Daily returns appear to be distributed equally, in a constant, symmetrical and serially independent (random) way either side of the average (0.02%). To the naked eye it appears the majority of the portfolio's daily returns (99.7%) fall within three standard deviations (3 x 1.85% = −5.5% to +5.5%) of the average (0.02%).

Daily returns appear to follow a random bell shape curve, or 'normal' distribution.

Or do they?

Do Markets' Daily Returns Fit Under a Bell Curve?

To test the accuracy of our naked eye its best to place a normal random 'bell' curve distribution over the histogram. If market daily returns are normally distributed (random), the histogram should fit snuggly under the bell curve.

To do this I created a normal distribution curve sharing the same average daily price change (0.02%), standard deviation (1.85%) and sample size (118,452) of my portfolio. I achieved this by again using

TABLE 3.4 The total number of daily up moves of my universal portfolio of 24 markets appear to have been cancelled out by the total number of down moves.

P24's Daily % Returns	Number of Days			
−6.50%	601			
−6.00%	186			
−5.50%	242			
−5.00%	378			
−4.50%	486			
−4.00%	704			
−3.50%	1044			
−3.00%	1442			
−2.50%	2067			
−2.00%	3267	Total		
−1.50%	4995	Zero to		
−1.00%	7853	Down		
−0.50%	12935	Moves	56671	48%
0.00%	20471			
0.50%	24762			
1.00%	13200	Total		
1.50%	8115	UP		
2.00%	4868	Moves	61781	52%
2.50%	3205			
3.00%	2206			
3.50%	1527			
4.00%	1083			
4.50%	709			
5.00%	527			
5.50%	371			
6.00%	236			
6.50%	972			
Total	118452			

Excel's random number generation function, which ensured 68% of all my daily price changes fell within one standard deviation of the average, 95% within two standard deviations and 99.7% within three standard deviations. I then placed my bell curve distribution over the histogram.

Here it is in Figure 3.12.

Well, how about that Mr RWT and Mr EMH?

I can see a double slap down coming!

Similar to our gold experience, at first glance my portfolio's histogram of daily returns appears to follow a normal random distribution. However, after overlaying a bell shape curve it suggests otherwise. As you can see the histogram *doesn't* fit snuggly under the bell curve. The middle low percentage daily moves appear to occur far more frequently than a normal random distribution would expect, far exceeding the top of the bell curve. In addition, my portfolio is showing far more daily returns beyond three standard deviation moves (−5.5% to +5.5%) than you would expect under a normal random distribution.

Looking at the data my portfolio of 24 markets daily returns are *not* normally distributed.

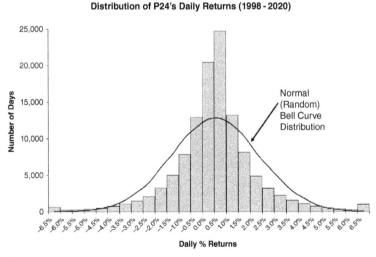

FIGURE 3.12 A normal random 'bell curve' distribution placed over the histogram of daily price changes, or returns, of my universal portfolio of 24 markets.

Thin Peaks and Fat Tails

In Figure 3.13 I've marked the middle high values and edges with 'thin peaks' and 'fat tails' respectively. Thin peaks represent far more smaller daily returns than you would expect if the markets were normally distributed. Fat tails represent far more larger daily returns than you would expect if the markets were normally distributed. The existence of thin peaks and fat tails in my portfolio's daily returns disproves the belief that market returns are normally distributed. There are too many smaller (validating the use of mean reversion trading strategies) and too many larger (validating the use of trend trading strategies) daily moves than you would expect if the markets were normally distributed.

This is the science behind the markets that validates the use of either mean reversion or trend trading strategies to pursue excess returns above market returns.

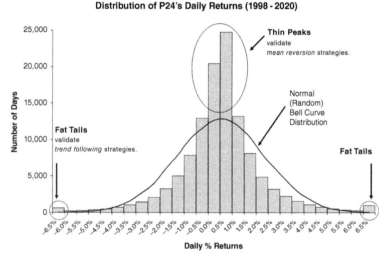

FIGURE 3.13 The existence of thin peaks and fat tails within the distribution of my universal portfolio of 24 markets' daily returns demonstrate daily price changes do not follow a normal random 'bell curve' distribution.

So, let's go back to the original key assumption embedded within the RWT and EMH.

Are markets normally distributed? Are we wasting our time developing mean reversion and trend trading strategies that use past prices to predict future prices?

According to my data above, no!

That's a loud NO, in case those in the ivory tower are hard of hearing.

Ok I hear you say, that's good to know for the daily timeframe. However, I hear your minds thinking that is all well and good but really profitable trend trades should last longer than a few days. Certainly, they should last at least a few weeks, if not months and if we're really onto a big winner, quarters?

Well I'm glad you're thinking like a trend trader! Good question. No. A great question. What you're thinking is whether markets are normally distributed over higher timeframes.

Well let me take a look for you.

Are Markets Fractal?

There is a belief that markets are fractal. Exhibiting similar behaviour or patterns over multiple timeframes, whether it's hourly, daily, weekly, monthly or higher and so on. The existence of thin peaks and fat tails in my portfolio of daily price changes disproves the notion that markets are normally distributed, on a daily timeframe. They justify traders' efforts to earn excess market returns by developing mean reversion and trend-trading strategies. However, do these market anomalies—thin peaks and fat tails—exist throughout all return dimensions, whether we're looking at weekly, monthly, quarterly or yearly price changes?

If they do, then any notion of market returns being normally distributed should be consigned to the dustbin (and the ivory tower ignored).

Let's first take a look at the histograms of higher timeframe price changes (returns) before I make any comments.

Weekly Return Distributions

The histogram in Figure 3.14 shows the distribution of my portfolio's weekly returns.

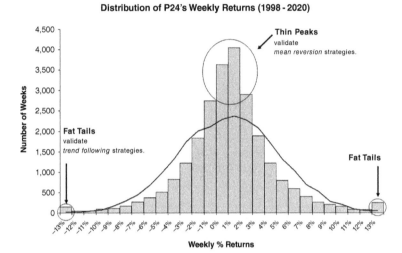

FIGURE 3.14 Distribution of P24's weekly price changes, or returns, do not follow a normal random 'bell curve' distribution.

Monthly Return Distributions

The histogram in Figure 3.15 shows the distribution of my portfolio's monthly returns.

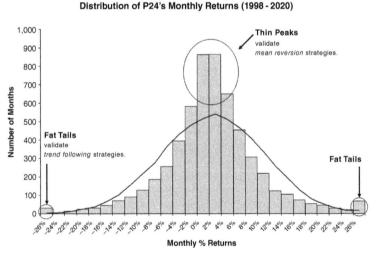

FIGURE 3.15 Distribution of P24's monthly price changes, or returns, do not follow a normal random 'bell curve' distribution.

Quarterly Return Distributions

The histogram in Figure 3.16 shows the distribution of my portfolio's quarterly returns.

Yearly Return Distributions

And finally, the histogram in Figure 3.17 shows the distribution of my portfolio's yearly returns.

Do Market Returns Follow a Normal Distribution?

So, do market returns, across multiple timeframe periods, follow a normal distribution as suggested by the academic theory? Well, let me think about for a nano second—ermm, NO!

As you can see from the histograms, market returns over the last 22 years have not followed a normal random bell curve distribution, despite major protests by the RWT and EMH. Maybe they did when these theories were first formulated, but they certainly haven't for the 22-year period between 1998 and 2020.

What these histograms show is that there is a greater probability of tail events on both sides of the return distribution, a situation called high kurtosis, across multiple timeframe periods than would be expected if they followed a normal random distribution. High kurtosis or fat tails is what validates the existence and purpose of trend trading.

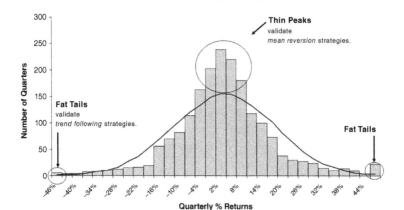

FIGURE 3.16 Distribution of P24's quarterly price changes, or returns, do not follow a normal random 'bell curve' distribution.

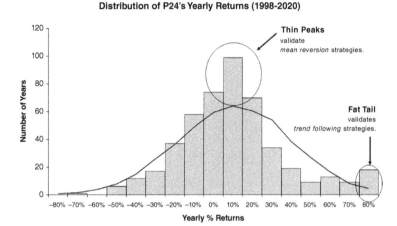

FIGURE 3.17   Distribution of P24's yearly price changes, or returns, do not follow a normal random 'bell curve' distribution.

If Prices Are Not Normally Distributed Then Why Do Models Rely on the Assumption?

If price changes are not normally distributed then why do models rely on the key assumption? Good question. I could argue that when these theories were developed prices were normally distributed; however, a quick analysis would suggest otherwise.

But first a little background. As mentioned earlier, the EMH was developed by Eugene Fama between 1965 and 1970. In 1965 he published a paper called 'The Behavior of Stock Market Prices' in *The Journal of Business*, where he argued support for the RWT. In 1970 he published a paper called the 'Efficient Capital Markets: A Review of Theory and Empirical Work' in *The Journal of Finance*. In this paper he formulated the EMH and its three forms of weak, semi-strong and strong.

To see whether prices were normally distributed back then when Fama's papers were published, I'll review the daily price changes of the SP500 cash index between 1928 and 1964. A period of data that Fama would have had access to.

Let me cut to the chase and show you, in Figure 3.18, the SP500's histogram of daily price changes or returns and see whether they did,

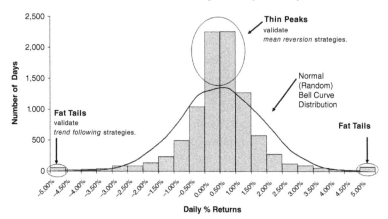

FIGURE 3.18 Distribution of SP500's daily price changes, or returns, between 1928 and 1964 do not follow a normal random 'bell curve' distribution.

or did not, fall nicely under a random bell curve distribution (as the RWT and EMH both assume).

Argh. Interesting. Scandal? Is that doors I hear slamming in the ivory tower?

At a time when key ideas were supported (RWT) and developed (EMH) there was evidence—and I know it's only one market, but still, there was evidence—that a key market in the world's largest economy at the time was not normally distributed. Yet RWT was strongly supported and the EMH heralded, where both relied on a key assumption that prices were normally distributed.

Weird, hey? Some may say they simply didn't know? But that is unlikely.

Sure, this was at a time before PCs, Excel and freely available data. However, they were very smart people with probably more time on their hands then we have today. So, why then did they embed such a fragile key assumption into their models?

Well, we can only guess. However, many believe the normal distribution assumption was accepted, embedded and used due to its convenient simplification and use of easy statistical methods. Or in two words: convenient and easy.

If we accept that reasoning, it appears the academics may have taken the line of least resistance. A decision that we're still dealing with today because of the unintended consequences:

- 'past performance is not indicative of future performance',
- 'it's impossible to time the market' and
- 'chasing manager performance is pointless'.

The normal distribution belief instilled and entrenched within academia has given many people a false sense of security and greatly underestimated market risk. The normal distribution mantra has led many people to believe the probability of market crashes is pretty low. However, histograms and history show us that they occur more frequently then you'd expect if price changes were in actual fact normally distributed.

Thus, all models relying on an assumption that price changes are normally distributed are underestimating the chance of large price changes. They're underselling risk. You'd think the entrenched belief that price changes follow a normal distribution would have been consigned to the dustbin following Long-Term Capital Management's (LTCM) demise in 1998 or when the 2008 and 2020 financial crises hit us. But nope. It's entrenched.

It's bewildering that data is being ignored. A histogram of fat tails clearly demonstrates that price changes are not normally distributed. They're not symmetrical, they have fat tails and they are not truly random because outsize moves occur more regularly then a normal distribution would expect.

Despite this, these models, based on an incorrect belief that price changes are normally distributed, are still being used today. They are still being used to explain the risk potential (or limited risk potential) of various financial instruments such as an inverse VIX ETN (Volatility Exchange Traded Notes). These instruments collected easy premium income by selling volatility short believing 99.9% of all daily price changes would occur within four standard deviations of the average. It didn't end well for the VIX ETN.

Let's take a look at Table 3.5, where I've summarized the distribution of the SP500's daily returns since 1928.

According to a normal random distribution, a price move beyond four standard deviations should almost be impossible (100.00% − 99.99% = 00.01%). From the data in Table 3.5 a four standard

TABLE 3.5   The frequency of SP500's daily returns show the occurrence of moves equal to or greater than four standard deviations being far more than what would be expected by a normal random distribution. Assuming daily returns follow a normal distribution greatly underestimates the risk of sudden sharemarket moves and crashes.

Distribution of SP500 Daily Returns (Since 1928)			
Standard	Deviations	*SP500 Daily Returns*	*Number of Days*
4 × STD	–4.7%	–5.0%	*75*
		–4.5%	*31*
		–4.0%	*40*
3 × STD	–3.5%	–3.5%	*58*
		–3.0%	*121*
2 × STD	–2.3%	–2.5%	*163*
		–2.0%	*296*
		–1.5%	*606*
1 × STD	–1.1%	–1.0%	*1,253*
		–0.5%	*2,665*
Average	0.0%	0.0%	*5,510*
		0.5%	*5,855*
		1.0%	*3,176*
1 × STD	1.2%	1.5%	*1,415*
		2.0%	*652*
2 × STD	2.4%	2.5%	*292*
		3.0%	*168*
		3.5%	*85*
3 × STD	3.5%	4.0%	*51*
		4.5%	*37*
4 × STD	4.7%	5.0%	*97*

deviation move should only occur on two days (22,646 days x 00.01%). However, as you can see, the SP500 has experienced a negative four standard deviation move on more than 75 occasions over the past

90+ years! That's a huge miss by the advocates of a normal random distribution. However, despite the data, the key normal distribution assumption is still being used and is still hugely underestimating risk. Like it did in early 2018. On 5 February 2018 the SP500 experienced an intraday −4.5% move that almost equalled four standard deviations (−4.7%). A move that should only occur, if prices were normally distributed, once in every 43 years. On that day holders of the inverse VIX ETNs saw the value of their notes decline between 80% and 90%. Billions in value were wiped out.

I can imagine many holders of the VIX ETN and holders of similar instruments collecting option premiums, not to mention the retail naked option sellers, would have been highly shocked believing such an event was unlikely to occur in their life time due to their strong belief in normal distributions. When the Coronavirus pandemic hit in 2020, between 19 February and 24 March the SP500 experienced six daily price moves greater than four standard deviations (−4.7% and +4.7%)! Take a look:

Date	Change in Daily Close
Mon 16 March 2020	−10.3%
Thu 12 Mar 2020	−9.9%
Mon 09 Mar 2020	−7.8%
Thu 27 Feb 2020	−4.9%
Fri 13 Mar 2020	8.5%
Tue 24 Mar 2020	9.5%

According to the theory, price moves beyond four standard deviations should only occur twice during a 90+-year period!

Crazy to believe prices follow a normal distribution.

But a study of distributions shows that larger than expected price moves can and do occur more frequently than a normal distribution would expect. Fat tails exist. But adherence to the RWT and EMH convinces people, like LTCM, the creators of the VIX ETN, naked option sellers and the advocates of 'buy-and-hold' strategies, to dismiss the risk of extreme data points as they do not conform to a normal random bell curve distribution.

Fat Tails—the Science Behind Trend Trading

Fat tails, or extreme market movements, across multiple timeframes not only validate the notion of trend trading but also make trend trading the most significant anomaly in financial markets.

Despite what the RWT and EMH theories say, the markets are not totally efficient and they're not totally random. Trends occur. They exist. They sit stacked up at the edge of distributions, begging to be traded. Traders can develop trading strategies that utilize past prices to generate buy and sell signals to predict future prices. It's our job to work out a sensible way to do just that.

Fat Tails—the Moral of Our Story So Far

The moral of fat tails is yes, there are trends to catch, but just as importantly, we should learn to respect the market's Mr Maximum Adversity and learn to expect the unexpected. Extreme price moves occur, and they occur more often than many expect. So, expect to be surprised and be prepared to be surprised, never trade without a stop. In addition, we should learn to resist the temptation of collecting easy premium income from selling naked options. Although it can provide a steady income for years, it can all be taken away, plus more, in the blink of one trading session. Just visualize the premium-collecting option seller picking up pennies in front of a steam roller. That can never end well. Best not to think of collecting easy premium income!

But for our purposes here, science has shown the existence of fat tails, which validates the pursuit of trend trading. Extreme price moves occur across multiple timeframes. They exist. It's our job to develop sensible trend-trading strategies to capture them.

So Why isn't Everyone Trading with the Trend?

Ok, I hear you. If the science of statistics proves that trend trading will always win due to the irrefutable existence of fat tails, why then don't all traders follow the trend and why aren't all trend traders making money from it? Good question. Without a doubt many have heard the old truism:

Trade with the trend, the trend is your friend.

And yet I know that many who attempt to trade with the trend fail to do so. There are many reasons for trader failure, which I discuss in *UPST*. However, since I've used science to validate trend trading, please let me use science again to explain why so many find it so hard.

It's to do with the bell curve—or more specifically, its construction. Although fat tails occur, which is wonderful for the trend follower, their occurrence is far less frequent then regular small price changes.

Remember the majority of price changes occur within two standard deviations of the average (95%). A huge challenge is that the 'bell curve' will only start to look good following many, many price changes. As a consequence, trend traders have to suffer through many losing trades before enjoying a good fat tail extreme winner. Now while markets can exist only on oxygen our trading accounts can't. So, if a trader is either not well capitalized or is not trading with a 0% ROR, then they'll run out of trading capital long before enough extreme fat tail events occur to make up for all their losing trades.

So, while the science of fat tails proves trend trading can't fail, it also explains the difficulty of absorbing many, many losing trades that sit under the almost perfect normal distribution bell curve. The many losing trades make it very difficult for most traders to stomach. Not impossible, but difficult. However, a well-designed robust positive expectancy trend-trading strategy, when combined with sensible money management that produces a 0% ROR, is traded over a diversified portfolio it will go a very long way to assisting a trader in suffering many losses before enjoying a few good wins.

Now that we understand the science of fat tails supports the pursuit of trend trading, it's time to see the 'money'. Understanding the science is all well and good, however, appreciating the science doesn't pay the bills.

Let's now look for the proof that trend trading works.

THE APPEALS OF TREND TRADING

It Works—the Evidence

Before there was any talk of distributions, randomness and efficiency, markets existed to facilitate the exchange of goods and services between buyers and sellers. Some markets have been in existence for centuries. Over the years many participants have collected and collated data to investigate the effectiveness of trend trading. Today there is a mountain of research supporting the effectiveness of trend following in earning excess market returns (please refer to Appendix A for literature on trend trading).

Rather than attempting to cover the evidence here, I'd like to point you in the direction of two sources.

The first being *Trend Following with Managed Futures: The Search for Crisis Alpha* (Wiley Trading, 2015), written by Alex Greyserman and Kathryn Kaminski. Don't be thrown by 'Managed Futures' in the title. It's all about trend trading. It's about the history, the performance and how it should fit within an investment portfolio. Be warned, it's not really a book aimed at retail traders but one more geared towards institutional investors and fund allocators. It is a little dry to read. It's full of statistics and tables. However, despite its academic appearance, it does give what I think is the most comprehensive deep dive into trend trading performance there is. It provides a thorough explanation of the rationale and benefit of trend trading. It's insightful. It's well researched (covering 800 years) and it's well written. However, it's not a book on how to develop trend trading strategies. So, don't go there for ideas, but if you want an in-depth look at the data supporting trend trading returns, it's the book for you. It's compelling.

Greyserman and Kaminski looked at 84 equity, fixed income, commodity and currency markets as they became available during the years from 1200 through to 2013. They established long or short equal risk sized positions based on whether prices were above or below their rolling 12-month past returns. The comparative performances are summarized in Table 3.6.

The annualized (CAGR) return of their trend trading strategy was 13%, with an annual volatility of 11% and a Sharpe ratio of 1.16. In contrast, the buy-and-hold strategy had an annualized return of only 4.8%, volatility of 10.3% and a Sharpe ratio of 0.47. Trend trading's risk-adjusted performance was twice that of the buy-and-hold strategy.

I think the following passage best sums up Greyserman and Kaminski's findings (from page 401):

> *Using roughly 800 years of market data, trend trading can be viewed from a long-term perspective. Over the centuries, empirically, trend trading has provided distinctly positive returns, a high Sharpe ratio, as well as low correlation with traditional asset classes, inflation, and interest rate regimes. The strategy provides consistently positive performance during crisis periods and the performance seems to be linked*

TABLE 3.6   Trend trading has not only been far more profitable than buy-and-hold over the last 800 years, but it has also been the most superior on a risk-adjusted basis as measured by the Sharpe Ratio.

Performance Statistics for Buy-and-Hold and Trend Following Portfolios (Period: 1223 to 2013)		
	Buy-and-Hold Portfolio	Trend Following Portfolio
Annualised Return	4.8%	13.0%
Annualised Std Deviation	10.3%	11.2%
Sharpe Ratio	0.47	1.16

Source: From Alex Greyserman, Kathryn Kaminski, Trend Following with Managed Futures: The Search for Crisis Alpha. © John Wiley & Sons.

to divergence across markets. From a portfolio perspective, the combination of trend trading with traditional portfolios such as a 60/40 portfolio significantly improves risk-adjusted performance.

In addition, I'd like to touch upon a paper updated in 2017 by its authors Brian Hurst, Yao Hua Ooi and Lasse Heje Pedersen titled *A Century of Evidence on Trend-Following Investing*. Although they don't cover 800 years, they do stretch their analysis back to 1880. They determined that between 1880 and 2013 trend trading, covering a global portfolio of 67 markets, achieved a grossed annualized (CAGR) return of 14.5% per year! They also found that for each decade since 1880 trend trading achieved positive results with low correlation with traditional asset classes like bonds, property and shares. They found that trend trading investing performed well in eight out of ten of the largest financial crises during the last century. Finally, they found trend trading investing performed well across all market cycles including periods of good growth and poor growth (recessions), war and peace, low and high interest rate environments and low and high inflation periods.

So far so good.

The science of fat tails validates the pursuit of trend trading while plenty of research papers (and books) offer ample empirical evidence of its effectiveness (once again please refer to Appendix A).

A Note of Caution

Just one note of caution here. Although compelling, academic papers and well-written books showing proof that trend trading works are open to the same criticism that simulated equity curves receive. It's easy to make a strategy look good in hindsight if you already have the data. Just as traders can fall victim to their own unintended excessive curve fitting and data mining, so can the academics.

Don't get me wrong. I welcome all the empirical evidence produced that supports trend trading. However, I just want to be a realist and acknowledge that most empirical papers are backward-looking projections, just like simulated equity curves.

As we'll shortly learn, simulated equity curves can come in different shapes and sizes offering various degrees of useful evidence. Most simulated equity curves are fragile constructs relying on attributed variable values. The only evidence they can provide is one of successful curve fitting and data mining where a trader has succeeded in fitting their trading idea to past data. This is similar to academic research papers where the author/s have only succeeded in producing a positive outcome based on their look-back trend-trading strategy.

It all comes down to in-sample data and out-of-sample data.

The best data to use, for both empirical research and reviewing trading strategies, is out-of-sample data. Data that has occurred after the strategy or idea was first developed or thought of.

On a holistic level, David Ricardo's insight to cut losses and let profits run underpins and validates the general testing of trend-trading strategies post 1800. However, the devil is in the detail. Unless a deliberate strategy has been communicated on a specific date on how to cut losses and let profits run, any attempt to develop such a strategy will receive criticism of curve fitting and data mining. Yes, the idea of cutting losses and letting profits run has been known since 1800; however, the exact strategy used to find entry and exit levels, unless previously and clearly articulated by someone, could simply have been a fluke by the researcher or author to find such a strategy to support the benefit of trend trading. And if not a fluke, then possibly the result of optimizing the various look-back variables used to produce the results that look most impressive. Or in two words, curve fitted.

Despite the insightfulness of their research papers and the degrees they have, academics' analysis can also fall victim to curve-fitting and data-mining criticism.

So yes, welcome the positive trend-trading message, but do so with your head up and eyes wide open and be conscious of whether in-sample or out-of-sample data was used. If out-of-sample, then all thumbs up. If in-sample, then be as wary of the research outcome as you would be of a perfect looking simulated equity curve.

Apologies for such a long monologue into normal distributions, bell curves, theories and fat tails. However, I hope I've given you a good insight into why trend trading works, which is one of its obvious and great appeals.

Next, I want to discuss another reason for its great appeal, it being best practice.

IT'S BEST PRACTICE

So far, I've covered the science behind why trend trading works. I have also pointed you towards research that documents the effectiveness of trend trading.

Another appeal of trend trading is that it is also best practice. Some of the best fund managers in the world are systematic trend traders. As I mentioned in Chapter 2, according to BarclayHedge, assets managed by systematic trend traders had grown from $22 billion in 1999 to over $298 billion by 2019. This is a huge growth over discretionary traders who, according to BarclayHedge, could only grow their assets under management over the same period from $8 billion to $12 billion. Please refer to Figure 2.2 in Chapter 2.

If we accept weight of money as an endorsement, then trend trading is certainly seen as best practice. So, if it's good enough for professional systematic trend traders, then surely, it's good enough for the rest of us? There is no shame in following the best!

I want to again point you to an external source of information, Michael Covel's book *Trend Following* (Wiley Trading, 2017). Covel not only gives a good account of the benefits of trend trading but he also provides an excellent insight in to some of the best money managers in the world who trade with the trend.

In Covel's book, to name just a few, you will read about the following managers who have achieved exceptional returns from following the trend:

- David Harding from Winton Capital,
- Bill Dunn from Dunn Capital Management,
- John W Henry from John W Henry & Co,
- Ed Seykota,
- Keith Campbell from Campbell & Co,
- Jerry Parker of Chesapeake Capital Management and
- Salem Abraham of Abraham Trading Company.

These best practice managers provide solid proof of the benefits of trend trading, as their results are all based on out-of-sample data. I say out-of-sample because the performance returns are their actual money in the bank results. They're not based on simulated equity curves. They're not based on academic research papers. They have used their trend-trading strategies live in the markets to earn good returns. All returns are post the development of their strategy, being traded live on out-of-sample data with real money.

So, not only do these managers support the idea that trend trading is best practice but their results also provide out-of-sample evidence that trend trading works and works well.

Another reason why trend trading appeals to me is because it simplifies the trading process.

It Simplifies the Trading Process

It's a daunting task for anyone who wants to trade. Even for those with experience.

Earlier I discussed how confusing the world was with the multitude of unanswered questions. Questions that every trader faces. From the helicopter macro view regarding key challenges facing Europe, North America and Asia down to the trader micro view of choosing between markets, instruments, timeframes and techniques. Every trader has what can appear to be an infinite array of choices and decisions to make, even down to the minute details of entry, stop and exit levels.

At times there can appear to be too many decisions to make. Without a complete trade plan, traders can be left with too many questions to answer. It can be overwhelming. However, I believe adopting a complete trade plan can help simplify the process. And, in my opinion, adopting a trend trading strategy can simplify the whole process even further.

So Many Decisions—Which Markets to Trade?

For most traders their first decision concerns which market or markets they'd like to trade. Selecting a preferred market isn't easy.

Some new or even experienced traders may believe they'll need to develop a worldview on global growth before they can hope to choose an appropriate market or markets to trade. Will global growth be expanding or contracting? What will be the resultant impact on various markets? Which ones are likely to be the winners, the property, equity, bond or commodity markets?

On a regional basis some may believe they'll need to develop country-specific views to successfully select an appropriate market or markets to trade. Questions I've raised before include:

- Will the European Union hold together?
- Will the United States get hold of its debt and deficit?
- Will China return to trend growth?
- Will Japan solve its demographic challenge?
- Will a full-scale currency and trade war with accompanying tariffs develop?
- Will global normalcy return after the Coronavirus pandemic?

What will be the likely impact on various markets given positive or negative outcomes?

Some may believe that to succeed in the markets they'll need to develop an opinion on whether a financial crisis will or will not occur and if one does, when and where and which markets will benefit or be disadvantaged. Some may believe they'll need to develop into deep thinkers and hopefully become more accurate forecasters then trained economists to successfully select an appropriate market or markets to trade.

So many questions.

Identifying and selecting an appropriate market or markets and companies to trade is both daunting and fraught with disappointment.

There is no guarantee that the markets or companies they'll select will perform as expected. Actually, there is every chance the market's Mr Maximum Adversity will ensure their selected markets and companies will do the opposite and tank!

But it doesn't stop at portfolio construction.

So Many Decisions—What Technique to Use?

After choosing an appropriate market or markets to trade the next question to answer is how to time their entry? When should they buy and sell? This isn't a straight forward question. Just like choosing a market there are multiple options available to assist traders with timing their entries.

First, they need to decide whether they should use fundamental or technical analysis, or a combination of both? If it's technical analysis they will need to decide which school of thought they should study and implement? For example, should they consider:

- cycles,
- pattern recognition:
  - chart patterns and
  - candle sticks,
- seasonals,
- astrology,
- moon phases,
- tidal rhythms,
- Dow Theory
- Elliott Wave Theory,
- WD Gann,
- Market Profile,
- Fibonacci analysis,
- fractals,
- sacred geometry,
- trend lines,
- indicator analysis for measuring:
  - price,
  - trend,
  - retracement,
  - momentum,
  - sentiment,

- volatility and
- volume,

... phew!

And it's not just a simple task of choosing a technique, because many don't work! With over 90% of active traders losing you could say over 90% of the above techniques don't work either. It's a mine field. A trader will have to hope their luck is in once they select a technique.

Once an approach is selected there is still the implementation: analysis, order preparation, entering, placing stops and exiting. There is so much to do and so much confusion. Which markets to trade? Which strategy to use? When to trade, where to enter, where to place stops and where to exit? There can be plenty of anxiety and confusion with investing and trading, but not when you decide to become a trend trader.

Trend Trading Makes it Easy

A key benefit of trend trading is that it does simplify the investment or trading decision.

Rather than trying to identify individual markets or companies, trend followers trade a diversified portfolio of liquid markets. There is no stress associated with selecting which market or company to trade above others. There is no lost sleep in pursing crude oil over gold or Netflix over Apple. There is no anxiety attached to deciding on whether global growth will expand or contract and the likely impact on markets.

Being a trend trader removes the pressure to unlock investment secrets. It removes the pressure to think like an economist. It removes the pressure to create a global macro narrative. It removes the pressure to understand why markets move. It removes the pressure to out think the market. It removes the pressure to be right. It removes the pressure to pick winners and avoid losers. It removes the uncertainty and procrastination. It removes any singular focus on any particular market. It removes the inflexibility of only being long, since you can also sell short

Trend trading, although difficult as we know, is relatively simple.

There is no agony over developing a view on global growth. You just trade a diversified portfolio of liquid markets.

There is no agony over finding answers to the big issues plaguing Europe, the United States, China and Japan. You just trade a diversified portfolio of liquid markets.

There is no agony over predicting the next financial crises or pandemic. You just trade a diversified portfolio of liquid markets.

There is no agony over making forecasts. You just trade a diversified portfolio of liquid markets.

There is no agony over market selection. You just trade a diversified portfolio of liquid markets.

There is no agony over having to pick the winners over the losers. You just trade a diversified portfolio of liquid markets.

There is no more worry about individual markets.

There is no agony over selecting and learning the right field of technical analysis to time when to buy and sell. You can just implement the three golden tenets of trend trading:

- Follow the trend:
  - buying those markets or companies moving up and
  - selling those markets or companies moving down,
- cut your losses short and
- let your profits run.

There is no agony in trying to understand why markets move. You just follow the trend.

There is no agony in trying to understand why some markets fail. You just cut your losses short.

There is no agony in trying to determine the right time to exit winning positions. You just let your profits run.

As I said, another strong appeal of trend trading is that it simplifies the investment and trading process in a big, big way (Figure 3.19).

The final appeal of trend trading for me is because it's difficult.

It's Difficult

Believe it or not, for me, the fact that it's hard to execute trend trading successfully makes it appealing to me. It should also make it appealing to you.

Hey, if trend trading was easy, everyone would be doing it and possibly the fat tails might disappear. It's difficult to handled six to seven losses out of every ten trades. It knocks out many retail trend

Trend Trading 101
Trend traders trade a diverse portfolio of markets.
Trend traders stick to their trade plans.
Trend traders do not need to know where or why the market moves to make money.
Trend traders just need to follow the trend.

Primary Benefit of Being a Trend Trader
Makes money - just look at the world's best investment/trading managers.

Secondary Benefits of Being a Trend Trader

Removes pressure to unlock investment secrets.	They follow their trade plan.
Removes pressure to think like an Economist.	They follow their trade plan.
Removes pressure to create a global macro narrative.	They follow their trade plan.
Removes pressure to understand why markets move.	They follow their trade plan.
Removes pressure to out think the market.	They follow their trade plan.
Removes pressure to be right.	They follow their trade plan.
Removes pressure to pick winners.	They follow their trade plan.
Removes pressure to avoid losers.	They follow their trade plan.
Removes uncertainly and procrastination.	They follow their trade plan.
Removes pressure to pick one market over another.	They follow their trade plan.
Removes focus on any particular market.	They follow their trade plan.
Removes inflexibility of only being long. Can sell short.	They follow their trade plan.

FIGURE 3.19 Trend trading simplifies the whole investment and trading process.

traders. Although trend trading is relatively simple, absorbing so many losing trades makes it both psychologically and financially difficult. Psychologically, because it's soul destroying absorbing and recording loss, after loss, after loss, after loss (you get the idea). Financially, as you have to have enough risk capital to not only fund trading a portfolio of diversified markets but also to fund the inevitable and continual drawdowns trend trading inflicts. Drawdowns and trend trading go hand in hand and are as regular as night follows day. Many retail trend traders can't handle the inevitable and constant drawdowns.

So, for me it makes trend trading appealing. It's a badge of honour to succeed where so many fail. You should also strive to succeed in an area where so many falter. It's an opportunity for you to show how determined you can be where so many take the soft option, throwing up their hands declaring either it's too hard (which is truthful for them) or doesn't work (which is a big fat lie).

I encourage you to accept the challenge and demonstrate the resilience and determination required to succeed where so many fail.

SUMMARY

I hope I have given you a good understanding of why trend trading is so appealing. Being known for over two centuries proves it's a durable strategy to follow. The science of fat tails proves it works, while research papers unanimously declare it as a profitable technique. The professionals embrace it as best practice and there are world renowned managers who have regularly outperformed the market for their investors. It helps to simplify the investing and trading process and being difficult presents it as a worthy challenge for the dedicated trader.

So, I hope I have everyone nodding along with me that trend trading is not only an obvious pursuit but also a worthwhile and profitable one.

However, I have to let you know that, for all the now obvious and good reasons to pursue trend trading, the majority of retail traders who do, fail at it!

Yep, that is the hard, cold truth about retail trend traders. Like swing, or counter-trend traders, most of them lose. Certainly, the number of losing trades, as I have discussed, helps to waylay many retail trend traders—however, there are other factors in play as well. But before I give you some additional perspectives into how the majority, despite the attraction, fail at trend trading, let me first share with you some insights as to why trends exist.

CHAPTER 4

Why Do Trends Exist?

CONFUSION REIGNS

There are many opinions as to why trends exist. On the one hand, there are the academics whose theories have difficultly explaining the existence of trends. On the other hand, there is plenty of empirical evidence to support them. At the end of the day, the existence of trends does not fit neatly into any theoretical financial model. So, despite their prevalence, there is no proper explanation for why they occur.

According to the Random Walk Theory (RWT), markets are random, where price changes are unrelated to previous price changes. There is no serial dependence between prices. There are no trends. As we know, the Efficient-Market Hypothesis (EMH) believes all markets are properly priced reflecting all available information, which is quickly, efficiently and correctly absorbed. Traders cannot use available information to predict future prices as it's already efficiently reflected in market prices. There are no trends.

Despite their objections, trends do exist as demonstrated by the occurrence of fat tail distributions.

BEHAVIOURAL FINANCE

Given this anomaly, another field of financial thinking is starting to challenge the mathematical view of financial markets. While the RWT and EMH still have their support there is a new model on the block called behavioural finance.

Behavioural finance is based on observations about human behaviour. It looks to join psychology with economics to explain traders' irrational decisions. It believes psychological factors such as behavioural and cognitive biases affect traders, which limits and distorts the information they receive. This distortion can cause them at times to behave like lemmings, making incorrect or irrational decisions.

Traders know emotions do affect financial decisions. We see it all the time in the markets. We see and feel how our fear and greed play havoc with our decision making. We can see how collectively our behaviour can drive prices way beyond normal limits as the crowd's greed pushes bubbles ever higher in fear of missing out. We can see how collectively our fear can drive prices even lower in fear of being wiped out, before reverting back. Without doubt fear and greed have an impact on market prices. Behavioural finance recognizes this.

Rather than accepting the belief that people make rational decisions because all information is efficiently, quickly and correctly absorbed, behavioural finance believes markets are influenced by peoples' emotions. Principally, fear and greed. It believes emotions cannot always be rational. People not only come in all sorts of different shapes and sizes but they also come carrying a wide variety of different psychological beliefs, prejudices and idiosyncrasies. According to behavioural finance, these individual quirks delay and hamper information being efficiently, quickly and correctly absorbed into market prices.

Behavioural finance's key takeaway is that people contain behavioural biases that slow down price discovery of new information. This creates market friction. This friction in turn perpetuates trends. These behavioural biases are part and parcel of our fabric and although at times they can serve us well they can also unintentionally have us behaving like lemmings, panicking rather than keeping our heads.

According to behavioural finance, information is not efficiently, quickly and correctly absorbed into prices. No. Us—you and I—being emotional beings, for better or worse, bring our human 'mind' baggage to the table. Our biases prejudice the efficient and correct absorption of new information allowing trends to emerge and perpetuate. What they're saying is that we're a bit dim. We're a bit slow. We get over excited. We're sometimes too exuberant. We're sometimes in denial. We're human. We're not rational machines. Yes, when challenged we can easily revert to our overly excited and overly panicky 6-year-old inner self.

So, there are now two schools of thought. The traditional RWT and EMH theories that rely on traders being rational (because all information is efficiently, quickly and correctly absorbed) and behavioural finance that believe traders are irrational (because information is not being efficiently, quickly or accurately absorbed due our inherent biases).

If we were all rational, then all information would be correctly reflected in prices. Traders would not be able to use existing information to predict future prices. Trends would not exist, as prices would adjust quickly to their correct fundamental levels. However, if instead of being rational we were the opposite, then our individual behavioural biases would slow down the price discovery process delaying the correct adjustment in prices. Our drip-feed reaction to new information would allow trends to emerge and build.

So, it comes down to whether you believe yourself to be rational or irrational. Interesting, hey?

Regardless of your personal thoughts behavioural finance at least makes an attempt to explain the existence of trends, unlike the RWT or EMH.

However, before we look at these behaviour biases it must be said that behavioural finance has faced a lot of resistance from academics (those untouchables who inhibit their ivory towers). No one knows for sure the reason for their resistance but many suspect it's due to behavioural finance not being 'scientific' enough. Many academics are keen to have their field of expertise recognized as a mathematically based science. They don't view behavioural finance as being hard edged enough. They see it more as a philosophy that has few controlled experiments to verify cause and effect. To them it is too general, too murky, too vague, too 'arty' and too soft. While the psychological basis of many investment decisions can be explained by principles that seem reasonable, there is no hard evidence that such principles actually explain the events studied. It's all a little bit vague.

Anyway, regardless of the resistance, we can at least have a look at these behavioural biases and gain some insight into why trends (fat tails) exist.

Figure 4.1 illustrates how behavioural finance explains trends.

Behavioural finance believes our cognitive biases cause delays in price discovery. The delays create friction, which in turn allows trends to develop. Got it? What they're implying is that we're slow to see the truth in information and it's our cognitive biases that blind us, slow us down.

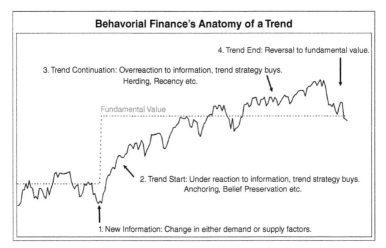

FIGURE 4.1 Unlike other theories behavioural finance at least attempts to explain the existence of trends.

Let's have a look at these biases we carry around. They are being held responsible for our tardy response to new information that enters the market. They cause us to either underreact or overreact to new information. This causes pricing inefficiencies that delay correct price discovery. Market friction delays price adjustments, which in turn allow trends to emerge and then perpetuate until they arrive at their correct fundamental level.

If you didn't already know yourself, please let me introduce you to the little nuances rattling around your head. These are the same cognitive biases swirling around the minds of those self-proclaimed market experts, the repeaters, amplifiers, infotainers, detractors and revisionists. Those peripheral market participants I've told you to ignore. Well, the havoc they cause combined with our own cognitive biases help perpetuate trends. Our cognitive biases, which also make it difficult to succeed as a discretionary trader, can lead to either underreaction or overreaction. Let's take a look.

Underreaction

Anchoring Bias

We apparently carry around an anchoring bias, where we tend to anchor our views to the first piece of information we receive. We're like ducklings being imprinted at birth. We're anchored to the first piece of information we have and we're very slow to adjust our views to new information. Our reluctance to react causes prices to underreact to news.

Belief Preservation Bias

Many of us have a religious faith, some stronger than others. What you probably don't know is that we can also develop a strong faith towards a trading strategy we use. So strong that we persist with it even after continuing poor performance. This causes us to ignore new information that may contradict our poor strategy. I know this first hand—when I persisted for too long with Elliott Wave. This faith to hang on to our losing strategies is referred to as the belief preservation bias. It causes us to adjust too slowly to new information, causing prices to again underreact to news.

Confirmation Bias

We have all done it. We've carried around biases against people, only focusing on their bad characteristics and not their good qualities. This is called confirmation bias. We only look at their bad behaviour, which confirms our ill feelings towards them, while ignoring their good. We do the same when trading. We tend to only look for information that confirms our positions. We'll ignore any contradictory news or information. If we're long gold we'll only pay attention to disturbing news about the end of fiat money, while dismissing news announcing major new gold discoveries. This causes us to adjust slowly to new information, causing prices to underreact to news, allowing trends to emerge.

Conservatism Bias

We're creatures of habit and the older we get the more entrenched our habits become. We become conservative. We resist changes to our daily routines. Hey, I may be the only person left on the planet not on Facebook. I delayed for a long time before switching to an electronic broker. As traders we're the same. We tend to hesitate in front of new information. We're not quick to digest and react to news. This hesitation is eventually replaced by action, but we all take action at different times, allowing trends to emerge as more traders start reacting to the news.

Loss Aversion Bias or Disposition Effect

Traders are bad losers. We've all done it. We hang on to losing trades far longer than we should. We do this because we hate realizing losses. We hate pain. While we don't mind a 'paper loss', we actually hate realizing losses because in our minds that is actual pain. This bias to loss aversion removes selling pressure when we're long, allowing downtrends to persist for longer periods. If we had collectively stopped ourselves out earlier, the 'stop losses' would have helped prices accelerate sooner to their correct fundament level.

On the other side, we're also bad winners. We've all done it when we've sold our winners too early. We do it as we like to realize profits. This early selling pressure dampens upward momentum allowing trends to continue until the new fundamental level is reached.

Overreaction

Herding Bias

We love the crowd. We crave acceptance and shy away from rejection. We hate being singled out, being seen as different. Welcome to our herding bias. As traders we love consensus, we like the comfort and feel of harmony it gives us. So, as traders we tend to follow the crowd. Which is good for us trend traders. This causes prices to overreact and move beyond where the real fundamental level is, causing trends to carry on. This herding effect feeds on itself and can lead to bubbles developing. I bet you didn't know that? I always thought central banks caused bubbles!

Recency Bias

Many of us are easily influenced by the last thought in our heads or our last experience. This refers to 'recency'. In trading we tend to place greater importance on more recent price moves compared to more distant ones. If we see prices rising, we'll expect prices to continue higher. This allows trends to march on causing prices to overreact and move beyond where the real fundamental level is.

PATH DEPENDENCY

Along with behavioural finance there is another idea gaining traction in finance called path dependency. It offers another explanation as to why trends exist. Path dependency refers to how the past can impact decisions, or simply, history matters.

The RWT believes price changes are totally independent of previous price changes. With a coin toss we know this is true. However, with market prices we can't be so sure. According to path dependency, prices are not random but incorporate path dependency.

Path dependency explains the continued use of a view based on historical use. It holds true even if new information becomes available. Path dependency occurs because it is often easier to simply continue with a previously held view than use the new information (similar to our conservatism bias). In other words, history matters when making decisions. So, if people have a memory based on their history, so do markets. They're path dependent, not random, so trends can and do exist as people have a memory of previous price action.

AND THE WINNER IS?

Well, there you have it. Accepted theory says trends do not exist, while the empirical evidence and new insights into our behaviour suggest they do! Got a headache yet? Well, I did mention the fuss surrounding trend trading was a little like a Punch and Judy show!

I suppose we have to accept economics is not a hard science but a soft mathematical construct with a difficult to quantify human element. Unfortunately, there isn't a single unified theory that can pull everything together. But not to worry, disagreements between the academics is their business, while ours is to seek out and take advantage of fat tails. Fat tails that we know exist! They can no longer argue about that!

SUMMARY

Now we're aware that our own behavioural idiosyncrasies regarding underreaction and overreaction are more than likely responsible for trends, it's time to understand more about why so many fail at trend trading. A failure rate that is at odds with both the existence and hard scientific data that proves trends exist. Let me now share my thoughts on how the majority, despite the attraction, despite the hard science, fail at trend trading.

CHAPTER 5

Why Do So Many Fail?

SCIENCE SAYS WE CAN'T LOSE

Despite what the academic models say, the science of large numbers demonstrates that extreme price moves occur, and they occur more frequently then we should expect. Prices are not random and do not follow a normal distribution. The existence of fat tails puts a mighty wrinkle in the bell curve theory and validates the pursuit of trend trading. Trend trading works. Yet despite the science proving trend trading can't lose, so many do! The question we have to ask ourselves is why?

OVERVIEW OF TREND TRADING

Before I attempt to answer the question, I first want to give an overview of trend trading for context purposes, to help you really understand all the nuances of trend trading. This will help highlight the irony of why so many fail in a pursuit backed by science.

Identify the Trend

So, let's take a few steps back. If I was to ask you what the most often quoted mantra for successful trading is, what do you think you would answer? Yes, that's correct …

trade with the trend, the trend is your friend.

And this is the number one execution rule for successful trend trading.

Let's now be conservative and assume that only 60% of all active traders have heard and understood this message (although I believe it's much higher). If this is the case, why is it that over 90% of trend traders still lose? Surely, if the majority of traders know the number one execution rule for successful trend trading is ...

trade with the trend ...

why is it that so many active traders lose?

Interesting, hey?

If you believe that over 60% of all traders know that they should be trading with the trend and yet over 90% of all active traders fail, don't you think that sounds ironic? This is a strong disconnect. There is something very strange going on when most know to trade with the trend yet most fail to do so.

Why Trend Trading Should be Simple

Despite so many experiencing failure, trading with the trend should be simple if you execute the three golden tenets:

- trade with the trend,
- cut your losses short and
- let your profits run.

Thanks to David Ricardo and others, these tenets have been known for over two centuries. They are not only old and durable but they are also very simple. All successful trend trading methodologies enshrine these three tenets in their strategy rules. Know these and you know how to trade with the trend. Easy! Trend trading is this simple. Nothing more and nothing less. If anyone suggests otherwise then I'd beg to differ. Yet so many fail in their pursuit of trading with the trend.

Four Important Observations about Trend Trading

To complete this overview let me share four very important observations about trend trading.

1. It's the safest way to trade—to trade with the trend.
2. Trends move markets and are the basis of all profits.
3. It's miserable being a trend trader, you lose on 67% of your trades!

4. Two popular ways to trade with the trend include:
   • trade breakouts or
   • trade retracements.

Firstly, trading with the trend is the safest way to trade. To do the opposite, to trade against the trend, is going against the market's grain. It's best to trade in the direction of least resistance where the profits are easiest.

Secondly, markets move because they trend. So, trends move markets and are therefore the basis of all profits. The longer you can hold onto a trend trade, the more potential you will have in earning a large profit. Trend traders can hold trades from a couple of weeks to a couple of months to much, much longer.

Thirdly, the irony of trend trading is that although it's the safest way to trade it's also one of the most miserable ways to trade. Since markets rarely trend a trend trader can usually expect to win only a third of their trades. Consequently, they will spend on average 67% of their time losing! If you wish to trade with the trend, and I hope you do, you'll have to accept the fact that it will be a miserable existence. You will not know when the profits will arrive. You will spend most of your time in drawdown. It will be painful. It will be depressing. It will be miserable. No ifs, no buts, no discussion. Trading with the trend is wretched. I've mentioned this ad infinitum.

However, if you can accept these first three observations then you'll be in a good position to succeed as a trend trader. If you can't then you'll need to reassess your interest in trading.

And finally. The two most popular approaches to trend trading include:

1. Trading breakouts in the direction of the trend:
   • never miss a big trend and
   • use larger stops.
2. Trading retracements in the direction of the trend:
   • can miss big trends and
   • use smaller stops.

Both strategies work.

Trading breakouts of higher prices or lower prices in the direction of the trend, like the popular Turtle Trading channel breakout strategy, is a successful strategy for trading with the trend. Breakout strategies do not wait for a retracement or pull back in an uptrend before entering the market on the long side. Nor do they wait for a relief rally or retracement in a downtrend before entering the market on the short side. They will buy much higher prices in an uptrend and they will sell much lower prices in a downtrend. The advantage of trading breakouts is that the trader will never miss a big trend. A disadvantage is that breakout trend trading requires larger stops relative to retracement trend trading.

Retracement trend trading requires the market to pause and experience a pullback in an uptrend, or a relief rally in a downtrend, before entering the market. A disadvantage of retracement trend trading is that sometimes strongly trending markets do not provide a retracement opportunity for a trader to enter. Retracement trend trading can and does miss some big trends. However, an advantage of retracement trend trading is that it does allow a trader to place much smaller initial stops.

In a Nutshell

Most have heard the phrase 'trade with the trend, the trend is your friend'—and despite it being a miserable existence, following the trend is as simple as trading with the trend, cutting losses short and letting profits run. And by the way, the science of hard data says you can't lose trading with the trend. It's a no brainer!

WHY DO SO MANY FAIL AT IT?

If trend trading is so simple, is backed by science and is so good, why is it that so many fail at it? I know, I know, I know, I hear you. Ok, if it's so easy and so great why do so many find it so difficult?

Well there are two broad reasons why so many fail at trend trading. I've mentioned each of them before; however, it doesn't hurt to re-examine them (I told you I'm repetitive):

1. The bell curve—its construction makes it tough—and
2. The trader—ignorance will always prevail.

The Bell Curve—it's Construction Makes it Tough

We now know statistics shows us that trend trading works, yet not every trader uses it and nor does every trader who attempts to follow the trend win. It's a conundrum. On the one hand, there is the hard, scientific data showing trend trading can't lose, while on the other hand, there is a sorry crowd of failed traders who curse trend trading. Confused? Let me first take a look at how the hard, scientific data makes it difficult to succeed at trend trading. Remember my mantra, 'It's a miserable existence being a trend trader'? Yes, well, it's all about the bell curve, or its construction to be precise.

Yes, we look at the bell curve of normal distributions and snigger behind our hands pointing at the fat tails while making faces at the academics. We can see those fat tails even if the academics can't. Yes, that is a boon for the trend traders. However, we can't point, snigger, make faces and feel superior to the academics without also acknowledging the complete distribution of returns. Yes, fat tails make trend trading exciting. However, there are many more returns that make up a complete (bell curve) distribution than just the extreme 'fat tail' returns. There are many, many returns (changes in prices) that occur within one, two and three standard deviations of the average. There is an abundance of positive and negative returns that are small, random, annoying, exhausting and soul destroying. A plethora of positive and negative returns that sit under the bell curve. They exist because markets don't tend to trend all the time. Those 'thin peaks' we identified demonstrate that markets are constantly rotating towards mean reversions, being range bound and creating a myriad of false breakouts. False breakouts and resultant empty wallets and heart ache for trend traders (Figure 5.1).

This is why trend trading is so miserable.

This is why trend traders can expect to lose on six to seven of their trades out of every ten. They have to suffer through a huge number of losers before they hit the big 'fat tail' winners. It's tough. And it's tough not only on the soul but also the wallet. Traders have to know what they're doing to fund the many losses and brokerage charges they have to absorb. They need sensible money management. They need to ensure they're trading with a 0% ROR.

The bell curve with its fat tails certainly proves, on the one hand, that trend trading is profitable in the long run; however, it simultaneously shows, on the other hand, that it's also challenging in the short

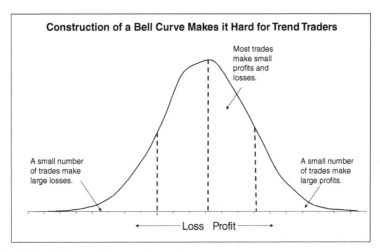

FIGURE 5.1 It takes an abundance of small market movements to make up a bell curve, which in turn makes it both frustrating and tough for trend traders.

to medium term. There is a lot of chaff that traders have to sort through, which is both psychologically and financial challenging for most trend traders.

Argh, the bell curve, its gives with the one hand and clobbers with the other!

The other reason why so many trend traders fail is themselves.

The Trader—Ignorance Will Always Prevail

The singular most important reason traders fail is because they trade with a ROR above 0%. Despite the best of intentions to succeed, ignorance will always slay the willing. There is no sidestepping, ducking or ignoring ROR. It's an immovable and immortal force that will not be ignored or denied. It exists, it's real and it's fatal. If we unpack ROR we can break down the fault into the two key weapons against ROR, money management and expectancy.

1. Poor money management: Most people over trade their account failing to use sensible money management. They trade with too few units of money lifting their individual ROR above 0% and pushing themselves towards their financial ruin.

2. Poor methodology: Most traders do not have a robust positive expectancy strategy with an out-of-sample positive upward sloping equity curve. Most have strategies that have fallen prey to the twin evils of data mining and excessive curve fitting resulting in an unstable, variable and downward sloping low to negative expectancy equity curve, which contributes to a ROR above 0% and their financial ruin. Phew, that was a mouth full.

As a side note, a poor mind set or poor psychology can also contribute to a trader's failure. However, if you have read *UPST* you will know that I rank psychology third behind money management and methodology in terms of importance. So yes, poor psychology can have an impact on a trader's performance, however, in my opinion, its influence is minor compared to the damaged done by utilizing poor money management and employing a poor methodology. In addition, it's my belief that if you fix both your poor money management and poor methodology you'll go a long way to diminishing the challenges psychology presents.

The central character in this tragic Shakespearean-like drama of trading failure is the main character themselves. The trader. And the trader's greatest singular fault that contributes to their downfall is simply their own ignorance.

Their ignorance of what ROR is and their ignorance of the importance ROR plays in their success or failure.

Ignorance will always defeat the best of intentions. Although trading, once knowledge and experience is acquired, is simple, it's not easy. And that is with the benefit of knowledge and experience.

Those without proper knowledge, despite their best of intentions to trade with the trend, will fail. Fact. They become cannon fodder for the winners. They inadvertently either trade with too few units of money or trade a low to negative expectancy strategy that when combined with their units of money produce a ROR above 0%, guaranteeing their failure. They trade towards their demise, blissfully unaware of what awaits. They usually take the wrong side of trades, exiting losing trades too late and exiting winning trades too early.

Despite the hard, scientific data proving trend trading is profitable, the majority of trend traders lose. We ask the question why and now know the simple answer is their ignorance. They're not aware that they trade with a ROR above 0%. Any percentage above 0% is fatal. Certainly, a trader with a lower percentage ROR will survive longer then a trader with a higher percentage. However, it will only stay their execution. Not remove it. Traders must commence trend trading with a 0% ROR and hope their strategy's equity curve is stable enough to keep their ROR at 0%. If they do, then they will survive and enjoy the profits when they come along.

Unfortunately, due to ignorance, the majority of trend traders are unaware of both the theory of ROR and their own individual levels of ROR given their personal money management and trading strategies.

They're unaware of ROR because they lack proper trading knowledge; and unaware of how to compute their individual ROR. They're unaware of how subjective variable dependent tools can lead them to fall victim to the twin evils of strategy development, namely data mining and excessive curve fitting.

Data mining occurs when traders only review and only trade those markets their strategy/s work best on. It's old-fashioned cherry picking. It gives false hope that a strategy is robust.

Excessive curve fitting occurs when traders include too many rules, filters and indicators with too many variables in their strategy/s to make them produce picture-perfect historical equity curves.

Data mining and excessive curve fitting are both key drivers to raising a trader's ROR above 0%. Even if they knew at the commencement of trading their strategy's expectancy was positive enough to deliver a 0% ROR, they're unaware of how the use of subjective variable dependent tools such as indicators can see them trade a strategy containing potentially wildly alternative equity curves. Equity curves with wildly alternative expectancies that can see their individual RORs lift above 0%.

Now let me tidy up and summarize how ignorance manifests itself.

Traders handicap themselves through their:

- - ignorance of ROR and
- - ignorance of trading poor methodologies.

Ignorance of ROR—it's the Math, Stupid

I know I'm about to repeat myself (again, I know), but this idea is core to my success, so please bear with me.

The majority of trend traders fail for the simple reason that they trade with a ROR above 0%. And they do this for the simple reason that they're ignorant of the concept of ROR. They lack the proper trading knowledge to succeed. They're unaware that all who wish to

Risk-of-Ruin = Fn [Units of Money + Strategy E[R]]

FIGURE 5.2   ROR is a function of the number of units of money a trader trades with and the expectancy of their strategy.

succeed in trading first need to survive, which requires trading with a 0% ROR (Figure 5.2).

With the correct knowledge they would know what ROR was and know how to calculate their own individual ROR. They would know and understand this math of trading, to trade with a 0% ROR. They would know that the two key weapons against ROR are money management and positive expectancy. They would know that money management refers to the number of units of money a trader has and whether it is enough to help keep their ROR at 0%. They would know that positive expectancy would come from their trading methodology, from how they find their setups, entry, stop and exit levels. They would know what percentage expectancy, or return, they would expect to earn for every dollar they risked according to their trading methodology. They would know that the number of units of money they trade with when combined with the percentage expectancy, or return of their methodology, would produce a statistical probability of the likelihood of them reaching their point of ruin. They would know this and they would know that they need to trade with a 0% ROR to first survive and then succeed.

In addition, they would know that they not only want to trade a positive expectancy strategy but also to trade a robust positive expectancy strategy with a stable and upward rising equity curve. They would know that the twin evils against an out-of-sample stable and upward rising equity curve are data mining and excessive curve fitting. They would know how to design a trend-trading methodology that eliminates data mining while avoiding excessive curve fitting, ensuring their individual ROR remains at 0%.

However, it's an unfortunate truth that the majority of trend traders are not aware of this proper trading knowledge. They inadvertently trade with too few units of money and they inadvertently trade with what they believe are positive expectancy strategies to only learn, at their peril, that through their lack of knowledge, lack of scrutiny or excessive curve fitting, they've developed and trade strategies with wildly alternative equity curves and expectancies that can see their ROR lift above 0%.

Too few units of money and/or an overly curve-fitted strategy will produce a ROR above 0% at some point during their trading. Any ROR above 0% is a guarantee, or constant, that a trader will reach their point of ruin, the only variable is when.

Quite simply the math of trading is to trade with a 0% ROR.

If you haven't already, please refer to *UPST* for more information on ROR.

Ignorance of Expectancy: Not Knowing Your Edge

The two key weapons against ROR are money management and expectancy. Since I wrote extensively about money management in *UPST*, I'll focus more on the second key weapon, expectancy. Expectancy comes from a trader's strategy. Hopefully, by the end of this chapter 1 will have offered some useful insights into why so many fail at trend trading. I hope to show why so many traders inadvertently develop and trade low to negative expectancies strategies that ultimately lift their ROR above 0% and see them lose. Traders are simply unaware of what their edge is, whether it's positive, low or negative.

Ignorance of Trading Poor Methodologies—Garbage in, Garbage Out

Most people develop and trade poor methodologies, and don't realize it.

If you accept, like I do, the science that shows fat tails exist, which in turn validates trend trading, and that successful trend trading is no more and no less than simply identifying the trend, cutting loses short and letting profits run, then you should also accept that trend trading can be broken down into four key words: trends, retracements, stops and exits. I would then suggest, if this is the case, and if the majority of traders have poor methodologies with low to negative expectancy equity curves that push traders' individual RORs above 0%, that you would have to believe that the majority of methodologies must be using poor trend tools, poor retracement tools, poor stop or poor exit techniques? Right?

Or simply, garbage in, garbage out.

Let's put it another way.

We know it's an unfortunate observation that over 90% of traders lose. We now know they lose because they simply trade with a ROR above 0%. Since a key weapon against ROR is a strategy's expectancy, then we can assume that 90% of trade plans must be poor or have a low to negative expectancy. If 90% of trade plans are poor, then that must imply 90% of tools used to develop those trade plans must also be poor. As I've said, garbage in, garbage out.

So, a big takeaway for you the reader is to be very wary of the majority of available trading tools. Like 90% of available trading tools! Therefore, the question as to why so many fail at trend trading when the science proves it works should be reframed as follows:

Why are 90% of available trading tools so poor?

My answer is a single word. Variability.

VARIABILITY KILLS INDICATORS

The majority of trading tools are indicators. They are by far the most popular type of tool. Their availability on multiple trading platforms and charting programs makes them the choice of convenience. To break down and help explain how 'variability' hurts indicators (and in turn trend traders) I have created an indictor-based trading strategy called Retracement Trend Trader (RTT). RTT incorporates the most popular indicator used by the majority of traders. I'll later dissect RTT according to my equity curve stability review to see whether we can gain any insights into why so many trend traders lose.

But first up, let's find out which indicators are the most popular.

POPULAR INDICATORS

There are hundreds of indicators available to help traders develop strategies. I've summarized a few of them in Figure 5.3.

Please note, Figure 5.3 is by no means an exhaustive list.

Generally, an indicator, or any trading tool, is designed to help identify a particular part of market structure. Some indicators are designed to identify the trend such as the moving average and MACD (moving average convergence divergence) indicators. Some indicators are designed to capture a retracement like the RSI (relative strength indicator), stochastics and Fibonacci ratios. Some indicators are designed to identify exhaustion or reversal points like reversal and divergence patterns. Some, like the VIX, are designed to pinpoint extremes in sentiment that can lead to reversals. Others are designed to measure a change in volatility like Bollinger Bands®.

Summary of Available Indicators

Accumulation Distribution	Equivolume Charts	Negative Volume	Standard Deviation Channels
ADX	Exponential Moving Average	On Balance Volume	Stochastic Oscillator
Aroon Oscillator	Fibonacci Extensions	Parabolic SAR	Trend Lines
ATR	Force Index	Percentage Trailing Stops	TRIX Indicator
Bollinger Bands	Heikin-Ashi Candlesticks	Pivot Points	True Range
Chaikin Money Flow	Ichimoku Cloud	Positive Volume	Twiggs Momentum Oscillator
Chaikin Oscillator	Keltner Channels	Price Comparison	Twiggs Money Flow
Chaikin Volatility	KST Indicator	Price Differential	Twiggs Smoothed Momentum
Chandelier Exits	Linear Regression	Price Envelope	Ultimate Oscillator
CCI	Least Squares	Price Ratio	Stochastic RSI
Coppock Indicator	Hull Moving Average	Price Volume Trend	Twiggs Volatility
Chande Momentum Oscillator	MA Oscillator	Percentage Bands	Twiggs Trend Index
Choppiness Index	MACD	Rainbow 3D Moving Averages	Volatility
Candlestick Patterns	Mass Index	Rate of Change (Price)	Volalilily Ratio
Detrended Price Oscillator	Median Price	Relative Strength	Volatility Stops
Directional Movement	Momentum	Relative Strength Index (RSI)	Volume Oscillator
Displaced Moving Average	Money Flow Index	Safezone Indicator	Weighted Moving Average
Donchian Channels	Moving Average	Simple Moving Average	Wilder Moving Average
Ease of Movement	Moving Average Filters	Slow Stochastic	Williams %R
Elder Ray Index	Multiple Moving Averages	Smoothed Rate of Change (SROC)	Williams Accumulate Distribute

FIGURE 5.3 Traders do not suffer from a lack of choice when it comes to indicators.

All tools are designed to help the trader identify a particular part of market structure.

Navigating, reviewing, selecting, trying out or eliminating indicators has generally been a difficult task for traders as there are so many of them to choose from.

To help determine which are the more popular indicators, we can thank Paul Ciana and his book *New Frontiers in Technical Analysis* (Wiley, 2011). Ciana identifies the four most popular indicators that were used by the majority of global traders using Bloomberg Professional Services between 2005 and 2010. I've summarized them in Figure 5.4.

Four Most Popular Indicators		
Rank	Indicator	Percentage Used by Traders
1	RSI Relative Strength Indicator	44%
2	MACD Moving Average Convergence Divergence	22%
3	BOLL Bollinger Bands	12%
4	STO Stochastic	9%

FIGURE 5.4 The four most popular indicators used by Bloomberg traders between 2005 and 2010.
Source: Based on Paul Ciana, *New Frontiers in Technical Analysis: Effective Tools and Strategies for Trading and Investing*, Volume 156 of Bloomberg Financial, John Wiley & Sons, 2011.

Within the four indicators there are two retracement, one trend and one volatility indicator.

Let me focus on the most popular indicator tool used by the majority of traders, the RSI.

RSI

The RSI was developed by J Welles Wilder in 1978. It's a simple retracement tool that measures a bar's close position relative to its look-back period. It looks for overbought or oversold conditions. If these overbought or oversold levels are set at 80% and 20% respectively, then at any time the current close is above 80% or below 20% of the look-back range it will suggest the current retracement is complete and a reversal is likely.

So, the RSI has two variables, its look-back period and its overbought and oversold levels.

The RSI, according to Ciana, is the most popular indicator used by the majority of their Professional Services subscribers. Being the most popular made it a perfect candidate to be part of my indicator-based RTT strategy. I'll shortly review RTT to see how 'variability' of the RSI (or any indicator) can hurt everyone; the tool, the strategy, the trader and their trading account!

But first, let me share with you how I appraise strategies according to my equity curve stability review. I do this to determine whether a strategy's equity curve (and trader's individual ROR) is stable enough to trade. Once completed I'll then take a look at RTT.

STRATEGY ROBUST REVIEW

Traders generally don't have a problem coming up with ideas on how to trade. What traders have difficulty with is developing robust strategies with positive upward sloping out-of-sample equity curves. They usually fall prey to the twin evils of development—data mining and excessive curve fitting. To help combat those challenges I've developed a review process that is designed to assist myself in reviewing and developing sensible strategies. The review includes the key attributes of winning strategies. In a nut shell they are:

- measurability and
- robustness.

Measurability

Measurability is important for calculating your ROR. Without precise and objective rules for setups, stops and exits a trader would not be able to build an evidence-based strategy and resultant historical equity curve to calculate both the strategy's expectancy and a trader's individual ROR.

Robustness

Robustness is important for avoiding data mining and excessive curve fitting. Robustness can be gauged by either actual evidence, such as out-of-sample performance, or by indication, such as being versatile and following good design principles. Versatility is important for avoiding data mining. Good robust strategies should be profitable over a diverse portfolio of markets, not just the best ones. Following good design principles will avoid excess curve fitting.

Excessively curve fitted strategies generally have a large universe of wildly alternative equity curves, expectancies and RORs and perform poorly on out-of-sample data. Robust strategies will generally have a narrow universe of alternative equity curves, expectancies and RORs and enjoy stable upward sloping equity curves and suffer little variability. Their minor variability helps to maintain a trader's ROR at 0%.

A key component to measuring robustness is to carry out an equity curve stability review. The whole purpose of the review is to determine whether a strategy's equity curve is stable enough to maintain a trader's ROR at 0% and be tradable. Figure 5.5 summarizes the review I follow. I'll go over each component as I review my RTT indicator strategy.

It's now time to introduce you to RTT.

RTT

RTT, as its name suggests, is a trend trading methodology that waits for a retracement before initiating a trade in the direction of the underlying trend. It uses two simple moving averages to define the medium-term (34-day) and long-term (250-day) trend. To identify a retracement, it will use the RSI with a ten-bar look back period and an 80% band for identifying overbought (>80%) and oversold (<20%) retracements. It will only initiate a trade in the direction of the medium-term and long-term trend following the completion of a retracement as defined by the RSI. Entry will occur on a break of the

Equity Curve Stability Review		
Strategy		Strategy
Setup		

Attributes of Winning Strategies

Measureable	Expectancy
	Units of money
	ROR
Robust	
Evidence	Out-of-sample performance
Indication	
Versatile	Profitable over a diversified portfolio
Good	Equity Curve Stability Review
Design	Number of indicator variables
Principles	Number of variable adjustments
	Number of possible equity curves
	Variation in equity curves
	Variation in expectancy
	Do any sets of variable values have ROR > 0%?
	Is equity curve stable enough to trade?

FIGURE 5.5 An equity curve stability review will determine whether or not a strategy's equity curve is stable enough to trade.

setup bar and an initial stop will occur at an opposite break of either the setup or entry bar, depending on which is furthest away. Winning positions will exit at a break of the nearest swing point.

Figure 5.6 illustrates an RTT trade example.

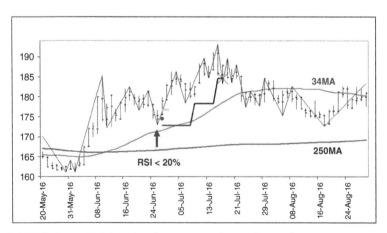

FIGURE 5.6 RTT is a simple strategy that will wait for a retracement before initiating a trade in the direction of the underlying trend.

RTT is a simple strategy. It uses only three indicators (two being the same) and has four variables.

Let me summarize the trading rules again:

Strategy:	RTT
Developed:	2015
Published:	2015
Data:	Daily
Approach:	Trend trading
Technique:	Retracement
Symmetry:	Buy and sell
Markets:	All
Indicators:	Moving Average
	RSI
Variables—Number:	4
	Moving average (34)
	Moving average (250)
	RSI (10 day, 80%)
Variables—Symmetry:	Same value for both buy and sell setups
Variables—Application:	Same value across all markets
Rules:	7
Buy Rules:	
Trend—Medium term:	Up—Previous close is above 34-day moving average
Trend—Long term:	Up—Previous close is above the 250-day moving average
Retracement:	RSI is below 20%
Entry:	Buy break of previous bar's high
	Avoid gap opening
Initial Stop:	Sell break of lowest low of either the setup or entry bar
Trailing Stop:	Sell break of closest swing low
Sell Rules:	
Trend—Medium term:	Down—Previous close is below 34-day moving average
Trend—Long term:	Down—Previous close is below the 250-day moving average
Retracement:	RSI is above 80%
Entry:	Sell break of previous bar's low
	Avoid gap opening
Initial Stop:	Buy break of highest high of either the setup or entry bar
Trailing Stop:	Buy break of closest swing high

Is RTT Suitable for Trading?

Now, remember the task at hand is to examine a typical indicator-based trend-trading strategy to gain some insights into why so many traders fail to trade with the trend. To help our understanding I've included the most popular indicator used by the majority of traders, the RSI. To help with this example I'll be completing an equity curve stability review (please refer to Figure 5.5).

Measurability

According to my review I first need to determine whether the strategy is measurable. Are the rules clear enough to build an historical equity curve and calculate both its expectancy and ROR?

As you can see in Figure 5.7, RTT is measurable. With 20 units of money and a 17.5% expectancy RTT delivers a 0% ROR. Big tick.

Robustness

Next, I have to determine whether RTT is robust enough to trade? Unfortunately, there is not enough actual evidence of out-of-sample performance data as I created this strategy back in 2015 for demonstration purposes. Since I have little evidence of robustness, I need to review the likelihood of whether robustness exists. A good indication of robustness is versatility. Versatility ensures a developer hasn't fallen into the trap of data mining where they only focus on the best markets. So, to avoid any issue of data mining I ran the strategy over my universal portfolio of 24 markets. As you can see in Figure 5.7, it has hypothetically been profitable over a portfolio of markets and is therefore versatile.

So far so go. Another big tick.

Another good indication of robustness is whether a strategy has followed good design principles. Principles that embrace simplicity. Simplicity of design can help avoid another trap of strategy development—excessive curve fitting. All strategies have an element of curve fitting, the less experienced traders will overdo it while the more experience will attempt to minimize it. The best way to minimize curve fitting is to have few rules with few indicators with few variables. The less variables there are, the less degree of freedom there is and the less likelihood a strategy can be curve fitted to past data. In addition, robust strategies will have the same variable values for both buy and sell setups and the same values across all markets.

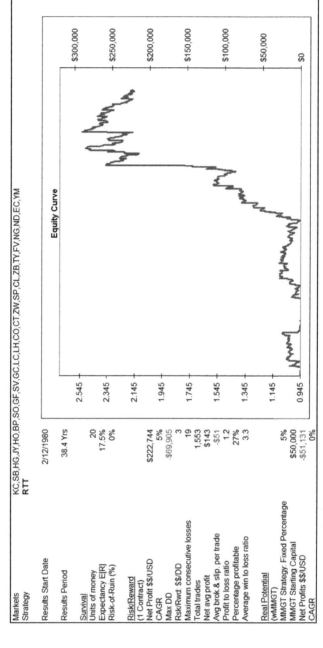

Markets	KC,SB,HG,JY,HO,BP,SO,GF,SV,GC,LC,LH,CO,CT,ZW,SP,CL,ZB,TY,FV,NG,ND,EC,YM
Strategy	RTT
Results Start Date	2/12/1980
Results Period	38.4 Yrs
Survival	
Units of money	20
Expectancy E[R]	17.5%
Risk-of-Ruin (%)	0%
Risk/Reward	
(1 Contract)	
Net Profit $$/USD	$222,744
CAGR	5%
Max DD	-$69,905
Rsk/Rwd $$/DD	3
Maximum consecutive losses	19
Total trades	1,553
Net avg profit	$143
Avg brok.& slip. per trade	-$51
Profit to loss ratio	1.2
Percentage profitable	27%
Average win to loss ratio	3.3
Real Potential	
(wMMGT)	
MMGT Strategy: Fixed Percentage	5%
MMGT Starting Capital	$50,000
Net Profits $$/USD	-$51,131
CAGR	0%

FIGURE 5.7 RTT is measurable and hypothetically profitable with a 0% ROR.

144

Looking at RTT you can see it has seven rules and contains three indicators with four variables.

Unfortunately, there is no cut and dry approach that can be used to determine whether or not excessive curve fitting exists. Ideally, there would be hard out-of-sample performance data to prove either way whether RTT was robust or not. In the absence of out-of-sample data the best approach I know to gauge the level of curve fitting is to undertake an equity curve stability review.

As a side note, another approach I could have followed is to split the data in half to provide in-sample-data and out-of-sample data. That is certainly one way to gauge the stability of a strategy's equity curve. However, I prefer to use all the data and perform an equity curve stability review instead. I want to know a strategy's universe of all possible alternative equity curves and expectancies and resultant RORs.

And on another side note: I'm not suggesting this is a preferred strategy to trade, because it's not. However, it's perfect for the exercise at hand to demonstrate the challenges faced by trend traders who use popular subjective variable dependent indicator-based tools to build their strategies.

Equity Curve Stability Analysis

At the end of the day, we as traders should want to know how sensitive our strategy is to changes in its variable values. Like the variables I've used in RTT's RSI and moving average indicators. As I hope to show you, it's important that we're aware of our strategy's universe of alternative equity curves, the resultant expectancies and RORs. I want to press upon you that believing you're trading a single equity curve based upon a single set of array variable values is naïve. It's almost guaranteed that you will in the future review and tweak your array of variable values. From my experience, traders are not good at leaving things well enough alone. Particularly men. They love to tinker. Well I want to forewarn traders of this so they will explore their strategy's universe of alternative equity curves, expectancies and ROR calculations with different arrays of variable values—so they'll be aware of all future possibilities. Traders need to trade with their eyes wide open. When their eyes are wide open, they'll see the traps ahead and start to understand why they have failed before to trade successfully with the trend.

How Large is the Universe of Alternative Equity Curves?

First up, traders need to be aware of the possible number of alternative equity curves there are. How large the universe is will be dependent upon the number of variables a strategy has and the number of adjustments allowed per variable. I (rightly or wrongly) limit the number of adjustments to four.

Generally, the more variables and the more adjustments allowed per variable, while keeping the other variables fixed, the larger the universe of alternative equity curves is. That is, the more variables there are, the more degrees of freedom that will exist. Too much freedom allows too much flexibility or too much wiggle room for a trader to curve fit their strategy to past data. It opens the door to excessive curve fitting and inevitable failure.

Now, I'm no mathematician and I can't say that using the following formula is correct, actually I'll say it's not. However, I can say its general thrust is spot on. For a four-variable strategy, which is limited to four adjustments per variable while keeping the other three fixed, I'll go with the following calculation:

$$4 \times 4 \times 4 \times 4 = 256$$

So, (I think) there are possibly 256 alternative equity curves to calculate. No doubt I have the wrong number, but regardless I know in my mind the universe is large!

(Note, if you are a mathematician please feel free to contact me via my website www.indextrader.com.au with the correct formula! Thank you.)

RTT's Universe of Alternative Equity Curves

Remember our exercise here is to examine the vulnerability of tools with variables as it's my belief that 'variability' of tools is a large reason why so many traders fail to trade with the trend. They're not aware of their strategy's universe of alternative equity curves, expectancies and RORs. 'Variability' is the reason why they inadvertently trade with a ROR above 0% and lose.

Let's look again at the values of RTT's four variables:

1. 34-day moving average,
2. 250-day moving average,

3. 10-bar RSI with

4. 80% overbought and oversold levels.

With 20 units of money and its current set of variable values (34-day, 250-day, 10-bar and 80%) RTT appears to be a positive expectancy strategy producing a 0% ROR (Figure 5.8).

With four variables and allowing four adjustments per variable I believe RTT's universe contains 256 possible alternative equity curves. Let's start looking at a few and see what we can learn.

To start my equity curve stability review I'll begin with changing the look-back value in the RSI from ten days to six days. Remember the RSI is one of the most popular indicators used by the majority of traders.

Wow, as you can see in Figure 5.9, the equity curve shifts by over 50%! Let's change the RSI's look-back period again from six days to five days.

And we have another shift in Figure 5.10. Not just in the equity curve but also in the trader's ROR calculation. The drop in expectancy has seen a significant shift in ROR from 0% to 21%.

Let's make one last change to the RSI's look-back period changing it from five days to four days.

Figure 5.11 sees another shift in the equity curve, expectancy and ROR.

Let's now shift our focus to the medium-term moving average and change it from 34 days to 50 days.

Woops, well that didn't go so well for Figure 5.12.

Let's now change the longer-term moving average from 250 days to 200 days.

Ouch says Figure 5.13, another change and another equity curve and another expectancy and ROR calculation.

Let me put these few alternative equity curves together in Figure 5.14.

Next, in Figure 5.15 I've measured the range of variability between equity curves.

Wow. With the original values and five subsequent variable changes I have produced six very different looking equity curves. The greatest variance between the best and worst equity curve was $180,000. When compared to the original historical performance that represents an 81% variation. In addition, we saw RTT's expectancy drop from 17.5% to 5.6%, a 68% fall—while its ROR lifted from 0% to a high of 32%!

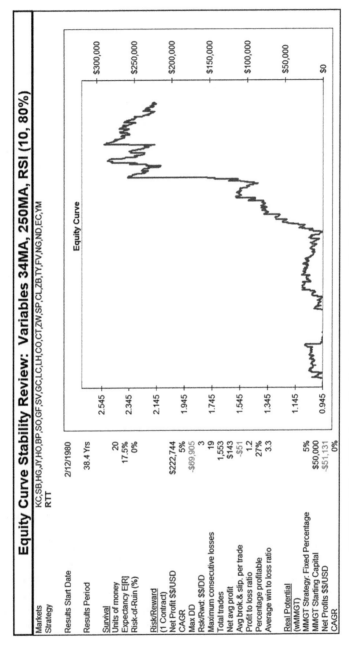

FIGURE 5.8 RTT's hypothetical performance with its original variable values.

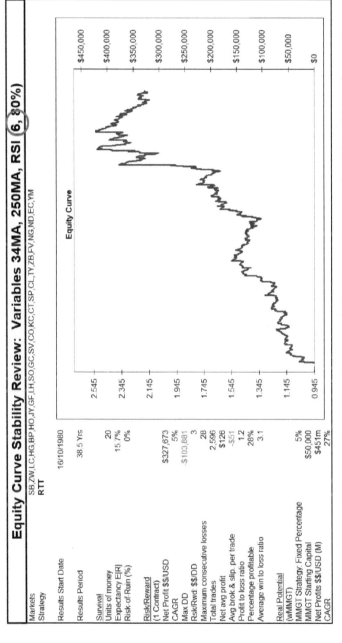

Equity Curve Stability Review: Variables 34MA, 250MA, RSI (6, 80%)

Markets: SB,ZW,LC,HG,BP,HO,JY,GF,LH,SO,GC,SV,CO,KC,GT,SP,CL,TY,ZB,FV,NG,ND,EC,YM
Strategy: RTT

Results Start Date	16/10/1980
Results Period	38.5 Yrs
Survival	
Units of money	20
Expectancy E[R]	15.7%
Risk-of-Ruin (%)	0%
Risk/Reward	
(1 Contract)	
Net Profit $$/USD	$327,673
CAGR	5%
Max DD	-$103,881
Rsk/Rwd: $$/DD	3
Maximum consecutive losses	28
Total trades	2,596
Net avg profit	$126
Avg brok & slip. per trade	-$51
Profit to loss ratio	1.2
Percentage profitable	28%
Average win to loss ratio	3.1
Real Potential	
(wMMGT)	
MMGT Strategy: Fixed Percentage	5%
MMGT Starting Capital	$50,000
Net Profits $$/USD (M)	$451m
CAGR	27%

Equity Curve values (right axis): $450,000 / $400,000 / $350,000 / $300,000 / $250,000 / $200,000 / $150,000 / $100,000 / $50,000 / $0

Left axis values: 2.545 / 2.345 / 2.145 / 1.945 / 1.745 / 1.545 / 1.345 / 1.145 / 0.945

FIGURE 5.9 RTT's hypothetical performance following a change in the RSI variable value to 6.

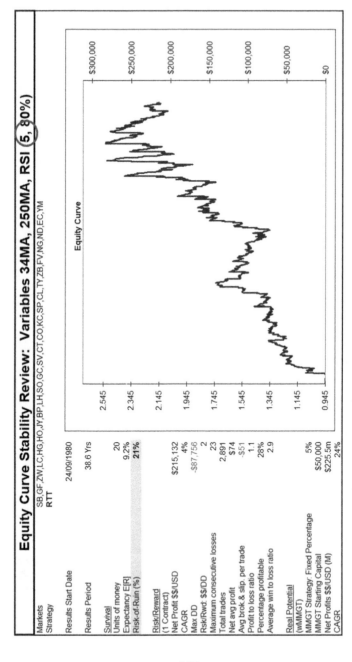

FIGURE 5.10 RTT's hypothetical performance following a change in the RSI variable value to 5.

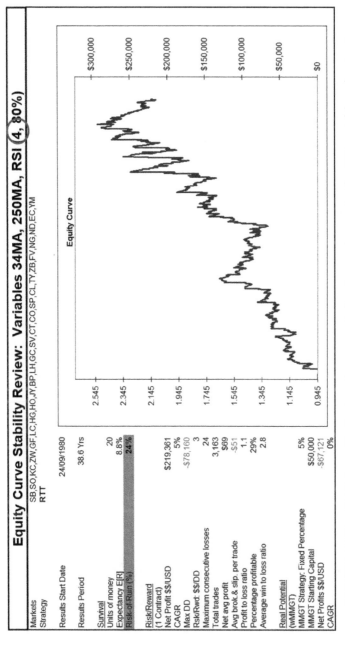

FIGURE 5.11 RTT's hypothetical performance following a change in the RSI variable value to 4.

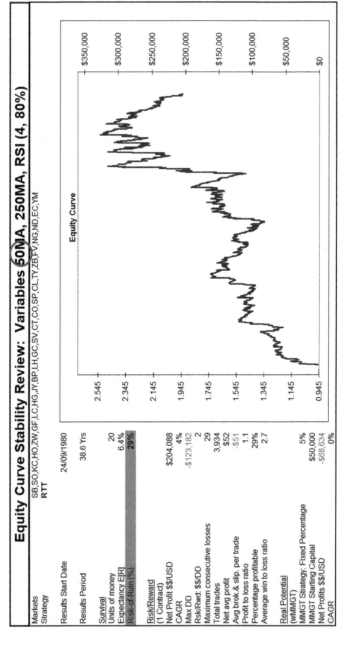

Equity Curve Stability Review: Variables 50MA, 250MA, RSI (4, 80%)

Markets SB,SO,KC,HO,ZW,GF,LC,HG,JY,BP,LH,GC,SV,CT,CO,SP,CL,TY,ZB,FV,NG,ND,EC,YM

Strategy RTT

Results Start Date	24/09/1980
Results Period	38.6 Yrs
Survival	
Units of money	20
Expectancy E[R]	6.4%
Risk-at-Ruin (%)	29%
Risk/Reward	
(1 Contract)	
Net Profit $$/USD	$204,088
CAGR	4%
Max DD	-$123,182
Rsk/Rwd: $$/DD	2
Maximum consecutive losses	29
Total trades	3,934
Net avg profit	$52
Avg brok.& slip. per trade	-$51
Profit to loss ratio	1.1
Percentage profitable	29%
Average win to loss ratio	2.7
Real Potential	
(wMMGT)	
MMGT Strategy: Fixed Percentage	5%
MMGT Starting Capital	$50,000
Net Profits $$/USD	-$68,634
CAGR	0%

FIGURE 5.12 RTT's hypothetical performance following a change in the moving average variable value to 50.

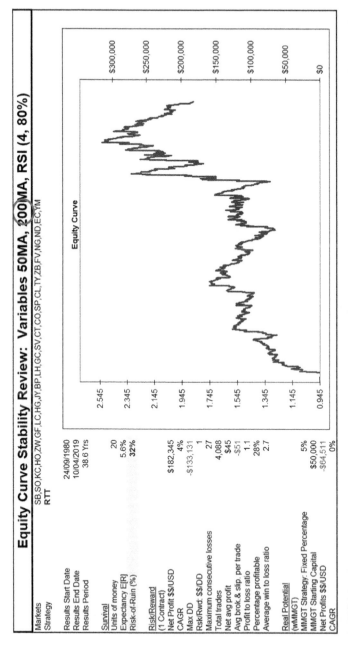

Equity Curve Stability Review: Variables 50MA, 200MA, RSI (4, 80%)

Markets: SB,SO,KC,HO,ZW,GF,LC,HG,JY,BP,LH,GC,SV,CT,CO,SP,CL,TY,ZB,FV,NG,ND,EC,YM
Strategy: RTT

Results Start Date	24/09/1980
Results End Date	10/04/2019
Results Period	38.6 Yrs
Survival	
Units of money	20
Expectancy E[R]	5.6%
Risk-of-Ruin (%)	**32%**
Risk/Reward	
(1 Contract)	
Net Profit $$/USD	$182,345
CAGR	4%
Max DD	-$133,131
Rsk/Rwd: $$/DD	1
Maximum consecutive losses	27
Total trades	4,088
Net avg profit	$45
Avg brok.& slip. per trade	-$51
Profit to loss ratio	1.1
Percentage profitable	28%
Average win to loss ratio	2.7
Real Potential	
(wMMGT)	
MMGT Strategy: Fixed Percentage	5%
MMGT Starting Capital	$50,000
Net Profits $$/USD	-$64,511
CAGR	0%

FIGURE 5.13 RTT's hypothetical performance following a change in the moving average variable value to 200.

153

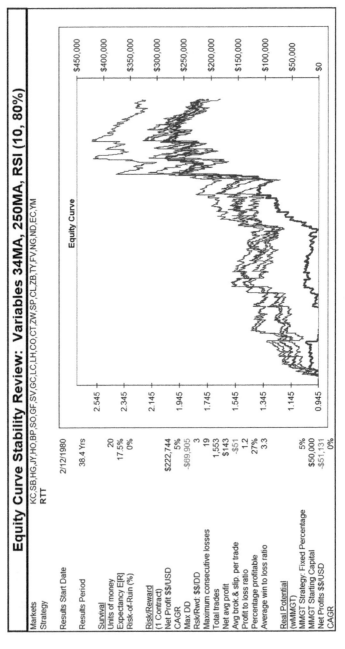

FIGURE 5.14 RTT's six alternative equity curves.

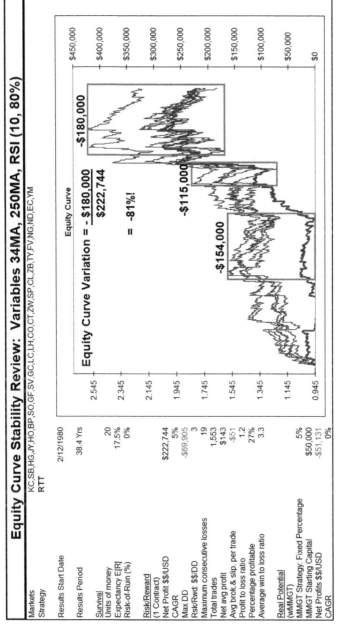

FIGURE 5.15 RTT's equity curves suffer large variability following only five variable adjustments.

Equity Curve Stability Review

Indicators	MA	MA	RSI Days	Level	E[R]		Units of $$		ROR
Variables	34	250	10	80%	17.50%	+	20	=	0%

Change in Variable Values

	MA	MA	RSI Days	Level	E[R]		Units of $$		ROR
	34	250	6	80%	15.70%	+	20	=	0%
	34	250	5	80%	9.20%	+	20	=	21%
	34	250	4	80%	8.80%	+	20	=	24%
	50	250	4	80%	6.40%	+	20	=	29%
	50	200	4	80%	5.60%	+	20	=	32%

FIGURE 5.16 Changes in RTT's variable values had an adverse impact on ROR.

That is an extraordinary amount of flex and I haven't produced anything like 256 alternative equity curves! Just viewing six equity curves tells me this is not a picture of stability.

TRADERS ALWAYS CHANGE VARIABLE VALUES

As a trader it's good to know the strategy was still profitable over different variable values. However, the amount of variation between the upper and lower equity curves is stomach churning. As a developer or trader, you won't know, without the benefit of hindsight or out-of-sample performance, whether the variable values you settle on will produce the best performance. You don't know and won't know until years down the track when you can look back and say, 'yeah, I choose right'. And knowing you'll know more years down the track is not comforting for the trader, you, in the 'now'. So far with only five limited changes in variable values the results have produced an 81% variation in historical performance, a 68% fall in expectancy and ROR blowing out to 32%. And the scary part is that I only made five changes to three variables, not four variables, which produced six different looking equity curves.

UNIVERSE OF ALTERNATIVE EQUITY CURVES, EXPECTANCIES AND ROR

Figure 5.16 summarizes the impact each change in variable value had on RTT's expectancy and ROR calculations.

With 20 units of money only the first two sets of array variable values produced a 0% ROR. Yet four sets of array values produced RORs above 0%, guaranteeing that anyone trading those combinations would lose.

Now, some may believe it's not relevant to know a strategy's universe of alternatives as they believe in their heart of hearts that they have struck upon a good, logical and sound combination of variable values. Actually, they're being too modest, because in the deepest recesses of their minds they're convinced they have settled upon the best set of values! Well, unfortunately, the market's Mr Maximum Adversity will ensure it is never that easy.

I've completed RTT's equity curve stability review in Figure 5.17.

I think RTT's review is self-explanatory. As you can see, there is so much variation that some of the possible alternative equity curves produced ROR calculations above 0%. Based on my small experiment here, you can see RTT does not have a stable equity curve and therefore it's not suitable for trading.

Now it's only when a trader undergoes this type of review that this information will reveal itself.

Equity Curve Stability Review

Strategy			RTT
Setup			MA (34)
			MA (250)
			RSI (4,80%)
Attributes of Winning Strategies			
Measureable		Expectancy	9%
		Units of money	20
		ROR	0%
Robust			
Evidence		Out-of-sample performance	No
Indication			
	Versatile	Profitable over a diversified portfolio	Yes
	Good	Equity Curve Stability Review	
	Design	Number of indicator variables	4
	Principles	Number of variable adjustments	4
		Number of possible equity curves	256
		Variation in equity curves	Large
		Variation in expectancy	Large
		Do any sets of variable values have ROR > 0%?	Yes
		Is equity curve stable enough to trade?	NO

FIGURE 5.17 An equity curve stability review determines whether or not a strategy's equity curve is stable enough to trade.

BEST SET OF VARIABLE VALUES ALWAYS CHANGE

Traders should not be ignorant of their strategy's parallel universe of alternative equity curves. They should not be smug in believing they've settled upon the best and correct variable values for their strategy. This is because there is every likelihood they'll slip in and out and all between a number of the alternative equity curves as they adjust their strategy's variable values to maximize historical performance. They may not plan on adjusting their variable values, but experience says they will because they will chase yesterday's best performance.

This is the great irony of subjective variable dependent tools like indicators and why so many trend traders come unstuck, despite the science saying trend trading can't lose.

Indicators allow too much flexibility to excessively curve fit models to past data. They provide traders with false comfort that they'll be safe from the market's Mr Maximum Adversity—as well as the false knowledge that they have hit upon the best or correct variable values. All they have done is allow the trader to massage their strategy to past data. To make them feel secure. Traders should not fall into this complacency trap. Variable values never stay constant. No. Traders always change them. Therefore, traders need to undertake an equity curve stability review to determine all possible variations in their strategy's equity curves, expectancies and ROR calculations. Although they may believe they'll only trade the initial agreed upon variable values, I can almost guarantee traders will inevitably adjust their variable values. I say this for two reasons:

1. greed and
2. human nature.

Greed

Markets change and the seduction of finding variables producing more profit and expectancy will be too hard to resist. Traders will alter their variable values accordingly, trying to catch the best historical fit. But unfortunately, looking backwards won't help the trader catch future profits. Markets are constantly changing as they cycle through bull and bear market phases. They're constantly being stretched during trending periods and compressed during range bound conditions. It's a fool's folly trying to capture yesterday's best variable values that produce the best results. But sadly, many traders cannot ignore the greed monster that resides within them.

So, we know greed or curiosity will see traders constantly tweak their variable values. And during that process they will cycle through and settle upon many combinations, which on the day are the most profitable (historically).

What traders will discover when looking above at the five alternative equity curves is that, at any one particularly point in time, each of the above variable combinations would have had its time in the sun. Each set of variable values would have been the best combination producing the most historical profit and expectancy at that particular point in time. So, if a trader ran the various combinations each day and ranked the profitability, you would notice that not one strategy ranked the best throughout the historical back-test period. Certainly not my original array values of 34-day, 250-day, 10-bar and 80%. No. Markets constantly change and so does the performance of various arrays of variables values. And this is what greed will do to a trader. Going forward they will regularly monitor their strategy's historical performance, and if they see more profit with another set of variable values, they'll change. But all they have done is found the best historical fit on that day. All they've accomplished is excessive curve fitting of their strategy to past data. They'll constantly rinse and repeat until they notice they've traded a wide range of variable values in their pursuit of maximizing historical opportunity. This is why it's so important to complete an equity curve stability review before trading so that all possible alternative equity curves and resultant expectancies and ROR values can be identified. And if one is a low or negative expectancy strategy with a ROR above 0%, then it will be identified before the commencement of trading. At which time a trader can make a conscious decision on whether or not to trade the strategy.

Human Nature

In addition, human nature, particularly the masculine type, cannot leave things well enough alone and love to tinker. So, I can almost guarantee anyone trading an indicator-based strategy will inevitably adjust their variable values. And why? Because they can.

KNOW YOUR STRATEGY'S UNIVERSE OF ALTERNATIVE EQUITY CURVE'S UPPER AND LOWER BANDS

So due to these two factors traders cannot believe they'll only be trading one set of variable values.

Accordingly, to ensure they have their eyes wide open, traders must examine their strategy's universe of potential alternative equity curves, expectancies and ROR calculations (Figure 5.18). This examination will reveal two key concerns every trader should be aware of:

1. possibilities of ruin and
2. tradability.

Possibilities of Ruin

Traders need to be aware if any of the potential alternative equity curves include ROR calculations above 0%. If they do then the trader should not trade the strategy. I can't say this enough. Traders need to be aware of their strategy's entire universe of alternative equity curves, expectancies and ROR calculations. Not just the single set of variable values they've settled on or are comfortable with. And if that complete universe includes equity curves with ROR calculations above 0%, then they shouldn't trade the strategy.

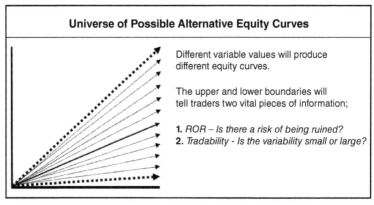

FIGURE 5.18 Exploring a strategy's universe of alternative equity curves is imperative for determining the possibility of ruin and tradability.

Tradability

In addition, traders should also examine whether the universe of alternative equity curves look tradable. If the range between the upper and lower bands of alternative equity curves is acceptable, and with little variation, the universe of possible equity curves may be possible to trade. However, if they're as variable as the example in Figure 5.15 where we've only seen six equity curves, a trader may decide the strategy is not tradable. They might liken it to rodeo riding and not like their chances of hanging on when the equity curve starts bucking. Too much variability would make it unlikely a trader would be able to hang on and continue trading a strategy.

STRATGEY ROBUSTNESS REVIEW

So, this is why trend traders fail when they should win. They're not aware of their strategy's universe of alternative equity curves, expectancies and ROR calculations. They're not aware that their variable dependent strategy has such a large and diverse universe of alternative equity curves where some may have ROR calculations above 0%. And they're not aware how variable and bumpy the ride will be, knocking many off their strategies, despite the strong possibility of positive long-term results. They only find out when they're on the sidelines watching their strategy trade out of its drawdown and reach new equity highs.

This is what brings the majority of trend traders unstuck. They're not aware of how to conduct an equity curve stability review. They generally use subjective variable dependent indicators. They settle on what they think is the best combination of values and inadvertently excessively curve fit their model to past data. They are ignorant of the magnitude of future possible performance variations as they invariably adjust their set of variable values to chase past performance. The swings in performance are so wild and so large they can push a strategy's expectancy south and their ROR north along with the real possibility of knocking them out of their saddle!

THE MORE VARIABLES, THE MORE ALTERNATIVES, THE MORE RISK

So, I hope you can see from this example of a simple indicator-based trend trading strategy that different sets of variable values can produce

Alternative Strategy 1		
	Indicator	Variables
Trend tool	MACD	3
Retracement tool	Stochastic	4
	Total	7

FIGURE 5.19 Even simple strategies with few indicators can introduce complexity and equity curve fragility.

a wide variation in performance. So wide that it confines RTT to the dustbin.

Let's look at some other trend trading strategies and see where the danger lies.

How about the strategy summarized in Figure 5.19 that employs two popular indicators?

This is also a relatively simple strategy using a very popular trend tool the MACD and a very popular retracement tool, the stochastic. The only problem is the total number of variables, seven.

How about a more complex strategy like the one I've outlined in Figure 5.20?

On one level this could be considered a very conservative approach, using dual trend and retracement tools to confirm each other. The only problem is the number of variables, 11. I'd hate to know the size of its parallel universe of alternative equity curves!

Alternative strategy 2		
	Indicator	Variables
Trend tool	Moving Average	1
	ADX	3
Retracement tool	Fibonacci Ratios	4
	RSI	3
	Total	11

FIGURE 5.20 Heavily laden indicator strategies generally experience greater variability in their alternative equity curves.

With both strategies the large number of variables, in my opinion, makes it too easy for a developer to massage their values to fit the strategy to past data. However, if an equity curve stability review is undertaken, any vulnerability would be exposed in their individual universe of alternative equity curves, expectancies and ROR calculations. A lot of work, but worthwhile if it prevents a trader reaching their point of ruin.

VARIABLE AND SUBJECTIVE TOOLS

No wonder the poor trend trader, who knows to trade with the trend because the trend is their friend, fails to successfully trade with the trend. Poor variable-laden tools make it almost impossible for them to succeed. Is it any wonder they fail? It's hard enough dealing with the many long sequences of losing trades without having to worry about the variability of trend and retracement tools. With variability it's garbage in, garbage out. What hurts the trader is the many long sequences of losing trades. What kills the trader is their ignorance of the universe of alternative equity curves that subjective variable dependent tools create.

These tools seduce the unsuspecting trend trader with their flexible appeal. They don't threaten a trader's fragile ego by attempting to supplant their opinion. They offer comfort and cooperative coexistence. They offer a warm and safe union. They offer a bright future through marriage. The subjective tool with its easy flexibility together with the ever knowing and bright trader. They offer a marriage made in heaven. And the trader falls for it lock, stock and barrel. The whole catastrophe.

Ah, we mere mortals—to be so easily seduced by the bright lights on our trading screens. What fools we are. What ignorant and happy fools we are to be so trusting.

So, in my opinion, any tool with a variable or variables represents huge risk to an unsuspecting trader unless it's properly investigated. They become too flexible, too unstable and too unreliable to rely upon. They allow too much fiddling by you giving you too much wiggle room to fit your strategy to past data. They are not objective or independent enough to rely upon without a detailed investigation. Variable dependent tools become all too willing collaborators in helping a trader to excessively curve fit their methodology to historical data.

INDEPENDENT OBJECTIVE TOOLS

And here we come to the key issue of the problem.

In my opinion, and please remember—as I've mentioned before—everything I write is only my opinion and you are welcome to disagree, no worries at all. Just remember to find objective evidence to support your position. But back to what I was saying. In my opinion effective trading tools should be independent of the trader. A good tool will be 100% objective and will not rely upon any subjective interpretation or input by the trader. A good tool will stand on its own feet and will not require any subjective massaging from the trader to make it work. A good tool will be independent of the trader. A good tool will be a trader-free zone where the trader can have no influence over its interpretation. A good tool cannot be tweaked or fiddled with by the trader. A good tool will have no variables that can be manipulated. Once, and only once, a trading tool can achieve these characteristics so I believe it should be considered for trading. Once it can stand free and be independent of the trader, a tool should then be evaluated for its own usefulness. A good independent tool will then either work or it won't. It won't need any variable massaging to make it appear to work. Simple.

A trading tool that requires any input from the trader becomes subjective. It's not objective and not independent. I believe they're too variable and too flexible to be used for trading. I believe 'variability' and 'subjectiveness' is dangerous. I believe 'variability' and 'subjectiveness' can kill a trader.

Only objective and independent tools should be considered.

As a trader, you know that you need assistance, so you look for tools that can assist you. In the beginning of your trading careers you believe the tools contained within your charting packages and trading platforms will assist. However, traders do not realize that variable flexibility of trading tools is not actually a benefit but is in fact a handicap. Traders don't learn this until much later, to their puzzlement, frustration and cost.

It's the cost of ignorance.

Although the moving average indicator is one of the best technical tools available (and one I use myself) it's easy to understand how subjective it can be and how varying and subjective its trend interpretations is. Is it any wonder then that traders struggle with the common trend tools available to them?

Popular trend tools—like the moving average, MACD and ADX indicators—all suffer from the same variable and subjective criticism. They can give two people trading the same markets two different trend interpretations depending on the variables they use. The traditional trend line also suffers from the same criticism when two different traders looking at the same chart can draw two different trend lines depending on the swing points they choose. Why would you use any tool that is so inconsistent with its trend interpretation? How can you objectively evaluate a trend tool for its effectiveness when its trend interpretation can differ so much between traders? These tools are like economists—they appear useful in explaining what has happen in the past but are less effective for giving objective and useful analysis for the future.

Unfortunately, trend traders do not learn of these vulnerabilities until it's too late. Their ignorance prevents them from questioning their effectiveness or identifying their handicaps and measuring their entire universe of alternative equity curves to discover any possibilities of ruin. Ignorance will defeat a trend trader's good intentions to follow the three golden tenets every time.

SO, WHAT TO DO?

It's best to use independent objective tools that are free of variables. However, if a variable dependent tool takes your interest in helping to locate setups by all means give it consideration. Undertake an equity curve stability review to discover its universe of alternative equity curves, expectancies and ROR calculations. In addition, it's best to develop a methodology that incorporates the attributes of winning strategies. Attributes such as measurability and robustness. I'll be talking more about these later in the book.

SUMMARY

Although a simple process, trend trading is plagued with many problems. The greatest challenge facing the trend trader is their ignorance of ROR and their use of subjective variable dependent tools. And unfortunately, only through their ignorance, they fall prey to the twin evils of strategy development—data mining and excessive curve fitting. Two evils that ultimately lead to their demise and ruin. So, despite knowing and implementing the three golden tenets, and despite the hard, scientific data backing trend trading, they fail.

Well, hopefully with this book I will assist those who are determined to succeed to know where the pot holes are so they can continue safely along their pathway towards sustainable trading. Now that we know trend trading is both durable and profitable, but not without its challenges, let me spend some time reviewing a number of alternative trend trading strategies.

CHAPTER 6

Strategies

I t's time now to look at some trend-trading strategies.
These strategies will use past prices to make buy and sell decisions.
They will buy markets going up and they will sell markets going
down. They adhere to the three golden tenets of trend trading:

- follow the trend,
- cut losses short and
- let profits run.

These golden tenets have been in use since 1800. Being old means
they're durable, which is a great appeal. As you'll see, the strategies all
adhere to the key principles according to their own interpretations
of the golden tenets. As I examine each strategy, I hope you'll notice
the variations in their execution. And as you do, you should make a
mental note of the ones that resonate. You may like to incorporate
them into your own methodology. As you'll see, the majority of strategies are profitable, reinforcing how resilient and effective the three
golden tenets are.

But despite their success, you will need to be aware that there are
no guarantees about the future. Although they have performed well in
the past, there can be no assurances that they'll perform equally as well
into the future. However, having said that, the odds and the existence
of fat tails suggest they will. But like anything associated with trading you need to have your head up and eyes wide open. Be prepared
for the unexpected. Respect the market's Mr Maximum Adversity and
ensure you commence and continue trading with a 0% ROR.

MARKETS

To see how effective the various trend-trading strategies are I will be running them over my universal portfolio of 24 markets, which I called 'P24'. To avoid data mining, the 24 markets have been independently and objectively selected based on their diversity and liquidity across eight market segments. The markets are summarized in Table 6.1.

TABLE 6.1   To avoid data mining the trend-trading strategies I'll review will be run over my P24 portfolio, which contains markets that have been independently and objectively selected based on their diversity and liquidity.

Markets

Market Sector/Segment	Futures Contract	Exchange	Avg Daily Volume*	Portfolio P24 3 Most Liquid	Symbol
Financials Currencies	Euro Currency	CME	188,888	EC	EC
	Japanese Yen	CME	138,000	JY	JY
	British Pound	CME	89,000	BP	BP
Interest Rates	10Yr T.Note	CME	1,249,000	10Yr T.Note	TY
	5Yr T.Note	CME	708,000	5Yr T.Note	FV
	30Yr T.Bond	CME	339,000	30Yr T.Bond	ZB
Indices	E-Mini S&P	CME	1,490,000	E-Mini S&P	SP
	E-Mini Nasdaq	CME	255,000	E-Mini Nasdaq	ND
	E-Mini Dow	CME	148,000	E-Mini Dow	DJ
Energy Energy	Crude Oil (WTI)	CME	253,000	Crude Oil	CL
	Natural Gas (H.Hub)	CME	115,000	Natural Gas	NG
	ULSD (Heating Oil)	CME	51,000	ULSD	HO
Metals Metals	Gold	CME	137,000	Gold	GC
	Copper	CME	45,000	Copper	HG
	Sliver	CME	44,000	Silver	SI
Food Grains	Corn	CME	129,000	Corn	CO
	Soybean	CME	104,000	Soybean	SO
	Wheat (SRW)	CME	55,000	Wheat	ZW
Softs	Sugar	ICE	58,000	Sugar	SB
	Coffee	ICE	15,000	Coffee	KC
	Cotton	ICE	14,000	Cotton	CT
Meat	Live Cattle	CME	23,000	Live Cattle	LC
	Lean Hog	CME	18,000	Lean Hog	LH
	Feeder Cattle	CME	3,000	Feeder Cattle	GF

* Volume Source: Premium Data from Norgate Investor Services
http://www.premiumdata.net/

Source: Data from Norgate Investor Services. www.norgatedata.com.

Please note, while many of the market symbols look familiar, many are not as they are not either the Chicago Mercantile Exchange's (CME) contract symbol or my broker's platform symbol, but mine that I've built into my VBA Excel trading model. For data I'll be using back-adjusted continuous futures contracts covering combined all sessions from Norgate Data (www.norgatedata.com). Their data covers 40 years of active trading, which will provide plenty of input for performance analysis.

Any smaller portfolio I use will be sourced from P24.

Before I begin reviewing the strategies, I'll first show you a naked strategy. A strategy without any hint of technical analysis. A strategy that I hope will demonstrate how powerful two of the golden tenets are.

TRADING NAKED WITHOUT TECHNICAL ANALYSIS

We now know hard scientific data tells us trend trading can't lose. The existence of fat tails and their regular appearance demonstrates that following the trend is a proven strategy to earn outsize returns.

I can demonstrate this with a simple strategy I'll call Random Trend Trader. The strategy will use Excel's random number generator, or coin toss, to signal either a buy or sell trade on the open. The model will hold a position without a stop for one day and then exit the following day on the open.

Here are the rules.

Rules

Strategy:	Random Trend Trader
Setup:	None
Entry:	Random (coin toss) entry, either buying or selling on the open.
Stop:	No stop
Exit:	Exit next day market on open
Brokerage:	None
Portfolio P8:	Japanese Yen, five-year treasury notes, e-mini Nasdaq, natural gas, copper, soybeans, coffee, lean hogs

Figure 6.1 shows the equity curve.

FIGURE 6.1   Random Trend Trader uses a coin toss to generate buy and sell signals.

Over the eight-market portfolio the strategy hypothetically made:

Results

| Portfolio P8: | SB, LC, GC, CO, TY, SP, CL & EC |
| Start: | 1980 |

Profit:	$264,429
Trades:	64,686
Avg Profit:	$4
Avg Brok & Slip per Trade:	$0

Although a profitable strategy, you'll notice it would quickly become unprofitable once brokerage and slippage is added. However, for the purpose of this exercise it will do. For a strategy, with a random entry, it's not bad. Now let's look at a histogram of its results in Figure 6.2.

You can see the distribution of results is almost normal, with individual trades being constant through time, falling symmetrically either side of an average value, and with half the trades positive and the other half negative. Where it's not 'normal' is in the fat tails. This is where Random Trend Trader can take advantage of both the science and

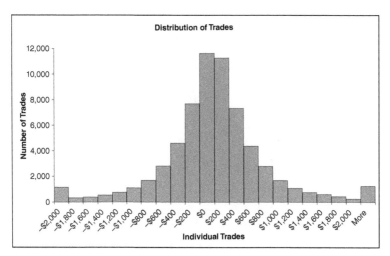

FIGURE 6.2 Random Trend Trader's histogram of individual trade results.

the three golden tenets to improve its results. Let's first look to see if cutting losses short will benefit our strategy.

Golden Tenet: Cut Your Losses Short

We can see from the histogram in Figure 6.2 that there are a significant number of large losses. If we can add say a 1% stop to our strategy to embrace the 'cut your losses short' golden tenet we should be able to chop off the large negative fat tails and instantly improve Random Trend Trader's profitability.

Figure 6.3 shows Random Trend Trader's new equity curve after the 1% stop has been added.

Over the eight-market portfolio the revised strategy made:

Results

Portfolio P8:	SB, LC, GC, CO, TY, SP, CL & EC
Start:	1980
Profit:	$243,121
Trades:	64,686
Avg Profit:	$3.76
Avg Brok & Slip per Trade:	$0

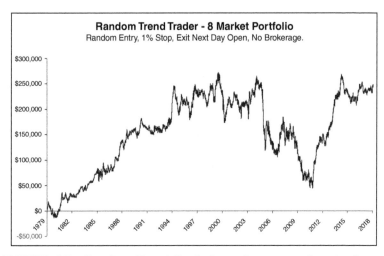

FIGURE 6.3   Random Trend Trader's performance after the introduction of a 1% stop.

Unfortunately, cutting losses short with the 1% stop doesn't appear to have improved performance with the average profit dropping to $3.76—or has it? Let's see if the histogram of individual trades in Figure 6.4 can show us more.

Well, how about that. Although the average profit has dropped, what the equity curve hasn't shown is the reduction in the large negative fat tails. Yes, the net profit is lower, however, Random Trend Trader has earned less profit with *far fewer* large negative losses, making it more comfortable to trade. So, one benefit of cutting your losses short is that it does make a strategy easier to trade. Let's now see if letting profits run will also benefit Random Trend Trader.

Golden Tenet: Letting Your Profits Run

Building on Random Trend Trader, we'll now look to add a trailing stop loss. Adding to the initial 1% stop Random Trend Trader will no longer exit on the next day's open, but will stay in a winning position until the previous week's low (for longs) or high (for shorts) is broken.

Figure 6.5 shows Random Trend Trader's new hypothetical equity curve once a trailing stop has been added to the initial 1% stop.

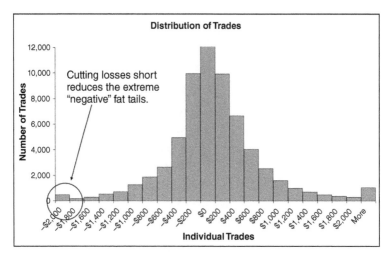

FIGURE 6.4 Introducing a 1% stop reduced Random Trend Trader's large losses.

FIGURE 6.5 Random Trend Trader's performance after the introducing a trailing one-week stop.

Wow, what an improvement it makes letting your profits run. Maybe this tenet should be called the 'golden, golden' tenet! Over the eight-market portfolio the new revised strategy (hypothetically) made:

Results

Portfolio P8:	SB, LC, GC, CO, TY, SP, CL & EC.
Start:	1980
Profit:	$618,000
Trades:	10,958
Avg Profit:	$56.40
Avg Brok & Slip per Trade:	$0

Let's see if Figure 6.6's histogram of individual trades can give us any additional insights?

The histogram clearly shows the benefit gained from the golden, golden tenet with the huge jump in extreme 'positive' fat tails. Letting profits run has shifted many of the positive results to the extreme edge where the big profitable trades are.

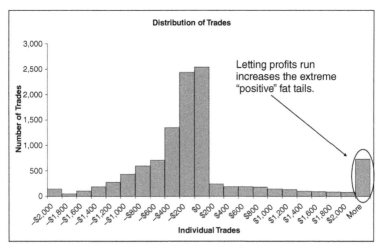

FIGURE 6.6 Introducing a one-week trailing stop increased the number of Random Trend Trader's large profits.

Random Trend Trader

Well, there you have it. A 'naked' strategy designed to avoid negative fat tails and to benefit from positive fat tails. A profitable trading strategy I've developed without even utilizing one piece of technical analysis. A profitable trading strategy with a random coin toss for its entry signal.

Let's recap the strategy's revised rules:

Rules

Strategy:	Random Trend Trader
Setup:	None
Entry:	Random (coin toss) entry, either buying or selling on the open
Initial Stop:	1%
Trailing Stop:	A break of the previous week's high (for shorts) and low (for longs)
Brokerage:	None

Results

Portfolio P8:	SB, LC, GC, CO, TY, SP, CL & EC.
Start:	1980
Profit:	$618,000
Trades:	10,958
Avg Profit:	$56.40
Avg Brok & Slip per Trade:	$0

Now, we can't get too excited as the profitability is marginal. If you deduct $50 for brokerage and slippage the average profit falls to $6.40 per trade.

However, the point here is not to suggest that Random Trend Trader is a preferred strategy to trade but to demonstrate how the hard science of mathematics proves following the trend is a proven strategy that can't lose. Random Trend Trader proves, even with a random and nonsensical entry technique, that just cutting losses short and letting profits run is a desirable and profitable approach to trading. You can't argue against the math, it is as inviolable as the laws of gravity!

But wait. Do I hear a few suspicious whispers suggesting I may be a little guilty of data mining since I've only selected eight markets? Have I just shown you the best eight markets to prove a point? Am I no different to those rainbow merchants who promote trading as the proverbial money tree offering effortless and boundless riches? No, I don't think so. So, let me run Random Trend Trader over my universal P24 portfolio, which contains 24 markets, being the three most liquid markets in each of eight diverse market segments. Figure 6.7 shows the results.

Results over the P24 Portfolio are as follows.

Results
_____

Portfolio P24:	SB, ZW, CO, SO, HO, LC, GF, BP, SV, KC, CT, ZB, GC, HG, JY, LH, SP, TY, CL, FV, NG, ND, EC, YM
Start:	1980
Profit:	$1,567,646
Trades:	31,953
Avg Profit:	$49
Avg Brok & Slip per Trade:	$0

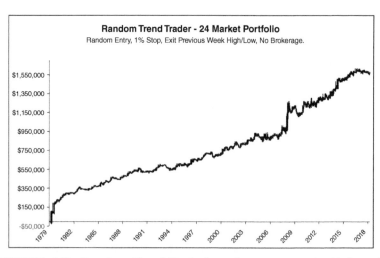

FIGURE 6.7 Random Trend Trader's performance on the Universal P24 Portfolio.

Well how about that. Although it would be a marginal proposition if brokerage and slippage were included, the model's performance based on a random coin toss and adhering to two golden tenets over a larger and well diversified portfolio, covering the most liquid markets in their segments, is outstanding. Didn't I say as inviolable as the laws of gravity? The math doesn't lie. Fat tails exist. Cutting losses short and letting profits run is a proven strategy 200-years young. A strategy with a nonsensical random coin toss entry without even a hint of technical analysis. It's all math.

Now that our little scientific experiment is complete, it's time to look at a number of different trend-trading strategies. Each using their preferred elements of technical analysis to embrace the three golden tenets of trend trading: follow the trend, cut losses short and let profits run.

TREND-TRADING STRATEGIES

There are essentially two types of trend-trading methodologies:

1. momentum trend trading and
2. relative strength trend trading.

Momentum strategies believe a new trend commences once prices are either above or below a particular price level.

Relative strength strategies believe a new trend commences once prices are either stronger or weaker when compared to similar peer securities within their universe of markets.

MOMENTUM TREND TRADING

Within momentum trend trading there are two categories:

- relative momentum trend trading and
- absolute momentum trend trading.

Relative Momentum Strategies

Relative momentum strategies believe a new trend commences once prices are either above or below previous prices. These strategies are less concerned with whether a market has broken out of a range and more concerned with whether prices are stronger or weaker than previous prices.

Examples include:

- rate of change strategies,
  - relative price move strategies,
    - moving average crossover strategies,
  - relative time move strategies and
    - period price move strategies.

Absolute Momentum Strategies

Absolute momentum strategies believe a new trend commences once a breakout of prices occur either above or below an absolute level or range.

Examples include:

- Breakout strategies:
  - price breakouts,
  - swing breakouts,
  - channel breakouts and
  - volatility breakouts.
- Retracement strategies:
  - rubber band mean reversion strategies.

RELATIVE STRENGTH TREND TRADING

Relative strength strategies believe a new trend commences once prices are either stronger or weaker when compared to similar peer securities within their universe of markets.

Each approach has its own variety of techniques as summarized in Figure 6.8.

In this book I'll only focus on what I do and know best, which is momentum trend trading. I will not be discussing relative strength trend trading.

Now, as we know trend trading relies on three golden tenets:

- follow the trend,
- cut losses short and
- let profits run.

TREND TRADING STRATEGIES

■ Momentum Trend Trading

    <u>Relative Momentum</u>
       ■ Rate of Change Systems

          ● Relative Price Move
            • Hearne 1% Rule (1850)
            • Gartley 3- and 6-Week Crossover (1935)
            • Donchian 5- and 20-Day Crossover (1960)
            • Golden 50- and 200-Day Crossover

          ● Relative Time Move
            • Calendar Rule (1933)

    <u>Absolute Momentum</u>
       ■ Breakout Systems

          ● Price Breakouts
            • Ricardo Rules (1800)

          ● Swing Breakouts
            • Dow Theory (1900)

          ● Congestion Breakouts
            • Livermore Reaction (1900)
            • Darvas Box (1950)
            • Arnold PPS (1987)

          ● Channel Breakouts
            • Donchian 4-Week Rule (1960)
            • Dreyfus 52-Week Rule (1960)
            • Turtle Trading (1983)

          ● Volatility Breakouts
            • Bollinger Bands (1993)
            • ATR Bands

       ■ Retracement Systems
            • Elder's Triple Screen Trading System (1985)
            • Mean Reversion

■ Relative Strength Trend Trading

FIGURE 6.8 There are multiple approaches to trading with the trend.

These are the three core value drivers behind successful trend-trading strategies. These tenets do not try to predict market moves but only react to them with the aim of capturing returns from large, outsized moves. Let's now examine a number of alternative trend-trading strategies to gain an understanding of how they each incorporate, embrace and execute the three golden tenets.

HYPOTHETICAL RESULTS

Please be aware the results shown for each strategy have all been run over the same P24 portfolio and are hypothetical. They've been computer generated by my VBA Excel trading model. In addition, please be aware that hypothetical results do not indicate future success and they may overestimate performance due to the impact of certain market conditions such as poor liquidity and poor execution.

RELATIVE MOMENTUM TREND TRADING

Relative momentum strategies focus on whether prices are either above or below previous prices. These strategies fall under the 'rate of change' category, which can either be price or time based. Let's begin with examining a few relative 'price' rate of change strategies.

Relative Price Rate of Change Momentum Trend Trading

I'll start with Pat Hearne's strategy.

Hearne's 1% Rule (1850)

William Fowler recorded Pat Hearne's trading strategy in his 1870 book *Ten Years on Wall Street*. Hearne was a notable American gambler and gangster. He would purchase 100 shares of a particular stock and continue to purchase a similar amount at every 1% rally. He would sell his complete holdings on 1% decline. Although technically pyramiding, its core idea is the essence of trend trading: follow the trend, cut losses short and let profits run. According to Fowler's observation, Hearne's approach appeared to be a buy only strategy.

Let's take a closer look. I'll begin with summarizing the rules.

Rules

Strategy:	Hearne 1% Rule
Developed:	1850
Published:	1870
Data:	Daily
Approach:	Trend trading
Technique:	Rate of price change
Symmetry:	Buy only
Markets:	All
Indicators:	None
Variables—Number:	1
Percentage movement:	(1%)
Variables—Symmetry:	Buy only
Variables—Application:	Same value across all markets
Setup:	None
Rules:	2

Buy Rules

Entry:	Buy break of a 1% rally off previous day's close
Stop:	Sell break of a 1% decline off previous day's close

Figure 6.9 illustrates a Hearne trade example.

Let's run this early trend-trading model over the P24 portfolio and see whether Hearne's idea has merit.

Results

Portfolio P24:	SB, ZW, CO, SO, HO, LC, GF, BP, SV, KC, CT, ZB, GC, HG, JY, LH, SP, TY, CL, FV, NG, ND, EC, YM
Start:	1980
Net Profit:	−$2,056,953
Total trades:	59,294
Avg Profit:	−$35
Avg Brok & Slip per Trade:	−$51

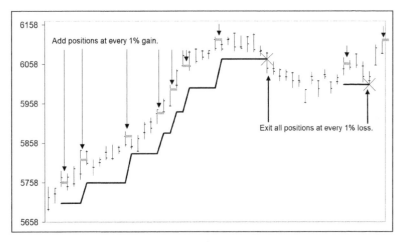

FIGURE 6.9 The Hearne 1% Rule strategy will add positions at every 1% rally while exiting all positions at a 1% loss.

Unfortunately, this is a losing proposition. Despite Figure 6.9's picture-perfect chart, when the idea is methodologically applied across a well-diversified portfolio of 24 markets and $51 is deducted for brokerage and slippage, Hearne's 1% Rule strategy loses, completely.

This result is no criticism of Hearne. Our recent markets over the last 40 years, I believe, are far more volatile and choppier than those Hearne would have traded back in the mid-nineteenth century, where trends were possibly more emerging and smoother. However it should be noted that without brokerage Hearne's 1% rule did average $16 gross per trade. So the idea does have merit, but not enough to cover brokerage.

Let's move on.

Gartley's Three- and Six-Week Crossover (1935)

Gartley is probably better known for his Gartley 1–2–3 retracement chart pattern. A pattern made popular by Larry Pesavento, who applied harmonic ratios. Gartley is not known for his dual moving average strategy unless you have a copy of his 1935 book *Profits in the Stock Market*. On page 266 you will see the chart illustration shown in Figure 6.10.

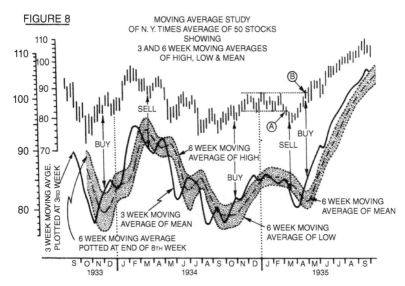

FIGURE 6.10 Gartley clearly illustrated his three and six week crossover strategy in his 1935 book *Profits in the Stock Market*.

Let me summarize the rules.

Rules

Strategy:	Gartley 3 and 6 week crossover
Developed:	Unknown
Published:	1935
Data:	Daily
Approach:	Trend trading
Technique:	Always in the market: a stop and reverse relative price rate of change
Symmetry:	Buy and sell
Markets:	All
Indicators:	Moving average (x 3)
Variables—Number:	3
	Short-term Moving average:
	High/Low
	3-week moving average of the weekly mean

	Mean is average of the weekly High/Low
	Longer-term Moving Average 1: 6-week moving average of the weekly high
	Offset (moved forward) by 2-weeks
	Longer-term Moving Average 2: 6-week moving average of the weekly low
	Offset (moved forward) by 2-weeks
	Weekly offset (2)
Variables—Symmetry:	Same value for both buy and sell setups
Variables—Application:	Same value across all markets

Buy Rules

Setup:	3-week moving average of mean > 6-week moving average of the highs
Entry:	Buy Monday market on open
Stop:	3-week moving average of mean < 6-week moving average of the lows
	Sell Monday Market on open

Sell Rules

Setup:	3-week moving average of mean < 6-week moving average of the lows
Entry:	Sell Monday market on open
Stop:	3-week moving average of mean > 6-week moving average of the highs
	Buy Monday market on open

Like the Hearne model, I've programmed Gartley's strategy into my VBA Excel trading model according to his rules as shown in Figure 6.11.

Being a relative momentum strategy the Gartley model watches for when prices are above or below previous prices. In Gartley's case, he uses three price series. When the three-week moving average of the mean closes on a Friday above the six-week moving average of the high (which is offset by two weeks), the model will go long on Monday's open. When the three-week moving average of the mean closes on Friday below the six-week moving average of the lows (which is offset by two weeks) the model will go short on Monday's open.

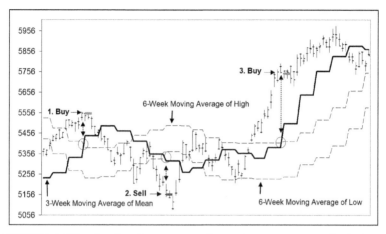

FIGURE 6.11 Gartley incorporated moving average calculations way before they became popular and way before the arrival of personal computers in the 1970s.

Let's see how his model, first published in 1935, has performed over my P24 portfolio since 1980?

Results

Portfolio P24:	SB, ZW, CO, SO, HO, LC, GF, BP, SV, KC, CT, ZB, GC, HG, JY, LH, SP, TY, CL, FV, NG, ND, EC, YM
Start:	1980
Net Profit:	$1,079,398
Total Trades:	3,387
Avg Profit:	$319
Avg Brok & Slip per Trade:	−$51

Well how about that. A strategy over 80 years old holding up exceedingly well over the last 40-odd years on out-of-sample data. Harold Gartley, take a bow! Straight off the pages from his 1935 book. Here is a trend-trading strategy that not only proves the golden tenets of trend trading work but also provides rock solid evidence of the methodology's robustness over 40+ years of out-of-sample data. Everyone, please stand and applaud Mr Harold Gartley.

Donchian's 5 and 20-Day Crossover (1960)

Another relative momentum moving average strategy is one published by Richard Donchian. Donchian is better known for his Four-Week Rule, which underpins the widely known and widely popular Turtle Trading strategy. This strategy is very similar to Gartley's but uses a shorter time period. It was published in 1960.

I've summarized the rules here.

Rules

Strategy:	Donchian's 5 and 20-Day Crossover
Developed:	Unknown
Published:	1960
Data:	Daily
Approach:	Trend trading
Technique:	Always in the market: a stop and reverse relative price rate of change
Symmetry:	Buy and sell
Markets:	All
Indicators:	Moving average (x 2)
Variables—Number:	2
	Short-term trend: 5-day moving average
	Long-term trend: 20-day moving average
Variables—Symmetry:	Same value for both buy and sell setups
Variables—Application:	Same value across all markets
Rules:	2

Buy Rules

Setup:	5-day moving average > 20-day moving average
Entry:	Buy next day market on open
Stop:	5-day moving average < 20-day moving average
	Sell next day market on open

Sell Rules

Setup:	5-day moving average < 20-day moving average
Entry:	Sell next day market on open
Stop:	5-day moving average > 20-day moving average
	Buy next day market on open

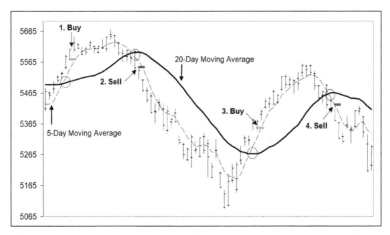

FIGURE 6.12 Richard Donchian's 5 and 20-Day strategy will stop and reverse positions following a cross over between a 5 and 20-day moving average.

Again, I have programmed this strategy into my VBA Excel trading model. Figure 6.12 illustrates four trade examples that have been triggered according to Donchian's rules.

Let's see how his model, known since 1960, has performed over my P24 portfolio since 1980.

Results

Portfolio P24:	SB, ZW, CO, SO, HO, LC, GF, BP, SV, KC, CT, ZB, GC, HG, JY, LH, SP, TY, CL, FV, NG, ND, EC, YM
Start:	1980
Net Profit:	$520,675
Total Trades:	13,306
Avg Profit:	$39
Avg Brok & Slip per Trade:	−$51

Well, the good news is that it's profitable. The bad news is that it's marginal. So, thumbs up as it is profitable. But no world beater, with an average profit of only $39. Still, it's a profit, so a nod of recognition to the golden tenets of trend trading. We should also throw in a respectful salute to Donchian, whose model, almost 60 years old, has produced an out-of-sample profit over the last 40-odd years. A profit that many other trading ideas, when objectively and systematically applied across a diversified portfolio of markets, would be jealous of. In a nut shell, even though it's not a world beater Donchian's 5 and 20-day model validates trend trading as a proven methodology.

Golden 50 and 200-Day Crossover

I'm not aware that this strategy has been attributed to any individual trader. However, due to its frequent appearance in the media and regular referencing by the 'talking' heads, I thought I should review it here.

No doubt you may have seen references to a 'Golden Cross' or 'Death Cross' occurring in a particular market, where the author has attributed its appearance as a monumental event. Many market protagonists believe that the appearance of either cross signals a seismic change in trend.

A 'Golden Cross' occurs when a 50-day moving average crosses above a 200-day moving average and is meant to confirm the existence of a bull market.

A 'Death Cross' occurs when a 50-day moving average crosses below a 200-day moving average and is meant to confirm the existence of a bear market.

I've summarized the rules here.

Rules

Strategy:	Golden 50 and 200-day Crossover
Developed:	Unknown
Published:	Unknown
Data:	Daily
Approach:	Trend trading
Technique:	Always in the market: A stop and reverse relative price rate of change
Symmetry:	Buy and sell
Markets:	All
Indicators:	Moving average (x 2)
Variables— Number:	2
	Medium-term trend: 50-day moving average
	Long-term trend: 200-day moving average
Variables—Symmetry:	Same value for both buy and sell setups
Variables—Application:	Same value across all markets
Rules:	2

Buy Rules

Setup:	50-day moving average > 200-day moving average
Entry:	Buy next day market on open
Stop:	50-day moving average < 200-day moving average
	Sell next day market on open

Sell Rules

Setup:	50-day moving average < 200-day moving average
Entry:	Sell next day market on open
Stop:	50-day moving average > 200-day moving average
	Buy next day market on open

This strategy is very similar to Richard Donchian's 5 and 20-day crossover methodology. The only difference is in the length of the respective moving averages. I've programmed it into my VBA Excel trading model where Figure 6.13 illustrates two trade examples.

Let's see how this Golden and Death Cross trend-trading strategy has performed over my P24 portfolio?

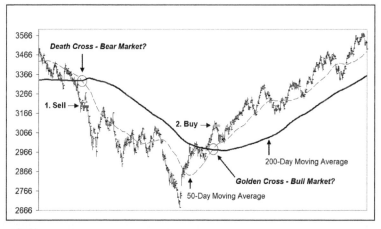

FIGURE 6.13 The Golden 50 and 200-day Crossover strategy will stop and reverse positions following a cross over between a 50 and 200-day moving average.

Results

Portfolio P24:	SB, ZW, CO, SO, HO, LC, GF, BP, SV, KC, CT, ZB, GC, HG, JY, LH, SP, TY, CL, FV, NG, ND, EC, YM
Start:	1980
Net Profit:	$1,715,940
Total Trades:	1,235
Avg Profit:	$1,389
Avg Brok & Slip per Trade:	−$51

Wow. Very nice indeed. With a high average profit of $1,389 the strategy is certainly consistent, making the Golden Crossover strategy the (current) chief cheer leader of the trend-trading faithful. It certainly pays to follow the trend, cut losses short and let profits run. It's a pity I can't attribute the strategy to a published source.

It's now time to look at another type of trend-trading strategy. Let's see how relative 'time' rate of change strategies look and perform.

Relative Time Rate of Change Momentum Trend Trading

These models look for a relative change in price over a specific time.

In 1933 Cowles and Jones released a research paper—'Some A Posteriori Probabilities in Stock Market Action'—examining momentum in share prices over various time horizons. They created and examined multiple time series from 20 minutes to three years. They concluded momentum existed in share prices where a positive or negative price movement had a 62.5% chance of seeing the movement continue over the next time period (and the academics say price changes are random!).

Let's examine relative rate of change over two popular time periods and see how effective 'time' is in identifying trend-trading opportunities. I'll begin with the monthly timeframe and then examine quarterly prices.

Monthly Close Model (1933)

This model will simply enter long if the current month closes above the previous month's close. It will reverse and go short if the current month closes below the previous month's close. The strategy is always in the market and is referred to as a stop and reverse strategy.

I've summarized the rules here.

Rules

Strategy:	Monthly Close Model
Developed:	1933
Published:	1933
Data:	Daily
Approach:	Trend trading
Technique:	Always in the market: a stop and reverse relative time rate of change
Symmetry:	Buy and sell
Markets:	All
Indicators:	None
Variables—Number:	0
Variables—Symmetry:	Not applicable
Variables—Application:	Not applicable
Rules:	2

Buy Rules

Setup:	Current monthly close > previous monthly close
Entry:	Buy next day, first day of the month, market on open
Stop:	Current monthly close < previous monthly close Sell next day, first day of the month, market on open

Sell Rules

Setup:	Current monthly close < previous monthly close
Entry:	Sell next day, first day of the month, market on open
Stop:	Current monthly close > previous monthly close Buy next day, first day of the month, market on open

While a monthly close continues in a trade's direction, the model will let profits run but will cut and reverse the position if a monthly close reverses.

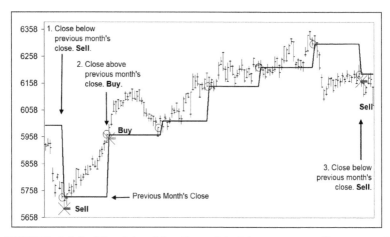

FIGURE 6.14 The Monthly Close Model strategy will stop and reverse positions following an opposite directional monthly close.

Like the other models, I've programmed this simple relative time model according to the rules above as shown in Figure 6.14.

Being a relative time momentum strategy the model watches for where the end-of-month price closes relative to the previous monthly close. If the model is short and the monthly close is up, the model will stop and reverse and go long on the open of the first day of the next month. If the model is long and prices close down the model will stop and reverse and go short on the open of the first day of the next month

Let's see how his model has performed over my P24 portfolio since 1980?

Results

Portfolio P24:	SB, ZW, CO, SO, HO, LC, GF, BP, SV, KC, CT, ZB, GC, HG, JY, LH, SP, TY, CL, FV, NG, ND, EC, YM
Start:	1980
Net Profit:	$1,003,526
Total Trades:	4,993
Avg Profit:	$201
Avg Brok & Slip per Trade:	−$51

Well how about that? Not bad for a simplistic model that waits for time and let's winning trades run, while cutting and reversing when losing. Again, this demonstrates the power of trend trading's three golden tenets. Cowles and Jones, hold hands and take a well-deserved bow.

Quarterly Close Model (1933)

Like the Monthly Close Model, this variation will simply enter long if the current quarterly close is above the previous quarterly close. It will reverse and go short if the current quarterly close is below the previous quarterly close.

The following rules are identical to the Monthly Close Model except for the quarterly time period.

<u>Rules</u>

Strategy:	Quarterly Close Model
Developed:	1933
Published:	1933
Data:	Daily
Approach:	Trend trading
Technique:	Always in the market: a stop and reverse relative time rate of change
Symmetry:	Buy and sell
Markets:	All
Indicators:	None
Variables—Number:	0
Variables—Symmetry:	Not applicable
Variables—Application:	Not applicable
Rules:	2

<u>Buy Rules</u>

Setup:	Current quarterly close > previous quarterly close
Entry:	Buy next day, first day of the quarter, market on open
Stop:	Current quarterly close < previous quarterly close Sell next day, first day of the quarter, market on open

Sell Rules

Setup:	Current quarterly close < previous quarterly close
Entry:	Sell next day, first day of the quarter, market on open
Stop:	Current quarterly close > previous quarterly close
	Buy next day, first day of the quarter, market on open

While a quarterly close continues in a trade's direction the model will let profits run, but will cut and reverse the position if a quarterly close reverses as shown in Figure 6.15.

Let's see how his model has performed over my P24 portfolio since 1980?

Results

Portfolio P24:	SB, ZW, CO, SO, HO, LC, GF, BP, SV, KC, CT, ZB, GC, HG, JY, LH, SP, TY, CL, FV, NG, ND, EC, YM
Start:	1980
Net Profit:	$611,092
Total Trades:	1,670
Avg Profit:	$366
Avg Brok & Slip per Trade:	−$51

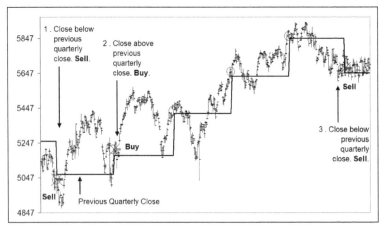

FIGURE 6.15 The Quarterly Close Model strategy will stop and reverse positions following an opposite directional quarterly close.

Good. Not as good as the Monthly Close Model due to the lower frequency of quarterly signals, but still good with a healthy net average profit. But regardless of the lower overall net profit, its methodology aligns with and confirms the three golden tenets of trend trading.

These momentum trend-trading strategies so far focus on prices' relative position to previous prices, whether they are above or below. The other class of momentum strategies look for prices enjoying a breakout beyond an absolute level. Let's now take a look at them.

ABSOLUTE MOMENTUM TREND TRADING

These momentum strategies believe a new trend commences once a breakout occurs either above or below a particular price level. These strategies are generally referred to as either breakout or retracement systems. Breakout systems include:

- price breakouts,
- swing breakouts,
- congestion breakouts,
- channel breakouts and
- volatility breakouts.

Retracement systems include popular models labelled mean reversion.

Let's take a look at a few of these absolute momentum trend-trading strategies.

Price Breakouts

I'll begin where it all started, with David Ricardo.

Ricardo Rules (1800)

James Grant wrote about David Ricardo in his 1838 book *The Great Metropolis, Volume 2*:

> *I may observe that he amassed his immense fortune by a scrupulous attention to what he called his own three golden rules, the observance of which he used to press on his private friends. These were,*
>
> - *Never refuse an option when you get it*
> - *Cut your losses short*
> - *Let your profits run on.*

Let me formulate a strategy to encapsulate these three golden rules.

Never Refuse an Option When You Get it
To capture Ricardo's belief to 'never refuse an option' I'll use the market's price action as the 'gift' of direction that should 'never' be refused. Simply, if there is no position and the market breaks a previous bar's high, Ricardo Rules should say 'go long'. A trader should listen to the market. If the market breaks a previous bar's low, the Ricardo Rules should say 'go short'. Once again, a trader should listen to the market. Its direction is the 'gift' a trader should 'never' refuse.

Cut Your Losses Short
Let's keep it simple. For an initial stop I'll use an opposite break of either the setup or entry bar, whichever one is further away. If prices breakup (taking out the previous setup bar's high) the Ricardo Rules will place an initial stop one tick below the lowest low of either setup bar or entry bar. If prices breakdown (taking out the previous setup bar's low) the Ricardo Rules will place an initial stop one tick above the highest high of either the setup bar or entry bar.

Let Your Profits Run on
If the market takes off, I'll use the closest swing point as a trailing stop. If the Ricardo Rules go long with prices rallying, a trailing stop will be raised to one tick below the nearest swing low. If the Ricardo Rules go short with prices falling, a trailing stop will be lowered to one tick above the nearest swing high. Simple.

Let me now summarize my interpretation of Ricardo Rules.

Rules

Strategy:	Ricardo Rules
Developed:	1800
Published:	1838
Data:	Daily
Approach:	Trend trading
Technique:	Price breakout
Symmetry:	Buy and sell
Markets:	All
Indicators:	None

Variables—Number:	0
Variables—Symmetry:	Not applicable
Variables—Application:	Not applicable
Rules:	3

Buy Rules

Setup:	Neutral daily bar
Entry:	Buy break of the previous bar's high
Initial Stop:	Sell break of the lowest low of either the setup or entry bar
Trailing Stop:	Sell break of the closest swing low

Sell Rules

Setup:	Neutral daily bar
Entry:	Sell break of the previous bar's low
Initial Stop:	Buy break of the highest high of either the setup or entry bar
Trailing Stop:	Buy break of the closest swing high

I've programmed the strategy into my VBA Excel trading model where Figure 6.16 illustrates a buy trade according to the rules.

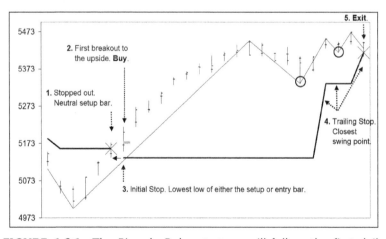

FIGURE 6.16 The Ricardo Rules strategy will follow the first daily bar breakout and remain in a position until the break of either its initial or trailing stop.

This simple representation of David Ricardo's approach to trading, used by him in the 1800s, reflects his core philosophy to accept all gifts of market direction (never to refuse an option), cut your losses short and let your profits run. Let's see how Ricardo Rules has performed over my P24 universal portfolio since 1980?

Results

Portfolio P24:	SB, ZW, CO, SO, HO, LC, GF, BP, SV, KC, CT, ZB, GC, HG, JY, LH, SP, TY, CL, FV, NG, ND, EC, YM
Start:	1980
Net Profit:	$622,552
Total Trades:	20,392
Avg Profit	$31
Avg Brok & Slip per Trade	−$51

Ok. Not a world beater. But not a loser either. Obviously, the average profit is low; however, for such a simple model the profitability is impressive. And its simplicity is a clear and obvious testament to the robustness of trend trading's three golden tenets.

Swing Breakouts

Dow Theory (1900)

Charles Dow is regarded as the father of technical analysis. A significant part of his work was his peak-and-trough trend analysis where a bull market was defined by higher highs and a bear market by lower lows. Each respective market remained in existence until a change in trend occurred.

Dow Theory's peak-and-trough trend analysis is possibly the first objective attempt at mechanically defining a 'trend' and potentially the second systematic trend-trading model to be devised after Hearne's 1% Rule strategy.

In a nut shell, Dow Theory believes higher highs and higher lows represents a trend up while lower highs and lower lows represents a trend down. For ease I'll refer to his peak-and-trough trend analysis as simply 'Dow Theory'.

Let me summarize the mechanical Dow Theory (peak-and-trough trend analysis) rules.

Rules

Strategy:	Dow Theory
Developed:	Unknown
Published:	1900
Data:	Daily
Approach:	Trend trading
Technique:	Always in the market: A stop and reverse swing breakout
Symmetry:	Buy and sell
Markets:	All
Indicators:	None
Variables—Number:	0
Variables—Symmetry:	Not applicable
Variables—Application:	Not applicable
Rules:	1

Buy Rules

Setup & Entry:	Change in daily Dow trend—from trend down to trend up
Stop:	Change in daily Dow trend—from trend up to trend down

Sell Rules:

Setup & Entry:	Change in daily Dow trend—from trend up to trend down
Stop:	Change in daily Dow trend—from trend down to trend up

I've programmed Dow Theory's mechanical peak-and-trough trend strategy as illustrated in Figure 6.17.

Let's see how Dow's peak-and-trough trend analysis, employed as a mechanical systemized model, has performed over my P24 portfolio since 1980?

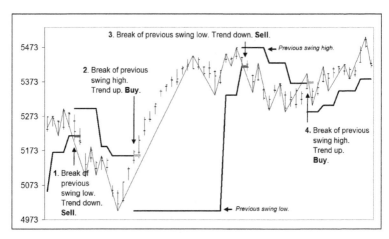

FIGURE 6.17 Dow Theory's peak-and-trough trend analysis is always in the market and will stop and reverse positions following a change in the daily Dow trend.

Results

Portfolio P24:	SB, ZW, CO, SO, HO, LC, GF, BP, SV, KC, CT, ZB, GC, HG, JY, LH, SP, TY, CL, FV, NG, ND, EC, YM
Start:	1980
Net Profit:	$1,090,346
Total Trades:	17,927
Avg Profit:	$61
Avg Brok & Slip per Trade:	−$51

Not bad, hey. Although the average profit is small, the results for a such a simple mechanical strategy containing one rule is impressive. Please remember Dow Theory is over 120 years old and is still performing well on 40+ years of out-of-sample data. It's an amazing testament to both trend trading and Dow Theory. For longevity and robustness, Charles Dow definitely deserves a hat tip and 21-gun salute.

Congestion Breakouts

Livermore Reaction (1900)

The Livermore Reaction model is the first of the congestion-type breakout models I'll be reviewing. Jess Livermore may just be the most celebrated trader I know of. I know Edwin Lefèvre's 1923 book *Reminiscences of a Stock Operator* had a profound impact on myself. I can still remember reading the book as a young trader when I was on Bank America's securities desk in Sydney, and believing he was referring to myself when he was categorizing all of his mistakes. I was thinking, 'that's me', 'yes, that's me, that's me!'. If you haven't got yourself a copy, do so now.

Jesse Livermore was a trend trader who summarized how he traded in his 1940 book *How to Trade in Stocks*. In his book he makes direct reference to following the trend:

> *It may surprise many to know that in my method of trading, when I see by my records that an upward trend is in progress, I become a buyer as soon as a stock makes a new high on its movement, after having had a normal reaction. The same applies whenever I take the short side. Why? Because I am following the trend at the time. My records signal me to go ahead!*

Livermore defined his 'normal reactions' as two pullbacks, or retracements, against the new trend. He used the term 'pivots' to describe swing points and defined trends according to the position of his 'pivots' or swing points. He defined an uptrend as being characterized by higher pivot (swing) highs and higher pivot (swing) lows. He defined a downtrend as being characterized by lower pivot (swing) highs and lower pivot (swing) lows. Since this is identical to Dow's peak-and-trough trend analysis I'll use the term 'Dow Theory'.

Livermore would look for a change in trend to occur (as defined by Dow Theory), wait patiently while two normal reactions (or retracements) occurred against the new trend, before entering on a break of the previous swing point, which would also reconfirm the new trend. He would stay in the trade until a change in Dow trend would stop him out. A change in Dow trend was simply an opposite break of previous pivot or swing point.

It's impossible to determine an accurate year for when he developed his approach. I'll assume he would have developed and traded it by his early to mid- twenties, so I'll haphazard a guess and say 1900.

Livermore gave consideration to other factors in his trading, however, in the interest of keeping it simple and comparable to the other strategies discussed here, my preference is to keep my discussion on his trading strategy to price alone.

I've summarized the rules below here.

Rules

Strategy:	Livermore Reaction
Developed:	1900
Published:	1940
Data:	Daily
Approach:	Trend trading
Technique:	Congestion breakout
Symmetry:	Buy and sell
Markets:	All
Indicators:	None
Variables—Number:	0
Variables—Symmetry:	Not applicable
Variables—Application:	Not applicable
Rules:	4

Buy Rules

Setup:	Change in Dow trend from trend down to trend up
	Two reactions/retracements swing down against the new Dow uptrend
Entry:	Buy break of the previous swing high
Stop:	Sell break of the closest swing low

Sell Rules

Setup:	Change in Dow trend from trend up to trend down
	Two reactions/retracements swing up against the new Dow down trend
Entry:	Sell break of the previous swing low
Stop:	Buy break of the closest swing high

I've programmed Livermore's Reaction strategy into my VBA Excel trading model as illustrated in Figure 6.18.

Let's see how Jesse Livermore's Reaction strategy, programmed as a mechanical systemized model, has performed over my P24 portfolio since 1980?

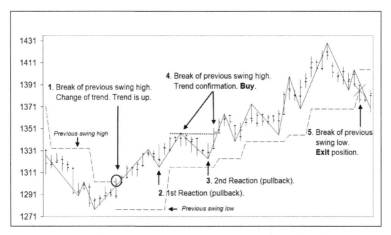

FIGURE 6.18   The Livermore Reaction strategy will only initiate a trade following a 'normal reaction' as defined by two retracements against a new trend.

Results

Portfolio P24:	SB, ZW, CO, SO, HO, LC, GF, BP, SV, KC, CT, ZB, GC, HG, JY, LH, SP, TY, CL, FV, NG, ND, EC, YM
Start:	1980
Net Profit:	$35,136
Total Trades:	1,279
Avg Profit	$27
Avg Brok & Slip per Trade:	−$51

Well that is disappointing. Given it's the renowned Jesse Livermore I was expecting (hoping) for more. But not to be. A positive is that it's at least profitable on out-of-sample data, demonstrating the core idea is robust. Not robust enough to trade as it is, but possibly robust enough to build upon by an energetic and enthusiastic trader. If that's you, remember to tread carefully and avoid falling into the trap of excessive curve fitting. Keep your focus on capturing market signals and not market noise.

As an aside it's interesting to note that Livermore's Reaction method is at direct odds with Ralph Elliott's Wave Theory. Elliott developed his approach in the 1930s and called it the Elliott Wave Theory. In its simplest form Elliott believed a trend is complete following a five-wave movement. Yet Livermore's Reaction is looking to enter the market on a fifth wave, just when Elliott is expecting the market to reverse. I know I can be accused of oversimplifying Elliott Wave, as there are many rules governing wave relationships and fractal layering; however, my observation is still valid. One approach is looking for a trend to continue, while the other is looking for a trend to reverse. They are diametrically opposed to each other. Interesting, hey? And it also gives a good insight into the difficulties that traders have in sorting out what works and what doesn't within the field of technical analysis. There are so many competing and opposing voices. Really, one could be forgiven for thinking technical analysis sometimes resembles a mad house!

The Darvas Box (1950)

The Darvas Box strategy is another congestion breakout strategy. Nicolas Darvas would (mentally) draw a box around congested prices to encapsulate range bound activity. He would enter the market on a break of the box.

Despite his book, Darvas did not specifically detail the exact rules for his method. He didn't specifically define the size or parameters of his box or his stop, except to infer he'd exit if the opposite box boundary was broken. He never actually drew any boxes on his charts, referring to himself as a mental chartist. In a nut shell, Darvas was looking for a congestion in prices, or consolidation. If prices broke out, he went long. In addition, Darvas was vague about the overall market condition he preferred to trade in. He made references to only examining shares trading at their all-time highs, and knowing a share's high and low over the preceding two or three years (making references to 52-week highs).

So, I need to define some hard rules if I hope to program and review the strategy. Now, although like many of his predecessors and contemporaries he used more than just price in his strategy (i.e. volume), it's my preference to keep my observations about these strategies I'm discussing both simple and consistent, so I'll just focus on price.

I've summarized the rules according to my interpretation of the Darvas Box Strategy.

Rules

Strategy:	Darvas Box
Developed:	1950
Published:	1960
Data:	Daily
Approach:	Trend trading
Technique:	Congestion breakout
Symmetry:	Buy and sell
Markets:	All
Indicators:	Average True Range (ATR)
Variables—Number:	5
	Darvas Box (4):
	Minimum length of box: (20) daily bars
	Maximum length of box: (100) daily bars
	Maximum height of box: as defined by a multiple (5) of the ATR (20)
Trailing Stop:	Number of weeks (2)
Variables—Symmetry:	Same value for both buy and sell setups
Variables—Application:	Same value across all markets
Rules:	4

Buy Rules

Setup:	Darvas Box
Trend:	Up—previous close must be above the previous year's high
Entry:	Buy a break of the Darvas Box's high
Stop:	Sell break of the 2-week low

Sell Rules

Setup:	Darvas Box
Trend:	Down—previous close must be below the previous year's low
Entry:	Sell a break of the Darvas Box's low
Stop:	Buy break of the 2-week high

I've programmed my interpretation of the Darvas Box strategy as illustrated in Figure 6.19.

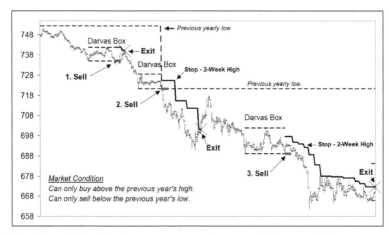

FIGURE 6.19 Nicolas Darvas used a mental box to define a congestion of prices. The Darvas strategy would trade a breakout of the congestion box.

Let's see how the Darvas Box strategy has performed over my P24 portfolio since 1980?

Results

Portfolio P24:	SB, ZW, CO, SO, HO, LC, GF, BP, SV, KC, CT, ZB, GC, HG, JY, LH, SP, TY, CL, FV, NG, ND, EC, YM
Start:	1980
Net Profit:	$136,731
Total Trades:	636
Avg Profit:	$215
Avg Brok & Slip per Trade:	−$51

Not bad compared to Livermore's Reaction Model. But not great compared to the others. The positive news is that for a 70+year-old strategy it's profitable. My only concern is the number of variables the strategy has. I've done no more than stipulate a minimum and maximum length for the box along with a maximum height. I've no doubt that if I changed those variables you'd see another alternative equity curve and resultant expectancy, ROR and average profit calculation.

How alternative? I don't know. But it's a consideration you need to be aware of. In addition, I can't say the results are out-of-sample as I've made up the variable values, not Nicolas Darvas. I've certainly utilized his 'box' philosophy, but the coded variables are mine. But, even with these reservations, the Darvas Box philosophy does enjoy an edge, and—along with many of the strategies above—validates the power of following the three golden tenets of trend trading.

This brings me to the last of the congestion-type breakout strategies I'll be discussing: Curtis Arnold's Pattern Probability Strategy.

Arnold's Pattern Probability Strategy (1987)

Curtis Arnold developed his Pattern Probability Strategy (PPS) in 1987 and later published it in his book *PPS Trading System* (Arnold, 1995). Unfortunately for Arnold, in 1997 he ran into trouble with the US Commodity Futures Trading Commission. He made a few claims they objected to. However, despite his misstep, I believe his PPS strategy is worth reviewing.

PPS is a very simple strategy looking to trade breakouts of price congestions in the direction of a medium-term and long-term trend as defined by the 18-day and 40-day moving average.

Price congestions are defined by traditional chart patterns such as triangles, rectangles, wedges, head and shoulders and double and triple tops and bottoms. For simplicity I'll focus on the triangle, rectangle and wedge patterns.

Arnold originally looked for patterns that contained at least ten days, and no more than 50 days. In his book he indicates that patterns with fewer than ten days may also be worth considering. So, it appears he's flexible on pattern size. For this exercise I'll focus purely on pattern and ignore any minimum or maximum number of days or bars.

PPS uses a combination of initial, breakeven and trailing stops. For its initial stop PPS uses the apex of the two converging connected trend lines. For simplicity I'll use an opposite break of either the setup or entry bar, depending on which is furthest away. PPS will move its initial stop to breakeven once the open profit is twice the initial risk or if on the fourth day there is an open profit. PPS uses two trailing stops. A break of the closest swing point or a break of a 45-degree trend line. For simplicity I'll stick with only using a break of the closest swing point.

Here are the rules according to my interpretations.

<u>Rules</u>

Strategy:	PPS
Developed:	1987
Published:	1995
Data:	Daily
Approach:	Trend trading
Technique:	Congestion breakout
Symmetry:	Buy and sell
Markets:	All
Indicators:	Moving average ($\times$ 2)
Variables—Number:	5
	Medium-term trend: Moving average (18)
	Long-term trend: Moving average (40)
	Breakeven stop: Open profit multiple (2) of trade risk
	Breakeven stop: Minimum open profit after minimum number of days (4)
	Number of swing points required to locate a setup pattern (4)
	Note: Each pair of swings is connected by a trend line
Breakeven Stop:	Open profit multiple (2) of trade risk
Breakeven Stop:	Minimum open profit after minimum number of days (4)
	Number of swing points required to locate a setup pattern (4)
	Note: Each pair of swings is connected by a trend line
Variables—Symmetry:	Same value for both buy and sell setups
Variables—Application:	Same value across all markets
Rules:	6

<u>Buy Rules</u>

Setup:	Chart pattern (Triangles, rectangles and wedges)
Trend:	Up—medium-term 18-day moving average is rising while the long-term 40-day moving average is either flat or rising.
Entry:	Buy break of pattern's top trend line

Initial Stop:	Sell break of the lowest low of either the setup or entry bar
Breakeven	
Stop:	Move stop to breakeven at the first of either: 1. Open profit is greater than twice the risk. 2. Open profit exists after 4 days.
Trailing Stop:	Sell break of the closest swing low

Sell Rules

Setup:	Chart pattern (Triangles, rectangles and wedges)
Trend:	Down—medium-term 18-day moving average is falling while the long-term 40-day moving average is either flat or falling.
Entry:	Sell break of pattern's bottom trend line
Initial Stop:	Buy break of the highest high of either the setup or entry bar
Breakeven	
Stop:	Move stop to breakeven at the first of either: 1. Open profit is greater than twice the risk. 2. Open profit exists after 4 days.
Trailing Stop:	Buy break of the closest swing high

I've programmed PPS into my VBA Excel trading model, according to my interpretation of the rules, to mechanically and systematically locate and trade breakouts of congestion patterns that are aligned with the underlying trend, as illustrated in Figure 6.20.

Let's see how my interpretation of Arnold's PPS strategy has performed over my P24 portfolio since 1980?

Results

Portfolio P24:	SB, ZW, CO, SO, HO, LC, GF, BP, SV, KC, CT, ZB, GC, HG, JY, LH, SP, TY, CL, FV, NG, ND, EC, YM
Start	1980
Net Profit:	$450,780
Total Trades:	2,586
Avg Profit:	$174
Avg Brok & Slip per Trade:	−$51

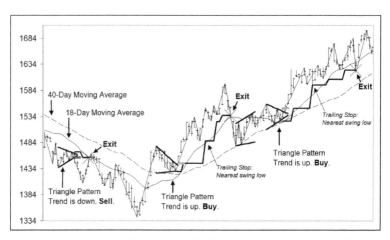

FIGURE 6.20   The PPS strategy looks to trade breakouts off traditional congestion patterns that are aligned with the trend.

Well, pretty good actually. We should also acknowledge Robert Edwards and John Magee with a hat tip for their help in popularizing congestion patterns in their seminal book *Technical Analysis of Stock Trends* (Martino Publishing, 1948). Arnold, despite his run in with the US Commodity Futures Trading Commission, has enveloped congestion patterns within a simple and logical trade plan. A trade plan whose performance, over a majority of out-of-sample data, not only demonstrates PPS's robustness but also helps validate the merits of trend trading.

Channel Breakouts

Another type of absolute momentum trend-trading methodologies are the popular channel breakout strategies. These strategies create a boundary, or channel either side of market prices. They believe a movement beyond, either to the upside or downside, constitutes the existence of a trend and must be traded.

Let's look at a few, beginning with Donchian's Four-Week Rule.

Donchian's Four-Week Rule (1960)

Donchian's Four-Week Rule methodology is the simplest strategy I know. It's a stop and reverse strategy that is always in the market, either long or short. It only has one rule, follow a four-week breakout. If the model is short and the market takes out the highest weekly high of the last four weeks, it will exit and reverse going long. If the model is long and the market takes out the lowest weekly low of the last four weeks, it will exit and reverse going short. Easy peasy.

I've summarize the rules here.

Rules

Strategy:	Donchian's Four-Week Rule
Developed:	Unknown
Published:	1960
Data:	Daily
Approach:	Trend trading
Technique:	Always in the market: a stop and reverse channel breakout
Symmetry:	Buy and sell
Markets:	All
Indicators:	None.
Variables—Number:	1
	Weekly Channel (4)
Variables—Symmetry:	Same value for both buy and sell setups
Variables—Application:	Same value across all markets
Rules:	1

Buy Rules

Setup & Entry:	Buy a break of the highest weekly high of the preceding 4 weeks
Stop:	Sell a break of the lowest weekly low of the preceding 4 weeks

Sell Rules:

Setup & Entry:	Sell a break of the lowest weekly low of the preceding 4 weeks
Stop:	Buy a break of the highest weekly high of the preceding 4 weeks

As you can see in Figure 6.21, I've programmed Donchian's Four-Week Rule strategy to stop and reverse following a four-week breakout.

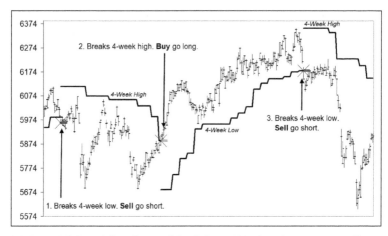

FIGURE 6.21   Richard Donchian's Four-Week Rule strategy will stop and reverse positions at a four-week breakout.

Let's see how Donchian's Four-Week Rule, first publish in 1960, has performed over my universal P24 portfolio since 1980?

Results
Portfolio P24:	SB, ZW, CO, SO, HO, LC, GF, BP, SV, KC, CT, ZB, GC, HG, JY, LH, SP, TY, CL, FV, NG, ND, EC, YM
Start:	1980
Net Profit:	$1,601,223
Total Trades:	6,120
Avg Profit:	$262
Avg Brok & Slip per Trade:	−$51

Outstanding. Definitely deserves a cartwheel celebration. I only have one word for a strategy with only one rule and one variable, which is 60+ years old with an out-of-sample performance like that. Extraordinary. And to use only a single rule to encapsulate the spirit of trend trading's three golden rules is exemplary. Take a bow Mr Richard Donchian. Actually, take two!

I personally believe this strategy is possibly one of the all-time best. Not because it makes the most, or has the best performance metrics, but because of the combination of longevity, simplicity (one rule) and performance. Outstanding with a capital 'O'.

Dreyfus's 52-Week Rule (1960)

No one knows for sure how Jack Dreyfus implemented his 52-Week Rule. So, for conservatism I'll keep it simple and similar to Donchian's Four-Week Rule. I've programmed the model according to the following rules, which, as you'll see, is similar to the Four-Week Rule, except for the number of weeks.

Rules

Strategy:	Dreyfus's 52-Week Rule
Developed:	Unknown
Published:	1960
Data:	Daily
Approach:	Trend trading
Technique:	Always in the market, a stop and reverse channel breakout
Symmetry:	Buy and sell
Markets:	All
Indicators:	None.
Variables—Number:	Weekly Channel (52)
Variables—Symmetry:	Same value for both buy and sell setups
Variables—Application:	Same value across all markets
Rules:	1

Buy Rules

Setup & Entry:	Buy a break of the highest weekly high of the preceding 52 weeks
Stop:	Sell a break of the lowest weekly low of the preceding 52 weeks

Sell Rules

Setup & Entry:	Sell a break of the lowest weekly low of the preceding 52 weeks
Stop:	Buy a break of the highest weekly high of the preceding 52 weeks

Similar to the other strategies, I've programmed Dreyfus's 52 Week Rule to systematically identify and enter trades according to its rules as shown in Figure 6.22.

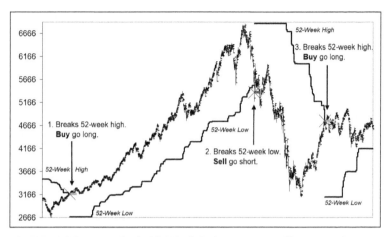

FIGURE 6.22 Dreyfus's 52-Week Rule strategy will stop and reverse positions at a 52-week breakout.

Below is Dreyfus's 52-Week Rule performance over my universal P24 portfolio since 1980.

Results
Portfolio P24:   SB, ZW, CO, SO, HO, LC, GF, BP, SV,
                            KC, CT, ZB, GC, HG, JY, LH, SP, TY,
                            CL, FV, NG, ND, EC, YM
Start: 1980

Net Profit: $1,442,906
Total Trades: 475
Avg Profit: $3,038
Avg Brok & Slip per Trade: −$51

Well how about that. Another exemplary performance from another 60+-year-old strategy. It not only displays robustness on out-of-sample data but again heralds the power of trend trading's three golden tenets. No wonder Jack Dreyfus was known as the 'Lion of Wall Street'!

Turtle Trading (1983)

The final channel breakout strategy is the Turtle Trading strategy made popular through Jack Schwager's book *Market Wizards: Interviews with Top Traders* (Simon & Schuster, 1989). The Turtle Trading strategy was developed by Richard Dennis and Bill Eckhardt. Together they taught it to a group of new traders in 1983, who became known as the 'Turtles'. Dennis and Eckhardt stood on the shoulders of Donchian, improving his Four-Week Rule by adding a few refinements. They introduced a two-week breakout stop and overlaid a filter requiring a previous losing signal to be in place before taking a trade. For a more detailed review of the strategy you can refer to Michael Covel's *The Complete Turtle Trader* (Harper Business, 2009). There are a number of variations in the model; however, for simplicity I'll restrict my review to the rules summarized here.

Rules

Strategy:	Turtle Trading
Developed:	Unknown
Published:	1983
Data:	Daily
Approach:	Trend trading
Technique:	Channel breakout
Symmetry:	Buy and sell
Markets:	All
Indicators:	None.
Variables—Number:	2
	Weekly Entry Channel (4)
	Weekly Stop Channel (2)
Variables—Symmetry:	Same value for both buy and sell setups
Variables—Application:	Same value across all markets
Rules:	3

Buy Rules

Setup:	Weekly Channel showing highest weekly high of the preceding 4 weeks
Filter:	Only trade signal if previous signal was a loss
Entry:	Buy a break of the highest weekly high of the preceding 4 weeks
Stop:	Sell a break of the lowest weekly low of the preceding 2 weeks

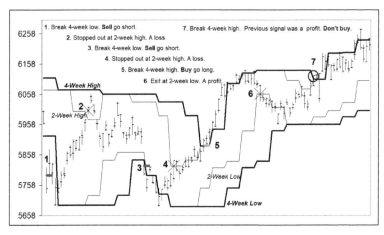

FIGURE 6.23 The Turtle Trading strategy will enter positions on a four-week breakout and exit positions on an opposite two-week breakout.

Sell Rules

Setup:	Weekly Channel showing lowest weekly low of the preceding 4 weeks
Filter:	Only trade signal if previous signal was a loss
Entry:	Sell a break of the lowest weekly low of the preceding 4 weeks
Stop:	Buy a break of the highest weekly high of the preceding 2 weeks

As shown in Figure 6.23, I've programmed the Turtle Trading strategy according to the rules above.

I've summarized the performance of Turtle Trading over my universal P24 portfolio since 1980.

Results

Portfolio P24:	SB, ZW, CO, SO, HO, LC, GF, BP, SV, KC, CT, ZB, GC, HG, JY, LH, SP, TY, CL, FV, NG, ND, EC, YM
Start:	1980
Net Profit:	$1,418,786

Total Trades:	5,212
Avg Profit:	$272
Avg Brok & Slip per Trade:	−$51

Another outstanding result. Is that applause I can hear? And well deserved it is. Turtle Trading has shown itself to be not only a solid but robust strategy. Although Dennis and Eckhardt are standing on the shoulders of Donchian, they should also be acknowledged for introducing their simple, logical and effective refinements. Refinements that improved the Four-Week Rule without falling into the trap of excessive curve fitting. Congratulations to both Richard Dennis and Bill Eckhardt.

The next absolute momentum trend-trading methodologies I'd like to share with you are the volatility breakout strategies. I'll begin with the Bollinger Band strategy.

Volatility Breakouts
Bollinger Bands (1993)

John Bollinger created his indicator in the 1980s. Bollinger Bands consist of three bands. A middle, upper and lower band. The bands contain two variables: the number of days, or length of period, and the number of standard deviations used to offset the upper and lower bands beyond the middle band. The middle band represents the moving average of the period in question while the upper and lower bands represent the standard deviation of prices away from the middle moving average value. When prices are range bound, rotating back and forth, the upper and lower standard deviation bands compress to reflect the lower volatility. When prices are directional and moving the upper and lower bands expand to reflect the higher volatility.

Band width is determined by the number of standard deviations the upper and lower bands are placed beyond the middle value.

If the upper and lower bands are drawn one standard deviation from the middle band, then one would expect prices to move within the upper and lower bands 68% of the time. Consequently, when prices close outside the bands it's a rare 32% occurrence and is possibly an indication of a new trend commencing.

If the upper and lower bands are drawn two standard deviations from the middle band then one would expect prices to move within the upper and lower bands 95% of the time. Consequently, when prices close outside the bands it's a very, very rare 5% occurrence and is possibly a strong indication of a new trend commencing.

So, the number of standard deviations used to offset the outer bands is an important variable. Certainly, the more standard deviations used the rarer the occurrence is of an outside close beyond the bands, and possibly a stronger indication of any potential trend. However, the downside is that the rarer the outside close is, the fewer trading opportunities will be presented.

Anyway, the idea is that a close outside the upper or lower bands is seen as an indication of a new trend commencing. So entries occur when a daily close occurs outside the bands while a stop is placed at an opposite close beyond the middle band.

Now, there are a number of various trading strategies that utilize Bollinger Bands. Both trend and counter-trend. Unfortunately, there isn't one standout *publicized* trend-trading Bollinger Band strategy that I can program and review and say, '*here are the out-of-sample results*'. Although Bollinger Bands have been around since the 1980s, a publicized model with clearly defined variable values does not.

However, having said that, there was a very popular and successful commercially available strategy based on Bollinger Bands that was developed in 1986 and first sold in 1993. The strategy was named as 'One of the Top 10 Trading Systems of All Time' by *Futures Truth* magazine. I never bought the strategy so I don't know what the variable values are, and even if I had, I wouldn't share them here as it would be a breach of trust. However, my point here is to let you know that even though there is no publicized strategy using Bollinger Bands I'm aware of that I can review and show out-of-sample results on, I can share with you that there was a very well-known and successful trend-trading strategy based on Bollinger Bands that was first sold in 1993.

Consequently I've used '1986' as the development date and '1993' as the 'release date', not to say my Bollinger Band strategy has been released since 1993, but to acknowledge Bollinger Bands as being the backbone of one of the most popular and successful trend-trading strategies from the 1990s.

With that being said, I'll program a trend-trading Bollinger Bands strategy using 80 days and one standard deviation. Here are the rules I'll use.

Rules

Strategy:	Bollinger Bands
Developed:	1986
Published:	1993

Data:	Daily
Approach:	Trend trading
Technique:	Volatility breakout
Symmetry:	Buy and sell
Markets:	All
Indicators:	Bollinger Bands
Variables—Number:	2
	Bollinger Bands (80)
	Standard deviation multiplier (1) used to create the upper and lower bands
Variables—Symmetry:	Same value for both buy and sell setups
Variables—Application:	Same value across all markets

Rules: 2
Buy Rules

Trend:	Up—previous close above the upper Bollinger band
Entry:	Buy next day market on open
Stop:	Previous close below the middle Bollinger band
	Sell next day market on open

Sell Rules

Trend:	Down—previous close below the lower Bollinger band
Entry:	Sell next day market on open
Stop:	Previous close above the middle Bollinger band
	Buy next day market on open

In Figure 6.24 I've programmed my Bollinger Bands strategy to mechanically and systematically identify trading opportunities according to the rules above.

Let's see how the Bollinger Band strategy has performed over my P24 portfolio.

Results

Portfolio P24:	SB, ZW, CO, SO, HO, LC, GF, BP, SV, KC, CT, ZB, GC, HG, JY, LH, SP, TY, CL, FV, NG, ND, EC, YM
Start:	1980

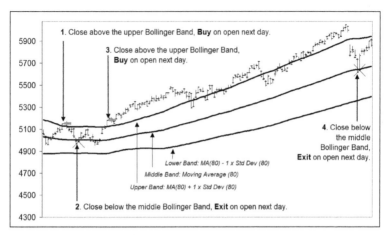

FIGURE 6.24 The Bollinger Band strategy will initiate positions following an expansion of prices beyond a one standard deviation movement, as defined by prices closing outside the upper and lower bands.

Net Profit:	$1,558,476
Total Trades:	2,954
Avg Profit:	$528
Avg Brok & Slip per Trade:	−$51

Wacko. Very good I'd say! Unfortunately, I can't say these results are out-of-sample, since I've made up the variable values. And consequently, I can't say these results demonstrate the robustness of the strategy. However, I think it's only fair to say well done to John Bollinger for developing a tool that uses the power of science to monitor and identify trend-trading opportunities. A tool used by a very popular and successful strategy that was first commercially sold in 1993. A strategy finding trading opportunities that embrace and celebrate the three golden tenets of trend trading.

ATR Bands (2020)

The other volatility breakout strategy I want to discuss is one based on ATR bands. It's identical to the Bollinger Bands strategy except that it uses the ATR, rather than the standard deviation, to measure volatility and create the upper and lower bands. Unfortunately, I can't attribute this strategy to any single trader with confidence.

Here are the rules I've programmed.

Rules

Strategy:	ATR Bands
Developed:	2020
Published:	2020
Data:	Daily
Approach:	Trend trading
Technique:	Volatility breakout
Symmetry:	Buy and sell
Markets:	All
Indicators:	Moving Average
	ATR
Variables—Number:	3
	Moving Average (80)
	ATR (80)
	ATR Multiplier (2) used to create the upper and lower bands
Variables—Symmetry:	Same value for both buy and sell setups
Variables—Application:	Same value across all markets
Rules:	2

Buy Rules

Trend:	Up—previous close above the upper ATR band
Entry:	Buy next day market on open
Stop:	Previous close below the moving average
	Sell next day market on open

Sell Rules

Trend:	Down—previous close below the lower ATR band
Entry:	Sell next day market on open
Stop:	Previous close above the moving average
	Buy next day market on open

Like the Bollinger Band breakout strategy, I've programmed the ATR breakout strategy in line with the rules above, as shown in Figure 6.25.

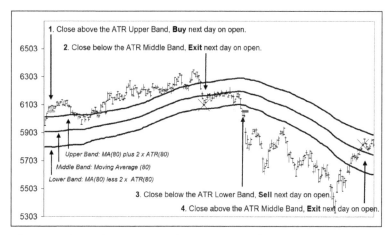

FIGURE 6.25 The ATR Bands strategy will initiate positions following an expansion of prices beyond a two average true range movement.

Let me now run the strategy over my universal P24 portfolio.

Results

Portfolio P24:	SB, ZW, CO, SO, HO, LC, GF, BP, SV, KC, CT, ZB, GC, HG, JY, LH, SP, TY, CL, FV, NG, ND, EC, YM
Start:	1980

Net Profit:	$1,193,319
Total Trades:	3,544
Avg Profit:	$337
Avg Brok & Slip per Trade:	−$51

It's also a winner. However, like the Bollinger Band strategy, these results don't demonstrate the strategy's robustness, as the figures are not out-of-sample because I made up the variable values. However, I've included it here alongside Bollinger Bands as an alternative measure of volatility.

That finishes my review of the absolute momentum 'breakout' trend-trading strategies. The other absolute momentum-type methodologies I want to look at are the 'retracement'-type strategies.

RETRACEMENT TREND TRADING

While breakout strategies will enter immediately following a breach of price, retracement strategies will patiently wait for a pause and pull back in prices before initiating a trade in the direction of the trend. Like the other strategies discussed already they also embrace the three golden tenets; however, their unique point of difference is to wait for a better price before entering.

Retracement Systems

I'll review two retracement strategies, which I hope will give you a good understanding of the approach. The first will be Dr Alexander Elder's Triple Screen Trading System (TSTS).

Elder's TSTS (1985)

Dr Alexander Elder developed his strategy in 1985 and first published it in *Futures* magazine in 1986. He later shared the strategy in his bestselling book *Trading for a Living* (Wiley, 1993). The strategy uses multiple timeframes to find trend-trading opportunities. It specifically looks for a retracement against a higher timeframe trend before entering a trade that is aligned with the trend. The main takeaway is to operate over three timeframes. For most private traders that would be weekly, daily and intra-day. The week would define the trend, the daily would define the retracement level and intra-day would define the entry level.

Trend   Elder uses the slope of the weekly MACD (moving average convergence divergence) histogram to define the trend. That is the relationship between the immediate weekly bar and the one prior. If the slope is up, the trend would be bullish and only buying opportunities would be considered. If the slope is down, the trend could be considered bearish and only selling opportunities would be considered. According to Elder, the best buy signals were the upward weekly MACD slopes that occurred below the centre line (negative numbers), while the best sell signals were the downward weekly MACD slopes that occurred above the centre line (positive numbers). On my testing I wasn't able to verify this so I didn't place any restrictions on defining the weekly trend except for the slope of the weekly MACD histogram.

Retracement   To identify an appropriate retracement against the weekly trend Elder used either his own Force Index or Elder-Ray oscillator indicators. He also mentioned traders could consider using either a Stochastic or Williams %R to identify suitable retracement levels. For this review I've used Elder's own Elder-Ray oscillator indicator.

Trade Plan   Elder enters on a break of the previous bar that satisfies both the trend and retracement condition. For buys an initial stop is placed at the lowest low of either the setup or entry bar. For sell trades an initial stop is placed at the highest high of either the setup or entry bar. The initial stop is adjusted to breakeven once an open profit appears. A 50% retracement of open profits is used as a trailing stop. Unfortunately, I found the strategy's trailing stop a little problematic. Certainly, the initial and break even stops are fine, and placing a trailing stop at the 50% retracement level of open profits appears sound and logical. However, the issue is practicality—where the strategy can keep a position open for multiple years, while the underlying market goes on a multiple year run. Some may feel that would be a strength of the strategy, to pick up unbelievable trades, and yes on a theoretical level it is, but on a practical level its nonsense. From my experience, traders find it difficult enough to hang on to a winning trade for three days let alone three weeks or three years. As a consequence, I've used the closest swing point as the trailing stop.

Here are the rules I'll use for my interpretation of Elder's TSTS.

Rules

Strategy:	TSTS
Developed:	1985
Published:	1986
Data:	Daily
Approach:	Trend trading
Technique:	Retracement
Symmetry:	Buy and sell
Markets:	All
Indicators:	MACD (12, 26, 9)
	Elder-Ray (13)
Variables—Number:	5
	MACD (3)
	Elder-Ray (1)
	Trailing Stop: Percentage (50%)
	protection of open profit

Variables—Symmetry:	Same value for both buy and sell setups
Variables—Application:	Same value across all markets
Rules:	6

Buy Rules

Trend:	Up—weekly MACD histogram bar is rising
	Last weekly histogram bar is above previous weekly histogram bar
Retracement:	Down—Elder-Ray Bear Power declines below zero & then ticks back up towards the centre line
Entry:	Buy break of the previous bar's high
Initial Stop:	Sell break of the lowest low of either the setup or entry bar
Breakeven Stop:	Move to breakeven at first open profit
Trailing Stop:	Sell break of the closest swing low

Sell Rules

Trend:	Down—weekly MACD histogram bar is falling
	Last weekly histogram bar is below previous weekly histogram bar
Retracement:	Up—Elder-Ray Bull Power rallies above zero & then ticks back down towards the centre line
Entry:	Sell a break of the previous bar's low
Initial Stop:	Buy break of the highest high of either the setup or entry bar
Breakeven Stop:	Move to breakeven at first open profit
Trailing Stop:	Buy break of closest swing high

In Figure 6.26 I've programmed TSTT to mechanically and systematically identify and trade those trend-trading opportunities that satisfy the above rules.

Just a quick note on the chart in Figure 6.26. Those familiar with MACD will detect that the representation is not how the MACD is usually shown. As I've mentioned, I do all my own programming in VBA

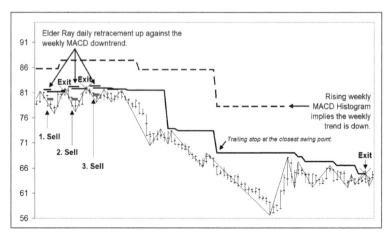

FIGURE 6.26 Elder's TSTS will wait for a retracement against a higher timeframe trend before initiating a trade.

for Excel. So, I've transposed the weekly MACD histogram into a daily representation that is shown here by the horizontal dashed line. When it appears above the daily bars it's telling me that the weekly histogram bar for the last complete week is below the previous week's histogram bar, or in other words, is falling. That is telling me, according to TSTT, that the weekly trend is down and TSTT can only look to sell after a retracement up has occurred as defined by the Elder-Ray indicator.

Here are TSTS's performance results over my universal P24 portfolio since 1980.

Results

Portfolio P24:	SB, ZW, CO, SO, HO, LC, GF, BP, SV, KC, CT, ZB, GC, HG, JY, LH, SP, TY, CL, FV, NG, ND, EC, YM
Start:	1980
Net Profit:	$336,473
Total Trades:	11,633
Avg Profit:	$29
Avg Brok & Slip per Trade:	−$51

The good news is that the majority of these results are out-of-sample and are positive. The bad news is that the average net profit is very low. However, I feel the greatest value to be derived from Elder's TSTS strategy is the important message to be in harmony with the higher timeframe trend. To know what the higher timeframe trend is and to ensure you're aligned with it.

Mean Reversion (2020)

Similar to TSTT, this strategy will wait for a retracement against the underlying trend before looking to initiate a trade in the direction of the trend. This strategy looks to take advantage of the market's tendency to revert to its mean. Markets will regularly move in one direction, suggesting further movement ahead, before inevitably reversing back. Much like the effect of stretching a rubber band, which will always snap back to its original position. The existence of 'thin peaks' demonstrates this tendency. I don't have a name for this strategy except to refer to it as mean reversion. I'll use two Bollinger Bands channels with one standard deviation. I'll use a longer length (30-day) Bollinger Band to define the trend and a shorter (15-day) Bollinger Band to define the retracement. The strategy will wait for a daily close outside the longer (30-day) Bollinger Band channel to identify the trend. It will then wait for an opposite daily close outside the shorter (15-day) Bollinger Band channel to signify that a retracement has occurred. Once a retracement has been identified, a trade will be initiated in direction of the trend at the first break of a daily bar. An initial stop will be placed at the opposite break of either the setup or entry bar, whichever is furthest away, while a trailing stop will be placed at the closest swing point. Similar to the ATR Band strategy, I can't attribute this methodology to any particular trader with confidence, so for conservatism I'll assume its existence began from the present.

Let me summarize the rules below.

<u>Rules</u>

Strategy:	Mean Reversion
Developed:	2020
Published:	2020
Data:	Daily
Approach:	Trend trading
Technique:	Retracement
Symmetry:	Buy and sell

Markets:	All
Indicators:	Bollinger Bands
Variables—Number:	3
	Length of the Bollinger Band trend channel (30)
	Length of the Bollinger Band retracement channel (15)
	Standard deviation multiplier (1) used to create the upper and lower bands
Variables—Symmetry:	Same value for both buy and sell setups
Variables—Application:	Same value across all markets
Rules:	5

Buy Rules

Trend:	Up—a previous close is above the trend upper Bollinger band
Retracement:	Down—previous close is below the retracement lower Bollinger band
Entry:	Buy first break of the previous bar's high
Initial Stop:	Sell break of the lowest low of either the setup or entry bar
Trailing Stop:	Sell break of the closest swing low

Sell Rules

Trend:	Down—a previous close is below the trend lower Bollinger band
Retracement:	Up—previous close is above the retracement upper Bollinger band
Entry:	Sell first break of the previous bar's low
Initial Stop:	Buy break of the highest high of either the setup or entry bar
Trailing Stop:	Buy break of the closest swing high

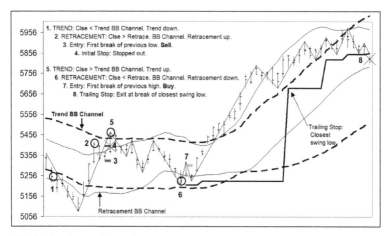

FIGURE 6.27 The mean reversion strategy will wait for a retracement against the trend before initiating a trade.

In Figure 6.27 I've programmed this mean reversion strategy to mechanically and systematically identify trading opportunities according to the rules above.

Below are the strategy's hypothetical performance results over my universal P24 portfolio since 1980.

Results

Portfolio P24:	SB, ZW, CO, SO, HO, LC, GF, BP, SV, KC, CT, ZB, GC, HG, JY, LH, SP, TY, CL, FV, NG, ND, EC, YM
Start:	1980
Net Profit:	$535,005
Total Trades:	5,163
Avg Profit:	$104
Avg Brok & Slip Per Trade:	−$51

Despite its good performance, I can't say these results demonstrate the robustness of the strategy as they're not out-of-sample. I've only just created this strategy along with the variable values. However,

I think the strategy presents a good demonstration of how a mean reversion retracement trend-trading strategy works. A strategy that finds trading opportunities that embrace and celebrate the three golden tenets of trend trading.

RETURN OF RANDOM TREND TRADER (2020)

Before I finish my review of strategies please let me circle back to my earlier scientific experiment, Random Trend Trader. It demonstrated the power of two golden tenets, 'cutting your losses short' and 'letting your profits run'. Let's see whether or not the third golden tenet, 'trade with trend', would have helped Random Trend Trader. And while we're at it, I'll add a charge for brokerage and slippage. I'll assume my experimental strategy's existence began from the present.

   To recap here are the rules, along with the new trend requirement.

Rules

Strategy:	Random Trend Trader
Developed:	2020
Published:	2020
Data:	Daily
Approach:	Trend trading
Technique:	Coin toss
Symmetry:	Buy and sell
Markets:	All
Indicators:	Moving Average
Variables – Number:	3
	Moving average (200)
	Initial stop (1%)
	Trailing weekly stop (1)
Variables—Symmetry:	Same value for both buy and sell setups
Variables—Application:	Same value across all markets
Rules:	4

Buy Rules

Setup:	Neutral daily bar
Trend:	Up—previous close is above the 200-day moving average
Entry:	If coin flip says buy, buy next day market on open
Initial Stop:	Sell a one % decline in price
Trailing Stop:	Sell break of previous weekly low

Sell Rules

Setup:	Neutral daily bar
Trend:	Down—previous close is below the 200-day moving average
Entry:	If coin flip says sell, sell next day market on open
Initial Stop:	Buy a one % rise in price
Trailing Stop:	Buy break of previous weekly high

Let's see how Random Trend Trader goes over my P24 Portfolio once a trend filter is attached.

Results

Portfolio P24:	SB, ZW, CO, SO, HO, LC, GF, BP, SV, KC, CT, ZB, GC, HG, JY, LH, SP, TY, CL, FV, NG, ND, EC, YM
Start:	1980

	No Trend	With 200dma
Profit:	−$61,957	$568,075
Trades:	31,953	15,871
Avg Profit:	−$2	$36
Avg Brok & Slip Per Trade:	−$51	−$51

Very well by the looks of it. What a difference trading with the trend makes. I think we can safely say that trading with the trend works as seen by the average loss of −$2 jumping to an average profit of $36. Not bad for a coin toss strategy. But also, not good enough to give further consideration to.

SUMMARY

Although not an exhaustive review, what I have shared here is a pretty good representation of strategies that inhibit the world of trend trading. In Table 6.2 I've summarized the strategies reviewed.

Where there is a known release date for each strategy, I have published it; however, for those strategies without one I've entered the year this book was published.

I hope my brief review has given you a good insight into how each strategy defines their trend, identifies their entry, stop and exit levels

TABLE 6.2   These strategies provide a good representation of the different approaches traders can use to trade with trend.

Model	Type	Published	Port.	Net $$	Trades	Avg $$	Brok/ Slip
Random Trend Trader	Coin toss	2020	P24	−$61,957	31,953	−$2	−$51
Hearne 1% Rule	Relative price ROC	1870	P24	−$2,056,953	59,294	−$35	−$51
Gartley's 3- and 6-Week Crossover	Relative price ROC	1935	P24	$1,079,398	3,387	$319	−$51
Donchian 5- and 20-Day Crossover	Relative price ROC	1960	P24	$520,675	13,306	$39	−$51
Golden 50- and 200-Day Crossover	Relative price ROC	2020	P24	$1,715,940	1,235	$1,389	−$51
Monthly Close Model	Relative time ROC	1933	P24	$1,003,526	4,993	$201	−$51
Quarterly Close Model	Relative time ROC	1933	P24	$611,092	1,670	$366	−$51
Ricardo Rules	Price breakout	1838	P24	$622,552	20,392	$31	−$51
Dow Theory	Swing breakout	1900	P24	$1,090,346	17,927	$61	−$51
Livermore Reaction	Congestion breakout	1940	P24	$35,136	1,279	$27	−$51
Darvas Box	Congestion breakout	1960	P24	$136,731	636	$215	−$51
Arnold PPS	Congestion breakout	1995	P24	$450,780	2,586	$174	−$51
Donchian 4-Week Rule	Channel breakout	1960	P24	$1,601,223	6,120	$262	−$51
Dreyfus 52-Week Rule	Channel breakout	1960	P24	$1,442,906	475	$3,038	−$51
Turtle Trading	Channel breakout	1983	P24	$1,418,786	5,212	$272	−$51
Bollinger Bands	Volatility breakout	1993	P24	$1,558,476	2,954	$528	−$51
ATR Bands	Volatility breakout	2020	P24	$1,193,319	3,544	$337	−$51
Elder Triple Screen Trading System	Retracement	1986	P24	$336,473	11,633	$29	−$51
Mean Reversion	Retracement	2020	P24	$535,005	5,163	$104	−$51
Random Trend Trader w200dma	Coin toss	2020	P24	$583,946	15,871	$37	−$51

and how holistically each does it according to their interpretation of the three golden tenets. As you have reviewed each strategy I hope you have made a mental note of all the individual ideas that have resonated. They may come in handy when you start to develop your own strategy.

Now that you have a better insight into what trend trading is and have a reasonable understanding of several strategies, it's time to give consideration to an approach you may like to follow. However, before we move further long the pathway towards trading a sensible and sustainable trading methodology, I want to first talk about the importance of measuring strategy performance within a risk-adjusted context.

CHAPTER

7

Measuring Risk

Before you can achieve sustainable trading you first need to survive the markets.

I'm only in the fortunate position to trade, and to continue to trade, because I have survived. And I've survived only because I've been effective at limiting my risk. I focus on managing it well. I'm a good risk manager. Not perfect. But good enough to survive the markets and be actively engaged every day so I'm present and in position to take advantage of the good opportunities when they arrive. I can only enter and adjust my orders and manage my open positions because I have first survived. Believe me. Survival comes before profit. So, my first objective in trading is to survive and I do this by ensuring I trade with a 0% ROR.

My second objective is to maximize my returns. For this I need a robust positive expectancy methodology. As I'll share later there are a number of tools that I use to help me review, develop and select worthy strategies to trade. One obvious desirable attribute of a good strategy is healthy returns. We all want profitable strategies. However, it's not a simple question of selecting the most profitable. It's not that easy. As traders we need to know the level of risk that was taken to earn the profit achieved.

In this chapter I want to discuss the importance of measuring strategy performance within the context of risk-adjusted returns rather than blindly focusing on maximum returns alone.

HOW TO MEASURE STRATEGY PERFORMANCE

A simple measure of performance would be net profit after brokerage and slippage, or a strategy's compound annual growth rate (CAGR).

As you know I highly rate the CAGR, or annualized return, as a key performance metric. However, it and net profit only provide a single dimensional view. They only describe the destination, not the journey of how profits or returns were derived. They make no mention of, or they do not address, what keeps us awake at nights, risk.

It's no good falling in love with a highly profitable strategy to only realize its day-to-day, week-to-week and month-to-month performance resembles a roller coaster. The views from up high, although spectacular, are only fleetingly attractive before they vanish amidst a gut-wrenching drop, which sees you reaching for the puke bucket. High profits aren't attractive if they're accompanied with high drawdowns. High equity swings aren't highly appealing.

A more sensible measure of performance should account for risk. You as the trader need to know whether a good performance was the result of high or low risk. Naturally, we all want good performances with low risk, the Holy Grail of performance. What we wouldn't give for a straight 45-degree 100% R-squared equity curve. I'd love two in my Christmas stocking thank you.

To avoid the mistake of pursuing a strategy based solely on its net profitability, or highest CAGR, we need to incorporate volatility into our analysis. We need to know what level of return is generated per unit of risk. We need to know how the returns came about. Were they the result of incurring excessive risk or were they the result of good strategy design? To help us we need to add a risk-adjusted performance metric to our analysis toolkit.

So how to do it?

Well there is plenty of choice within the universe of risk-adjusted measurements. While some traders will focus on volatility, system quality and drawdowns, others will investigate their strategy's Sharpe and Sortino ratios. And if you listen carefully enough, you'll also hear talk of Calmar, Mar, Treynor, Martin, Jensen and Modigliani.

Now I don't want to scare you, or overly confuse myself, by going too deep into this particular rabbit hole. So, I'll stick to the basics as I unpack this very important risk-adjusted return requirement.

RISK-ADJUSTED RETURN MEASUREMENTS

As I've alluded to, there are many risk-adjusted return measurements. The more popular ones divide a strategy's annual return by their preferred measurement of risk. Their objective is to measure a strategy's return per unit of risk.

Normalizing return by risk results in a return value per unit of risk (Figure 7.1). A strategy with a higher return value per unit of risk is superior, on a risk-adjusted basis, to another strategy with a lower return value per unit of risk.

Take the following two trading methodologies summarized in Figure 7.2.

Methodology A has a high 20% annual return with a high 40% annual risk (volatility). It's only able to make 0.5% return per unit of risk. Methodology B has a lower 10% annual return with a low 5% annual risk (volatility). It's able to make 2% return per unit of risk. On a risk-adjusted basis, methodology B is superior to methodology A. Methodology A is riskier and is less efficient at producing returns on a per-unit-of-risk basis.

$$\text{Risk Adjusted Returns} = \frac{\text{Annual Returns}}{\text{Annual Risk}}$$

FIGURE 7.1   Traders need to know a strategy's return per unit of risk to gain an insight into how returns are generated.

Risk-Adjusted Return Measurement			
	Annual Return	Annual Risk	Return Per Unit of Risk
Method A	20%	40%	0.50%
Method B	10%	5%	2.0%

FIGURE 7.2   Methodology B, on a risk-adjusted return basis, is superior to methodology A.

As I've mentioned, there are quite a few of tools that exist within the universe of risk-adjusted measurements. Two of the more popular ones are the Sharpe and Sortino ratios, while a third, less accepted one, is the Ulcer Performance Index (UPI).

These measures are almost identical. They all agree on the same numerator, using the annual excess returns generated by a strategy over a risk-free rate. And they all evaluate dispersion of the annual excess returns around a baseline. Where they differ is in the proxy they use for their risk denominator. Each of these measures normalizes returns with a denominator that represents their own proxy for risk. By doing this they each scale a strategy's performance down to a return figure per unit of risk (volatility). A strategy with a higher return per unit of risk is superior on a risk-adjusted basis.

So, the key difference is their proxy for risk.

The Sharpe ratio (Figure 7.3) uses the standard deviation of all returns, both positive and negative.

The Sortino ratio (Figure 7.4) uses the standard deviation of only the downside, or negative returns.

The Ulcer Performance Index (Figure 7.5) uses the Ulcer Index (UI), which measures a methodology's average percentage drawdown.

$$\text{Sharpe Ratio} = \frac{\text{Annual Excess Returns}}{\substack{\text{Standard Deviation} \\ \text{Annual Excess Returns}}}$$

FIGURE 7.3 The Sharpe ratio is the industry standard for risk-adjusted returns.

$$\text{Sortino Ratio} = \frac{\text{Annual Excess Returns}}{\substack{\text{Standard Deviation} \\ \text{Annual Negative Returns}}}$$

FIGURE 7.4 The Sortino ratio improves on the Sharpe ratio by only focusing on downside risk.

$$\frac{\text{Ulcer}}{\text{Perf.}} = \frac{\text{Annual Excess Returns}}{\text{Ulcer Index}}$$

FIGURE 7.5   The UPI improves on the Sortino ratio and others by focusing on the depth and breadth of downside risk (average drawdowns) as defined by the UI.

STANDARD DEVIATION—PROXY FOR RISK

Out of the three the most quoted metrics are the Sharpe and Sortino ratios. Out of those two the Sharpe ratio is the most popular. It's the industry standard. Sharpe's popularity makes its denominator, the standard deviation of returns, the most often used proxy for risk.

So, for the majority within finance the standard deviation is the accepted measurement for risk, or volatility. However, does its consensus acceptance make it the best arbiter of strategy risk?

Let's take a closer look.

STANDARD DEVIATION—CALCULATION AND INTERPRETATION

The standard deviation simply measures the dispersion of returns from its average (Figure 7.6). It's an easy calculation, particularly when you have a spreadsheet. For those curious it involves the following calculations:

1. Calculate the average.
2. Subtract each data point from the average.
3. Square the difference between the data point and average.
4. Calculate average of the squared differences.
5. Calculate square root of the average of squared differences.

If a strategy's returns follow a normal distribution (and as we know, that 'if' is questionable) then one would expect 68% of returns to fall within ±1 standard deviation from the average return. For example, if a strategy's average annual return was 10% and the dispersion of

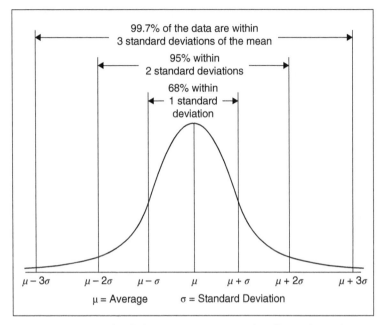

99.7% of the data are within
3 standard deviations of the mean

95% within
2 standard deviations

68% within
1 standard
deviation

$\mu - 3\sigma$ $\mu - 2\sigma$ $\mu - \sigma$ μ $\mu + \sigma$ $\mu + 2\sigma$ $\mu + 3\sigma$

μ = Average σ = Standard Deviation

FIGURE 7.6 Standard deviation measures the dispersion of returns from the average and is the industry proxy for measuring risk.

returns around the average was 30%, then one would expect in 68% of years that the strategy's annual return will fall within a range of −20% (10% − 30%) to +40% (10% + 30%).

STANDARD DEVIATION—ADVANTAGES

Using standard deviation as the proxy for risk has two advantages. Firstly, it's easy to calculate and understand. Armed with historical return data and a spreadsheet it's a straight forward calculation. Secondly, it provides traders with a predictive model they can use to estimate future annual returns. Whether they wish to use a single standard deviation (68%), two standard deviations (95%) or three standard deviations (99.7%) traders can estimate the likely range their annual returns will fall within. It provides them with a looking glass into the future.

STANDARD DEVIATION—IS IT THE BEST PROXY?

Despite its acceptance as the industry's measurement for volatility, we need to question whether it's the best risk proxy for traders. Despite the popularity of the Sharpe ratio, its use of the standard deviation of returns to measure risk has come under heavy, and deserved, criticism.

STANDARD DEVIATION—DISADVANTAGE

Although standard deviation is the industry standard for measuring risk, it suffers from one catastrophic weakness. It fails the reality test. It fails to understand the reality of market returns and it fails to understand the reality of traders. It's a flawed measure of market risk where it fails to understand how the market and participants behave and feel towards individual and sequential upside (profits) and downside (losses) risk. It simply ignores the reality of risk.

It Ignores Market Reality—Prices are not Normally Distributed

The effectiveness of standard deviation as a measure of risk depends on the assumptions of the statistical properties of market prices. Standard deviation assumes changes in market prices or returns follow a bell-shaped curve, or normal distribution. So, for standard deviation to be an accurate measure of risk we have to assume market prices follow a normal (random) distribution. Unfortunately, as we now know from Chapter 3, market prices do not follow a normal distribution (remember those high kurtosis fat tails). If that wasn't bad enough, strategy returns also don't follow a normal distribution. In particular, trend trading strategies suffer from positive skewness where they experience a higher percentage of small losses and a lower percentage of profits. In addition, they enjoy an abnormally high kurtosis, or fat tails, where they record lovely large profits. Skewness and fat tails distorts the distribution curve from what a normal 'bell-shape' curve should look like. Consequently, the distribution of strategy results is not constant through time, they do not fall symmetrically either side of an average, and half the results are not positive and the other half negative. Strategy results do not follow a normal (random) distribution.

With these realities it becomes obvious that standard deviation can't accurately measure risk. To use a risk measure that relies on results following a normal distribution when in actual fact they don't is nonsensical and bewildering as to why so many still persist with it.

And not only does standard deviation fail to recognize the reality of strategy result distributions but it also fails to reflect how traders feel about risk.

Ignores Trader Reality—not all Risk is Created Equal

Standard deviation treats all individual results equally, regardless of whether they're positive (profits) or negative (losses), and ignores their sequence of occurrence (drawdowns). This is at complete odds with how you and I treat results. Traders are not concerned with profits. It's not what keeps us awake at nights. It's the losses that bite and can cause insomnia for some. Winning trades just take off, look after themselves and don't cause us any pain. We don't worry about them. We do worry about the losses. And traders do care about the sequence of results, as a string of losses causes drawdowns and cerebral pain. Standard deviation doesn't share the same worries.

So, to cut a long story short, not all risk is created equal in our eyes, but according to standard deviation it is. Standard deviation's homogenous treatment of risk ignores the realty that:

1. Traders desire upside risk (profits) while abhorring downside risk (losses).
2. Traders care deeply about the sequence of negative returns because drawdowns hurt.

Let's take a closer look.

Penalizes Profits

Risk is defined as volatility in returns, both positive and negative. The standard deviation does a perfect job of capturing all dispersions. However, traders are generally not worried about upside profit volatility. They are more worried about the downside loss volatility. Traders are only concerned about avoiding downside risk (or the potential for losses). Upside return volatility, aka profits, is what we traders want!

So, standard deviation does not discern between upside (good profits) and downside (bad losses) volatility. It focuses solely on volatility but not its direction.

The consequence of this is that using standard deviation as the proxy for risk penalizes strategies that generate upside volatility (big positive results) even if their drawdowns are small.

For example, a positive-skewed trend-following strategy with a large dispersion of results, which involve many small losses with irregular large profits, will have a larger standard deviation calculation and hence smaller risk-adjusted return. The strategy is penalized because of its success. Madness.

On the other side a negative-skewed mean-reversion strategy with a small dispersion of results, which involve many small gains with irregular large losses, will have a smaller standard deviation calculation and hence higher risk-adjusted return. The strategy is rewarded despite the inherent risk of incurring irregularly large losses. It's a mad, mad world.

So, even though measures using standard deviation as their proxy for risk suggest they are calculating a 'risk-adjusted' return they in actual fact are not. They aren't 'adjusting' returns correctly for the 'actual' risk that matters to traders.

Given that most trading strategy's result distributions display positive skewness and fat tails, any risk-adjusted return measure that uses standard deviation, like the popular Sharpe and Sortino ratios, cannot be relied on to accurately measure risk-adjusted performance. So unfortunately, it's out the door for those types of measurements.

I'll say it again. Standard deviation ignores a trader's reality. Traders care deeply about capturing upside profitability while avoiding downside losses.

Ignores Drawdowns

The other major practical consideration standard deviation ignores is the sequence of results and their resultant drawdowns. While standard deviation ignores them, traders don't. We are particularly sensitive to drawdowns. Although we know they are as inevitable as the sun rising each day, it's our preference to trade strategies that have historically had manageable drawdowns. It's the major risk we face, trading through a huge accumulative loss, so it is in our interest that we use a risk measure that takes into account drawdowns.

Unfortunately, the standard deviation calculation is not affected by the sequence in which profits and losses occur. Consequently, it does not recognize strings of losses and their resultant drawdowns. As a result, it cannot distinguish drawdown riskiness between strategies. For example, take the three strategies summarized in Figure 7.7. All three strategies produce the same net profit, while suffering three completely different drawdowns. Despite their different drawdowns, standard deviation sees them as all having the same risk.

Figure 7.8 illustrates the three very different equity curves across the three strategies.

What is surprising is that despite three very different looking equity curves and drawdowns, all three strategies produced the same standard deviation of 7.8%. The madness continues. Despite the math saying their risks are equal, no traders, certainly not you or I, would ever consider the strategies having the same risk.

Strategy C endured a horrible, life extinguishing drawdown.

Strategy B suffered a state of perpetual drawdown for almost 20 years.

Strategy A behaved well, producing minor and easily recoverable drawdowns as it steadily grew its equity curve.

These three strategies, despite producing the same net profit, have three clearly distinct and different maximum drawdowns and risk profiles. Traders, if given the choice, would prefer strategy A over B and C as it appears to have the lowest volatility. Yet, according to standard deviation, they all have the same risk. Madness.

This is a major flaw of standard deviation as a proxy for risk.

While the sequence of returns and the resultant drawdowns have a huge impact on you and I as traders, it has no impact on standard deviation. It does nothing to distinguish between strategies based on

Standard Deviation Cannot Distinguish Riskiness Between Strategies			
	Strategy A	Strategy B	Strategy C
Net Profit	$124,400	$124,400	$124,400
Maximum Drawdown	−$32,500	−$56,700	−$432,225
Standard Deviation	7.8%	7.8%	7.8%

FIGURE 7.7 Standard deviation cannot distinguish riskiness between strategies.

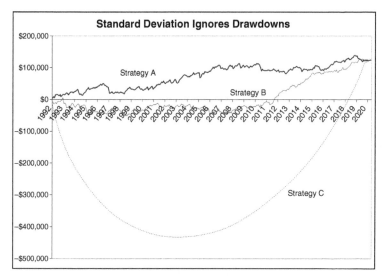

FIGURE 7.8   Despite three very different looking equity curves, all three strategies have the same standard deviation.

'real' traders' risk. The risk of downside volatility (losses), both the individual and sequential and their resulting drawdowns. It's extraordinary and nonsensical that the standard deviation continues to be the industry proxy for risk.

Let me say it one more time. Standard deviation ignores a trader's reality. Traders care deeply about downside losses, their sequence and the resultant drawdowns.

Can't Identify Low Drawdown Strategies

Another drawback of ignoring drawdowns is that standard deviation can't help you and I in identifying strategies that manage to avoid deep drawdowns, a very desirable attribute that traders value. Its blindness to sequences and drawdowns cuts both ways, not correctly measuring a strategy's real risk-adjusted return and not helping traders identify low drawdown strategies.

Fails Everyone—the Market and the Trader

Well you'd think two strikes and standard deviation would be out. But due to incumbency it remains the industry standard for measuring

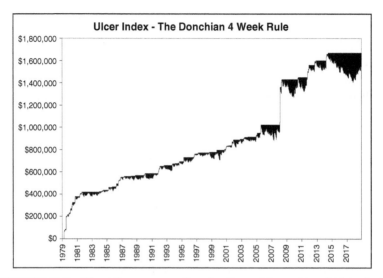

FIGURE 7.9   The UI measures the depth and breadth of historical drawdowns as represented by the dark regions.

risk. However, as traders we don't need to follow the herd this time. There is another more appropriate measure of risk, one that reflects the reality of trading, focusing on and measuring the relative pain of downside volatility, its sequence and resultant drawdowns. It's appropriately called the UI.

The UI, as you'll see, is a superior measurement of risk.

THE ULCER INDEX—A SUPERIOR RISK PROXY

The Ulcer Index (UI) was developed by Peter Martin in 1987 and first published in his book, co-authored with Byron McCann, *The Investor's Guide to Fidelity Funds* (Wiley, 1989). As its name appropriately implies, the UI measures and identifies the average drawdown traders can expect to stomach if they trade a particular strategy. As you'll see, the UI reflects the reality of trading, measuring the depth and breadth of negative downside volatility, making it the superior proxy for 'real' risk. The UI can be calculated on any investment that fluctuates in value, whether it's an individual security, index, fund or trading strategy.

THE ULCER PERFORMANCE INDEX—A SUPERIOR RISK-ADJUSTED RETURN MEASUREMENT

Due to the flaws of standard deviation as a proxy for risk and the resultant complications in the risk-adjusted measurements that use it, like the Sharpe and Sortino ratios, Peter Martin developed his own risk-adjusted return measurement. He called it the Ulcer Performance Index (UPI). Unlike the Sharpe and Sortino ratios, where the annual excess returns are divided by the standard deviation, Martin instead normalizes the annual excess returns by his UI. His UPI, or Martin Ratio as some prefer to call it, is a far more accurate risk-adjusted return measurement as it recognizes and focuses on real individual and sequential (drawdown) downside risk. The objective is to find, develop or trade strategies with the highest UPI, which means the highest risk-adjusted return per unit of average drawdown risk.

Let's begin by taking a look at how the UI is calculated.

THE UI—CALCULATION

The UI measures the depth and breadth of percentage drawdowns from equity highs. The greater the number of drawdowns and their time taken to recover to new equity highs, the greater the UI is, or the greater the average drawdown is. Ideally, we want to trade strategies that have lower average drawdowns, or have a lower UI (and hence higher UPI), as it suggests future drawdowns should also be lower. Lower drawdowns mean less worry and less aggravation for our stomachs.

The UI is calculated according to the formula in Figure 7.10.

The UI represents the square root of the mean of the squared percentage drawdowns.

The UI can be calculated for any period (day, week, monthly, quarterly or yearly) although for longer periods, like the quarterly and yearly, it may fail to measure some drawdowns if they occur inter-period.

The UI requires the following calculations:

1. Select your preferred period (day, week, month, quarterly or yearly).
2. Calculate the period drawdown from the period equity high.

$$\begin{array}{c}\text{Percentage} \\ \text{Drawdown} \\ \text{Per Period} \\ \text{(DPP)}\end{array} = \dfrac{\begin{array}{c}\text{Current Period} \\ \text{Equity Value}\end{array} - \begin{array}{c}\text{Current Period} \\ \text{Equity High}\end{array}}{\begin{array}{c}\text{Current Period} \\ \text{Equity High}\end{array}} \times 100$$

$$\begin{array}{c}\text{Ulcer} \\ \text{Index}\end{array} = \sqrt{\dfrac{DPP_1{}^\wedge 2 + DPP_2{}^\wedge 2 + \ldots DPP_N{}^\wedge 2}{N}}$$

FIGURE 7.10 The UI measures a strategy's average percentage drawdown.

$$\begin{array}{c}\text{Ulcer} \\ \text{Perf.} \\ \text{Index}\end{array} = \dfrac{\text{Annual Excess Returns}}{\text{Ulcer Index}}$$

FIGURE 7.11 The UPI measures the amount of excess returns per unit of average drawdown risk (the UI).

3. Convert the period drawdown to a percentage and multiple it by 100.
4. Square the period percentage drawdown.

(Note: The squaring penalizes larger drawdowns proportionally more than smaller drawdowns.)

5. Sum up all the squared percentage drawdowns.
6. Calculate the average squared percentage drawdowns.
7. Calculate the square root of the average squared percentage drawdowns.
8. The square root becomes the UI.

Table 7.1 illustrates how to calculate the UI for the SP 500. It shows that between 1992 and 2019 the SP 500's average percentage yearly drawdown was 14.5%.

Note that when calculating the UI for a trading strategy it's important when measuring historical drawdowns to reset the equity curve to zero at the start of each year. Or, in other words, commence each year with just your starting account balance. If you don't, then using the accumulative equity curve penalizes earlier drawdowns, when there

TABLE 7.1 Armed with a spreadsheet it's straight forward to calculate the UI.

			Calculating Ulcer Index for SP500 1992–2019				Ulcer Index
Year	Close	Max Close	Percentage Drawdown	Percentage Drawdown Squared	Sum Percentage Drawdown Squared	Average Sum Percentage Drawdown Squared	Square Root Average Sum Percentage Drawdown Squared
1 1992	435.70	435.7	0.00%	0.00%			
2 1993	466.40	466.4	0.00%	0.00%			
3 1994	459.30	466.4	−1.52%	0.02%			
4 1995	615.90	615.9	0.00%	0.00%			
5 1996	740.70	740.7	0.00%	0.00%			
6 1997	970.40	970.4	0.00%	0.00%			
7 1998	1229.20	1,229.2	0.00%	0.00%			
8 1999	1469.20	1,469.2	0.00%	0.00%			
9 2000	1320.30	1,469.2	−10.13%	1.03%			
10 2001	1148.10	1,469.2	−21.86%	4.78%			
11 2002	879.80	1,469.2	−40.12%	16.09%			
12 2003	1111.90	1,469.2	−24.32%	5.91%			
13 2004	1211.90	1,469.2	−17.51%	3.07%			
14 2005	1248.30	1,469.2	−15.04%	2.26%			
15 2006	1418.30	1,469.2	−3.46%	0.12%			

TABLE 7.1 continued

Calculating Ulcer Index for SP500 1992–2019

	Year	Close	Max Close	Percentage Drawdown	Percentage Drawdown Squared	Sum Percentage Drawdown Squared	Average Sum Percentage Drawdown Squared	Ulcer Index — Square Root Average Sum Percentage Drawdown Squared
16	2007	1468.40	1,469.2	−0.05%	0.00%			
17	2008	903.20	1,469.2	−38.52%	14.84%			
18	2009	1115.10	1,469.2	−24.10%	5.81%			
19	2010	1257.60	1,469.2	−14.40%	2.07%			
20	2011	1257.60	1,469.2	−14.40%	2.07%			
21	2012	1426.20	1,469.2	−2.93%	0.09%			
22	2013	1848.40	1,848.4	0.00%	0.00%			
23	2014	2058.90	2,058.9	0.00%	0.00%			
24	2015	2043.90	2,058.9	−0.73%	0.01%			
25	2016	2238.80	2,238.8	0.00%	0.00%			
26	2017	2673.60	2,673.6	0.00%	0.00%			
27	2018	2506.80	2,673.6	−6.24%	0.39%			
28	2019	2986.20	2,986.2	0.00%	0.00%	58.6%	2.09%	14.5%

249

is less accumulative profit built up, while favouring later drawdowns, when there is plenty of accumulative profit in the bank. It's best to reset the equity curve at the start of each year.

The UI—Interpretation

The UI measures the depth and breadth of percentage drawdowns from equity highs (Table 7.2). It shows a strategy's average historical percentage drawdown. A strategy with a higher percentage UI suggests higher drawdowns ahead. A strategy with a lower percentage UI suggests lower drawdowns ahead. The idea is to prefer strategies with a low UI.

So, a perfect theoretical strategy, such as the Holy Grail that never loses money, would have a UI value of 0%. A nasty theoretical strategy, such as the Perpetual Drawdown (DD) strategy that always loses money, would have an UI value of +100%.

Basically, the higher the UI, the more painful the historical average drawdown has been.

The UI is ideal for comparing the relative pain of competing shares, indices, funds, markets and trading strategies. For example,

TABLE 7.2   The UI measures the average percentage drawdown.

Ulcer Index	
The Average Percentage Drawdown	
Yearly Performance: 1992–2019	
Strategy: Holy Grail	0%
10 Year Treasury Notes	6%
SP500	15%
SPI200	15%
Gold	18%
Ftse100	21%
Hang Seng	22%
Dax	23%
Copper	27%
Crude Oil	29%
Nikkei225	31%
Shanghai SSE	36%
Strategy: Perpetual DD	100%

according to the UI, the SP500 between 1992 and 2019 has been one of the less painful share markets to invest in, the Shanghai Stock Exchange one of the most painful to possess while ten-year treasury notes have lived up to their risk-free status as being the least painful market to own.

The UI—Advantages

The UI has many advantages.

Focuses on Practical Risk that Matters to Traders

The UI overcomes the main criticism of standard deviation, as it distinguishes between good (upside profits) and bad (downside loss) risk. By focusing only on downside losses, their sequences and resultant drawdowns, the UI gives the best indication of real historical risk. It gives the best indication of how it's going to feel, real world, when trading a particular strategy.

Measures 100% of Negative Returns

By measuring from equity highs rather than an average like the standard deviation, the UI is able to include every negative drop in performance that occurred over the period in question. It measures complete downside risk.

Captures More Than Maximum Drawdown

The UI, by measuring the depth and breadth of all drawdowns, regardless of the degree, contains much more information than the maximum drawdown alone. By focusing on the complete depth and breadth of all drawdowns the UI is able to capture much of a strategy's nonlinearities.

Helps to Identify Low Drawdown Strategies

Unlike the standard deviation the UI is able to identify low downside volatility strategies that are good at avoiding excessive drawdowns. This is terribly important due to the asymmetrical nature of losses and drawdowns. Remember as I discussed in *UPST* a 50% loss requires a 100% gain to recover. Avoiding deep drawdowns is as good as enjoying a rising equity curve.

Consistent across all Periods

The UI is a robust measurement that is consistent across periods. Take the UI calculations in Table 7.3 for the SP500 between 1992 and 2019.

The UI—Disadvantages

The major criticism aimed at the UI, and a major argument supporting standard deviation, is that the UI is backward looking and has no predictive powers. Measuring the average historical drawdown only tells us what has happened in the past. No more. Whereas supporters of standard deviation will point to their predictive statistical model and tell us knowledge of a strategy's standard deviation can tell the trader the likely range of where their strategy's future annual returns will land. Without circling back to all the flaws of standard deviation, one only has to point out the singularly most important flaw in their standard deviation 'predictive' argument. Market prices and strategy results, due to skewness and kurtosis (fat tails), *do not* follow a normal distribution. And even if market returns did, a working normal distribution would not give any indication of the likely sequence of future negative results and resultant drawdowns. So, traders cannot rely on the statistical properties of normal distributions to gain any insight into real risk that matters to traders—possible future drawdowns.

So, neither approach to measuring risk has any predictive powers that traders can rely on. But at least the UI does give an insight into real downside risk that matters most to traders—historical drawdowns.

TABLE 7.3   UI is consistent across all periods.

Ulcer Index	
SP500	
1992–2019	
Weekly	17.3%
Monthly	16.9%
Quarterly	16.4%
Yearly	14.5%

UPI—A SUPERIOR RISK-ADJUSTED RETURN MEASUREMENT

Just as standard deviation is a poor proxy for risk, so are the risk-adjusted return measures that use it, like the industry standard Sharpe ratio and the popular Sortino ratio. By using the standard deviation as their risk proxy, they also fall victim to the same criticisms directed towards standard deviation.

As already discussed, to overcome the standard deviation problem Martin created his own risk-adjusted return measurement and called it the UPI.

UPI—CALCULATION

By dividing excess returns over a risk-free rate by his UI Martin has created a far more accurate measurement of 'real' risk-adjusted returns. By measuring a strategy's return per unit of average drawdown risk it focuses on what matters to traders. What has been the unit of reward for per unit of average drawdown pain?

UPI—AN EXAMPLE

Let's circle back to the three strategies. Despite three very different looking equity curves and drawdowns, they appeared identical according to their net profit and standard deviation. Let's see how Martin's UPI measures up against the popular risk-adjusted measures such as the Sharpe and Sortino ratios.

As a recap, the Sharpe ratio divides the annual excess return over a risk-free rate by the standard deviation of all annual excess returns. Sharpe does not distinguish between downside or upside risk, treating all volatility the same. The Sortino ratio is identical to the Sharpe ratio except they use the standard deviation of the annual downside volatility as their proxy for risk. It does not penalize upside volatility.

Table 7.4 calculates the UPI for five strategies.

For the risk-free rate I have used the ten-year treasury note yield.

Beside the three original strategies I've included two additional methodologies, Retracement Trend Trader (RTT; from Chapter 5) and Richard Donchian's Four-Week Rule (from Chapter 6). These methodologies represent five very different strategies, with varying

TABLE 7.4 The UPI measures the amount of excess return per unit of average drawdown risk.

| | The Ulcer Performance Index | | | | |
| | A Superior Risk-Adjusted Return Measurement | | | | |
	Strategy A	Strategy B	Strategy C	Retracement Trend Trader	Donchian 4-Week Rule
Net Profit	$124,400	$124,400	$124,400	$222,744	$1,554,739
Maximum Drawdown	–$32,500	–$56,700	–$432,225	–$69,905	–$261,907
Standard Deviation	7.8%	7.8%	7.8%	43.8%	159.6%
Popular Risk Metrics					
Sharpe Ratio	0.2	0.2	0.1	0.2	0.4
Sortino Ratio	0.3	0.4	0.1	0.4	1.2
Alternative Risk Metric					
Ulcer Index (Avg % DD)	19.50%	19.70%	49.3%	22.7%	50.0%
Ulcer Performance Index	**0.2**	**0.2**	**0.1**	**0.3**	**1.4**

254

profitability, with five very diverse equity curves and historical risk profiles. They couldn't be more different.

Examining Table 7.4 shows us that all three measures rightfully acknowledge RTT and the Four-Week Rule as being superior to strategies A, B and C on a risk-adjusted basis, with the Four-Week Rule being the best.

Let's look at each metric individually.

According to the Sharpe ratio, there is very little difference between the strategies, with all five recording low values between 0.1 and 0.4. According to Sharpe, they're all poor, while Donchian's Four-Week Rule is little better, on a risk-adjusted basis, than strategy C with its life-extinguishing deep drawdown. Let me tell you, that is nonsense from a trader's perspective. The Four-Week Rule only has a low Sharpe ratio because of its wonderful upside profitability—volatility that traders want—yet it's being punished for it. It's total nonsense with a capital 'N'. If we were solely relying on the Sharpe ratio as our guide not one of the five strategies, including the Four-Week Rule, would receive any further attention from us.

The Sortino ratio sees more distinction, and is an improvement on Sharpe, as it only focuses on downside risk, recording values from 0.1 to 1.2. It gives more granularity and records a bigger distinction between Donchian's Four-Week Rule and the other strategies. It would encourage us to give further investigation to the Four-Week Rule. So, well done Sortino.

The UPI, on a risk-adjusted drawdown basis, records the largest distinction between the strategies. It rightfully sees the Four-Week Rule strategy as the standout methodology among the five, producing 1.4 units of excess return for every unit of average percentage drawdown. Despite its large historical average drawdown, the Four-Week Rule strategy rewards the trader with proportionally more return per unit of drawdown risk suffered. In addition, the UPI correctly views the other four strategies as poor on a risk-adjusted basis. In my opinion, the UPI is by far the superior risk-adjusted return measurement. Peter Martin, take a bow.

Let's review the trend-trading strategies I discussed in Chapter 6. Apart from the losing Hearne 1% Rule strategy, I've summarized and ranked the methodologies in Table 7.5. I first rank them according to their straight profitability, with no consideration given to the risk incurred, and then by their risk-adjusted performance according to the UPI.

TABLE 7.5 The UPI offers a superior risk-adjusted return measurement.

	Alternative Performance Measures				
Rank	Model's Ranked by Profitability	Net Profit	Rank	Model's Ranked by Risk-adjusted Performance	UPI
1	Golden 50- and 200-Day Crossover	$1,715,940	1	Turtle Trading	2.2
2	Donchian 4-Week Rule	$1,601,223	2	Bollinger Bands	1.7
3	Bollinger Bands	$1,558,476	3	Golden 50- and 200-Day Crossover	1.5
4	Dreyfus 52-Week Rule	$1,442,906	4	Donchian 4-Week Rule	1.4
5	Turtle Trading	$1,418,786	5	Dow Theory	1.4
6	ATR Bands	$1,193,319	6	Dreyfus 52-Week Rule	1.3
7	Dow Theory	$1,090,346	7	ATR Bands	1.1
8	Gartley's 3- and 6-Week Crossover	$1,079,398	8	Gartley's 3- and 6-Week Crossover	1.1
9	Monthly Close Model	$1,003,526	9	Monthly Close Model	0.8
10	Ricardo Rules	$622,552	10	Arnold PPS	0.7
11	Quarterly Close Model	$611,092	11	Mean Reversion	0.6
12	Random Trend Trader w200dma	$583,946	12	Ricardo Rules	0.5
13	Mean Reversion	$535,005	13	Quarterly Close Model	0.4
14	Donchian 5- and 20-Day Crossover	$520,675	14	Random Trend Trader w200dma	0.4
15	Arnold PPS	$450,780	15	Donchian 5- and 20-Day Crossover	0.4
16	Elder Triple Screen Trading System	$336,473	16	Elder Triple Screen Trading System	0.3
17	Darvas Box	$136,731	17	Darvas Box	0.1
18	Livermore Reaction	$35,136	18	Livermore Reaction	0.1

As you can see, the UPI offers a different ranking to profitability. Although the Golden 50- and 200-day crossover strategy was the most profitable, it only ranked third when it was measured on a risk-adjusted basis. Turtle Trading managed to move from fifth position on the profitability table to number one on a risk-adjusted basis, earning 2.2 units of excess returns for every unit of average drawdown risk. Turtle Trading, Bollinger Bands, Golden 50- and 200-day crossover, Four-Week Rule and Dow Theory were the most efficient at earning excess returns given the level of average drawdown risk incurred. According to the UPI they are the superior risk-adjusted performing trend-trading methodologies. On the UPI criterion alone, traders would prefer Turtle Trading over the others.

NOT ALL STRATEGIES ARE CREATED EQUAL

Naturally, the higher the UPI is, the more superior a strategy is on a risk-adjusted basis. Although higher vs lower is better, it's not always possible to develop or select a good strategy with a high UPI. The metric needs to be seen as a relative measurement.

This is because not all strategies are created equal.

Some strategies, like the ones discussed in this book, are trend trading, while others are counter-trend. Within the trend-trading universe there are relative and absolute momentum trend-trading methodologies. Within the absolute there are breakout and retracement strategies. Within the former there are numerous techniques including price, swing, congestion, channel and volatility breakout strategies.

Each strategy 'type' attempts to capture a particular part of market structure.

Trend trading attempts to capture long sustainable movements. Some trend-trading techniques will enter following a break of an absolute level, whether it's measured by price or volatility. Some will wait for a retracement before entering. Counter-trend strategies will attempt to capture trend terminations, whether they're temporary or permanent. Trends can terminate due to a loss of momentum, exhaustion or extreme sentiment.

So not all strategies are the same and accordingly they should not have their UPI values compared to each other. It's important to compare apples with apples (Figure 7.12).

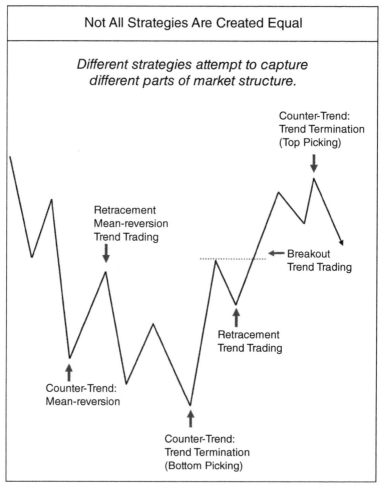

FIGURE 7.12 When comparing UPI values it's important you are comparing similar strategies types to each other.

I personally trade strategies with UPI values ranging between 2.8 to less than 1. Less than 1 may not sound significant; however, for those strategies they are the best I have for the particular part of market structure I'm attempting to capture. On an apples-vs-apples basis they are my best.

As a rule of thumb, an UPI over 2 is very good. A value less than 0.5 is low. However, the important point is to ensure you compare like with like. And the real magic occurs when you bundle up your uncorrelated but complimentary strategies—where you will enjoy risk-adjusted UPI values of over 3 as the combined strategies start smoothing out your equity curve and dampening average historical drawdown risk.

SUMMARY

Although the UPI is a superior risk-adjusted return measurement, it is not a silver bullet for identifying or selecting the best trading strategy. As I'll discuss later, there is no single magic metric that can be relied upon to select the best strategy. In my opinion, and as I'll later show, strategy review and selection require a mixture of robustness and performance analysis. I tend to lend more weight to the former, and how much weight depends more on experience, or art, then science. However, for a single risk-adjusted return measurement, Martin's UPI is an improvement on the popular Sharpe and Sortino ratios.

Now that you're forearmed about the importance of measuring strategy performance within the context of 'real' drawdown risk, it's almost time to move you forward towards developing a sensible trading solution. But before I do, I want to arm you with a suitable trader's toolkit that will help you in the nuts and bolts of strategy review, development and selection.

CHAPTER 8

Moving Forward

At this point you will now have a good understanding of the appeal of trend trading: Why trends exist. How trend trading works. Why so many fail at it. And the importance of measuring strategy performance within the context of traders' real drawdown risk. Hopefully I've done enough to encourage you to seriously consider it as a preferred approach to trading.

At this point, given the strategies I've reviewed, you may have developed some preferences for different trend, entry, stop and exit techniques. Your next step is to develop those preferences into a tangible and sensible strategy. And it's fine if you haven't developed any preferences yet, as I hope to offer some suggestions. But first I need to arm you with a suitable toolkit that will assist you in reviewing, developing and selecting a sensible trading solution.

THE TOOLKIT

A proper toolkit will hopefully delivery you safely to a sensible and sustainable trading destination and includes:

- portfolio construction,
- data,
- software,
- attributes of winning strategies,
- strategy review,
- strategy benchmark and
- strategy development.

PORTFOLIO CONSTRUCTION

Every trader's twin evils when developing strategies are excessive curve fitting and data mining (and haven't I said that ad infinitum). Curve fitting will always be present, while data mining can be eliminated. Data mining can be avoided by objectively selecting a universal portfolio of markets that are well diversified and have minimal correlation. As you know from Chapter 6, I use a universal portfolio of 24 diverse markets spread across eight market segments including:

- currencies,
- interest rates,
- indices,
- energy,
- metals,
- grains,
- softs and
- meats.

Within each market segment I select the three most liquid futures contracts based on their average daily volume. Please refer to Figure 8.1.

Using diversification and volume as the selection criteria provides me with an objectively and independently selected portfolio of diversified markets. A portfolio of markets that is absent of any data mining or cherry picking. I'd encourage you to do the same. For your research you should create a comprehensive portfolio like mine, which will ensure your strategy results will be absent of any data mining. For your actual trading select a progressive portfolio, adding markets according to diversity and liquidity, like the mini portfolios P2, P4, P8 and P16. The portfolio you create should be appropriate given your level of risk capital and risk appetite (drawdown).

If you trade shares you should follow the same process and create a portfolio of shares based on diversification and volume. Select the top one, two, three or more most actively traded shares by average daily volume across different market segments, such as:

- consumer discretionary,
- consumer staples,
- energy,
- financials,

Portfolio Construction

To Avoid "Data Mining" let Diversification and Liquidity Select Your Portfolio

The Most Liquid US Futures Contracts By Market Segment
Selected by diversity and liquidity

Market Sector/Segment	Futures Contract	Exchange	Avg Daily Volume*	Portfolio P2 Most Liquid	Portfolio P4 Most Liquid	Portfolio P8 Most Liquid	Portfolio P16 2 Most Liquid	Portfolio P24 3 Most Liquid
Financials Currencies	Euro Currency	CME	188,888			EC		EC
	Japanese Yen	CME	138,000				JY	JY
	British Pound	CME	89,000					BP
Interest Rates	10Yr T.Note	CME	1,249,000			10Yr T.Note	10Yr T.Note	10 Yr T.Note
	5Yr T.Note	CME	708,000				5Yr T.Note	5Yr T.Note
	30Yr T.Bond	CME	339,000					30Yr T.Bond
Indices	E-Mini S&P	CME	1,490,000	E-Mini S&P	E-Mini S&P	E-Mini S&P	E-Mini S&P	E-Mini S&P
	E-Mini Nasdaq	CME	255,000				E-Mini Nasdaq	E-Mini Nasdaq
	E-Mini Dow	CME	148,000					E-Mini Dow
Energy Energy	Crude Oil (WTI)	CME	253,000	Crude Oil	Crude Oil	Crude Oil	Crude Oil	Crude Oil
	Natural Gas (H.Hub)	CME	115,000				Natural Gas	Natural Gas
	ULSD (Heating Oil)	CME	51,000					ULSD
Metals Metals	Gold	CME	137,000		Gold	Gold	Gold	Gold
	Copper	CME	45,000				Copper	Copper
	Silver	CME	44,000					Silver
Food Grains	Corn	CME	129,000		Corn	Corn	Corn	Corn
	Soybean	CME	104,000				Soybean	Soybean
	Wheat (SRW)	CME	55,000					Wheat
Softs	Sugar	ICE	58,000			Sugar	Sugar	Sugar
	Coffee	ICE	15,000				Coffee	Coffee
	Cotton	ICE	14,000					Cotton
Meat	Live Cattle	CME	23,000			Live Cattle	Live Cattle	Live Cattle
	Lean Hog	CME	18,000				Lean Hog	Lean Hog
	Feeder Cattle	CME	3,000					Feeder Cattle

* Volume Source: Premium Data from Norgate Investor Services
http://www.norgatedata.com

FIGURE 8.1   Creating portfolios based on independent and objective criterion such as diversity and liquidity avoids data mining. Source: Premium data from Norgate Investor Services. https://www.norgatedata.com

- health care,
- industrials,
- information technology,
- materials,
- metals/mining,
- telecommunications services,
- utilities and
- real estate.

For your actual trading you will then need to select a group of markets from your research portfolio, based on diversity and liquidity, that is appropriate given your level of risk capital and risk appetite (drawdown).

DATA

To gather evidence, you'll need reliable data. Although I trade a diversified and complementary portfolio of multiple timeframe strategies over a portfolio of diversified and liquid markets, I begin with daily data. From the daily data I'll create the higher timeframe periods; weekly, monthly, quarterly and yearly.

There are plenty of data sources. I've been using Norgate Data for over 15 years and have never had a problem with their futures and share (Australian and US) data. The majority of their futures data begins from contract commencement and I use the following format and sessions:

Data:	Futures data
Period:	Start 1980
Source:	https://norgatedata.com/
Format:	Back-adjusted continuous future contract data
Sessions:	Combined all-sessions data

SOFTWARE

One of my key messages from Chapter 3 was to develop your verification skills. Unfortunately, developing coding skills will be the only way you'll be able to independently verify and validate trading ideas. There are no shortcuts. Yes, you could rely on others—however, you'll always be limited by their knowledge, skills, level of proficiency and availability.

I'm reluctant to write too much about software as I really have no current experience in third-party trading/charting packages. I've been using VBA (Visual Basic Application) for Excel for over 20 years. All the charts and performance metrics in this book are courtesy of my VBA Excel trading model. I can certainly sing the praises of VBA for Excel, no worries at all. But I can't really comment on commercial packages.

As I mentioned in Chapter 3, students of mine use the following packages:

- AmiBroker,
- Channalyze,
- MultiCharts,
- Trade Navigator,
- Tradeguider,

- TradeStation and
- Trading Blox.

The more popular packages being used among my students are:

- TradeStation,
- MultiCharts,
- AmiBroker and
- Trading Blox.

Those of my students who have elected to code my strategies straight from programming languages use:

- Visual Basic,
- Python,
- Java and
- Ruby.

This is obviously not an exhaustive list. Google will probably be of more help than me. My only advice is to get skilled up so you can independently gather evidence and verify trading ideas.

ATTRIBUTES OF WINNING STRATEGIES

Next, you need to be aware of the attributes of winning strategies. I've mentioned these before. If you wish to either review an existing methodology or develop your own, you'll need to know what to look out for. I've summarized the attributes in Figure 8.2.

Winning strategies have two chief attributes:

- Measurability and
- Robustness.

Measurability

To measure your methodology (whether it's an old or new idea) the strategy requires clear and objective rules. No subjective opinion can be allowed. There have to be black and white rules for when to trade, where to enter, where to place stops and how to exit. If you wish to trade a traditional chart pattern like the head and shoulder formation

Attributes of Winning Strategies				
Attribute	How?	Benefit	Outcome	ROR
Measureable	Clear rules w money mgt.	Build equity curve	Evidence based	0%
Robust Evidence	Out-of-sample performance	Robustness	Stable equity curve	0%
Indication Versatile	Profitable over a diversified portfolio	Avoid data mining	Stable equity curve	0%

Good
      Design
      Principles
	Simple
	Few rules
	Few indicators
	Few variables
	- same value for buy/sell
	- same value across mkts
		Avoid curve fitting	Stable equity curve	0%

FIGURE 8.2 Winning strategies have common attributes that all traders should look for in their own methodologies.

you'll need to articulate exactly how a head and shoulder pattern is defined.

Saying,

I'll just wait for a head and shoulder pattern to appear and enter on a break of the neck line,

isn't good enough.

When I programmed Curtis Arnold's Pattern Probability Strategy to trade triangles, rectangles and wedges I defined them as having at least four swing points where each pair of swing points had to be connected by a trend line. Entry was off a break of a pattern's trend line. You need to understand that programming languages require explicit instructions so vague observations won't do. Without specific rules you won't be able to calculate a strategy's expectancy and hence your ROR.

Robustness

A tradable robustness should be the Holy Grail objective of all strategies.

Tradable implies reality and practicality. Would a trader in all likelihood be able to stay committed to a strategy and trade it through the inevitable drawdowns? And drawdowns are the key. It's not practical to select the most profitable strategy over out-of-sample data if it has the potential, based on its historical performance, to suffer from deep drawdowns. Large drawdowns may be fine for institutional traders and hedge funds, but it's not for you and I. So, 'tradable' is all about being sensible and practical.

Robustness simply refers to a strategy working as well in the present as it has worked in the past. Robustness implies a positive upward sloping out-of-sample equity curve.

As I've mentioned before, there are two ways to gauge robustness:

1. Evidence and
2. Indication.

Evidence   Evidence of robustness manifests itself as a stable upward sloping equity curve over out-of-sample data. The strategy is robust. Proof is in the pudding. And obviously the more time since the strategy was developed or published the better.

Indication   If there is no out-of-sample evidence you can look for indications of the likelihood robustness should be present in a strategy. There are two good indication of robustness;

1. Versatility and
2. Good design principles

Versatility   Versatility is a sign of robustness if a strategy can be profitable over a diversified portfolio of markets. Versatility is a positive sign a strategy has not been data mined to fit a few well-chosen markets.

Good Design Principles   Another indication of robustness is if the strategy has been developed following good design principles. As I've mentioned ad infinitum good design principles embrace simplicity. Simplicity ensures there is less chance you'll fall victim to excessive curve fitting. Now curve fitting exists in all strategies. Without an idea to capture market movements there wouldn't be any strategies. Experienced traders look to minimize curve fitting while inexperienced ones overdo it, searching for that perfect, painless to trade, perfectly straight 45-degree historical equity curve.

Good design principles embrace simplicity. Simplicity minimizes the risk of excessive curve fitting. Simple ideas with few rules, few indicators and few variables. Variables whose values are the same for both buy and sell setups and across all markets. Robustness isn't found in complexity. Please remember Tom DeMark's earlier remark.

Strategy Benchmark

You now know what to look for in a good strategy. The next important and key tool you require in your trader's toolkit is a strategy benchmark.

You need a strategy benchmark to help you avoid falling into the relevancy trap.

You know all about the relevancy trap, focusing on and trading only those strategies developed by your own hands. You want to matter. You want to be relevant. You want your efforts to be acknowledged and rewarded. In your mind, the best way to do that is to trade your own strategy. However, for most traders their best efforts fall far short of what is necessary to succeed in real markets, with real money. This is why it's always important to benchmark your development efforts against an established and robust methodology. A methodology that has worked well in the past and in all likelihood will continue to work in the future. The strategy benchmark should be the minimum hurdle your own strategy must clear before consideration is given to trading it.

If your efforts cannot surpass the benchmark, then you should consider trading it. Not your own designed strategy. Do not believe that your self-esteem, your relevancy, is attached to your development efforts. Your self-esteem and relevancy should be tied to your account balance. The objective in trading is to avoid ROR, survive, make money and build your trading account. Not pander to your narcissistic self to have your development efforts admired.

The trick is to select an appropriate strategy benchmark. And ensure it contains many of the attributes of winning strategies, where the single best attribute it can have is robustness.

To help you select either an appropriate benchmark or your preferred strategy to trade you should follow an objective and structured review process, like the one I'm about to show you.

STRATEGY REVIEW

Unfortunately, there is no single super metric that can be used to rank one strategy above another.

Whereas I use hard mathematics for calculating ROR, I use a combination of qualitative and quantitative measures when reviewing a strategy. There isn't a right or wrong combination. It's really up to the individual trader. When reviewing a strategy, I undertake a robustness and performance analysis to help me weigh up my opinion on a strategy. Between the two I usually give more weight to the robustness metrics, because—as I've indicated—a strategy's robustness profile will keep me alive far longer than any compelling performance metric.

Robustness Analysis

First up, I'll review a strategy's robustness by examining the usual suspects as shown in Figure 8.3.

Straight up, I want to see what evidence there is of a strategy's robustness. Positive out-of-sample performance. The more time, the more out-of-sample performance there is, the more confidence I'll have in the strategy.

If there is no evidence of robustness, I'll look for indications that robustness is likely to exist. Even when there is plenty of evidence, I'll

Robustness Analysis		
Evidence		Out-of-sample performance
Indication		
	Versatility	Profitability over a diversified portfolio
		Avoids data mining
	Good	Simple
	Design	Few rules
	Principles	Few indicators
		Few variables
		- same value for buy/sell
		- same value across all markets
		Avoids excessive curve fitting

FIGURE 8.3 Good methodologies will have either or both evidence or indications of robustness.

still examine the likely indicator 'markers' to gain a better understanding of the strategy.

One positive indication of the likelihood of robustness is versatility. A versatile strategy is one that is less likely to have been data mined. So, I will want to know whether a strategy is profitable over a diverse portfolio of markets. And is it profitable on out-of-sample markets, markets the strategy was never designed to trade?

Another good indication of robustness is whether a strategy has embraced good design principles to avoid excessive curve fitting. Is it complex or simple? Are there many or few rules? Are there many or few indicators? Are there many or few variables? Do the variables have the same value for both buy and sell setups and across all markets? How large is the parallel universe of alternative equity curves given the number of variables and adjustments allowed? Do any of the alternative equity curves produce ROR calculations above 0%? Is the strategy's equity curve stable enough to trade over various sets of variable values?

Once I've completed my robustness analysis, I'll review a number of performance measures.

Performance Analysis

You can get lost in the encyclopedia of performance metrics. It's one rabbit hole that you don't want to fall into. Over the years I have learned to rely on a few key metrics as shown in Figure 8.4.

For my performance analysis I'm keen to gain a good insight into five important areas of strategy performance:

- survival,
- reward/risk ratio,
- risk,
- efficiency with money management and
- difficulty in trading.

Let's have a look at each.

Survival   My number one objective in trading is to survive. Nothing comes a close second. So, right away I want to know what a strategy's ROR is when its expectancy is combined with my preferred money management strategy. Unless it's 0%, I'm not interested in pursuing it.

Performance Analysis

Survival
    Risk-of-ruin

Reward/Risk
    Net profit (with no money management position sizing)
    Maximum drawdown (DD)
    Reward/Risk ratio (Net profit/Max DD)
    Ulcer Peformance Index (UPI)

Risk
    Average risk per trade (Stops)

Efficiency with Money Management
    Net profit (with money management position sizing)
    Compound Annual Growth Rate (CAGR)

Difficulty in Trading
    Maximum drawdown (Days)
    Maximum consecutive losses
    Smoothness of equity curve R^2

FIGURE 8.4   Over the years I have learned to rely on a number of key performance metrics.

Reward/Risk Ratio   My next concern is to know what a strategy's reward to risk payoff is. How much return has the strategy produced for its worst's historical drawdown? It's the old fashion cornerstone of economics. Why consider a strategy if in the past it has not produced a good enough return for the amount of risk it has incurred?

While the reward/risk ratio is good it only focuses on a single point in time when the worst historical drawdown occurred. The Ulcer Performance Index (UPI), although more complex to calculate, gives me more granularity to the reward/risk payoff. By measuring drawdowns, it delivers a more accurate risk-adjusted return picture telling me how efficient a strategy is in producing each unit of excess return per unit of average drawdown risk. The higher the better.

Risk   Next, I'm super keen to know what a strategy's average risk, or average stop, per trade is. I do this because I want to avoid the risk of big stops. Naturally, my preference is for lower risk (smaller stops) and this is for two very important reasons. One, I naturally prefer to risk less capital than more and, two, *its cuts to a strategy's efficiency in making money.*

No doubt you may have heard or read a comment similar to the following:

> *Getting into a trade is not important. What is important is where you get out. Don't worry about the entry, it's all about the exit.*

For me that's a red flag.

It suggests to me that the person responsible for the comment in all probability doesn't trade because the entry and stops (and hence trade risk) are *both* terribly important. You can't rank one above the other. Your entry and stop represents the risk per setup. It's the lynch pin to your position sizing and the potential money you can make.

Remember, money management is the secret behind both your survival (lowering your ROR) and your prosperity. As your account balance grows, money management allows you to increase your position size. A larger position size means more profit. A higher average risk will have a smaller position size relative to a lower average risk. It's my preference to prefer a strategy with a lower average risk per trade. It will allow me to trade larger position sizes and ultimately enjoy greater profit potential. This leads me straight into the importance of my next measure, a strategy's efficiency.

Efficiency with Money Management   If we survive in trading, our second objective is to make money. And since we know the secret behind earning big money is money management, we as traders want to know how efficient a strategy is when money management is applied.

This is terribly important because looking at a strategy's single contract (or single position size) results can hide the existence of big stops. Many strategies only look good because of their use. Developers can use big stops to avoid their strategies from being stopped out by taking profits quickly, or only when a profitable close occurs, regardless of how many days, weeks or months have gone by!

By examining the efficiency of a strategy, by reviewing its profitability with money management applied, *the existence of big stops can no longer be hidden* and the real power of a strategy (or lack of power) is revealed. Remember, if we have the same amount of risk capital allocated to trade, our position size for a strategy with larger stops will be smaller relative to a strategy with smaller stops.

The key metric I used to measure a strategy's efficiency is the compound annual growth rate (CAGR), or annualized returns. Large stops or a lack of trades, can't hide from it. Remember, if 0% ROR is king, CAGR is queen.

Difficultly in Trading

Lastly, I want a quick understanding of how difficult a strategy would be to trade? How long was the worst historical drawdown? How many consecutive losses has there been in the past? How smooth is the equity curve? Is it peaceful looking or gut wrenching? The R-squared measurement gives me a fair idea of how difficult a strategy will be to trade. A reading of 100% represents a straight-line equity curve, while a low 50% reading represents a rough curve. It's preferable to trade strategies with 90+% R-squared reading.

Tying it All Together—Hard Science or Art?

Following both analyses you will need to tie them together. How you weigh up each is your business. For myself, I usually give more weight to a strategy's robustness over performance (Figure 8.5). The more robust a strategy is, the more believable the performance measures will be. The more robust a strategy is, the more confidence I'll have in trading it during a drawdown.

Out of the robustness analysis, I rank evidence of robustness over indications. Out of the five performance metrics, I rank survival (ROR), reward/risk and efficiency as my top three.

If I review a strategy with little or no out-of-sample performance but it shows good indications of robustness, through its versatility and good design, I'd allow a few of the performance measures to be less than desirable.

If I feel a strategy, through its complexity, has been overly curve fitted I'd put it aside for no further consideration, despite how bright and shiny it is and how irresistible it looks. No amount of compelling performance metrics will sway me.

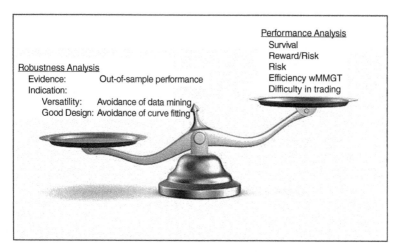

FIGURE 8.5 In the final analysis I usually give more weight to robustness attributes over performance metrics.

Whichever way you review a strategy there will be a balancing between robustness and performance measures. It will be one-part science and one-part art. As I've said, there is no single super metric that can rank all strategies. Certainly, positive out-of-sample performance provides hard evidence of robustness. Certainly, profitability over a diverse portfolio of markets demonstrates versatility and the absence of data mining. Certainly, simplicity of few rules, with few indicators and few variables, demonstrates good design principles and the possible absence of excessive curve fitting. However, there is no single insight, technique or metric you can use to detect excessive curve fitting. Determining both the amount of and the impact of curve fitting is subjective. Is it excessive or is it reasonable? This is where the trader will have to rely on their experience and move more into the realm of 'art' than science.

Once a trader has worked their alchemy, the final step is to determine the size of a strategy's universe of alternative equity curves. To know the upper and lower boundary curves with their resultant expectancies and ROR calculations, not to mention the level of variance. Will it be a smooth or bumpy ride to trade?

Equity Curve Stability Review

This is the final piece of the puzzle and final hurdle. For strategies with no out-of-sample evidence of robustness we need to know how sensitive the methodology's equity curve is to changes in its variable values. To do this we need to complete an equity curve stability review.

As an example, I'll complete a review of the Bollinger Band volatility breakout strategy I shared with you in Chapter 6.

Remember, even though there was a very popular and successful commercially available strategy based on Bollinger Bands from the 1990s, the variables I used were made up. So, despite the strategy being named as 'One of the Top 10 Trading Systems of All Time' by *Futures Truth* magazine, I can't rely on the performance figures. They're not out-of-sample.

Without evidence I need to rely on indications of robustness. And it looks good. The Bollinger Band strategy has every indication of robustness by being versatile over a diverse portfolio of markets and by following good design principles through its simplicity. However, it does contain two variables that suggest its equity curve could be fragile or unstable. To find out how much we need to complete the review.

So, this makes the Bollinger Band strategy ideal to undergo an equity curve stability review.

Here are its rules again:

Rules

Strategy:	Bollinger Bands
Developed:	1986
Published:	1993
Data:	Daily
Approach:	Trend trading
Technique:	Volatility breakout
Symmetry:	Buy and sell
Markets:	All
Indicators:	Bollinger Bands
Variables—Number:	2
	Bollinger Band length (80)
	Standard deviation multiplier (1) used to create the upper and lower bands

| Variables—Symmetry: | Same value for both buy and sell setups |
| Variables—Application: | Same value across all markets |

| Rules: | 2 |

Buy Rules

Trend:	Up—previous close above the upper Bollinger band
Entry:	Buy next day market on open
Stop:	Previous close below the middle Bollinger band
	Sell next day market on open

Sell Rules

Trend:	Down—previous close below the lower Bollinger band
Entry:	Sell next day market on open
Stop:	Previous close above the middle Bollinger band
	Buy next day market on open

The strategy contains one indicator, which has two variables. The first is its 80-day length and the second is its standard deviation multiplier (1) that is used to construct the upper and lower bands. I will restrict the number of adjustments of each variable to four. With two variables and four adjustments I know the strategy's universe of alternative equity curves will be 24. If the original variable values are included the total universe consists of 25 possible equity curves.

I'll use a 10% adjustment for each variable, making two adjustments above and two below the original value. The adjustment factor for the Bollinger Band length will be eight days, being 10% of 80 days. The adjustment factor for the standard deviation multiplier will be 0.1, being 10% of one. Accordingly, the Bollinger Band lengths I'll be using are 64 days, 72 days, 80 days (original value), 88 days and 96 days. For the standard deviation multiplier used to create the upper and lower bands I'll use 0.8, 0.9, 1.0 (original value), 1.1 and 1.2.

I've run all the additional 24 equity curves and overlaid them in Figure 8.6.

It certainly looks much better than the Retracement Trend Trader's review I completed in Chapter 5.

Although it doesn't appear so, there are 25 equity curves displayed in Figure 8.6. I found the strategy was insensitive to changes in the standard deviation multiplier, where many alternate equity curves resembled each other. The majority of variation you can see was caused by changes in the length.

Operating within my arbitrary limit of only four adjustments, we can clearly see the upper and lower boundaries of alternative equity curves. The question we need to answer is whether any of the lower boundary equity curves produce a ROR calculation above 0%.

I've summarized the values in Table 8.1.

As you can see, I'm pleased to report that no alternative equity curve produced a ROR calculation above 0%. So, it's two thumbs up for Bollinger Bands.

Let me now complete the equity curve stability review as shown in Figure 8.7.

For comparison purposes I've included the Retracement Trend Trader's review. In my opinion the variation in the Bollinger Band strategy's alternative equity curves is medium. The variation in expectancy is small. When they are combined with no variable values producing a ROR calculation above 0%, one could make a strong case for arguing that the strategy's equity curve is stable enough to trade.

So, there you have it. Bollinger Bands Strategy, despite no evidence of robustness due to the absence of out-of-sample performance, is worth your consideration. Not only does it exhibit good indications of robustness through its versatility and simplicity but it also appears to have a stable equity curve with a universal absence of any ROR calculations above 0%. Bollinger Bands appears to be a robust strategy. I say 'appears' as there can never be any guarantees about an unknowable future. And I suppose we shouldn't be surprised, knowing Bollinger Bands was the backbone of a very successful commercially available strategy back in the 1990s.

The equity curve stability review completes the process I follow in reviewing strategies. Let's now use this new strategy review tool to select your next tool, a strategy benchmark.

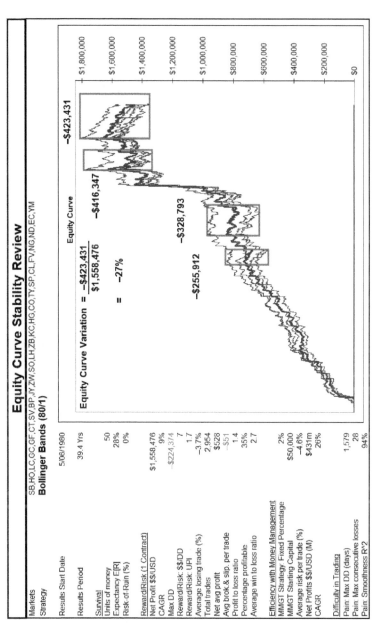

FIGURE 8.6 An equity curve stability review requires the examination of a strategy's parallel universe of alternative equity curves.

TABLE 8.1   Not one of Bollinger Band's alternative equity curves produced a ROR calculation above 0%.

Equity Curve Stability Review

Indicator	Bollinger Band		E[R]		Units of $$		ROR
	Days	Multiplier					
Variables	80	1	28%	+	50	=	0%

Change in Variable Values

	64	0.8	21%	+	50	=	0%
	64	0.9	21%	+	50	=	0%
	64	1	21%	+	50	=	0%
	64	1.1	21%	+	50	=	0%
	64	1.2	21%	+	50	=	0%
	72	0.8	27%	+	50	=	0%
	72	0.9	27%	+	50	=	0%
	72	1	27%	+	50	=	0%
	72	1.1	27%	+	50	=	0%
	72	1.2	27%	+	50	=	0%
	80	0.8	28%	+	50	=	0%
	80	0.9	28%	+	50	=	0%
	80	1	28%	+	50	=	0%
	80	1.1	28%	+	50	=	0%
	80	1.2	28%	+	50	=	0%
	88	0.8	27%	+	50	=	0%
	88	0.9	27%	+	50	=	0%
	88	1	27%	+	50	=	0%
	88	1.1	27%	+	50	=	0%
	88	1.2	27%	+	50	=	0%
	96	0.8	29%	+	50	=	0%
	96	0.9	29%	+	50	=	0%
	96	1	29%	+	50	=	0%
	96	1.1	29%	+	50	=	0%
	96	1.2	29%	+	50	=	0%

Equity Curve Stability Review

Strategy		RTT	Bollinger B
Setup		MA (34) MA (250) RSI (4,80%)	Bollinger Bands (80,1)
Attributes of Winning Strategies			
Measureable	Expectancy	9%	28%
	Units of money	20	50
	ROR	0%	0%
Robust			
Evidence	Out-of-sample performance	No	No
Indication			
Versatile	Profitable over a diversified portfolio	Yes	Yes
Good	Equity Curve Stability Review		
Design	Number of indicator variables	4	2
Principles	Number of variable adjustments	4	4
	Number of possible equity curves	256	25
	Variation in equity curves	Large	Medium
	Variation in expectancy	Large	Small
	Do any sets of variable values have ROR > 0%?	Yes	None
	Is equity curve stable enough to trade?	**NO**	**YES**

FIGURE 8.7 If fragility exists an equity curve stability review will reveal it.

STRATEGY BENCHMARK—WHICH STRATEGY WILL IT BE?

Let's now examine the strategies I reviewed in Chapter 6 to see if one of them would be suitable for selection as your strategy benchmark. Remember, the idea of having a strategy benchmark is to help you avoid falling into the relevancy trap. This strategy will become your benchmark. The strategy to beat. It will become your line in the sand. The baseline that you'll need to surpass if you wish to trade a strategy developed by your own efforts.

In Chapter 6 I reviewed 19 strategies, which included my coin-tossing scientific-based Random Trend Trader. From that group only one strategy failed to make money, Hearne's 1% Rule. Let me remove Hearne's strategy and rank the group by net profit (Table 8.2).

Based on what many would believe to be a fair basis for selection, the Golden 50- and 200-Day Crossover would appear to be the stand-out strategy. The strategy worthy of selection. However, you now know that looking at a single, one dimensional metric doesn't scratch the surface when it comes to strategy review. It's not enough. A robustness and performance analysis has to be carried out. So, let's do it.

TABLE 8.2 Chapter 6's alternative trend trading strategies ranked by net profitability.

Model	Type	Published	Port.	Net $$	Trades	Avg $$	Brok/Slip
Golden 50- and 200-Day Crossover	Relative price ROC	2020	P24	$1,715,940	1,235	$1,389	–$51
Donchian 4-Week Rule	Channel breakout	1960	P24	$1,601,223	6,120	$262	–$51
Bollinger Bands	Volatility breakout	1993	P24	$1,558,476	2,954	$528	–$51
Dreyfus 52-Week Rule	Channel breakout	1960	P24	$1,442,906	475	$3,038	–$51
Turtle Trading	Channel breakout	1983	P24	$1,418,786	5,212	$272	–$51
ATR Bands	Volatility breakout	2020	P24	$1,193,319	3,544	$337	–$51
Dow Theory	Swing breakout	1900	P24	$1,090,346	17,927	$61	–$51
Gartley's 3- and 6-Week Crossover	Relative price ROC	1935	P24	$1,079,398	3,387	$319	–$51
Monthly Close Model	Relative time ROC	1933	P24	$1,003,526	4,993	$201	–$51
Ricardo Rules	Price breakout	1838	P24	$622,552	20,392	$31	–$51
Quarterly Close Model	Relative time ROC	1933	P24	$611,092	1,670	$366	–$51
Random Trend Trader w200dma	Coin toss	2020	P24	$583,946	15,871	$37	–$51
Mean Reversion	Retracement	2020	P24	$535,005	5.163	$104	–$51
Donchian 5- and 20-Day Crossover	Relative price ROC	1960	P24	$520,675	13,306	$39	–$51
Arnold PPS	Congestion breakout	1995	P24	$450,780	2,586	$174	–$51
Elder Triple Screen Trading System	Retracement	1986	P24	$336,473	11,633	$29	–$51
Darvas Box	Congestion breakout	1960	P24	$136,731	636	$215	–$51
Livermore Reaction	Congestion breakout	1940	P24	$35,136	1,279	$27	–$51

Gather the Data

In Table 8.3 I've summarized the 18 remaining strategies eligible for becoming a strategy benchmark. For my robustness analysis I've summarized both the evidence and indication of robustness for each strategy.

Table 8.3 contains all the robustness information I use. The published data indicates the amount of out-of-sample performance data there is. Data that can offer me hard evidence of a strategy's robustness. Apart from four, the majority of strategies have plenty of evidence to demonstrate their robustness. To complement the evidence, I've summarized the important indicator markers of robustness. As you can see, and it's no surprise due to the level of out-of-sample evidence, the majority of strategies possess good indications of robustness. They're all versatile, being profitable over a diverse portfolio of 24 markets. This gives a strong indication that they haven't been data mined. Another indication is whether or not they have followed good design? Are they simple or complex? Is there excessive curve fitting or not? Well, three strategies at first glance look to have quite a number of rules:

- Mean Reversion,
- Arnold's Pattern Probability Strategy and
- Elder's Triple Screen Trading System (TSTS).

Certainly, more than the others. This unfortunately suggests the possibility of excessive curve fitting. However, despite their number of rules, they all have symmetrical rules that are applicable to both buy and sell setups, and across all markets, suggesting there isn't excessive curve fitting present. It's pleasing to see that the strategies are generally light on indicators. However, I can't say the same about the number of variables contained within three strategies:

- Arnold's Pattern Probability Strategy,
- Elder's TSTS and
- Darvas's Box.

Each contains five variables. This is nearly twice the average of the remaining strategies. However, in their defence, where variables exist, they all have the same value for both buy and sell setups and across all

TABLE 8.3 Key evidence of robustness is out-of-sample performance, while key indications are versatility and simplicity of design.

Model	Published	Robustness Analysis						Indication							
		Evidence					Data Mining?	Excessive Curve Fitting?							
		Out-of-sample Yrs	Net $$	Trades	Avg $$	Brok & Slip	Port.	Rules		Indicators		Variables			
								No.	Sym.	No.	Sym.	No.	Sym.	Mkts	
Golden 50- and 200-Day Crossover	2020	0	$1,715,940	1,235	$1,389	$51	P24	2	Yes	1	Yes	2	Yes	Yes	
Donchian 4-Week Rule	1960	60	$1,601,223	6,120	$262	$51	P24	1	Yes	0	Yes	1	Yes	Yes	
Bollinger Bands	1993	27	$1,558,476	2,954	$528	$51	P24	2	Yes	1	Yes	2	Yes	Yes	
Dreyfus 52-Week Rule	1960	60	$1,442,906	475	$3,038	$51	P24	1	Yes	0	Yes	1	Yes	Yes	
Turtle Trading	1983	37	$1,418,786	5,212	$272	$51	P24	3	Yes	0	Yes	2	Yes	Yes	
ATR Bands	2020	0	$1,193,319	3,544	$337	$51	P24	2	Yes	1	Yes	2	Yes	Yes	
Dow Theory	1900	120	$1,090,346	17,927	$61	$51	P24	1	Yes	0	Yes	0	NA	NA	
Gartley's 3- and 6-Week Crossover	1935	85	$1,079,398	3,387	$319	$51	P24	2	Yes	1	Yes	3	Yes	Yes	
Monthly Close Model	1933	87	$1,003,526	4,993	$201	$51	P24	2	Yes	0	NA	0	NA	NA	
Ricardo Rules	1838	182	$622,552	20,392	$31	$51	P24	3	Yes	0	Yes	0	NA	NA	
Quarterly Close Model	1933	87	$611,092	1,670	$366	$51	P24	2	Yes	0	Yes	0	NA	NA	
Random Trend Trader w200dma	2020	0	$583,946	15,871	$37	$51	P24	4	Yes	1	Yes	3	Yes	Yes	
Mean Reversion	2020	0	$535,005	5,163	$104	$51	P24	5	Yes	1	Yes	3	Yes	Yes	
Donchian 5- and 20-Day Crossover	1960	60	$520,675	13,306	$39	$51	P24	2	Yes	1	Yes	2	Yes	Yes	
Arnold PPS	1995	25	$450,780	2,586	$174	$51	P24	6	Yes	1	Yes	5	Yes	Yes	
Elder Triple Screen Trading System	1986	34	$336,473	11,633	$29	$51	P24	6	Yes	2	Yes	5	Yes	Yes	
Darvas Box	1960	60	$136,731	636	$215	$51	P24	4	Yes	1	Yes	5	Yes	Yes	
Livermore Reaction	1940	80	$35,136	1,279	$27	$51	P24	4	Yes	0	Yes	0	NA	NA	

markets. This again suggests the unlikelihood of excessive curve fitting being present. But then we shouldn't be too surprised given the level of out-of-sample performance present.

In Table 8.4 I've summarized my key performance metrics.

I've tabulated the key performance metrics I rely on when reviewing a strategy. Based on the initial net profit ranking the top five candidates for a strategy benchmark are:

1. Golden 50- and 200-Day Crossover,
2. Donchian's Four-Week Rule,
3. Bollinger Bands,
4. Dreyfus's 52-Week Rule and
5. Turtle Trading.

Let's now get down to the granulate level to see which strategy should really be ranked number one for selection.

Initial Robustness and Performance Analysis

The number one attribute for any strategy is robustness. My preference is for out-of-sample evidence. Given these criteria, I'll remove the following strategies:

1. Golden 50- and 200-Day Crossover,
2. ATR (average true range) bands,
3. Random Trend Trader and
4. Mean reversion.

It's bad luck for the Golden 50- and 200-Day Crossover, as it's gone from hero to zero in one click. But unfortunately, I don't have any reliable record to say when it was first originally published and by whom? No doubt there may be traders who have followed and traded it successfully for years and would be laughing at my decision to remove it. I've personally been using the 200-day moving average as my dominant trend tool for over 30 years. I think it does a good job. But I haven't been applying a 50-day moving average to generate trading signals. So, without reliable proof of when it was first published, I can't rely on favourable hindsight to keep it in. It's also hard on both my ATR bands and mean reversion strategies, because they had some of the highest CAGR of 22% and 24% respectively.

TABLE 8.4 Key indicators of good performance include metrics measuring survival, reward/risk pay-off, efficiency and difficulty in trading.

| Model | Robustness | | Performance Analysis | | | | | | | | | | | | |
| | | | Survival | | | Reward/Risk | | | | EfficiencywMMgt | | | Difficulty in trading | | |
	Published	Out-of-sample Yrs	E[R]	Units $$	ROR	Net $$	D/D	R/R	UPI	Risk	MMgt	CARG	DD Days	Losses	R^2
Golden 50- and 200-Day Crossover	2020	0	39%	50	0%	$1,715,940	$196,367	9	1.5	4.4%	$17m	16%	1,197	22	97%
Donchian 4-Week Rule	1960	60	14%	50	0%	$1,601,223	$261,817	6	1.4	5.6%	$69m	20%	1,608	18	93%
Bollinger Bands	1993	27	28%	50	0%	$1,558,476	$224,374	7	1.7	4.6%	$431m	26%	1,579	28	94%
Dreyfus 52-Week Rule	1960	60	47%	50	0%	$1,442,906	$113,469	13	1.3	16.7%	$2m	10%	1,600	9	98%
Turtle Trading	1983	37	21%	50	0%	$1,418,786	$95,107	15	2.2	4.7%	$257m	24%	1,637	20	96%
ATR Bands	2020	0	18%	50	0%	$1,193,319	$298,392	4	1.1	4.2%	$130m	22%	3,036	22	92%
Dow Theory	1900	120	5%	50	0%	$1,090,346	$250,428	4	1.4	3.3%	$167m	23%	2,238	24	95%
Gartley's 3- and 6-Week Crossover	1935	85	12%	50	0%	$1,079,398	$295,771	4	1.1	6.2%	$30m	18%	2,972	18	83%
Monthly Close Model	1933	87	10%	50	0%	$1,003,526	$382,027	3	0.8	5.0%	$582m	27%	3,556	22	83%
Ricardo Rules	1838	182	3%	50	100%	$622,552	$449,550	1	0.5	1.9%	$116m	21%	2,237	27	77%
Quarterly Close Model	1933	87	9%	50	0%	$611,092	$261,974	2	0.4	7.5%	$5m	12%	4,472	17	74%
Random Trend Trader w200dma	2020	0	7%	50	0%	$583,946	$197,797	3	0.4	1.0%	$0m	0%	3,257	53	87%
Mean Reversion	2020	0	13%	50	0%	$535,005	$121,869	4	0.6	1.8%	$219m	24%	3,441	27	92%
Donchian 5- and 20-Day Crossover	1960	60	3%	50	100%	$520,675	$311,061	2	0.4	3.0%	$0m	0%	6,689	25	36%
Arnold PPS	1995	25	31%	50	0%	$450,780	$62,059	7	0.7	2.2%	$35m	18%	2,494	23	95%
Elder Triple Screen Trading System	1986	34	4%	50	100%	$336,473	$330,350	1	0.3	1.8%	$5m	12%	5,039	32	51%
Darvas Box	1960	60	15%	50	0%	$136,731	$75,614	2	0.1	5.5%	$0m	0%	3,089	17	82%
Livermore Reaction	1940	80	3%	50	100%	$35,136	$101,554	0	0.1	2.8%	$0m	0%	3,827	17	30%

But this is central to the main issue of why we need to objectively review all strategies before consideration can be given to trading them.

Despite how nice and shiny a strategy looks with good performance, good versatility and good design principles, without evidence of robustness it's hard to keep them. Especially when there are so many other strategies available with plenty of out-of-sample evidence of robustness to choose from. Maybe someone could publish a book in 20 years' time and revisit both my strategies, who knows, they may just hold up. But to keep them today would be based on hope and not evidence. It would be plain foolishness. Let's stick to the evidence, when so many of the other strategies have it in spades.

It's disappointing to see Random Trend Trader go; however, it has served its purpose, to demonstrate the power of trend trading's three golden tenets.

Removing the four strategies reduces the selection pool down to 14.

My number one performance metric is ROR. I applied my preferred fixed percentage money management strategy to each strategy. I risked a fixed 2% to create 50 units of money and began each calculation with a $50,000 account balance. I defined my point of ruin as being an entire 100% loss. To calculate each strategy's ROR I used my simulator, as described in *UPST*. Based on the simulated ROR calculations I removed the following strategies, as their respective values were above 0%.

1. Ricardo Rules,
2. Donchian's 5- and 20-Day Crossover,
3. Elder's TSTS and
4. Livermore Reaction.

Removing these four strategies reduces the selection pool down to a top ten.

I have to say it's disappointing to lose Jesse Livermore's Reaction strategy. For such a legendary name it's a sorry outcome. However, it should not be seen as a vote of no confidence in the person or his approach to the markets. His Reaction method was in all probability only one of a number of approaches he used. The same should be said for Richard Donchian and Dr Alexander Elder. Dropping them only indicates that the particular idea, according to my simulated ROR calculation, had a ROR above 0%. It says nothing more.

It doesn't say anything about their other strategies and contributions, like Donchian's Four-Week Rule and Elder's highly popular and bestselling book, *Trading for a Living* (Wiley, 1993). It just says the strategy in question did not pass my robustness review. That's all.

I should also note that if my ROR calculations did not remove these strategies, some of my other performance metrics would have.

For instance, they all have very poor reward/risk payoff and risk-adjusted return metrics:

	Reward/Risk Ratio	UPI
• Ricardo Rules	1	0.5
• Donchian's 5- and 20-Day Crossover	2	0.4
• Elder's TSTS	1	0.3
• Livermore Reaction	0	0.1

Apart from Ricardo Rules they also have poor efficiency in making money:

	Efficiency with Money Mgt	CAGR
• Ricardo Rules	$116m	21%
• Donchian's 5- and 20-Day Crossover	$0m	0%
• Elder's TSTS	$5m	12%
• Livermore Reaction	$0m	0%

They have particularly long drawdown periods which would test the patience of any trader:

	Length of Drawdown (Days)
• Ricardo Rules	2,237
• Donchian's 5- and 20-Day Crossover	6,689
• Elder's TSTS	5,039
• Livermore Reaction	3,827

And lastly, they all have very rough looking equity curves with poor R-squared values making each strategy almost impossible to trade:

	R-Square
• Ricardo Rules	77%
• Donchian's 5- and 20-Day Crossover	36%
• Elder's TSTS	51%
• Livermore Reaction	30%

So, although it's a pity to see these strategies go, their performance over out-of-sample data, despite providing hard evidence of their robustness, also provides hard evidence of poor performance, and so warrants their removal.

The Top Ten

So, here we have the final top ten strategies, with Table 8.5 summarizing their robustness analysis.

Table 8.6 summarizes their performance analysis.

Each strategy deserves its place in my top ten. They all have ample out-of-sample performance, with Arnold's Pattern Probability Strategy being the youngest with only 25 years. They're all versatile. They're all profitable over a universal diverse portfolio of 24 markets demonstrating that each strategy has not been data mined. The only area where a few look vulnerable is whether or not they have been developed following good design principles?

Arnold's Pattern Probability Strategy, Darvas's Box strategy and Gartley's Three- and Six-Week Crossover could be removed due to their number of variables (five, five and three respectively). Gartley's strategy could be argued as being fine as his variables of using three and six weeks were clearly published in 1935 and they have stood the test of time with their out-of-sample performance. Arnold's Pattern Probability Strategy could also be argued as being fine. Although he has five variables, they also were well defined back in 1995, where three of the variables concern his well-thought-out trade plan, following sensible logic.

So, I'd keep both Arnold's and Gartley's strategies for the moment.

However, Nicholas Darvas never explicitly recorded his rules, or the value of his variables. I made them up as my interpretation of his strategy. Given their fragile nature I'd vote to remove Darvas's Box for not following good design principles, which require clearly defined rules. However, I'm happy to keep the Darvas Box strategy in the top ten, as it's unlikely to challenge for the top placing.

The trick now is to select one of the top ten as your strategy benchmark. As I've mentioned numerous times, our primary objective as traders is to survive the markets first. We do that by trading with a 0% ROR. If we survive, our next objective is to make money. And knowing that the real secret behind big profits is money management,

TABLE 8.5 The top ten strategies all have good evidence and indications of robustness.

Model	Type	Robustness Analysis												
		Evidence						Data Mining?	Indication					
									Excessive Curve Fitting?					
		Published	Out-of-sample Yrs	Net $$	Trades	Avg $$	Brok & Slip	Port.	Rules		Indicators	Variables		
									No.	Sym.	No.	No.	Sym.	Mkts
Donchian 4-Week Rule	Channel breakout	1960	60	$1,601,223	6,120	$262	–$51	P24	1	Yes	0	1	Yes	Yes
Bollinger Bands	Volatility breakout	1993	27	$1,558,476	2,954	$528	–$51	P24	2	Yes	1	2	Yes	Yes
Dreyfus 52-Week Rule	Channel breakout	1960	60	$1,442,906	475	$3,038	–$51	P24	1	Yes	0	1	Yes	Yes
Turtle Trading	Channel breakout	1983	37	$1,418,786	5,212	$272	–$51	P24	3	Yes	0	2	Yes	Yes
Dow Theory	Swing breakout	1900	120	$1,090,346	17,927	$61	–$51	P24	1	Yes	0	0	NA	NA
Gartley's 3- and 6-Week Crossover	Relative price ROC	1935	85	$1,079,398	3,387	$319	–$51	P24	2	Yes	1	3	Yes	Yes
Monthly Close Model	Relative time ROC	1933	87	$1,003,526	4,993	$201	–$51	P24	2	Yes	0	0	NA	NA
Quarterly Close Model	Relative time ROC	1933	87	$611,092	1,670	$366	–$51	P24	2	Yes	0	0	NA	NA
Arnold PPS	Congestion breakout	1995	25	$450,780	2,586	$174	–$51	P24	6	Yes	1	5	Yes	Yes
Darvas Box	Congestion breakout	1960	60	$136,731	636	$215	–$51	P24	4	Yes	1	5	Yes	Yes

TABLE 8.6 Most, but not all, of the top ten strategies have good performance metrics.

Model	Type	Robustness		Performance Analysis										Difficulty in trading		
				Survival			Reward/Risk				Efficiency wMMgt					
		Published	Out-of-sample Yrs	E[R]	Units	ROR $$	Net $$	D/D	R/R	UPI	Risk	MMgt	CARG	DD Days	Losses	R^2
Donchian 4-Week Rule	Channel breakout	1960	60	14%	50	0%	$1,601,223	*$261,817	6	1.4	*5.6%	$69m	20%	1,608	18	93%
Bollinger Bands	Volatility breakout	1993	27	28%	50	0%	$1,558,476	*$224,374	7	1.7	*4.6%	$431m	26%	1,579	28	94%
Dreyfus 52-Week Rule	Channel breakout	1960	60	47%	50	0%	$1,442,906	*$113,469	13	1.3	*16.7%	$2m	10%	1,600	9	98%
Turtle Trading	Channel breakout	1983	37	21%	50	0%	$1,418,786	*$95,107	15	2.2	*4.7%	$257m	24%	1,637	20	96%
Dow Theory	Swing breakout	1900	120	5%	50	0%	$1,090,346	*$250,428	4	1.4	*3.3%	$167m	23%	2,238	24	95%
Gartley's 3- and 6-Week Crossover	Relative price ROC	1935	85	12%	50	0%	$1,079,398	*$295,771	4	1.1	*6.2%	$30m	18%	2,972	18	83%
Monthly Close Model	Relative time ROC	1933	87	10%	50	0%	$1,003,526	*$382,027	3	0.8	*5.0%	$582m	27%	3,556	22	83%
Quarterly Close Model	Relative time ROC	1933	87	9%	50	0%	$611,092	*$261,974	2	0.4	*7.5%	$5m	12%	4,472	17	74%
Arnold PPS	Congestion breakout	1995	25	31%	50	0%	$450,780	*$62,059	7	0.7	*2.2%	$35m	18%	2,494	23	95%
Darvas Box	Congestion breakout	1960	60	15%	50	0%	$136,731	*$75,614	2	0.1	*5.5%	$0m	0%	3,089	17	82%

we need to look at each strategy's efficiency in making money. This is why CAGR is in my top three performance metrics. It's the final arbiter on a strategy's superiority, or efficiency in making money, assuming all the other robustness criterion are fine. So, let me rank the strategies according to their individual CAGR.

Ranked by CAGR

In Tables 8.7 and 8.8 I've ranked the top ten strategies by their efficiency in making money as measured by CAGR.

Within the Top ten, our new top five now looks quite different:

1. Monthly Close Model,
2. Bollinger Bands,
3. Turtle Trading,
4. Dow Theory and
5. Donchian's Four-Week Rule

It looks quite different to our original top five:

1. Golden 50- and 200-Day Crossover,
2. Donchian's Four-Week Rule,
3. Bollinger Bands,
4. Dreyfus's 52-Week Rule and
5. Turtle Trading.

Well done to Donchian's Four-Week Rule, Bollinger Bands and Turtle Trading for remaining in the top five list. Particularly Richard Donchian, who has two strategies in the top five, as the Turtle Trading Strategy was built upon the shoulders of his Four-Week Rule.

Commiserations should be given to Dreyfus's 52-Week Rule strategy for dropping out of the top five. Despite its impressive single position size net profit of $1,442,906, it ended up dropping to ninth position in my table with a CAGR of only 10%. This is despite having one of the smoothest equity curves with an R-squared reading of 98% (note 100% would be a straight 45-degree equity curve) and having one of the shortest drawdown period of 1,600 days.

The reason for its fall from grace is its use of *large* stops.

Being a stop and reverse strategy it's always in the market. A 52-week breakout creates enormous risk, like an average −16.7% risk

TABLE 8.7 The top ten robustness metrics ranked by CAGR.

Model	Type	Robustness Analysis						Data Mining?	Indication					
		Evidence							Excessive Curve Fitting?					
									Rules		Indicators	Variables		
		Published	Out-of-sample Yrs	Net $$	Trades	Avg $$	Brok & Slip	Port.	No.	Sym.	No.	No.	Sym.	Mkts
Monthly Close Model	Relative time ROC	1933	87	$1,003,526	4,993	$201	–$51	P24	2	Yes	0	0	NA	NA
Bollinger Bands	Volatility breakout	1993	27	$1,558,476	2,954	$528	–$51	P24	2	Yes	1	2	Yes	Yes
Turtle Trading	Channel breakout	1983	37	$1,418,786	5,212	$272	–$51	P24	3	Yes	0	2	Yes	Yes
Dow Theory	Swing breakout	1900	120	$1,090,346	17,927	$61	–$51	P24	1	Yes	0	0	NA	NA
Donchian 4-Week Rule	Channel breakout	1960	60	$1,601,223	6,120	$262	–$51	P24	1	Yes	0	1	Yes	Yes
Arnold PPS	Congestion breakout	1995	25	$450,780	2,586	$174	–$51	P24	6	Yes	1	5	Yes	Yes
Gartley's 3- and 6-Week Crossover	Relative price ROC	1935	85	$1,079,398	3,387	$319	–$51	P24	2	Yes	1	3	Yes	Yes
Quarterly Close Model	Relative time ROC	1933	87	$611,092	1,670	$366	–$51	P24	2	Yes	0	0	NA	NA
Dreyfus 52-Week Rule	Channel breakout	1960	60	$1,442,906	475	$3,038	–$51	P24	1	Yes	0	1	Yes	Yes
Darvas Box	Congestion breakout	1960	60	$136,731	636	$215	–$51	P24	4	Yes	1	5	Yes	Yes

TABLE 8.8 The top ten performance metrics ranked by CAGR.

| Model | Type | Robustness | | Performance Analysis | | | | | | | | | | | | |
| | | Published | Out-of-sample Yrs | Survival | | | Reward/Risk | | | | Efficiency wMMgt | | | Difficulty in trading | | |
				E[R]	Units $$	ROR $$	Net $$	D/D	R/R	UPI	Risk	MMgt	CARG	DD Days	Losses	R^2
Monthly Close Model	Relative time ROC	1933	87	10%	50	0%	$1,003,526	−$382,027	3	0.8	−5.0%	$582m	27%	3,556	22	83%
Bollinger Bands	Volatility breakout	1993	27	28%	50	0%	$1,558,476	−$224,374	7	1.7	−4.6%	$431m	26%	1,579	28	94%
Turtle Trading	Channel breakout	1983	37	21%	50	0%	$1,418,786	−$95,107	15	2.2	−4.7%	$257m	24%	1,637	20	96%
Dow Theory	Swing breakout	1900	120	5%	50	0%	$1,090,346	−$250,428	4	1.4	−3.3%	$167m	23%	2,238	24	95%
Donchian 4-Week Rule	Channel breakout	1960	60	14%	50	0%	$1,601,223	−$261,817	6	1.4	−5.6%	$69m	20%	1,608	18	93%
Arnold PPS	Congestion breakout	1995	25	31%	50	0%	$450,780	−$62,059	7	0.7	−2.2%	$35m	18%	2,494	23	95%
Gartley's 3- and 6-Week Crossover	Relative price ROC	1935	85	12%	50	0%	$1,079,398	−$295,771	4	1.1	−6.2%	$30m	18%	2,972	18	83%
Quarterly Close Model	Relative time ROC	1933	87	9%	50	0%	$611,092	−$261,974	2	0.4	−7.5%	$5m	12%	4,472	17	74%
Dreyfus 52-Week Rule	Channel breakout	1960	60	47%	50	0%	$1,442,906	−$113,469	13	1.3	−16.7%	$2m	10%	1,600	9	98%
Darvas Box	Congestion breakout	1960	60	15%	50	0%	$136,731	−$75,614	2	0.1	−5.5%	$0m	0%	3,089	17	82%

per trade! That's big. Having such larger stops prevented the strategy from building its position size. Remember, when we trade we have a fixed amount of capital we're prepared to risk. The amount of capital is defined by our money management strategy. If a setup's stop is small, it means we can put on a relatively larger position size vis-à-vis a setup with a larger stop. Dreyfus's 52-Week strategy has enormous stops. As a result, it's not efficient in making money. Large stops kills it. This is why it's so important when reviewing a strategy to see how it performs when money management is applied. Looking at an equity curve based on a single contract or position sizing can hide the existence of large stops and poor efficiency. Remember, CAGR is queen!

At this stage of my system review, based on my robustness and performance analysis, the Monthly Close Model would be your toolkit's preferred strategy benchmark. It's not only robust but it's the most efficient at making money with a 27% CAGR. A win–win.

Or is it?

Remember, there is no single super metric that can rank strategies. Not even the CAGR. Despite its remarkable annualized return, the Monthly Close Model has suffered poor performance across a number of key metrics. It has a very low reward/risk payoff ratio of only 3:1 and a low UPI. It only earned 0.8 units of excess returns over the risk-free rate for each unit of average drawdown risk. It has suffered the second longest drawdown period of 3,556 days and does not enjoy a smooth equity curve, recording a lower 83% R-squared. Well, not to worry. There are nine other strategies to choose from—which brings us to the next logical strategy in line for selection, Bollinger Bands. With its high 26% CAGR, improved reward/risk ratio of 7:1 and a healthy UPI of 1.7, along with a reasonable drawdown period of 1,579 days and smoother 94% R-squared equity curve, it looks like our next obvious choice.

Or does it?

Well, despite its position in my table, you have to remember I made up its core variable value of 80 for my review. I gave it a generous publishing date to acknowledge its use in one of the all-time best commercially available trading strategies from the 1990s. The strategy was named as 'One of the Top 10 Trading Systems of All Time' by *Futures Truth* magazine. But despite its impressive credentials, I don't know the variable value that came with the system. So, despite its heritage and despite my positive equity curve stability review, I have to overlook its outstanding performance. Its results are not out-of-sample. Even though it's both versatile and well designed, with a stable enough equity curve to trade, I have to ignore it when there are so many other alternative strategies with plenty of out-of-sample evidence of robustness to choose from.

So, for me, I have to skip Bollinger Bands. This leads me to the next highest ranked strategy, Turtle Trading. It has a healthy 24% CAGR and a superior risk-adjusted performance. It has the best of both worlds. It enjoys both a strong reward/risk ratio of 15:1 and an excellent UPI of 2.2. And it achieved both with a reasonable draw-down period of 1,637 days along with a smooth 96% R-squared equity curve. For me, Turtle Trading appears to have the strongest combination of robustness and performance metrics, which produces the best risk-adjusted performance, making it an ideal candidate to become a strategy benchmark.

Equity Curve Stability Review—Turtle Trading

Before I consider recommending Turtle Trading as your strategy benchmark, I first want to review how sensitive its equity curve is to changes in its variable values. Not because it's necessary, as any further analysis is superfluous to its 37+ years of out-of-sample performance. Performance that provides irrefutable evidence of its robustness. No, but because it'll be a good illustrative exercise to go through. So, to review its sensitivity to changes in variable values I'll complete an equity curve stability review.

Let's review the strategy rules that we first saw in Chapter 6.

Rules

Strategy:	Turtle Trading
Developed:	Unknown
Published:	1983
Data:	Daily
Approach:	Trend trading
Technique:	Channel breakout
Symmetry:	Buy and sell
Markets:	All
Indicators:	None.

Variables—Number:	2
	Weekly Entry Channel (4)
	Weekly Stop Channel (2)
Variables—Symmetry:	Same value for both buy and sell setups
Variables—Application:	Same value across all markets

Rules: 3

<u>Buy Rules</u>

Setup:	Weekly Channel showing highest weekly high of the preceding 4 weeks
Filter:	Only trade signal if previous signal was a loss
Entry:	Buy a break of the highest weekly high of the preceding 4 weeks
Stop:	Sell a break of the lowest weekly low of the preceding 2 weeks

<u>Sell Rules</u>

Setup:	Weekly Channel showing lowest weekly low of the preceding 4 weeks
Filter:	Only trade signal if previous signal was a loss
Entry:	Sell a break of the lowest weekly low of the preceding 4 weeks
Stop:	Buy a break of the highest weekly high of the preceding 2 weeks

The strategy contains two variables. The first being the length of the entry breakout channel (four weeks) and the second being the length of the opposite stop breakout channel (two weeks).

I will restrict the number of adjustments of each variable to four. With two variables and four adjustments, like the Bollinger Band review, I know the strategy's universe of alternative equity curves will be 25 when the original variable values are included.

Unfortunately, I can't use a 10% adjustment for each variable like I did with the Bollinger Band review, as weeks are not easily divisible. For this review I'll use a single week as the adjustment factor, making two adjustments above and two below the original value. Accordingly, for the weekly entry breakout channel length I'll be using two weeks, three weeks, four weeks (original value), five weeks and six weeks. For the opposite weekly stop breakout channel, I'll use zero weeks, one week, two weeks (original value), three weeks and four weeks. Naturally a zero-week stop is impossible as it would imply the strategy being stopped out immediately upon entry. Consequently, I'll remove the zero- week stop, which will reduce Turtle Trading's universe of alternative equity curves from 25 to 20. In addition, Turtle Trading restricts the length of the opposite 'stop' channel to being less than the length of the breakout 'entry' channel. For example, a two-week breakout entry signal cannot have a three-week opposite breakout stop because another two-week breakout entry signal can occur before the prior position is stopped out at the three-week channel. As a consequence, this will remove three equity curves (a two-week entry with three-week stop, a two-week entry with four-week stop and a three-week entry with four-week stop). This will reduce the universe of alternative equity curves from 20 to 17. Still enough to gauge its stability.

I've run all the additional 16 equity curves and overlaid them in Figure 8.8.

Operating within my arbitrary limit of only four adjustments, we can clearly see the upper and lower boundaries of alternative equity curves. The question we need to answer is whether any of the lower boundary equity curves produce ROR calculations over 0%.

I've summarized the results in Table 8.9.

As you can see, there are no alternative equity curves producing ROR calculations above 0%. So, it's two thumbs up as well for Turtle Trading.

Let me now complete the equity curve stability review as shown in Figure 8.9.

Based on my one-week adjustment factor the variation in alternate equity curves and expectancies is large. In defence of Turtle Trading, my adjustment factor is large in itself, where one week on a four-week breakout represents a 25% adjustment. Much larger than the 10% adjustment I used in my Bollinger Band review. But regardless, being a weekly breakout strategy where the smallest denominator is a weekly unit, I had no alternative but to adjust the variables in weekly increments. So, the variance between the upper and lower boundaries is large. But regardless of the variance, no variable values produced an ROR calculation above 0% making Turtle Trading's equity curve stable enough to trade.

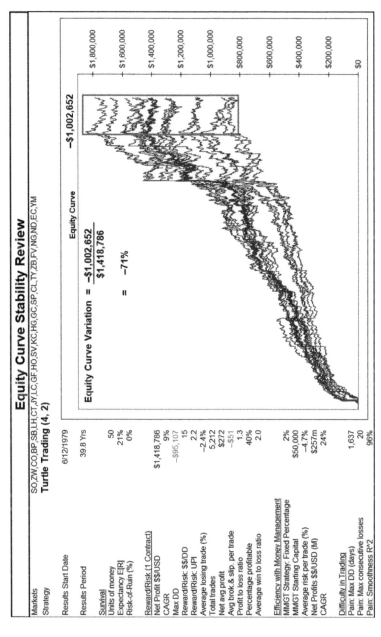

FIGURE 8.8 Turtle Trading's universe of alternative equity curves.

TABLE 8.9   Turtle Trading's universe of alternative equity curves are absent of any ROR calculations above 0%.

Equity Curve Stability Review

Indicator	Breakout Channels		E[R]		Units of $$		ROR
	Entry Week	Stop Week					
Variables	4	2	21%	+	50	=	0%
Change in Variable Values							
	2	1	8%	+	50	=	0%
	2	2	15%	+	50	=	0%
	3	1	14%	+	50	=	0%
	3	2	19%	+	50	=	0%
	3	3	23%	+	50	=	0%
	4	1	16%	+	50	=	0%
	4	2	21%	+	50	=	0%
	4	3	25%	+	50	=	0%
	4	4	24%	+	50	=	0%
	5	1	15%	+	50	=	0%
	5	2	21%	+	50	=	0%
	5	3	23%	+	50	=	0%
	5	4	24%	+	50	=	0%
	6	1	15%	+	50	=	0%
	6	2	23%	+	50	=	0%
	6	3	23%	+	50	=	0%
	6	4	24%	+	50	=	0%

In addition, as I said before, this review is superfluous because Turtle Trading, in its basic configuration as taught by Richard Dennis and Bill Eckhardt to their student traders in 1983, has 37+ years of out-of-sample performance. Performance that provides indisputable

Equity Curve Stability Review			
Strategy		RTT	Turtle Trading
Setup		MA (34)	Channel (4)
		MA (250)	Channel (2)
		RSI (4,80%)	
Attributes of Winning Strategies			
Measureable	Expectancy	9%	21%
	Units of money	20	50
	ROR	0%	0%
Robust			
Evidence	Out-of-sample performance	No	Yes
Indication			
Versatile	Profitable over a diversified portfolio	Yes	Yes
Good	Equity Curve Stability Review		
Design	Number of indicator variables	4	2
Principles	Number of variable adjustments	4	4
	Number of possible equity curves	256	17
	Variation in equity curves	Large	Large
	Variation in expectancy	Large	Large
	Do any sets of variable values have ROR > 0%?	Yes	None
	Is equity curve stable enough to trade?	**NO**	**YES**

FIGURE 8.9   Turtle Trading's review confirms its equity curve is stable enough to trade.

evidence of its robustness. That is enough to confirm it as a suitable strategy benchmark. However, if you decide your preference is to trade the strategy and elect to alter the variables, at least you'll know the size of its universe of alternative equity curves.

In my mind, Turtle Trading becomes the next best strategy suitable for selection as a strategy benchmark.

Back to the 1980s—Turtle Trading   Accordingly, Turtle Trading is the strategy benchmark I'd select for your trader's toolkit. It's the highest ranked strategy according to my robustness and performance analysis and equity curve stability review. It should now become the benchmark against which you judge your own efforts. If you can't surpass it and you wish to trade, then you should seriously consider trading it.

Now, does my analysis make Turtle Trading the perfect strategy? No. Despite its ranking, which is deserved, it's not perfect. A big issue for me is the size of its stops, -4.7%. It may not be as large as -16.7%, but it's still relatively large. However, as for being a benchmark, it's perfect. It's the best from my list and it has far more attractive attributes than the majority of self-made failed trading strategies. If your own efforts can't surpass Turtle Trading, and you wish to trade, then you should seriously consider trading it, even with the relative large stops.

And I hope the irony hasn't escaped the more experienced traders among you. When you've been scratching your heads looking for answers, hunting for strategies that work, devouring books, attending seminars and workshops and feverishly coding, the answer has been hiding in plain sight. The Turtle Trading strategy.

Now that I have selected a strategy benchmark, the final addition to your toolkit is a strategy development blueprint.

STRATEGY DEVELOPMENT

This is the final addition to your toolkit.

All the hard work has already been completed. You have everything you need in your toolkit to develop a strategy:

- portfolio construction,
- data,
- software,
- attributes of winning strategies,
- strategy review and
- strategy benchmark.

You know the importance of having an objectively selected portfolio based on diversity and average daily volume. You will need to secure a reliable data source. Software, if it isn't already, should be on your shopping list. You know the attributes you want in your trading strategy and you know how to review and benchmark your efforts against the Turtle Trading strategy.

The last piece to this puzzle is a blueprint for strategy development. This simply consists of a six-step plan:

1. Find a methodology.
2. Code the methodology.
3. Review the methodology.
4. Compare the methodology.
5. Adjust the methodology:

- without excessive curve fitting,
- review again and
- compare again.
6. Complete an equity curve stability review.

Rinse and repeat. That's it.

Dust off your old trading books. It will be preferable to review books published before 2000, as they will give you 20+ years of out-of-sample performance. Start reading and if an idea grabs your attention code it up and run an historical back test over a universal portfolio of diverse markets. That will produce an historical equity curve and generate the performance metrics I've used. If it doesn't, do it manually with a spreadsheet. Do a strategy review and compare it to Turtle Trading. If it deserves further attention, give consideration to how you can improve it without falling into the trap of excessive curve fitting. Try to be minimal with the number of rules, indicators and variables used. Review the modified strategy and compare it again to Turtle Trading.

The difficult part will be to recognize when your 'adjustments' have strayed too far into excessive curve fitting. When you've crossed that Rubicon it's all over red rover. There's no cigar. It's back to the drawing board.

If you believe you haven't crossed that line of excessive curve fitting, and the strategy appears superior to Turtle Trading, the last step is to undertake an equity curve stability review. You will need to determine how large the strategy's parallel universe of alternative equity curves is given the number of variables and adjustments you'll allow. You will need to determine if any of the alternative equity curves produce ROR calculations above 0%. You will need to determine how much variation exists between the upper and lower boundaries of alternative equity curves and gauge whether the variation is reasonable enough to trade. You will need to determine if the strategy's equity curve is stable enough to trade over various sets of variable values.

If the answer is yes, its hip, hip hooray and your next objective will be to compete a T.E.S.T. If your T.E.S.T is successful then you're on your way. It's time to pop open the champagne.

If the answer is no, don't worry. There are plenty of old ideas to keep you busy. Just rinse and repeat.

Data Splitting

As I've mentioned before, another approach to gauging a strategy's robustness is to split your data in half, developing an idea on the in-sample set of data and then seeing how it goes on the out-of-sample set of data. As I've said, I prefer using the whole data set for an equity curve stability review. I like to gauge the size and breadth of a strategy's parallel universe of alternative curves. To be aware of the upper and lower boundary of equity curves. To see what is revealed in between. Another reason why I don't bother data splitting is that by concentrating on old and established ideas the majority of my historical data beyond 1980 is already 'out'-of-sample!

SUMMARY

Well, here you are. You're now equipped with the correct tools you'll need as you venture into the exciting world of strategy development. It's a toolkit that should never leave your side. You now know how to select and construct a portfolio and secure data. You know the importance of software to help you gather evidence. You now know what to look out for in a winning strategy. You now know how to conduct a strategy review. You now know how to select a strategy benchmark to help you avoid falling into the relevancy trap. Hey, you actually now have a strategy benchmark.

Now that you're properly equipped, it's time to try your hand at developing a sensible trading strategy, one that will (hopefully) surpass your benchmark and move you firmly along your pathway towards sustainable trading.

CHAPTER

Back to the Future

The more markets change, the more they stay the same.

It's now time to go backwards to move forwards.

As an aside I want to dedicate this chapter to the early technicians. Those traders who generously shared their market insights. To recognize those shoulders we all stand upon. Although they're no longer with us in person, I want to demonstrate that they're certainly still with us in spirit. Helping to guide us through the fog of trading that accompanies us in the volatile world of global markets. I hope this chapter will do justice to their past service as I examine one particular gem that can be found among the rarely useful, scarcely ever supported by evidence, generally misleading and at times often contradictive field of technical analysis.

The objective of this chapter, apart from offering a sincere salute of thanks to those who have gone before us, is to develop a sensible and sustainable trading strategy. To do this I'll be following my strategy development blueprint.

STRATEGY DEVELOPMENT

I'll be following the six-step plan I shared with you in Chapter 8:

1. Find a methodology.
2. Code the methodology.

3. Review the methodology.
4. Compare the methodology.
5. Adjust the methodology:
   - without excessive curve fitting,
   - review again and
   - compare again.
6. Complete an equity curve stability review.

FIND A METHODOLOGY

It's time to take a walk down memory lane. I certainly believe you need to look backwards to move forwards. To take the time to look in the rear-view mirror for inspiration. You now know it's the old ideas that can give you the greatest gift a trader desires, proof of robustness from positive out-of-sample performance. New ideas can't. But old ideas can.

Review Trading Books Published Before 2000

Now there are plenty of old ideas on trading. You just need to search for them. One simple approach is to review all trading books published before 2000. If an idea grabs your attention, code it up for review. Being published before 2000 will give you 20+ years of out-of-sample performance. That's plenty enough to gauge an idea's robustness.

Top Ten Trend Trading Strategies

For myself, I'll start by reviewing my list of top ten trend trading strategies, which I have summarized in Tables 9.1 and 9.2.

These tables commenced as a list of 18 alternative trend trading strategies. The list grew to 19 when I introduced Random Trend Trader. Through my robustness and performance analysis the list was trimmed down to a top ten. As you know, my original list was not exhaustive so please don't think your search for established ideas should be restricted to my top ten strategies.

So, the question becomes, which established methodology should I review? Well, since the key word here is 'established', I can see one strategy that is a standout in terms of age, Dow Theory. It's certainly the oldest at 120 years young. That will do me. Dow Theory is it.

TABLE 9.1 Key robustness metrics for the top ten strategies.

Model	Type	Robustness Analysis											
		Evidence						Data Mining?	Indication				
									Excessive Curve Fitting?				
		Published	Out-of-sample Yrs	Net $$	Trades	Avg $$	Brok & Slip	Port.	Rules		Indicators	Variables		
									No.	Sym.	No.	No.	Sym.	Mkts
Monthly Close Model	Relative time ROC	1933	87	$1,003,526	4,993	$201	*$51	P24	2	Yes	0	0	NA	NA
Bollinger Bands	Volatility breakout	1993	27	$1,558,476	2,954	$528	*$51	P24	2	Yes	1	2	Yes	Yes
Turtle Trading	Channel breakout	1983	37	$1,418,786	5,212	$272	*$51	P24	3	Yes	0	2	Yes	Yes
Dow Theory	Swing breakout	1900	120	$1,090,346	17,927	$61	*$51	P24	1	Yes	0	0	NA	NA
Donchian 4-Week Rule	Channel breakout	1960	60	$1,601,223	6,120	$262	*$51	P24	1	Yes	0	1	Yes	Yes
Arnold PPS	Congestion breakout	1995	25	$450,780	2,586	$174	*$51	P24	6	Yes	1	5	Yes	Yes
Gartley's 3- and 6-Week Crossover	Relative price ROC	1935	85	$1,079,398	3,387	$319	*$51	P24	2	Yes	1	3	Yes	Yes
Quarterly Close Model	Relative time ROC	1933	87	$611,092	1,670	$366	*$51	P24	2	Yes	0	0	NA	NA
Dreyfus 52-Week Rule	Channel breakout	1960	60	$1,442,906	475	$3,038	*$51	P24	1	Yes	0	1	Yes	Yes
Darvas Box	Congestion breakout	1960	60	$136,731	636	$215	*$51	P24	4	Yes	1	5	Yes	Yes

TABLE 9.2 Key performance metrics for the top ten strategies.

| Model | Type | Robustness | | Performance Analysis | | | | | | | | | | | | |
| | | | | Survival | | | Reward/Risk | | | | Efficiency wMMgt | | | Difficulty in trading | | |
		Published	Out-of-sample Yrs	E[R]	Units $$	ROR	Net $$	D/D	R/R	UPI	Risk	MMgt	CARG	DD Days	Losses	R^2
Monthly Close Mode	Relative time ROC	1933	87	10%	50	0%	$1,003,526	−$382,027	3	0.8	−5.0%	$20m	27%	3,556	22	83%
Bollinger Bands	Volatility breakout	1993	27	28%	50	0%	$1,558,476	−$224,374	7	1.7	−4.6%	$431m	26%	1,579	28	94%
Turtle Trading	Channel breakout	1983	37	21%	50	0%	$1,418,786	−$95,107	15	2.2	−4.7%	$257m	24%	1,637	20	96%
Dow Theory	Swing breakout	1900	120	5%	50	0%	$1,090,346	−$250,428	4	1.4	−3.3%	$85m	23%	2,238	24	95%
Donchian 4-Week Rule	Channel breakout	1960	60	14%	50	0%	$1,601,223	−$261,817	6	1.4	−5.6%	$69m	20%	1,608	18	93%
Arnold PPS	Congestion breakout	1995	25	31%	50	0%	$450,780	−$62,059	7	0.7	−2.2%	$113m	18%	1,875	31	95%
Gartley's 3- and 6-Week Crossover	Relative price ROC	1935	85	12%	50	0%	$1,079,398	−$295,771	4	1.1	−6.2%	$30m	18%	2,972	18	83%
Quarterly Close Model	Relative time ROC	1933	87	9%	50	0%	$611,092	−$261,974	2	0.4	−7.5%	$5m	12%	4,472	17	74%
Dreyfus 52-Week Rule	Channel breakout	1960	60	47%	50	0%	$1,442,906	−$113,469	13	1.3	−16.7%	$2m	10%	1,600	9	98%
Darvas Box	Congestion breakout	1960	60	15%	50	0%	$136,731	−$75,614	2	0.1	−5.5%	$0m	0%	3,089	17	82%

Dow Theory

The Background

Dow Theory is attributed to Charles Dow (1851–1902), who is regarded as the father of technical analysis and trend analysis in particular. Which is lucky for me since my book is about trend trading. Apart from his theory he was very much part of the market's fabric. He established Dow Jones & Company in 1882 with Edward Jones and became a part owner and editor of *The Wall Street Journal*. He was certainly a pillar of Wall Street having created the Dow Jones Rail Index in 1884 (which is now the Transportation Index) and the Dow Jones Industrial Index in 1896. Dow's ideas on market behaviour came to light in 1900 when he published a series of articles for *The Wall Street Journal*. What is interesting is that he never published his complete theory on the markets. He never wrote a book sharing his insights and he never used the term 'Dow Theory'. It was Dow's close friend Samuel Nelson who refined his theory and first coined the term Dow Theory. Notable publications supporting Dow's ideas include:

- 1902—*The ABC of Stock Speculation* by Samuel Nelson.
- 1922—*The Stock Market Barometer* by William P. Hamilton.
- 1932—*The Dow Theory* by Robert Rhea.
- 1960—*How I Helped More Than 10,000 Investors to Profit in Stocks* by E. Schaefer.
- 1961—*The Dow Theory Today* by Richard Russell.

In a Nutshell

So, what is it? With the risk of oversimplifying it, Dow Theory can be encapsulated by the seven points I've summarized in Figure 9.1. Please take a moment to read them.

Got it? Maybe? No, not really? Don't worry, as I'm going to simplify it.

Peak and Trough Trend Analysis

For my purposes, I want to distil Dow Theory down to its simplest interpretation. One that encapsulates Dow Theory and one that will allow me to code up a model with clear and objective rules.

Dow Theory in a Nutshell

---

1. Markets contained all information.
   Price reflects all relevant fundamental, political, and psychological information.
   Believe what you see, not what you think.

2. Market trends are defined by peaks and troughs.
   Uptrend is defined by higher peaks and higher troughs. Higher prices, trend up.
   Down trend is defined by lower peaks and lower troughs. Lower prices, trend down.

3. Market trends comprise 3 trends.

Primary trend:	Major trend.	Trade in its direction, not against it.
		Lasts between one to three years.
Secondary trend:	Intermediate trend.	Is a retracement against the primary trend.
		Lasts between three weeks and three months.
Minor trend:	Small trend.	Is s retracement against the secondary trend.
		Is alinged with the primary trend.
		Lasts less than three weeks.

4. Market primary trends comprise 3 phases;

Accumulation:	Astute participants are entering, feeling a change in trend.
Public:	Majority of investors are entering, seeing the new trend.
Distribution:	Public are entering, trend is well publicized in the news.

5. Market trends must confirm each other.
   Each index requires a confirmed trend change, to confirm a primary trend change.

6. Market trend volume must confirm the trend.
   Primary trend volume > Secondary trend volume. Price more important than volume.

7. Primary trend is considered in place until a confirmed reversal takes place.

FIGURE 9.1   Dow Theory comprises seven key insights.

I want to focus on point 2:

2. Market trends are defined by peaks and troughs.

Uptrend is defined by higher peaks and higher troughs.
Higher prices, trend up.

Downtrend is defined by lower peaks and lower troughs.
Lower prices, trend down.

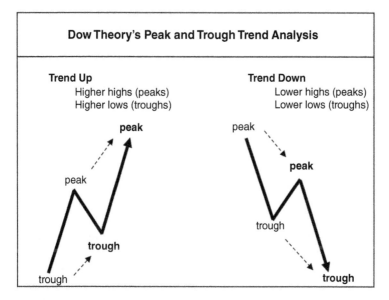

FIGURE 9.2 Dow's peak and trough trend analysis is a key component of Dow Theory.

This refers to Dow's peak and trough trend analysis. This was the analysis upon which he earned his mantle of being the father of trend analysis. It was a simple yet effective analysis for determining the trend as shown in Figure 9.2.

Although Dow used the terms 'peaks' and 'troughs', my preference is to use 'highs' and 'lows'. While the market is in an uptrend it should be making higher highs and higher lows. Similarly, if the market is in a downtrend it should be making lower lows and lower highs.

Simplification

I know Dow Theory is more than the peak and trough trend analysis. However, for my purposes, when I use the term 'Dow Theory', I will simply be referring to just the peak and trough trend analysis. Not the entire theory. In addition, I will be using swing charts overlaid on daily bar charts to help identify trends. Swing charts smooth prices and help identify market highs and lows, which in turn help to identify trends and changes in trends as defined by Dow Theory (i.e. the peak and trough trend analysis).

Dow Theory—101

Dow Theory is simple once you define how you'll identify the 'highs' and 'lows'. As I said, I use swing charts overlaid on daily bar charts. There are only three key rules to remember when working out a market's trend according to Dow Theory:

1. Dow Theory is always in the market, the trend is either up or down.
2. Trend is up when the market is making higher highs.
3. Trend is down when the market is making lower lows.

Simple, hey? It really is as simple as counting one–two–three, as I've shown in Figure 9.3.

If you can understand Figure 9.3, then you can consider yourself an expert in Dow Theory (i.e. the peak and trough trend analysis). As you can see, the swing chart overlaid on the daily bar chart helps to define the 'highs' and 'lows', smoothing out prices.

Dow Theory is always in the market with a trend interpretation. The trend is either up or down, or the model is either long or short.

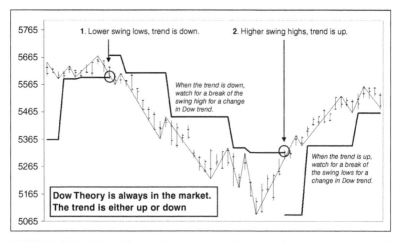

FIGURE 9.3   Dow Theory is a stop and reversal strategy where it's always in the market, either long or short.

The chart begins in an uptrend. The market is making higher (swing) highs and higher (swing) lows. When the trend is up you need to watch for a break of the swing lows. When a break occurs, there is a change in Dow trend where Dow Theory switches from long to short. When the trend is down the market should be making lower lows and lower highs. When this happens, you need to watch for a break of the swing highs. When such a break occurs, there is a change in Dow trend where Dow Theory switches from short to long. The chart finishes in an uptrend, where the trader should be watching for a break of the swing lows to herald a change in Dow trend from up to down.

That's it. Dow Theory 101.

Now that you have a better understanding of Dow Theory, it's time to code it up.

CODE THE METHODOLOGY

Lucky for me I've already coded up Dow Theory from Chapter 6. Since I will be developing a Dow Theory strategy based on daily bars, I'll start referring to the model as 'Daily Dow Trader' or DDT. The model will enter positions on a change in the daily Dow trend.

I've summarized the rules here.

<u>Rules</u>

Strategy name:	DDT
Core—Methodology:	Dow Theory
Core—Published:	1900
Markets:	All
Indicators:	None
Variables—Number:	0
Rules:	1

<u>Buy Rules</u>

Setup & Entry:	Change in daily Dow trend—from trend down to trend up.
Stop:	Change in daily Dow trend—from trend up to trend down.

<u>Sell Rules</u>

Setup & Entry:	Change in daily Dow trend—from trend up to trend down.
Stop:	Change in daily Dow trend—from trend down to trend up.

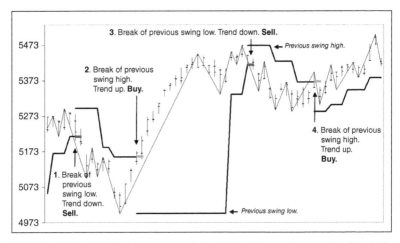

FIGURE 9.4   DDT changes position following a change in the daily Dow trend.

Let's revisit my Dow Theory chart example from Chapter 6, which I've shown here again in Figure 9.4.

As you can see, DDT is always in the market, either long or short. It will enter a position on a change in the daily Dow trend. Once in a position, it will place an initial and trailing stop at an opposite break of the nearest swing point. A break will initiate a change in Dow trend. Once stopped out, it will automatically enter a new position. This type of strategy is referred to a stop and reversal (SAR) model.

REVIEW THE METHODOLOGY

Let's have a look at DDT's performance results as shown in Figure 9.5. There are no surprises here as we have already seen many of the figures from Chapter 6.

COMPARE THE METHODOLOGY

Table 9.3 compares DDT's performance against Turtle Trading.

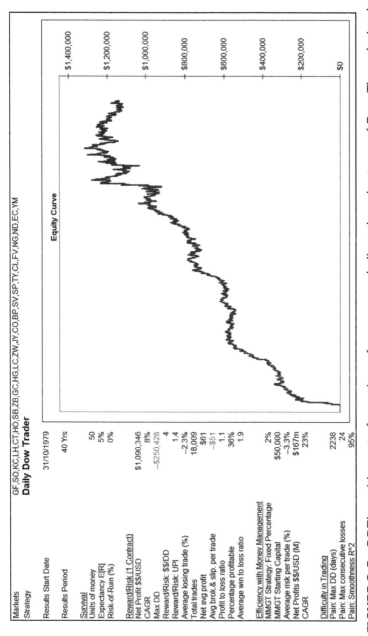

| Markets | GF,SO,KC,LH,CT,HO,SB,ZB,GC,HG,LC,ZW,JY,CO,BP,SV,SP,TY,CL,FV,NG,ND,EC,YM |
| Strategy | **Daily Dow Trader** |

| Results Start Date | 31/10/1979 |
| Results Period | 40 Yrs |

Survival	
Units of money	50
Expectancy E[R]	5%
Risk-of-Ruin (%)	0%

Reward/Risk (1 Contract)	
Net Profit $$/USD	$1,090,346
CAGR	8%
Max DD	–$250,428
Reward/Risk: $$/DD	4
Reward/Risk: UPI	1.4
Average losing trade (%)	–2.3%
Total trades	18,009
Net avg profit	$61
Avg brok.& slip. per trade	–$51
Profit to loss ratio	1.1
Percentage profitable	36%
Average win to loss ratio	1.9

Efficiency with Money Management	
MMGT Strategy: Fixed Percentage	2%
MMGT Starting Capital	$50,000
Average risk per trade (%)	–3.3%
Net Profits $$/USD (M)	$167m
CAGR	23%

Difficulty in Trading	
Pain: Max DD (days)	2238
Pain: Max consecutive losses	24
Pain: Smoothness R^2	95%

FIGURE 9.5 DDT's positive out-of-sample performance underlines the robustness of Dow Theory's simple yet effective peak and trough trend analysis.

At this stage I'm happy with DDT's robustness. The results are all out-of-sample, proving the strategy (and Dow Theory) is robust. Being profitable over a diversified portfolio of 24 markets demonstrates its versatility and the absence of data mining. Its simplicity demonstrates good design principles and ensures the absence of excessive curve fitting. So, it's all good regarding robustness.

What concerns me as a trader is the level of drawdown.

Remember a 'tradable' robustness should be the Holy Grail objective of every strategy and unfortunately DDT's large drawdown is not tradable. Very few private traders would be able to stomach it. So, for the moment it's a deal breaker for me as its drawdown makes the strategy unattractive to trade.

ADJUST THE METHODOLOGY

Now comes the tinkering and the challenge. Developing ideas to improve DDT while avoiding excessive curve fitting. As a core idea Dow Theory is pretty hard to improve on due to its longevity, durability, simplicity, effectiveness and efficiency. Let's keep DDT as it is and create a new Dow Theory model based on a higher weekly timeframe. Let's see if a higher timeframe model can result in a lower drawdown?

Code Weekly Dow Trader

I'll call the new model Weekly Dow Trader or WDT and its rules are identical to DDT's except for the weekly timeframe.

Rules
Strategy name:	WDT
Core—Methodology:	Dow Theory
Core—Published:	1900
Markets:	All
Indicators:	None
Variables—Number:	0
Rules:	1

TABLE 9.3 DDT's large historical drawdown makes it unsuitable for a private trader.

Model	Type	Robustness		Performance Analysis												
				Survival			Reward/Risk				Efficiency wMMgt			Difficulty in trading		
		Published	Out-of-sample Yrs	E[R]	Units $$	ROR	Net $$	D/D	R/R	UPI	Risk	MMgt	CARG	DD Days	Losses	R^2
Turtle Trading	Channel breakout	1983	37	21%	50	0%	$1,418,786	–$95,107	15	2.2	–4.7%	$257m	24%	1,637	20	96%
Daily Dow Trader	Swing breakout	1900	120	5%	50	0%	$1,090,346	–$250,428	4	1,4	–3.3%	$167m	23%	2,238	24	95%

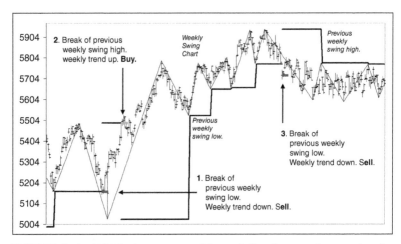

FIGURE 9.6 WDT changes positions following a change in the weekly Dow trend.

Buy Rules

Setup & Entry:	Change in weekly Dow trend—from trend down to trend up
Stop:	Change in weekly Dow trend—from trend up to trend down

Sell Rules

Setup & Entry:	Change in weekly Dow trend—from trend up to trend down
Stop:	Change in weekly Dow trend—from trend down to trend up

I've programmed WDT in my Visual Basic for Applications (VBA) Excel trading model to mechanically and systematically locate and trade the change in weekly Dow trend, as shown in Figure 9.6.

Review WDT

WDT's performance is summarized in Figure 9.7. Switching from a daily timeframe to weekly has certainly boast returns, doubling the net profit. So far it looks good to me.

Compare WDT

Table 9.4 compares WDT to both DDT and Turtle Trading.

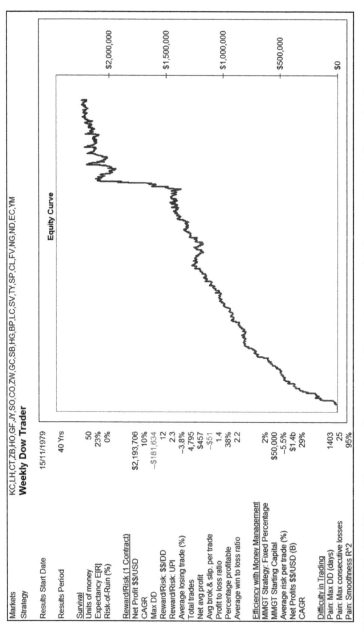

| Markets | KC,LH,CT,ZB,HO,GF,JY,SO,CO,ZW,GC,SB,HG,BP,LC,SV,TY,SP,CL,FV,NG,ND,EC,YM |
| Strategy | **Weekly Dow Trader** |

| Results Start Date | 15/11/1979 |
| Results Period | 40 Yrs |

Survival
Units of money	50
Expectancy E[R]	23%
Risk-of-Ruin (%)	0%

Reward/Risk (1 Contract)
Net Profit $$/USD	$2,193,706
CAGR	10%
Max DD	−$181,634
Reward/Risk: $$/DD	12
Reward/Risk: UPI	2.3
Average losing trade (%)	−3.8%
Total trades	4,795
Net avg profit	$457
Avg brok.& slip. per trade	−$51
Profit to loss ratio	1.4
Percentage profitable	38%
Average win to loss ratio	2.2

Efficiency with Money Management
MMGT Strategy: Fixed Percentage	2%
MMGT Starting Capital	$50,000
Average risk per trade (%)	−5.5%
Net Profits $$/USD (B)	$1.4b
CAGR	29%

Difficulty in Trading
Pain: Max DD (days)	1403
Pain: Max consecutive losses	25
Pain: Smoothness R^2	95%

Equity Curve

FIGURE 9.7 WDT's positive out-of-sample performance on a higher weekly timeframe further underscores the robustness of Dow Theory's simple yet effective peak and trough trend analysis.

TABLE 9.4 While WDT's worst drawdown is an improvement on DDT, it's still not low enough to challenge Turtle Trading.

Model	Type	Robustness		Performance Analysis												
				Survival			Reward/Risk				Efficiency wMMgt			Difficulty in trading		
		Published	Out-of-sample Yrs	E[R]	Units $$	ROR	Net $$	D/D	R/R	UPI	Risk	MMgt	CARG	DD Days	Losses	R^2
Turtle Trading	Channel breakout	1983	37	21%	50	0%	$1,418,786	−$95,107	15	2.2	−4.7%	$257m	24%	1,637	20	96%
Daily Dow Trader	Swing breakout	1900	120	5%	50	0%	$1,090,346	−$250,428	4	1.4	−3.3%	$167m	23%	2,238	24	95%
Weekly Dow Trader	Swing breakout	1900	120	23%	50	0%	$2,193,706	−$181,634	12	2.3	−5.5%	$1.4b	29%	1,403	25	95%

Across the board WDT is generally ahead of DDT, which is really pleasing. Expectancy, net profit, drawdown, reward/risk ratio, risk-adjusted returns (a huge jump in the Ulcer Performance Index (UPI)) efficiency (amazingly better) and time during worst historical drawdown are all improved. It's a remarkably good start. However, even though WDT's drawdown is lower than DDT, it's still too large for me and continues to be a deal breaker.

Adjust WDT

Time for more tinkering. Since changing the timeframe from daily to weekly worked so well, I want to create another Dow Theory model. I'll base it on the monthly timeframe and call it Monthly Dow Trader, or MDT.

Code MDT

The rules are identical to DDT and WDT except for the monthly time-frame.

Rules
Strategy name:	MDT
Core—Methodology:	Dow Theory
Core—Published:	1900
Markets:	All
Indicators:	None
Variables—Number:	0
Rules:	1

Buy Rules
Setup & Entry:	Change in monthly Dow trend—from trend down to trend up
Stop:	Change in monthly Dow trend—from trend up to trend down

Sell Rules
Setup & Entry:	Change in monthly Dow trend—from trend up to trend down
Stop:	Change in monthly Dow trend—from trend down to trend up

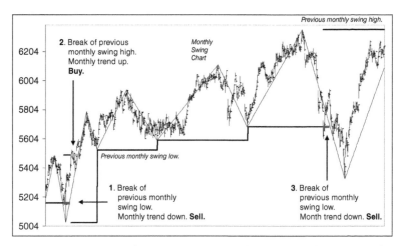

FIGURE 9.8 MDT changes position following a change in the monthly Dow trend.

I've programmed MDT to mechanically and systematically locate and trade the change in monthly Dow trend, as shown in Figure 9.8.

Review MDT

MDT's performance is summarized in Figure 9.9. Moving to a monthly timeframe certainly gives us another insight into the robustness of Dow Theory. Although some metrics have improved, others have not.

Compare MDT

With my tinkering I now have three versions of Dow Theory stacked against Turtle Trader, as shown in Table 9.5.

So far, moving up timeframes has improved Dow Theory's Achilles' heel, its maximum historical drawdown. It's also good to see improvements in expectancy, time in drawdown, number of consecutive losses and smoothness of equity curve. Where it drops disappointingly is in its efficiency. MDT large −10.1% average risk (stops) hampers its ability to increase position sizing and hence profits. It records a disappointingly low 13% compound annual growth rate (CAGR). It's inefficient in making money compared to DDT, WDT and Turtle Trading.

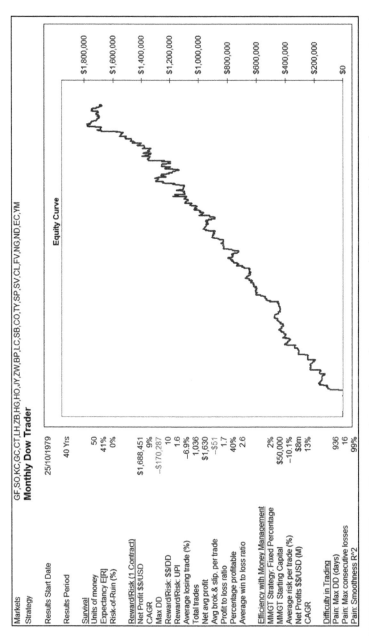

Markets	GF,SO,KC,GC,CT,LH,ZB,HG,HO,JY,ZW,ZW,BP,LC,SB,CO,TY,SP,SV,CL,FV,NG,ND,EC,YM
Strategy	**Monthly Dow Trader**
Results Start Date	25/10/1979
Results Period	40 Yrs
Survival	
Units of money	50
Expectancy E[R]	41%
Risk-of-Ruin (%)	0%
Reward/Risk (1 Contract)	
Net Profit $$/USD	$1,688,451
CAGR	9%
Max DD	–$170,287
Reward/Risk: $$/DD	10
Reward/Risk: UPI	1.6
Average losing trade (%)	–6.9%
Total trades	1,036
Net avg profit	$1,630
Avg brok.& slip. per trade	–$51
Profit to loss ratio	1.7
Percentage profitable	40%
Average win to loss ratio	2.6
Efficiency with Money Management	
MMGT Strategy: Fixed Percentage	2%
MMGT Starting Capital	$50,000
Average risk per trade (%)	–10.1%
Net Profits $$/USD (M)	$8m
CAGR	13%
Difficulty in Trading	
Pain: Max DD (days)	936
Pain: Max consecutive losses	16
Pain: Smoothness R^2	99%

FIGURE 9.9 MDT's positive out-of-sample performance on a higher monthly timeframe once again reinforces the robustness of Dow Theory's simple yet effective peak and trough trend analysis.

321

TABLE 9.5 While MDT's worst drawdown is an improvement over both DDT and WDT, it's still not low enough to challenge Turtle Trading.

Model	Type	Robustness		Performance Analysis												
		Published	Out-of-sample Yrs	Survival			Reward/Risk				Efficiency wMMgt			Difficulty in trading		
				E[R]	Units	ROR $$	Net $$	D/D	R/R	UPI	Risk	MMgt	CARG	DD Days	Losses	R^2
Turtle Trading	Channel breakout	1983	37	21%	50	0%	$1,418,786	−$95,107	15	2.2	−4.7%	$257m	24%	1,637	20	96%
Daily Dow Trader	Swing breakout	1900	120	5%	50	0%	$1,090,346	−$250,428	4	1.4	−3.3%	$167m	23%	2,238	24	95%
Weekly Dow Trader	Swing breakout	1900	120	23%	50	0%	$2,193,706	−$181,634	12	2.3	−5.5%	$1.4b	29%	1,403	25	95%
Monthly Dow Trader	Swing breakout	1900	120	41%	50	0%	$1,688,451	−$170,287	10	1.6	−10.1%	$8m	13%	936	16	99%

Due to its poor efficiency, MDT is a perfect example of the danger of large stops.

Just look at its equity curve. As you can see, it's to die for. With an R-squared value of 99%, it's almost the proverbial straight arrow. Who wouldn't want a strategy like this? The only problem is the existence of large stops. I know you can clearly see it here in the efficiency metrics, but not every developer will show their strategy's average risk or performance when money management is applied.

So, although MDT looks compelling on the surface with its amazing equity curve, the continuing high drawdown and the existence of large stops makes it a deal breaker.

Adjust the Methodology with Loss Filter

Well, I was thinking of doing a rinse and repeat. Trying Dow Theory on another higher timeframe. However, the exercise would be pointless knowing the average risk would jump again, creating larger stops and grinding down Dow Theory's efficiency in making money.

So, what to do? What can I do to combat Dow Theory's large drawdown without falling into the trap of excessive curve fitting? Since the spirit of this chapter, and the thrust of my beliefs, is to re-examine old ideas, I should continue to look for established insights for help. Ideas and insights that have stood the test of time. With that in mind, I want to take a leaf out of Richard Dennis and Bill Eckhardt's Turtle Trading book and examine if their losing signal filter can help reduce Dow Theory's various drawdowns? Remember Turtle Trading doesn't take a four-week breakout unless the previous signal was a loss.

Code DDT with Loss Filter

I'll return to DDT and insert a new line of code. It will ensure a daily Dow signal is only taken if the previous change in daily Dow trend was a loss. Here are the rules with the additional losing signal filter.

Rules
Strategy name:	DDT
Core—Methodology:	Dow Theory
Core—Published:	1900
Markets:	All
Indicators:	None.
Variables—Number:	0
Rules:	2

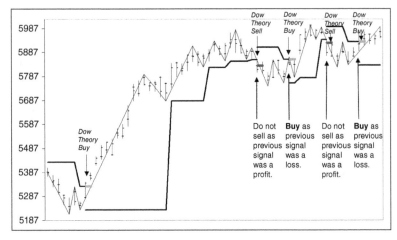

FIGURE 9.10 DDT will only trade a change in the daily Dow trend if the previous change in daily Dow trend was a loss.

Buy Rules

Filter:	Only trade if the previous change in daily Dow trend was a loss
Setup & Entry:	Change in daily Dow trend—from trend down to trend up
Stop:	Change in daily Dow trend—from trend up to trend down.

Sell Rules

Filter:	Only trade if the previous change in daily Dow trend was a loss
Setup & Entry:	Change in daily Dow trend—from trend up to trend down
Stop:	Change in daily Dow trend—from trend down to trend up

I've altered DDT's program to mechanically and systematically locate and trade only those changes in the daily Dow trend that follow a losing Dow signal. Please refer to Figure 9.10.

Review DDT with Loss Filter

Figure 9.11 summarizes DDT's performance with loss filter (LF). I have to say its introduction certainly appears to have hit the ball out of the park.

Markets	LH,HG,SB,CT,ZB,KC,ZW,JY,HO,LC,GF,CO,BP,GC,SO,SV,SP,TY,CL,FV,NG,ND,EC,YM
Strategy	**Daily Dow Trader with LF**

Results Start Date	29/11/1979
Results Period	39.9 Yrs

Survival	
Units of money	50
Expectancy E[R]	14%
Risk-of-Ruin (%)	0%

Reward/Risk (1 Contract)	
Net Profit $$/USD	$1,684,485
CAGR	9%
Max DD	–$149,512
Reward/Risk: $$/DD	11
Reward/Risk: UPI	2.4
Average losing trade (%)	–2.3%
Total trades	11,306
Net avg profit	$149
Avg brok.& slip. per trade	–$51
Profit to loss ratio	1.2
Percentage profitable	39%
Average win to loss ratio	1.9

Efficiency with Money Management	
MMGT Strategy: Fixed Percentage	2%
MMGT Starting Capital	$50,000
Average risk per trade (%)	–3.4%
Net Profits $$/USD (B)	$2.3b
CAGR	31%

Difficulty in Trading	
Pain: Max DD (days)	1685
Pain: Max consecutive losses	21
Pain: Smoothness R^2	96%

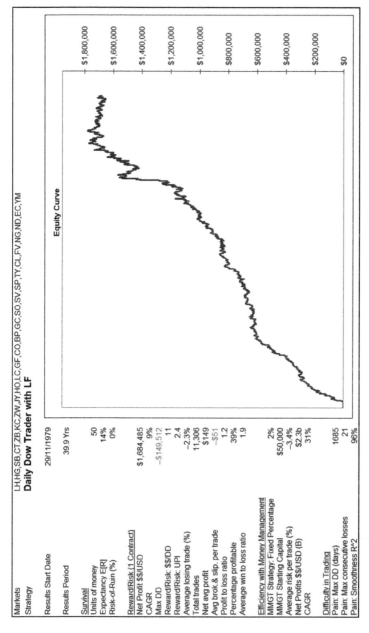

FIGURE 9.11 Waiting for a losing signal has a positive impact on DDT's performance.

Compare DDT with Loss Filter

Table 9.6 compares the models so far against Turtle Trading. I think Richard Dennis and Bill Eckhardt deserve a big thank-you for their simple filter. A filter they taught their students back in 1983.

It appears the loss filter has had a signification impact across DDT's performance metrics:

	DDT	DDT with Loss Filter	Impact with Loss Filter
• Expectancy	5%	14%	+180%
• Net profit	$1.090m	$1.684m	+55%
• Drawdown	−$0.250m	−$0.150m	−40%
• Reward/risk	4	11	+175%
• UPI	1.4	2.4	+71%
• Net profit with money mgt	$167m	$2.3b	+1,277%
• CAGR	23%	31%	+35%
• Consecutive losses	24	21	−12.5%
• Smoothness (R^2)	95%	96%	+1%

That is an extraordinary impact on performance. And it's pleasing to see it comes from another 'old' idea.

Unfortunately, as extraordinary as it is, the sad reality is that the drawdown is still too large. Although it has dropped by 40%, it's still too large for the average private trader. Our search continues.

Adjust WDT with Loss Filter

Since the loss filter worked so well on DDT, I want to see whether its impact is similar on WDT and MDT. I want to see whether it's enough to reduce the drawdown to a manageable level?

TABLE 9.6 Introduction of a loss filter has seen a significant improvement in DDT's performance.

| Model | Type | Robustness | | Performance Analysis | | | | | | | | | | | | | |
| | | | | Survival | | | | Reward/Risk | | | | Efficiency wMMgt | | | Difficulty in trading | | |
		Published	Out-of-sample Yrs	E[R]	Units	ROR	$$	Net $$	D/D	R/R	UPI	Risk	MMgt	CARG	DD Days	Losses	R^2
Turtle Trading	Channel breakout	1983	37	21%	50	0%	0%	$1,418,786	-$95,107	15	2.2	-4.7%	$257m	24%	1,637	20	96%
Daily Dow Trader	Swing breakout	1900	120	5%	50	0%	0%	$1,090,346	-$250,428	4	1.4	-3.3%	$167m	23%	2,238	24	95%
Weekly Dow Trader	Swing breakout	1900	120	23%	50	0%	0%	$2,193,706	-$181,634	12	2.3	-5.5%	$1.4b	29%	1,403	25	95%
Monthly Dow Trader	Swing breakout	1900	120	41%	50	0%	0%	$1,688,451	-$170,287	10	1.6	-10.1%	$8m	13%	936	16	99%
Daily Dow Trader wLF	Swing breakout	1900	120	14%	50	0%	0%	$1,684,485	-$149,512	11	2.4	-3.4%	$2.3b	31%	1,685	21	96%

Code WDT with Loss Filter

I've added the line of code to WDT to match the new rules. Here they are.

<u>Rules</u>

Strategy name:	WDT
Core—Methodology:	Dow Theory
Core—Published:	1900
Markets:	All
Indicators:	None
Variables—Number:	0
Rules:	2

<u>Buy Rules</u>

Filter:	Only trade if the previous change in weekly Dow trend was a loss
Setup & Entry:	Change in weekly Dow trend—from trend down to trend up
Stop:	Change in weekly Dow trend—from trend up to trend down

<u>Sell Rules</u>

Filter:	Only trade if the previous change in weekly Dow trend was a loss
Setup & Entry:	Change in weekly Dow trend—from trend up to trend down
Stop:	Change in weekly Dow trend—from trend down to trend up

As you can see in Figure 9.12, I've altered WDT's program to mechanically and systematically locate and trade only those changes in the weekly Dow trend that follow a losing weekly Dow signal.

Review WDT with Loss Filter

Figure 9.13 summarizes WDT's performance with loss filter. Its introduction has certainly reduced the drawdown, smoothed out the equity curve and lessens the number of days during the worst drawdown. It certainly appears to make it an easier strategy to trade.

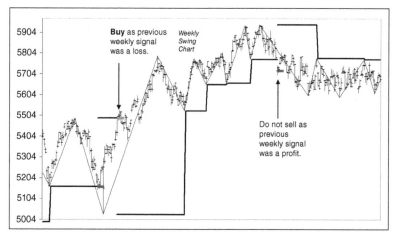

FIGURE 9.12 WDT will only trade a change in the weekly Dow trend if the previous change in weekly Dow trend was a loss.

Compare WDT with Loss Filter

Unfortunately, Table 9.7 shows that the improvement in tradability has come at a considerable cost in performance.

On a profitability comparison it doesn't look so good:

	WDT	WDT with Loss Filter	Impact with Loss Filter
• Net profit	$2.2m	$1.6m	−27%
• Net profit with money mgt	$1.4b	$474m	−66%

While on other metrics there is improvement:

	WDT	WDT with Loss Filter	Impact with Loss Filter
• Expectancy	23%	27%	+15%
• Drawdown	−$0.182m	−$0.131m	−28%
• UPI	2.3	2.0	−15%
• Consecutive losses	25	18	−28%
• Smoothness (R^2)	95%	97%	+2%

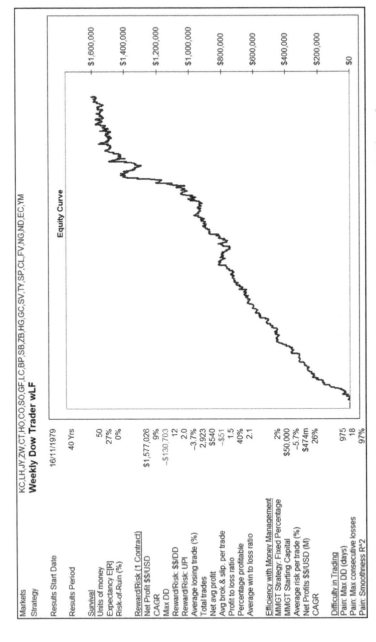

Markets	KC,LH,JY,ZW,CT,HO,CO,SO,GF,LC,BP,SB,ZB,HG,GC,SV,TY,SP,CL,FV,NG,ND,EC,YM
Strategy	**Weekly Dow Trader wLF**

Results Start Date	16/11/1979
Results Period	40 Yrs
<u>Survival</u>	
Units of money	50
Expectancy E[R]	27%
Risk-of-Run (%)	0%
<u>Reward/Risk (1 Contract)</u>	
Net Profit $$/USD	$1,577,026
CAGR	9%
Max DD	-$130,703
Reward/Risk: $$/DD	12
Reward/Risk: UPI	2.0
Average losing trade (%)	-3.7%
Total trades	2,923
Net avg profit	$540
Avg brok.& slip. per trade	-$51
Profit to loss ratio	1.5
Percentage profitable	40%
Average win to loss ratio	2.1
<u>Efficiency with Money Management</u>	
MMGT Strategy: Fixed Percentage	2%
MMGT Starting Capital	$50,000
Average risk per trade (%)	-5.7%
Net Profits $$/USD (M)	$474m
CAGR	26%
<u>Difficulty in Trading</u>	
Pain: Max DD (days)	975
Pain: Max consecutive losses	18
Pain: Smoothness R^2	97%

Equity Curve

FIGURE 9.13 Waiting for a losing signal has a positive impact on WDT's performance.

TABLE 9.7 Despite the loss filter lowering WDT's worst drawdown, it's not enough to dislodge Turtle Trading as the preferred strategy.

Model	Type	Robustness		Performance Analysis												
				Survival			Reward/Risk				Efficiency wMMgt			Difficulty in trading		
		Published	Out-of-sample Yrs	E[R]	Units $$	ROR	Net $$	D/D	R/R	UPI	Risk	MMgt	CARG	DD Days	Losses	R^2
Turtle Trading	Channel breakout	1983	37	21%	50	0%	$1,418,786	−$95,107	15	2.2	−4.7%	$257m	24%	1,637	20	96%
Daily Dow Trader	Swing breakout	1900	120	5%	50	0%	$1,090,346	−$250,428	4	1.4	−3.3%	$167m	23%	2,238	24	95%
Weekly Dow Trader	Swing breakout	1900	120	23%	50	0%	$2,193,706	−$181,634	12	2.3	−5.5%	$1.4b	29%	1,403	25	95%
Monthly Dow Trader	Swing breakout	1900	120	41%	50	0%	$1,688,451	−$170,287	10	1.6	−10.1%	$8m	13%	936	16	99%
Daily Dow Trader wLF	Swing breakout	1900	120	14%	50	0%	$1,684,485	−$149,512	11	2.4	−3.4%	$2.3b	31%	1,685	21	96%
Weekly Dow Trader wLF	Swing breakout	1900	120	27%	50	0%	$1,577,026	−$130,703	12	2.0	−5.7%	$474m	26%	975	18	97%

The most pleasing metric to see is the −28% drop in drawdown. But unfortunately, it's still too high for an average private trader. Let's look at introducing the loss filter to MDT and see whether we can work with it.

Code MDT with Loss Filter

I've added the loss filter code to MDT to match the new rules. Here they are.

Rules

Strategy name:	MDT
Core—Methodology:	Dow Theory
Core—Published:	1900
Markets:	All
Indicators:	None
Variables—Number:	0
Rules:	2

Buy Rules

Filter:	Only trade if the previous change in monthly Dow trend was a loss
Setup & Entry:	Change in monthly Dow trend—from trend down to trend up
Stop:	Change in monthly Dow trend—from trend up to trend down

Sell Rules

Filter:	Only trade if the previous change in monthly Dow trend was a loss
Setup & Entry:	Change in monthly Dow trend—from trend up to trend down
Stop:	Change in monthly Dow trend—from trend down to trend up

I've altered MDT's program to mechanically and systematically locate and trade only those changes in the monthly Dow trend that follows a losing monthly Dow signal. Please refer to Figure 9.14.

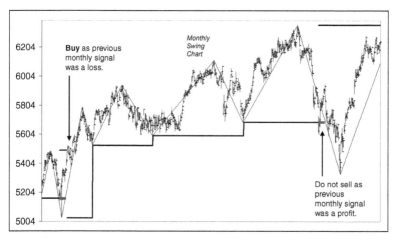

FIGURE 9.14 MDT will only trade a change in the monthly Dow trend if the previous change in monthly Dow trend was a loss.

Review MDT with Loss Filter

Figure 9.15 summarizes MDT's performance with loss filter.

Compare MDT with Loss Filter

Introduction of a loss filter has a positive impact on MDT's worst drawdown. However, as Table 9.8 shows, the filter comes at a cost to performance.

Certainly, a lower drawdown is positive. However, for the strategy overall it's not a positive contribution. Expectancy, profitability, reward/risk ratio, the UPI, efficiency, days in drawdown and smoothness of equity curve have all been adversely impacted.

Loss Filter

While the loss filter has reduced profitably for WDT and MDT, it made a significant impact for DDT. The disproportional impact is due to the higher frequency of Dow trades on the daily timeframe.

Table 9.9 summarizes the loss filter's impact on each of the Dow models. It's interesting to compare the impact on those trades following a loss and those following a profit. For DDT and WDT we can see

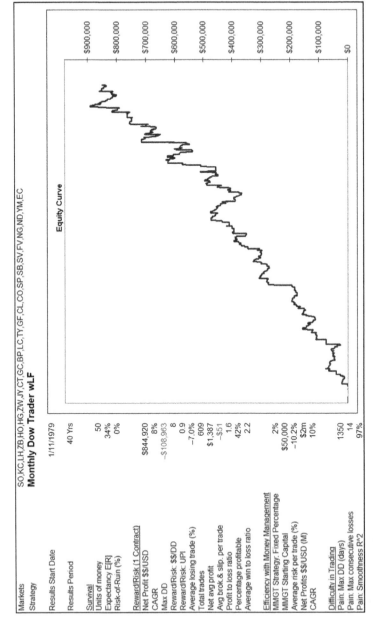

Markets: SO,KC,LH,ZB,HO,HG,ZW,JY,CT,GC,BP,LC,TY,GF,CL,CO,SP,SB,SV,FV,NG,ND,YM,EC
Strategy: **Monthly Dow Trader wLF**

Results Start Date	1/11/1979
Results Period	40 Yrs
Survival	
Units of money	50
Expectancy E[R]	34%
Risk-of-Ruin (%)	0%
Reward/Risk (1 Contract)	
Net Profit $$/USD	$844,920
CAGR	8%
Max DD	–$108,963
Reward/Risk: $$/DD	8
Reward/Risk: UPI	0.9
Average losing trade (%)	–7.0%
Total trades	609
Net avg profit	$1,387
Avg brok.& slip. per trade	–$51
Profit to loss ratio	1.6
Percentage profitable	42%
Average win to loss ratio	2.2
Efficiency with Money Management	
MMGT Strategy: Fixed Percentage	2%
MMGT Starting Capital	$50,000
Average risk per trade (%)	–10.2%
Net Profits $$/USD (M)	$2m
CAGR	10%
Difficulty in Trading	
Pain: Max DD (days)	1350
Pain: Max consecutive losses	14
Pain: Smoothness R^2	97%

Equity Curve

FIGURE 9.15 Waiting for a losing signal has a positive impact on MDT's worst historical drawdown.

TABLE 9.8 Despite the loss filter lowering MDT's worst drawdown, it's negative impact across the other performance metrics does not make MDT superior to Turtle Trading.

Model	Type	Robustness		Survival			Reward/Risk				Efficiency wMMgt			Difficulty in trading		
		Published	Out-of-sample Yrs	E[R]	Units $$	ROR	Net $$	D/D	R/R	UPI	Risk	MMgt	CARG	DD Days	Losses	R^2
Turtle Trading	Channel breakout	1983	37	21%	50	0%	$1,418,786	−$95,107	15	2.2	−4.7%	$257m	24%	1,637	20	96%
Daily Dow Trader	Swing breakout	1900	120	5%	50	0%	$1,090,346	−$250,428	4	1.4	−3.3%	$167m	23%	2,238	24	95%
Weekly Dow Trader	Swing breakout	1900	120	23%	50	0%	$2,193,706	−$181,634	12	2.3	−5.5%	$1.4b	29%	1,403	25	95%
Monthly Dow Trader	Swing breakout	1900	120	41%	50	0%	$1,688,451	−$170,287	10	1.6	−10.1%	$8m	13%	936	16	99%
Daily Dow Trader wLF	Swing breakout	1900	120	14%	50	0%	$1,684,485	−$149,512	11	2.4	−3.4%	$2.3b	31%	1,685	21	96%
Weekly Dow Trader wLF	Swing breakout	1900	120	27%	50	0%	$1,577,026	−$130,703	12	2.0	−5.7%	$474m	26%	975	18	97%
Monthly Dow Trader wLF	Swing breakout	1900	120	34%	50	0%	$844,920	−$108,963	8	0.9	−10.2%	$2m	10%	1,350	14	97%

Performance Analysis

a respective 268% and 64% improvement. Unfortunately for MDT, it suffers a 30% drop in average profit. The lack of trades impacts MDT, as it appears that the higher the occurrence of signals, the greater the positive impact is for the loss filter.

Not Enough

Despite its positive impact on DDT and WDT, the loss filter was unable to reduce the drawdown to a manageable level. So, I need to continue my tinkering.

What to do?

So far, I've been looking at Dow's signals, gauging whether or not to trade a change in Dow trend. I've looked at how a loss filter impacts each strategy. Next, I want to examine if a change in trade plan can help lower the various models' drawdowns?

Adjust the Methodology with an Initial Stop

To this point the trade plan has employed straight Dow Theory. Both the entry and stop have occurred at a change in Dow trend. With DDT, WDT and MDT all being derived from Dow Theory, albeit on different timeframes (daily, weekly and monthly), it's my strong preference for the model to remain 100% Dow. So far, I've been going up in timeframes as I've reviewed both the raw Dow model and loss filter. What I haven't done is moved lower to an intra-day timeframe. So, next I want to examine the impact of introducing an initial intra-day Dow stop. To see whether it may have a positive impact on lowering historical drawdowns.

The idea is that winning trades should just take off and not look back. So, the purpose of introducing an initial stop is to exit losing trades quickly. To bow deeply to the 'cut losses short' golden tenet and to firmly embrace the only real secret to successful trading—to become a good loser by losing early. Rather than wait for a change in Dow trend to exit a losing trade, I want to use a closer initial stop. For this I'll use a lower timeframe intra-day change in Dow trend. Since I don't collect intra-day data, I'll use a proxy. I'll use an opposite break of either the daily setup or entry bar, whichever is furthest away, to act as my intra-day swing high or low. The setup bar is the bar prior to the entry bar. I'm happy to use a daily bar's high or low as a proxy for an intra-day swing high or low because generally (but not always) the daily high or low does represent an intra-day swing point.

TABLE 9.9 The loss filter has a greater impact on higher trade frequency models.

Markets	KC,LH,CT,ZB,HO,GF,JY,SO,CO,ZW,GC,SB,HG,BP,LC,SV,TY,SP,CL,FV,NG,ND,EC,YM								
Strategy	Daily Dow Trader			Weekly Dow Trader			Monthly Dow Trader		
Results Start Date	31/10/1979	with Loss Filter	with Profit Filter	15/11/1979	with Loss Filter	with Profit Filter	25/10/1979	with Loss Filter	with Profit Filter
Reward/Risk (1 Contract)									
Net Profit $$/USD	$1,090,346	$1,684,485	–$594,139	$2,193,706	$1,577,026	$616,680	$1,688,451	$844,920	$843,531
Total trades	18,009	11,306	6,703	4,795	2,923	1,872	1,036	609	427
Net avg profit	$61	$149	–$89 268%	$457	$540	$329 64%	$1,630	$1,387	$1,975 –30%

337

Code DDT with Loss Filter and Two-Stop Trade Plan

I've amended DDT to introduce an initial daily stop so the model now trades according to the following rules.

<u>Rules</u>

Strategy name:	DDT
Core—Methodology:	Dow Theory
Core—Published:	1900
Markets:	All
Indicators:	None
Variables—Number:	0
Rules:	3

<u>Buy Rules</u>

Filter:	Only trade if the previous change in daily Dow trend was a loss
Setup & Entry:	Change in daily Dow trend—from trend down to trend up
Initial Stop:	Sell break of the lowest low of either the daily setup or entry bar
Trailing Stop:	Change in daily Dow trend—from trend up to trend down

<u>Sell Rules</u>

Filter:	Only trade if the previous change in daily Dow trend was a loss
Setup & Entry:	Change in daily Dow trend—from trend up to trend down
Initial Stop:	Buy break of the highest high of either the daily setup or entry bar
Trailing Stop:	Change in daily Dow trend—from trend down to trend up

I've modified DDT to trade with both an initial and trailing stop as shown in Figure 9.16.

Review DDT with Loss Filter and Two-Stop Trade Plan

Figure 9.17 summarizes DDT's performance following inclusion of both a loss filter and initial daily stop. The inclusion of an initial daily stop continues to see DDT perform strongly.

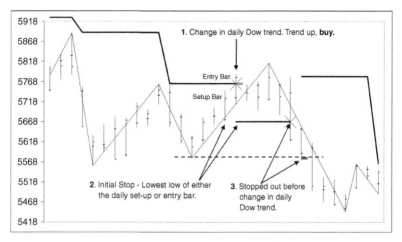

FIGURE 9.16 Introducing an initial daily stop allows DDT to exit losing trades sooner.

Compare DDT with Loss Filter and Two-Stop Trade Plan

Table 9.10 summarizes our growing list of possible alternative models. As you can see, the introduction of an initial daily stop has had a positive impact on DDT.

Introducing an initial daily stop has improved DDT's expectancy, the risk-adjusted UPI (very nicely) and efficiency. Unfortunately, it has not managed to lower the worst historical drawdown to a manageable level. Let's see if the introduction of an initial daily stop can help lower either WDT's or MDT's worst drawdown.

Code WDT with Loss Filter and Two-Stop Trade Plan

I've introduced an initial daily stop for WDT so the model now trades according to the following rules.

<u>Rules</u>
Strategy name: WDT
Core—Methodology: Dow Theory
Core—Published: 1900
Markets: All
Indicators: None
Variables—Number: 0

Rules: 3

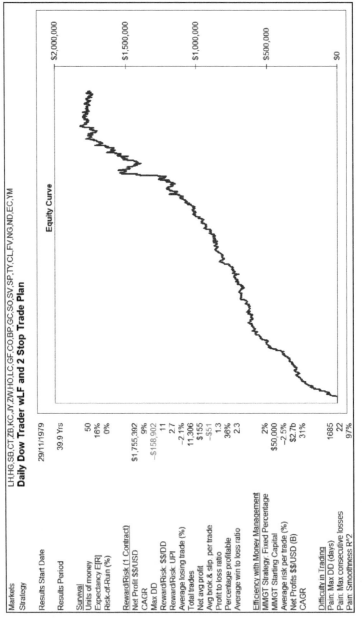

| Markets | LH,HG,SB,CT,ZB,KC,JY,ZW,HO,LC,GF,CO,BP,GC,SO,SV,SP,TY,CL,FV,NG,ND,EC,YM |
| Strategy | **Daily Dow Trader wLF and 2 Stop Trade Plan** |

Results Start Date	29/11/1979
Results Period	39.9 Yrs
Survival	
Units of money	50
Expectancy E[R]	16%
Risk-of-Ruin (%)	0%
Reward/Risk (1 Contract)	
Net Profit $$/USD	$1,755,392
CAGR	9%
Max DD	–$158,902
Reward/Risk: $$/DD	11
Reward/Risk: UPI	2.7
Average losing trade (%)	–2.1%
Total trades	11,306
Net avg profit	$155
Avg brok.& slip. per trade	–$51
Profit to loss ratio	1.3
Percentage profitable	36%
Average win to loss ratio	2.3
Efficiency with Money Management	
MMGT Strategy: Fixed Percentage	2%
MMGT Starting Capital	$50,000
Average risk per trade (%)	–2.5%
Net Profits $$/USD (B)	$2.7b
CAGR	31%
Difficulty in Trading	
Pain: Max DD (days)	1685
Pain: Max consecutive losses	22
Pain: Smoothness R^2	97%

FIGURE 9.17 Introduction of an initial daily stop has a positive impact on DDT's performance metrics, particularly with its UPI reaching 2.7, illustrating how cutting losses can reduce the average breadth and depth of drawdowns, improving a model's risk-adjusted returns.

TABLE 9.10 Introducing an initial daily stop sees an almost universal improvement across DDT's performance metrics.

Model	Type	Robustness		Performance Analysis												
		Published	Out-of-sample Yrs	Survival			Reward/Risk				Efficiency wMMgt			Difficulty in trading		
				E[R]	Units $$	ROR	Net $$	D/D	R/R	UPI	Risk	MMgt	CARG	DD Days	Losses	R^2
Turtle Trading	Channel breakout	1983	37	21%	50	0%	$1,418,786	−$95,107	15	2.2	−4.7%	$257m	24%	1,637	20	96%
Daily Dow Trader	Swing breakout	1900	120	5%	50	0%	$1,090,346	−$250,428	4	1.4	−3.3%	$167m	23%	2,238	24	95%
Weekly Dow Trader	Swing breakout	1900	120	23%	50	0%	$2,193,706	−$181,634	12	2.3	−5.5%	$1.4b	29%	1,403	25	95%
Monthly Dow Trader	Swing breakout	1900	120	41%	50	0%	$1,688,451	−$170,287	10	1.6	−10.1%	$8m	13%	936	16	99%
Daily Dow Trader wLF	Swing breakout	1900	120	14%	50	0%	$1,684,485	−$149,512	11	2.4	−3.4%	$2.3b	31%	1,685	21	96%
Weekly Dow Trader wLF	Swing breakout	1900	120	27%	50	0%	$1,577,026	−$130,703	12	2.0	−5.7%	$474m	26%	975	18	97%
Monthly Dow Trader wLF	Swing breakout	1900	120	34%	50	0%	$844,920	−$108,963	8	0.9	−10.2%	$2m	10%	1,350	14	97%
Daily Dow Trader wLF W2STP	Swing breakout	1900	120	16%	50	0%	$1,755,392	−$158,902	11	2.7	−2.5%	$2.7b	31%	1,685	22	97%

Buy Rules

Filter:	Only trade if the previous change in weekly Dow trend was a loss
Setup & Entry:	Change in weekly Dow trend—from trend down to trend up
Initial Stop:	Sell break of the lowest low of either the daily setup or entry bar
Trailing Stop:	Change in weekly Dow trend—from trend up to trend down

Sell Rules

Filter:	Only trade if the previous change in weekly Dow trend was a loss
Setup & Entry:	Change in weekly Dow trend—from trend up to trend down
Initial Stop:	Buy break of the highest high of either the daily setup or entry bar
Trailing Stop:	Change in weekly Dow trend—from trend down to trend up

I've modified WDT to trade with both an initial and trailing stop, as shown in Figure 9.18.

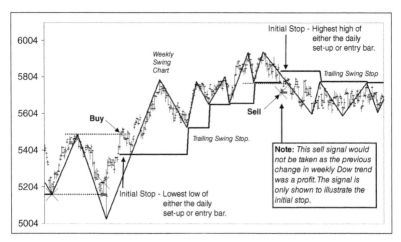

FIGURE 9.18 Introducing an initial daily stop allows WDT to exit losing trades sooner.

Review WDT with Loss Filter and Two-Stop Trade Plan

Figure 9.19 summarizes WDT's performance following inclusion of both a loss filter and initial daily stop. The introduction of an initial daily stop has seen WDT's average risk per trade halve from −5.7% to −2.7%.

Compare WDT with Loss Filter and Two-Stop Trade Plan

Table 9.11 summarizes the impact an initial daily stop has on WDT. As you know, the benefit of smaller stops is the boost it delivers to a strategy's position sizing and efficiency. The introduction of an initial daily stop has reduced WDT's average risk by half from −5.7% to −2.7%, boasting profits from $474 million to a staggering $1.3 billion. This saw WDT's CAGR jumping from 26% to 29%. Simply outstanding.

Not only has the performance improved significantly but the drawdown has dropped by 38% from −$130,703 to −$80,520. A win–win. The only disappointment is seeing the risk-adjusted UPI falling from 2 units of excess returns per unit of average drawdown risk to 1.8 units. A disappointment, but not a deal breaker given the enormous boast in profitability. Cutting losses short has certainly worked for WDT.

Code MDT with Loss Filter and Two-Stop Trade Plan

Let's see how the introduction of an initial daily stop helps MDT. I've amended MDT so that the model now trades according to the following rules.

Rules
Strategy name:	MDT
Core—Methodology:	Dow Theory
Core—Published:	1900
Markets:	All
Indicators:	None
Variables—Number:	0
Rules:	3

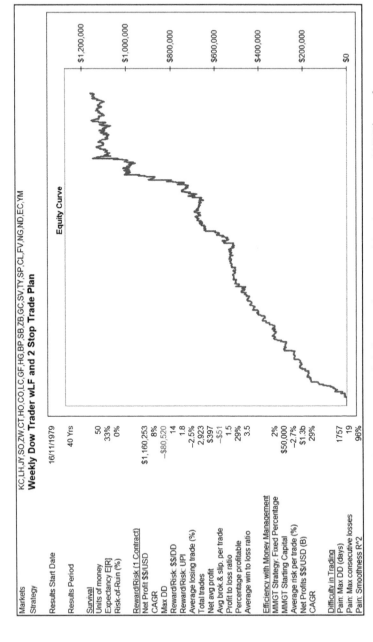

| Markets | KC,LH,JY,SO,ZW,CT,HO,CO,LC,GF,HG,BP,SB,ZB,GC,SV,TY,SP,CL,FV,NG,ND,EC,YM |
| Strategy | **Weekly Dow Trader wLF and 2 Stop Trade Plan** |

| Results Start Date | 16/11/1979 |
| Results Period | 40 Yrs |

Survival	
Units of money	50
Expectancy E[R]	33%
Risk-of-Ruin (%)	0%

Reward/Risk (1 Contract)	
Net Profit $$/USD	$1,160,253
CAGR	8%
Max DD	–$80,520
Reward/Risk: $$/DD	14
Reward/Risk: UPI	1.8
Average losing trade (%)	–2.5%
Total trades	2,923
Net avg profit	$397
Avg brok & slip. per trade	–$51
Profit to loss ratio	1.5
Percentage profitable	29%
Average win to loss ratio	3.5

Efficiency with Money Management	
MMGT Strategy: Fixed Percentage	2%
MMGT Starting Capital	$50,000
Average risk per trade (%)	–2.7%
Net Profits $$/USD (B)	$1.3b
CAGR	29%

Difficulty in Trading	
Pain: Max DD (days)	1757
Pain: Max consecutive losses	19
Pain: Smoothness R^2	96%

FIGURE 9.19 Introducing an initial daily stop has a positive impact on WDT's performance.

TABLE 9.11 Introduction of an initial daily stop has lowered WDT's worst drawdown to below Turtle Trading's, while at the same time giving a significant boost to its efficiency in making money. A win–win.

Model	Type	Robustness		Performance Analysis												
				Survival			Reward/Risk				Efficiency wMMgt			Difficulty in trading		
		Published	Out-of-sample Yrs	E[R]	Units $$	ROR	Net $$	D/D	R/R	UPI	Risk	MMgt $$	CARG	DD Days	Losses	R^2
Turtle Trading	Channel breakout	1983	37	21%	50	0%	$1,418,786	−$95,107	15	2.2	−4.7%	$257m	24%	1,637	20	96%
Daily Dow Trader	Swing breakout	1900	120	5%	50	0%	$1,090,346	−$250,428	4	1.4	−3.3%	$167m	23%	2,238	24	95%
Weekly Dow Trader	Swing breakout	1900	120	23%	50	0%	$2,193,706	−$181,634	12	2.3	−5.5%	$1.4b	29%	1,403	25	95%
Monthly Dow Trader	Swing breakout	1900	120	41%	50	0%	$1,688,451	−$170,287	10	1.6	−10.1%	$8m	13%	936	16	99%
Daily Dow Trader wLF	Swing breakout	1900	120	14%	50	0%	$1,684,485	−$149,512	11	2.4	−3.4%	$2.3b	31%	1,685	21	96%
Weekly Dow Trader wLF	Swing breakout	1900	120	27%	50	0%	$1,577,026	−$130,703	12	2.0	−5.7%	$474m	26%	975	18	97%
Monthly Dow Trader wLF	Swing breakout	1900	120	34%	50	0%	$844,920	−$108,963	8	0.9	−10.2%	$2m	10%	1,350	14	97%
Daily Dow Trader wLF w2STP	Swing breakout	1900	120	16%	50	0%	$1,755,392	−$158,902	11	2.7	−2.5%	$2.7b	31%	1,685	22	97%
Weekly Dow Trader wLF w2STP	Swing breakout	1900	120	33%	50	0%	$1,160,253	−$80,520	14	1.8	−2.7%	$1.3b	29%	1,757	19	96%

Buy Rules

Filter:	Only trade if the previous change in monthly Dow trend was a loss
Setup & Entry:	Change in monthly Dow trend—from trend down to trend up
Initial Stop:	Sell break of the lowest low of either the daily setup or entry bar
Trailing Stop:	Change in monthly Dow trend—from trend up to trend down.

Sell Rules

Filter:	Only trade if the previous change in monthly Dow trend was a loss
Setup & Entry:	Change in monthly Dow trend—from trend up to trend down
Initial Stop:	Buy break of the highest high of either the daily setup or entry bar
Trailing Stop:	Change in monthly Dow trend—from trend down to trend up

I've modified MDT to trade with both an initial and trailing stop, as shown in Figure 9.20.

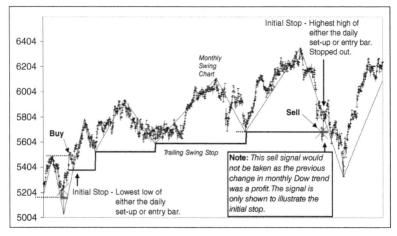

FIGURE 9.20 Introducing an initial daily stop allows MDT to exit losing trades sooner.

Review MDT with Loss Filter and Two-Stop Trade Plan

Figure 9.21 summarizes MDT's performance following inclusion of both a loss filter and initial daily stop.

Compare MDT with Loss Filter and Two-Stop Trade Plan

Table 9.12 shows that the introduction of an initial daily stop has seen a significant reduction in MDT's worst drawdown.

What is really pleasing is seeing the worst historical drawdown fall 44% to below −$63,000, while only seeing a 22% impact on the single position sizing net profit. In addition, the dramatic 70% drop in the average risk from −10.2% to −2.9% has seen its efficiency lift from $2 million to $15 million. It certainly pays to trade with smaller stops.

However, despite seeing the drawdown finally drop to a more manageable level, and certainly below Turtle Trading's drawdown, to my mind it still doesn't represent a final sensible trading destination. Firstly, with the tighter stop, its accuracy drops to 20%, making it a hard methodology to follow. I know traders should only trade for the opportunity to earn expectancy, however, in all reality, a 20% accuracy strategy may just be too hard for the average private trader to follow. And secondly, and more importantly, Turtle Trading is still by far much more efficient in making money.

However, as an aside, MDT with loss filter and daily initial stop is my personal pinup strategy for championing the three golden tenets. Using a change in the monthly Dow trend is definitely aligning the strategy with a strong trend. Using an initial daily stop with a monthly entry signal is definitely cutting losses short. Using a monthly swing point as the trailing stop is definitely letting profits run. MDT is definitely the poster child for trend trading's three golden tenets. I wouldn't say it's the best child, as there are better performing Dow models—however, it's certainly a poster child for demonstrating the essence of trend trading; trading with the trend, cutting losses short and letting profits run.

So far, I've managed to achieve my primary objective of lowering Dow Theory's drawdown, but sometimes at a cost to performance. Let me try another idea.

Adjust the Methodology by Introducing Multiple Timeframes

Next, I want to combine multiple timeframe Dow models. I'd like to know how combining a higher timeframe entry signal would work with

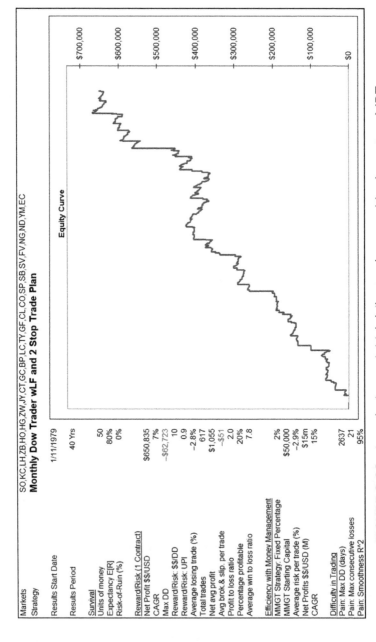

| Markets | SO,KC,LH,ZB,HO,HG,ZW,JY,CT,GC,BP,LC,TY,GF,CL,CO,SP,SB,SV,FV,NG,ND,YM,EC |
| Strategy | **Monthly Dow Trader wLF and 2 Stop Trade Plan** |

| Results Start Date | 1/11/1979 |
| Results Period | 40 Yrs |

Survival	
Units of money	50
Expectancy E[R]	80%
Risk-of-Ruin (%)	0%

Reward/Risk (1 Contract)	
Net Profit $$/USD	$650,835
CAGR	7%
Max DD	–$62,723
Reward/Risk: $$/DD	10
Reward/Risk: UPI	0.9
Average losing trade (%)	–2.8%
Total trades	617
Net avg profit	$1,055
Avg brok.& slip. per trade	–$51
Profit to loss ratio	2.0
Percentage profitable	20%
Average win to loss ratio	7.8

Efficiency with Money Management	
MMGT Strategy: Fixed Percentage	2%
MMGT Starting Capital	$50,000
Average risk per trade (%)	–2.9%
Net Profits $$/USD (M)	$15m
CAGR	15%

Difficulty in Trading	
Pain: Max DD (days)	2637
Pain: Max consecutive losses	21
Pain: Smoothness R^2	95%

FIGURE 9.21 Introducing an initial daily stop has a positive impact on MDT.

348

TABLE 9.12 While the introduction of an initial daily stop has a positive impact in lowering MDT's worst drawdown, it comes at a high cost with accuracy dropping to 20%. A low level that may be a bridge too far for the private trader.

Model	Type	Robustness		Performance Analysis												
		Published	Out-of-sample Yrs	Survival			Reward/Risk				Efficiency wMMgt			Difficulty in trading		
				E[R]	Units $$	ROR	Net $$	D/D	R/R	UPI	Risk	MMgt	CARG	DD Days	Losses	R^2
Turtle Trading	Channel breakout	1983	37	21%	50	0%	$1,418,786	−$95,107	15	2.2	−4.7%	$257m	24%	1,637	20	96%
Daily Dow Trader	Swing breakout	1900	120	5%	50	0%	$1,090,346	−$250,428	4	1.4	−3.3%	$167m	23%	2,238	24	95%
Weekly Dow Trader	Swing breakout	1900	120	23%	50	0%	$2,193,706	−$181,634	12	2.3	−5.5%	$1.4b	29%	1,403	25	95%
Monthly Dow Trader	Swing breakout	1900	120	41%	50	0%	$1,688,451	−$170,287	10	1.6	−10.1%	$8m	13%	936	16	99%
Daily Dow Trader wLF	Swing breakout	1900	120	14%	50	0%	$1,684,485	−$149,512	11	2.4	−3.4%	$2.3b	31%	1,685	21	96%
Weekly Dow Trader wLF	Swing breakout	1900	120	27%	50	0%	$1,577,026	−$130,703	12	2.0	−5.7%	$474m	26%	975	18	97%
Monthly Dow Trader wLF	Swing breakout	1900	120	34%	50	0%	$844,920	−$108,963	8	0.9	−10.2%	$2m	10%	1,350	14	97%
Daily Dow Trader wLF W2STP	Swing breakout	1900	120	16%	50	0%	$1,755,392	−$158,902	11	2.7	−2.5%	$2.7b	31%	1,685	22	97%
Weekly Dow Trader wLF w2STP	Swing breakout	1900	120	33%	50	0%	$1,160,253	−$80,520	14	1.8	−2.7%	$1.3b	29%	1,757	19	96%
Monthly Dow Trader wLF w2STP	Swing breakout	1900	120	80%	50	0%	$650,835	−$62,723	10	0.9	−2.9%	$15m	15%	2,637	21	95%

a lower timeframe trade plan? That is, have a model enter on a higher timeframe change in Dow trend, like the weekly or monthly, and then use a change in the daily Dow trend as the trailing stop. The idea is to see whether such a combination will lower drawdowns. Let's have a look.

Code WDT with Loss Filter and Daily Two-Stop Trade Plan

I've amended WDT to use a daily initial and daily trailing swing stop. WDT now trades according to the following rules.

Rules
Strategy name:	WDT
Core—Methodology:	Dow Theory
Core—Published:	1900
Markets:	All
Indicators:	None
Variables—Number:	0
Rules:	4

Buy Rules
Filter:	Only trade if the previous change in weekly Dow trend was a loss
Setup & Entry:	Change in weekly Dow trend—from trend down to trend up
Initial Stop:	Sell break of the lowest low of either the daily setup or entry bar
Trailing Stop:	Change in <u>daily</u> Dow trend—from trend up to trend down

Sell Rules
Filter:	Only trade if the previous change in weekly Dow trend was a loss
Setup & Entry:	Change in weekly Dow trend—from trend up to trend down
Initial Stop:	Buy break of the highest high of either the daily setup or entry bar
Trailing Stop:	Change in <u>daily</u> Dow trend—from trend down to trend up

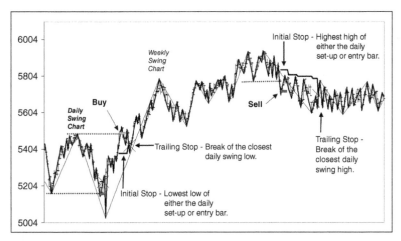

FIGURE 9.22 Introducing a trailing daily swing stop switches WDT into a dual timeframe Dow model.

I've modified WDT to trade with a daily initial and daily trailing swing stop, as shown in Figure 9.22.

Review WDT with Loss Filter and Daily Two-Stop Trade Plan

Figure 9.23 summarizes WDT's performance following inclusion of a loss filter with a daily initial and trailing swing stop.

Compare WDT with Loss Filter and Daily Two-Stop Trade Plan

Table 9.13 summarizes the growing list of alternative models.

Introducing a daily initial and daily trailing swing stop to WDT has certainly achieved my primary objective of seeing a reduction in drawdown from −$80,520 to −$69,487, a 14% fall. However, the improvement has come at a high price. Performance sees net profits drop 62% from $1.3 billion to $488 million. A heavy cost to pay. In addition, the risk-adjusted UPI has dropped 33% to 1.2.

Let's see what is revealed when we run MDT with a daily two-stop trade plan.

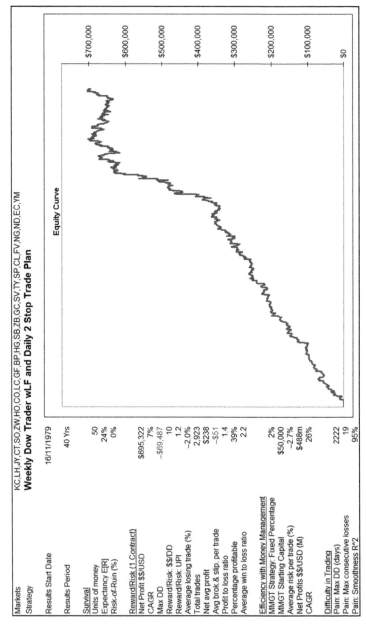

| Markets | KC,LH,JY,CT,SO,ZW,HO,CO,LC,GF,BP,HG,SB,ZB,GC,SV,TY,SP,CL,FV,NG,ND,EC,YM |
| Strategy | **Weekly Dow Trader wLF and Daily 2 Stop Trade Plan** |

Results Start Date	16/11/1979
Results Period	40 Yrs
Survival	
Units of money	50
Expectancy E[R]	24%
Risk-of-Ruin (%)	0%
Reward/Risk (1 Contract)	
Net Profit $$/USD	$695,322
CAGR	7%
Max DD	–$69,487
Reward/Risk: $$/DD	10
Reward/Risk: UPI	1.2
Average losing trade (%)	–2.0%
Total trades	2,923
Net avg profit	$238
Avg brok & slip. per trade	–$51
Profit to loss ratio	1.4
Percentage profitable	39%
Average win to loss ratio	2.2
Efficiency with Money Management	
MMGT Strategy: Fixed Percentage	2%
MMGT Starting Capital	$50,000
Average risk per trade (%)	–2.7%
Net Profits $$/USD (M)	$488m
CAGR	26%
Difficulty in Trading	
Pain: Max DD (days)	2222
Pain: Max consecutive losses	19
Pain: Smoothness R^2	95%

FIGURE 9.23 Introducing a trailing daily swing stop reduces WDT worst drawdown.

TABLE 9.13 The good news is that introducing a daily trailing swing stop lowers WDT's worst drawdown—however, the bad news is that it comes at a cost of lower performance.

| Model | Type | Robustness | | Performance Analysis | | | | | | | | | | | | |
| | | | | Survival | | | Reward/Risk | | | | Efficiency wMMgt | | | Difficulty in trading | | |
		Published	Out-of-sample Yrs	E[R]	Units	ROR $$	Net $$	D/D	R/R	UPI	Risk	MMgt	CARG	DD Days	Losses	R^2
Turtle Trading	Channel breakout	1983	37	21%	50	0%	$1,418,786	−$95,107	15	2.2	−4.7%	$257m	24%	1,637	20	96%
Daily Dow Trader	Swing breakout	1900	120	5%	50	0%	$1,090,346	−$250,428	4	1.4	−3.3%	$167m	23%	2,238	24	95%
Weekly Dow Trader	Swing breakout	1900	120	23%	50	0%	$2,193,706	−$181,634	12	2.3	−5.5%	$1.4b	29%	1,403	25	95%
Monthly Dow Trader	Swing breakout	1900	120	41%	50	0%	$1,688,451	−$170,287	10	1.6	−10.1%	$8m	13%	936	16	99%
Daily Dow Trader wLF	Swing breakout	1900	120	14%	50	0%	$1,684,485	−$149,512	11	2.4	−3.4%	$2.3b	31%	1,685	21	96%
Weekly Dow Trader wLF	Swing breakout	1900	120	27%	50	0%	$1,577,026	−$130,703	12	2.0	−5.7%	$474m	26%	975	18	97%
Monthly Dow Trader wLF	Swing breakout	1900	120	34%	50	0%	$844,920	−$108,963	8	0.9	−10.2%	$2m	10%	1,350	14	97%
Daily Dow Trader wLF w2STP	Swing breakout	1900	120	16%	50	0%	$1,755,392	−$158,902	11	2.7	−2.5%	$2.7b	31%	1,685	22	97%
Weekly Dow Trader wLF w2STP	Swing breakout	1900	120	33%	50	0%	$1,160,253	−$80,520	14	1.8	−2.7%	$1.3b	29%	1,757	19	96%
Monthly Dow Trader wLF w2STP	Swing breakout	1900	120	80%	50	0%	$650,835	−$62,723	10	0.9	−2.9%	$15m	15%	2,637	21	95%
Weekly Dow Trader wLF wDay2STP	Swing breakout	1900	120	24%	50	0%	$695,322	−$69,487	10	1.2	−2.7%	$488m	26%	2,222	19	95%

Code MDT with Loss Filter and Daily Two-Stop Trade Plan

I've amended MDT to use a daily initial and daily trailing swing stop. The model now trades according to the following rules.

Rules
Strategy name:	MDT
Core—Methodology:	Dow Theory
Core—Published:	1900
Markets:	All
Indicators:	None
Variables—Number:	0
Rules:	4

Buy Rules
Filter:	Only trade if the previous change in monthly Dow trend was a loss
Setup & Entry:	Change in monthly Dow trend—from trend down to trend up
Initial Stop:	Sell break of the lowest low of either the daily setup or entry bar
Trailing Stop:	Change in <u>daily</u> Dow trend—from trend up to trend down

Sell Rules
Filter:	Only trade if the previous change in monthly Dow trend was a loss
Setup & Entry:	Change in monthly Dow trend—from trend up to trend down
Initial Stop:	Buy break of the highest high of either the daily setup or entry bar
Trailing Stop:	Change in <u>daily</u> Dow trend—from trend down to trend up

I've modified MDT to trade with a daily initial and daily trailing swing stop, as shown in Figure 9.24.

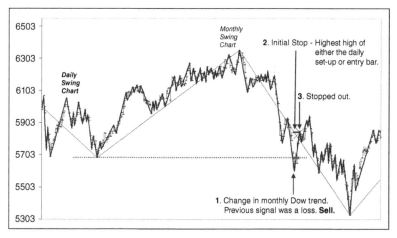

FIGURE 9.24 Introducing a trailing daily swing stop switches MDT into a dual timeframe Dow model.

Review MDT with Loss Filter and Daily Two-Stop Trade Plan

Figure 9.25 summarizes MDT's performance following inclusion of a loss filter with a daily initial and daily trailing swing stop. Marrying MDT with a daily two-stop trade plan doesn't appear to be positive.

Compare MDT with Loss Filter and Daily Two-Stop Trade Plan

Table 9.14 shows that the introduction of a daily initial and daily trailing swing stop has seen a significant reduction in MDT's worst drawdown. It's the lowest drawdown achieved so far.

Based on my primary objective of reducing drawdowns, MDT with a daily initial and daily trailing swing stop looks like the strategy to topple Turtle Trading. It certainly has the lowest drawdown at −$33,057. However, it comes at a huge price. Profitability has been flattened. Risk-adjusted performance has almost vanished with a UPI dropping to 0.3. Days in the longest drawdown have blown out to an uncomfortable 4,362 days. The bad news is that this combination will suffer the ignominy of being the least attractive, despite meeting my objective of

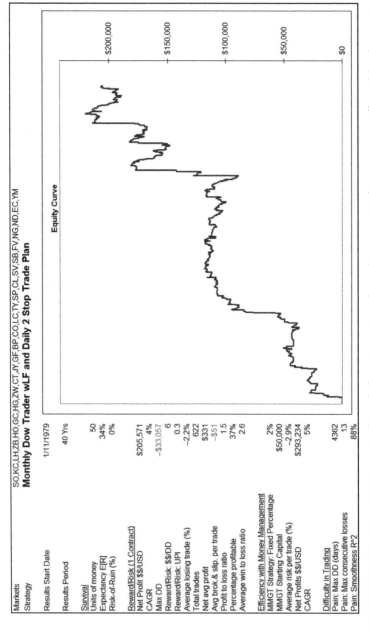

| Markets | SO,KC,LH,ZB,HO,GC,HG,ZW,CT,JY,GF,BP,CO,LC,TY,SP,CL,SV,SB,FV,NG,ND,EC,YM |
| Strategy | **Monthly Dow Trader wLF and Daily 2 Stop Trade Plan** |

Results Start Date	1/11/1979
Results Period	40 Yrs
Survival	
Units of money	50
Expectancy E[R]	34%
Risk-of-Ruin (%)	0%
Reward/Risk (1 Contract)	
Net Profit $$/USD	$205,571
CAGR	4%
Max DD	-$33,057
Reward/Risk: $$/DD	6
Reward/Risk: UPI	0.3
Average losing trade (%)	-2.2%
Total trades	622
Net avg profit	$331
Avg brok.& slip. per trade	-$51
Profit to loss ratio	1.5
Percentage profitable	37%
Average win to loss ratio	2.6
Efficiency with Money Management	
MMGT Strategy: Fixed Percentage	2%
MMGT Starting Capital	$50,000
Average risk per trade (%)	-2.9%
Net Profits $$/USD	$293,234
CAGR	5%
Difficulty in Trading	
Pain: Max DD (days)	4362
Pain: Max consecutive losses	13
Pain: Smoothness R^2	88%

FIGURE 9.25 Introducing a trailing daily swing stop doesn't appear to have an overall positive impact on MDT, despite lowering its worst drawdown.

TABLE 9.14 Despite producing the lowest drawdown, introducing a daily initial and daily trailing swing stop has had an overall negative impact on MDT's performance.

Model	Type	Robustness		Performance Analysis												
		Published	Out-of-sample Yrs	Survival			Reward/Risk				Efficiency wMMgt			Difficulty in trading		
				E[R]	Units $$	ROR	Net $$	D/D	R/R	UPI	Risk	MMgt	CARG	DD Days	Losses	R^2
Turtle Trading	Channel breakout	1983	37	21%	50	0%	$1,418,786	-$95,107	15	2.2	-4.7%	$257m	24%	1,637	20	96%
Daily Dow Trader	Swing breakout	1900	120	5%	50	0%	$1,090,346	-$250,428	4	1.4	-3.3%	$167m	23%	2,238	24	95%
Weekly Dow Trader	Swing breakout	1900	120	23%	50	0%	$2,193,706	-$181,634	12	2.3	-5.5%	$1.4b	29%	1,403	25	95%
Monthly Dow Trader	Swing breakout	1900	120	41%	50	0%	$1,688,451	-$170,287	10	1.6	-10.1%	$8m	13%	936	16	99%
Daily Dow Trader wLF	Swing breakout	1900	120	14%	50	0%	$1,684,485	-$149,512	11	2.4	-3.4%	$2.3b	31%	1,685	21	96%
Weekly Dow Trader wLF	Swing breakout	1900	120	27%	50	0%	$1,577,026	-$130,703	12	2.0	-5.7%	$474m	26%	975	18	97%
Monthly Dow Trader wLF	Swing breakout	1900	120	34%	50	0%	$844,920	-$108,963	8	0.9	-10.2%	$2m	10%	1,350	14	97%
Daily Dow Trader wLF W2STP	Swing breakout	1900	120	16%	50	0%	$1,755,392	-$158,902	11	2.7	-2.5%	$2.7b	31%	1,685	22	97%
Weekly Dow Trader wLF w2STP	Swing breakout	1900	120	33%	50	0%	$1,160,253	-$80,520	14	1.8	-2.7%	$1.3b	29%	1,757	19	96%
Monthly Dow Trader wLF w2STP	Swing breakout	1900	120	80%	50	0%	$650,835	-$62,723	10	0.9	-2.9%	$15m	15%	2,637	21	95%
Weekly Dow Trader wLF wDay2STP	Swing breakout	1900	120	24%	50	0%	$695,322	-$69,487	10	1.2	-2.7%	$488m	26%	2,222	19	95%
Monthly Dow Trader wLF wDay2STP	Swing breakout	1900	120	34%	50	0%	$205,571	-$33,057	6	0.3	-2.9%	$0.3m	5%	4,332	13	88%

minimizing drawdown. The good news is that I've come to the end of my adjustments.

Your Choice

It's up to the individual trader to decide whether or not, in their opinion, any of the combinations I have given are good enough to surpass the Turtle Trading benchmark. For myself, I believe the modified WDT (MWDT) with loss filter, daily initial stop and weekly trailing swing stop, even with its still large drawdown, is superior.

Let's compare the performances:

	MWDT with loss filter with initial daily stop	Turtle Trading	Impact
• Expectancy	33%	21%	+57%
• Net profit	$1.160m	$1.419m	−18%
• Drawdown	−$0.080m	−$0.095m	−16%
• Reward/risk ratio	14	15	−7%
• UPI	1.8	2.2	−18%
• Average risk per trade	−2.7%	−4.7%	+42%
• Net profit with money mgt	$1.3b	$257m	+406%
• CAGR	29%	24%	+21%
• Longest drawdown	1,757 days	1,637 days	+7%
• Consecutive losses	19	20	−5%
• Smoothness (R^2)	96%	96%	+0%

First up, from a typical private trader's perspective, MWDT's lower drawdown is a big attraction. Secondly, although it falls behind Turtle Trading on the reward/risk metrics, it makes up for it in spades with its smaller stops and superior 29% CAGR making $1.3 billion compared to Turtle Trading's $257 million. It's far more efficient in making money as its lower initial risk of −2.7% allows the trader to build up their position size far quicker compared to Turtle Trading's initial risk of −4.7%. In addition, without question, MWDT is more robust. Dow Theory has been in existence much longer then Richard

Donchian's powerful Four-Week Rule strategy (which Turtle Trading is built upon). And please remember that after you achieve your first objective of surviving the markets, your second objective is to make money, which MWDT achieves in spades—achieving a 29% CAGR with its loss filter, daily initial stop and weekly trailing swing stop.

EQUITY CURVE STABILITY REVIEW

The final step in my strategy development blueprint is to undertake an equity curve stability review. Now this step is really redundant for MWDT. Apart from a 1983 loss filter, MWDT is 100% Dow Theory making the majority of its results out-of-sample. Out-of-sample performance that delivers undeniable proof the model is robust. However, in the interests of demonstrating my development process, I'll complete an equity curve stability review.

Purpose

The whole purpose of a review is to determine whether a strategy's equity curve is stable. Stable enough to maintain a 0% ROR across various variable values and be tradable. To achieve this, it's necessary to know a strategy's entire universe of alternative equity curves, expectancies and ROR calculations. The size of the universe will be a function of the number of variables in the strategy and the number of adjustments allowed. The more variables and more adjustments, the larger the universe is. The larger the universe, the higher the likelihood that one or more of the alternative equity curves will produce a ROR calculation above 0%. Not a good outcome. But you won't know that until an equity curve stability review is completed.

Figure 9.26 summarizes my equity curve stability review for MWDT.

To help appreciate how robust MWDT is I've included the Retracement Trend Trader (RTT) review from Chapter 5 as a comparison. As you can see, it was a relatively straight forward exercise. MWDT, with loss filter and daily initial stop trade plan, unlike RTT, *does not contain any subjective variable dependent indicators.* MWDT has only one equity curve and it will either work or it won't. As you can see, it does. It doesn't need favourable variable values to produce

Equity Curve Stability Review			
Strategy		RTT	MWDT
Setup		MA (34)	WDT
		MA (250)	Loss Filter
		RSI (4,80%)	2 STP
Attributes of Winning Strategies			
Measureable	Expectancy	9%	33%
	Units of money	20	50
	ROR	0%	0%
Robust			
Evidence	Out-of-sample performance	No	Yes
Indication			
Versatile	Profitable over a diversified portfolio	Yes	Yes
Good	Equity Curve Stability Review		
Design	Number of indicator variables	4	0
Principles	Number of variable adjustments	4	0
	Number of possible equity curves	256	1
	Variation in equity curves	Large	None
	Variation in expectancy	Large	None
	Do any sets of variable values have ROR > 0%?	Yes	None
	Is equity curve stable enough to trade?	NO	YES

FIGURE 9.26 A review shows MWDT, with loss filter, initial daily stop and weekly trailing swing stop, has a stable equity curve.

favourable results. Dow Theory passes the objective and independence test. Dow Theory deals with 100% price. Dow Theory is 100% objective. No one can tweak, adjust, fiddle or wiggle a change in Dow trend. No one. Not you. Not me. Not central banks. And not even the market's Mr Maximum Adversity. It's pure 100% market behaviour. You can have no influence. I can have no say. Either it will work or it won't. Dow Theory works.

SENSIBLE TRADING DESTINATION

I certainly believe that MWDT presents a sensible and sustainable approach to trading the markets. Layering a weekly change in Dow trend with a simple loss filter, an initial daily stop and a weekly trailing swing stop has a verifiable and evidence-based edge. The model wraps its flag firmly around the golden tenet pole of trend trading. Using the higher weekly timeframe, the model ensures a trader is (hopefully) 'following the trend', as defined by Dow Theory. Using a much lower intra-day initial stop is firmly 'cutting losses short', while using a weekly change in Dow trend as the trailing stop certainly honours 'letting profits run'. Not only does it tick all three boxes, it does so with great efficiency—enjoying a healthy 29% CAGR. I encourage you to consider the model and, if you do, to first independently verify it and complete a T.E.S.T before implementing it in the market. If you'd like a performance update please feel free to contact me via my website www.indextrader.com.au. Just write MWDT's current performance in the subject line and I'll send it to you, no worries.

DRAWDOWN

Despite my efforts, MWDT's −$80,520 drawdown on my P24 portfolio is probably still too large for most private traders. If you're happy with your strategy review, like I am with MWDT, but are not comfortable with the level of drawdown, the next logical step is to construct a portfolio where the level of historical drawdown is acceptable for your trading account and risk appetite. To construct a smaller portfolio, you will need to avoid falling into the trap of data mining. You should not select or cherry pick just the best performing markets out of the P24 portfolio. That's a no– no. Better to construct a progressive portfolio based on diversification and liquidity as I showed in Chapter 8. Please refer to the mini portfolios P2, P4, P8 and P16 shown in Figure 8.1. Those portfolios are constructed on the objective criterion of diversity and liquidity. I've run MWDT over the various portfolio configurations, as shown in Figure 9.27.

It's good to see the strategy performing well across all portfolios. Please understand that performance improves as portfolios gets larger. Smaller portfolios are always disadvantaged because they have fewer chances to catch good trading opportunities due to less markets. In Table 9.15 I've summarized MWDT's individual performance across each portfolio combination.

MWDT's performance is consistent across the portfolios underlining the robustness of both Dow Theory and the strategy. Across all portfolios the profit to loss ratio, accuracy and average win to average loss ratio and resultant expectancy are uniform, illustrating that the strategy's performance is not reliant on a handful of key markets. The benefit of trading larger portfolios is evident in the improving reward/risk metrics and efficiency, as each portfolio increases in size.

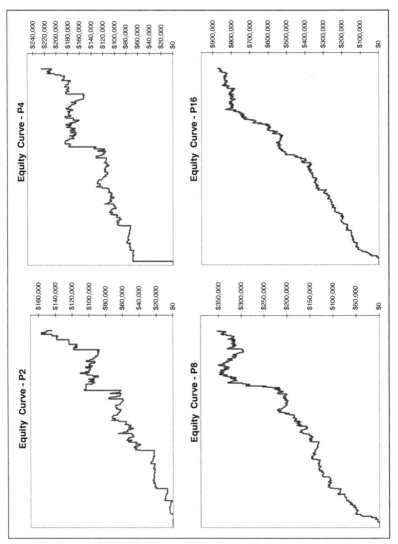

FIGURE 9.27 MWDT demonstrates consistent performance across all portfolios.

TABLE 9.15 MWDT's performance is not reliant upon a handful of good performing markets.

Strategy	Modified Weekly Dow Trader wLF and 2 Stop Trade Plan				
Results Start Date	16/11/1979				
Results Period	40 Yrs				
Portfolio	P2	P4	P8	P16	P24
Survival					
Units of money	50	50	50	50	50
Expectancy E[R]	40%	38%	38%	41%	33%
Risk-of-Ruin (%)	0%	0%	0%	0%	0%
Reward/Risk (1 Contract)					
Net Profit $$/USD	$144,190	$219,530	$352,733	$871,470	$1,160,253
CAGR	4%	4%	5%	8%	8%
Max DD	-$22,405	-$32,948	-$56,288	-$55,262	-$80,520
Reward/Risk: $$/DD	6	7	6	16	14
Reward/Risk: UPI	0.2	0.4	0.7	1.7	1.8
Average losing trade (%)	-1.8%	-1.6%	-1.8%	-2.6%	-2.5%
Total trades	258	501	929	1,900	2,923
Net avg profit	$559	$438	$380	$459	$397
Avg brok.&slip. per trade	-$51	-$51	$51	-$51	-$51
Profit to loss ratio	1.6	1.6	1.5	1.6	1.5
Percentage profitable	33%	34%	31%	30%	29%
Average win to loss ratio	3.3	3.1	3.5	3.8	3.5
Efficiency with Money Management					
MMGT Strategy: Fixed Percentage	2%	2%	2%	2%	2%
MMGT Starting Capital	$50,000	$50,000	$50,000	$50,000	$50,000
Average risk per trade (%)	-2.0%	-1.7%	-2.0%	-2.8%	-2.7%
Net Profits $$/USD	$277,365	$2m	$22m	$813m	$1.3b
CAGR	5%	10%	17%	27%	29%
Difficulty in Trading					
Pain: Max DD (days)	1599	2884	2509	1800	1757
Pain: Max consecutive losses	11	14	16	17	19
Pain: Smoothness R^2	93%	95%	93%	98%	96%

CHARLES DOW (1851–1902)

Charles Dow, take a bow. I can attest, not only through simulated historical equity curves over out-of-sample data, but through my own trading, that his peak and trough trend analysis is as effective today as it was when he first shared it through his articles in *The Wall Street Journal* in 1900. I can attest that it has stood the test of time. Not the 1987 sharemarket crash or Asian currency crisis, not the dotcom bubble, not the US housing bubble or global financial crisis, not quantitative easing or high frequency trading, not disruptive tech unicorns, not weaponized tweets and not even a global pandemic popping another central bank fuelled bubble have derailed its effectiveness. Dow Theory, as I label it, is timeless and without a doubt proves the old adage that:

The more markets change, the more they stay the same.

Dow Theory may be old and may be unfashionable to many. However, its undeniable performance over out-of-sample data, across multiple timeframe periods and under all market conditions and black swan events, makes it a robust methodology that should be reviewed and actively considered by the serious market participant. Where many study the markets and only see uncertainty, Dow Theory sees opportunities. The big question is whether Dow Theory will continue to perform as well into the future as it has in the past. Well, no one, not me and not you, knows. However, if it's past performance under all market conditions, across all bull and bear market cycles, across all timeframes and across all markets is any guide to go by, the odds look pretty positive. However, you don't need the odds to survive the markets. Just keep your ROR firmly at 0% to ensure survival and the Dow Theory compass may just guide you through the volatile and unpredictable maze called world markets.

Thank you Charles Dow, this chapter is dedicated to you and your peers.

BACK TO THE FUTURE TO MOVE FORWARD

I hope you are now familiar with how I go about developing strategies. I'm a stickler for looking backwards to move forwards, as only old ideas can gift me with substantial out-of-sample data and hard evidence of robustness. Once you've found an old idea to review it becomes a prescriptive process. Use your software to code the idea, review and compare it with your strategy benchmark. To avoid data mining ensure it's versatile across a diverse portfolio of universal markets. If it looks interesting enough make adjustments without falling into the trap of excessive curve fitting. If the strategy still looks favourable, complete an equity curve stability review. If you're still smiling, complete a T.E.S.T and if it's positive, celebrate by taking the family out to dinner! Easy peasy!

EMBRACE DIVERSIFICATION

Once completed your aim is to eventually build a portfolio of uncorrelated strategies that comprise both trend and counter-trend techniques that can be traded over multiple timeframes and multiple markets. Diversification works. Diversification of techniques, timeframe and markets will smooth out your equity curve.

As Ray Dalio, the head of Bridgewater Associates, one of the world's largest hedge funds, wrote in his book *Principles* (Simon & Schuster, 2017), building a portfolio of uncorrelated strategies, or using diversification, was the

> ... *Holy Grail of Investing* ...'

Multiple uncorrelated strategies over multiple timeframes over multiple markets will give you more trading opportunities, diversification against individual strategy and individual market failure and a smoother equity curve. Diversification provides better risk management. But first, focus on achieving sustainable trading by following the trend.

THANK YOU

Thank you for buckling up and putting time aside to read my thoughts on trend trading. I know everyone's time is limited so I do appreciate you reading this. I can't expect you to agree with everything I've written and I do apologize if at times my opinions are polar opposite to yours. However, I do hope you have been able to agree with enough of my ideas to justify your time taken to read this book.

I know I was hard at the beginning, painting an unflattering picture of being a trend trader: how most of the time it's a miserable existence. I wanted to keep it real. To help you avoid giving up after a few losses. I wanted you to know, expect and start welcoming the pain ahead to steel yourself for the inevitable. The inevitable drawdowns that inhabit the world of trend trading. I did this because I want you to survive your first drawdown. To see you safely to the other side where new equity highs await. Do that and you'll be in a good position to succeed.

And you can. You are now equipped with all the knowledge to recognize or create your own robust positive expectancy methodology. One that should be able to survive the inescapable drawdowns ahead. So, I hope my forthright and realistic discussion about trend trading, with the ideas I have reviewed, will see you riding a rising, although at times bumpy, equity curve that is backed by hard scientific data as you chase those fat tails.

You should now have a good understanding and appreciation of the contradictory nature of trading. You should now be prepared to expect the unexpected, as very little is as it appears. There are so many contradictions wherever you look in the world of trading. While it may appear to be the best of times given the advancements in technology, the internet and smart devices, it's still the worst of times, where over 90% of active traders still lose. It's a world where our constant companions are not comfort, certainty and security, but pain, change and uncertainty. It's a world where its most persuasive language, technical analysis, has little persuasion. It's a world where thinking doesn't make you the money, but costs you. It's a world where being the best loser makes you the best winner. It's a world where picking winners, being accurate, having a good entry technique and being right doesn't lead to success, but knowing maths does. It's a world where convenience can kill. Beware of gift-bearing indicators. It's a world where informative sounding people are the least informed. It's a world where being relevant is irrelevant for success. It's a world where excessive creativity and ingenuity is excessively punished. It's a world where substance is frowned upon and simplicity is cherished. It's a world where less is more. It's a world where going backwards is seen as going forwards. It's a world where the old is favoured over the new. It's an upside-down world. It's a world where nothing is as it appears to be. It's a world where success isn't celebrated, but humility is. It's a world where, on one hand, we're told the trend is our friend, follow the trend, while, on the other hand, we're told past performance is not indicative of future performance. We're told distributions are normal, but wherever we look they're anything but normal. Dietary books say fat is bad, while trading success loves fat tails. It's a world where hard science says trend trading can't lose, yet so many do. It's a world where standard deviation is the universally accepted proxy of risk, yet receives universal criticism. It's a world that cherishes more rather than less ulcers. It's a weird, weird and contradictory world us traders live in. It's a world where opportunity is found not in certainty but uncertainty. Acknowledging, accepting, embracing and executing these contradictions will go a long way to keeping you firmly planted on your pathway to sustainable trading.

Before I go, please remember I've only shown you one road that leads to Rome. If it's not for you, don't worry—there are alternative approaches to trading. I apologize again for my repetitive style and please remember to question and independently verify any idea of mine you'd like to consider.

And finally, I want to say (again) that the ideas in this book alone are not enough for you to succeed. Not only will you need a robust positive expectancy methodology to trade but you'll also need the universal principles of successful trading. If you haven't already, I'd encourage you to get yourself a copy of my previous book *The Universal Principles of Successful Trading* (Wiley, 2010). I actually rank my previous book above this one as the universal principles take precedence over methodology. However, I highly value what I have shared here, particularly as I see this book as the missing chapter, or companion to *The Universal Principles of Successful Trading*. Together, I truly believe they'll put you firmly on your pathway to sensible and sustainable trading. And please remember, if you'd like an update on MWDT's performance do not hesitate to contact me via my website.

I wish you every success.

APPENDIX

Literature on Trend Trading

This is a brief summary of literature discussing momentum investing and trend trading.

COWLES AND JONES (1933)

In 1933 Cowles and Jones released a research paper titled 'Some A Posteriori Probabilities in Stock Market Action' (published in July 1937 in *Econometrica*). They catalogued two types of sequences, positive and reversals, on individual shares. Positive (trend) sequences occurred when positive returns were followed by positive returns and negative returns were followed by negative returns. Reversal (counter-trend) sequences occurred then positive returns were followed by negatives returns, and vice versa.

They examined an array of time series of prices, ranging from 20 minutes up to and including three years. They found for every time series the positive (trend) sequences outnumbered the reversal (counter-trend) sequences. For example, on their monthly time series ranging from 1835 to 1935, if the market had risen there was a 62.5% probability of the market rising again in the next month. Momentum begets momentum.

LEVY (1967)

In 1967 Levy published an article in *The Journal of Finance* titled 'Relative Strength as a Criterion for Investment Selection'. Levy found there was 'good correlation between past performance groups and future performance groups' over a 26-week period. He wrote:

> *the [26-week] average ranks and ratios clearly support the concept of continuation of relative strength. The stocks which historically were among the 10 per cent strongest appreciated in price by an average of 9.6 per cent over a 26-week future period. On the other hand, the stocks which historically were among the 10 per cent weakest appreciated in price an average of only 2.9 per cent over a 26-week future period.*

Relative strength implies stronger momentum.

JEGADEESH AND TITMAN (1993)

In 1993 Jegadeesh and Titman published an article in *The Journal of Finance* titled 'Returns to Buying Winners and Selling Losers: Implications for Stock Market Efficiency'. They showed a momentum strategy, which bought shares that had performed well in the past and sold shares that had performed poorly in the past, generating significant positive returns over one to four quarterly holding periods. They discovered the existence of strong and persistent momentum.

ASNESS, LIEW AND STEVENS (1997)

In 1997 Asness, Liew and Stevens published a paper in *The Journal of Portfolio Management* titled 'Parallels between the Cross-Sectional Predictability of Stock and Country Returns'. They discovered strong and persistent momentum existed in US shares and international equity indices.

ROUWENHORST AND GEERT (1998)

In 1998 Rouwenhorst and Geert published an article in *The Journal of Finance* titled 'International Momentum Strategies'. They examined shares across international markets including Austria, Belgium, Denmark, France, Germany, Italy, the Netherlands, Norway, Spain, Sweden, Switzerland and the United Kingdom. They discovered the existence of strong and persistent momentum.

LEBARON (1999)

In 1999 LeBaron published an article in *The Journal of International Economics* titled 'Technical Trading Rule Profitability and Foreign Exchange Intervention'. He examined the currency markets employing a stop and reverse 150-day moving average crossover strategy. LeBaron found that using a simple momentum model created 'unusually large profits in foreign exchange series'. He discovered the existence of strong and persistent momentum.

MOSKOWITZ AND GRINBLATT (1999)

In 1999 Moskowitz and Grinblatt published an article in *The Journal of Finance* titled 'Do Industries Explain Momentum?'. They discovered the existence of strong and persistent momentum across industries.

ROUWENHORST (1999)

In 1999 Rouwenhorst published an article in *The Journal of Finance* titled 'Local Return Factors and Turnover in Emerging Stock Markets'. He examined 1,700 shares across 20 countries and found that emerging market shares experienced strong momentum. He discovered the existence of strong and persistence momentum.

GRIFFIN, JI AND MARTIN (2003)

In 2003 Griffin, Ji and Martin 2003 published an article in *The Journal of Finance* titled 'Momentum Investing and Business Cycle Risk: Evidence from Pole to Pole'. They discovered the existence of strong and persistent momentum during periods of both positive and negative growth.

HWANG AND GEORGE (2004)

In 2004 Hwang and George published an article in *The Journal of Finance* titled 'The 52-Week High and Momentum Investing'. They used a 52-week high breakout to test and demonstrate the existence of momentum in shares between 1963 and 2001. They discovered the existence of strong and persistent momentum.

WILCOX AND CRITTENDEN (2005)

In 2005 Wilcox and Crittenden wrote a paper titled 'Does Trend trading Work on Stocks?'.

They examined over 24,000 shares between 1983 and 2004. They employed a long only strategy, which bought shares at their all-time highs with a ten-day average true range stop loss. They showed their strategy materially outperformed the S&P 500 over the same period. They discovered the existence of strong and persistent momentum.

FABER (2006)

In 2006 Faber published an article in *The Journal of Wealth Management* titled 'A Quantitative Approach to Tactical Asset Allocation'. He applied a simple monthly crossover strategy, which would buy when the month closed above a ten-month moving average and revert to cash when the month closed below the ten-month moving average. He applied his crossover strategy to US and foreign shares, commodities and bonds between 1972 and 2005. He discovered the existence of strong and persistent momentum across all asset classes.

SZAKMARY, SHEN AND SHARMA (2010)

In 2010 Szakmary, Shen and Sharma published an article in *The Journal of Banking & Finance* titled 'Trend-following Trading Strategies in Commodity Futures: A Re-Examination'. They examined 28 futures markets over 48 years applying several trend-following strategies such as moving average crossovers and channel breakouts. They discovered the existence of strong and persistent momentum.

LIU, LIU AND MA (2010)

In 2010 Liu, Liu and Ma published an article in *The Journal of International Money and Finance* titled 'The 52-Week High Momentum Strategy in International Stock Markets'. They employed a strategy to buy the 52-week high across 20 international markets and discovered the existence of strong and persistent momentum.

HURST, OOI AND PEDERSEN (2010)

In 2010 Hurst, Ooi and Pedersen published an article in *The Journal of Investment Management* titled 'Demystifying Managed Futures'. They examined the returns of managed futures funds from 1985 to 2012 and demonstrated that a significant component of their returns could be explained by simple trend trading strategies. In doing so they demonstrated the consistency of trend-following during both bull and bear markets. They discovered the existence of strong and persistent momentum.

MOSKOWITZ, OOI, HUA AND PEDERSEN (2011)

In 2011 Moskowitz, Ooi Hua, and Pedersen published a research paper titled 'Time Series Momentum' in *Journal of Financial Economics*. They examined 58 markets from 1985 to 2010 covering equity indices, currencies, commodities and bonds. They discovered the existence of strong and persistence momentum across all sectors.

ANTONACCI (2012)

In 2012 Antonacci published an article in *The Journal of Management & Entrepreneurship* titled 'Risk Premia Harvesting Through Dual Momentum'. He examined data from 1974 covering shares, gold, corporate and government bonds. He discovered the existence of strong and persistent momentum across all markets.

LUU AND YU (2012)

In 2012 Luu and Yu published an article in *The Journal of Fixed Income* titled 'Momentum in Government-Bond Markets'. They examined government bonds from 1987 to 2011 and discovered the existence of strong and persistent momentum.

HURST, OOI AND PEDERSEN (2012)

In 2012 AQR Capital Management LLC published a paper by Hurst, Ooi and Pedersen titled 'Century of Evidence of Trend Trading Investing'. They undertook an exhaustive examination of momentum across commodities, equity indices and currency pairs. Their research covered 1903 to 2011. They found the existence of strong and persistent momentum across all markets. They also found that incorporating a momentum approach into a traditional 60/40 share/bond portfolio increased returns, while reducing both volatility and maximum drawdown.

LEMPÉRIÈRE, DEREMBLE, SEAGER, POTTERS AND BOUCHARD (2014)

In 2014 Lempérière, Deremble, Seager, Potters and Bouchard published a paper titled 'Two Centuries of Trend Trading' in *The Journal of Investment Strategies*. This was another exhaustive study that covered commodities and shares back to 1800. They discovered the existence of strong, stable and persistent momentum across time and across all asset classes.

GREYSERMAN AND KAMINSKI (2014)

Well, this might just be the definitive in-depth book to advocate trend trading. In 2014 Greyserman and Kaminski published their book *Trend Trading with Managed Futures: The Search for Crisis Alpha* (Wiley Trading, 2014). They applied a trend-trading strategy over 84 markets covering shares, bonds, currencies and commodities as they became available from 1223 to 2013. That's almost 800 years of data. They discovered the existence of strong and persistent momentum across all asset classes and across all centuries. In particular, they showed momentum enjoyed a 13% annual return compared to buy-and-hold's 4.8% annual return. Go momentum!

CLARE, SEATON, SMITH AND THOMAS (2014)

In 2014 Clare, Seaton, Smith and Thomas published a paper titled 'Size Matters: Tail Risk, Momentum and Trend trading in

International Equity Portfolios' in *The Journal of Investing*. Their study compared the effectiveness of relative momentum against absolute momentum over a wide range of international share markets. They only found limited effectiveness of relative momentum, while they discovered strong and persistent momentum existed with absolute momentum (trend trading) strategies.

GLABADANIDIS (2016)

In 2016 Glabadanidis published an article in *The International Review of Finance* titled 'Timing the Market with a Combination of Moving Averages'. He demonstrated the existence of strong and persistent momentum in US shares when applying a moving average trend-trading strategy.

GEORGOPOULOU AND WANG (2016)

In 2016 Georgopoulou and Wang published a paper titled 'The Trend is Your Friend: Time-Series Momentum Strategies Across Equity and Commodity Markets' in *Review of Finance*. Their research covered conventional asset classes from 1969 to 2015. They discovered the existence of strong and persistent momentum.

HAMILL, RATTRAY AND VAN HEMERT (2016)

In 2016 Hamill, Rattray and Van Hemert produced a paper for Man AHL titled 'Trend Trading: Equity and Bond Crisis Alpha'. They examined a global diversified portfolio consisting of bonds, commodities, currencies and equity indices from 1960 to 2015. They discovered the existence of strong and persistent momentum. They also found momentum was particularly strong during bear markets.

D'SOUZA, SRICHANACHAICHOK, WANG AND YAO (2016)

In 2016 D'Souza, Srichanachaichok, Wang and Yao published a paper titled 'The Enduring Effect of Time Series Momentum on Stock

Returns Over Nearly 100 Years' in *The Financial Management Journal*. They reviewed US shares from 1927 to 2014 and international shares from 1975. They applied both relative and absolute momentum strategies to their data set. They discovered the existence of strong and persistent momentum when the absolute momentum strategies were applied. They did not find strong and persistent momentum when the relative momentum strategies were used.

GECZY AND SAMONOV (2017)

In 2017 Geczy and Samonov published a paper titled 'Two Centuries of Multi-Asset Momentum (Equities, Bonds, Currencies, Commodities, Sectors and Stocks)' in *Financial Analysts Journal*. They examined a wide range of asset classes over 215 years covering equity indices, bonds, currencies, commodities and US shares. They discovered the existence of strong and persistent momentum.

HURST, OOI AND PEDERSEN (2017)

In 2017 these authors wrote an extension of their previous 2012 paper 'A Century of Evidence on Trend-Following Investing' in *The Journal of Portfolio Management*. Their earlier paper covered 1903 to 2011. In this paper they extended their research back to 1880. They discovered the existence of strong and persistent momentum in each decade since 1880. They also discovered momentum performed well across all market conditions from recessions to booms, from war and to peace time, from high to low interest rate regimes and from high to low inflation periods. Go momentum!

INDEX